THERE'S
A
COUNTRY
IN MY
CELLAR

Books by Russell Baker

Russell Baker

THERE'S
A
COUNTRY
IN MY
CELLAR

WILLIAM MORROW AND COMPANY, INC.
New York

1722

Library of Congress Cataloging-in-Publication Data

Baker, Russell, 1925-
   There's a country in my cellar / Russell Baker.
      p.   cm.
   Newspaper columns published since 1962.
   ISBN 0-688-09598-4
   I. Title.
   PS3552.A4343A6   1990
   814'.54—dc20   90-36699
                                                                   CIP

Printed in the United States of America

First Edition

1   2   3   4   5   6   7   8   9   10

BOOK DESIGN BY PAUL CHEVANNES

Contents

Introduction

Most of these pieces were written under the influence of desperation, which is the newspaperman's normal state of mind. Deadlines do that to him. He lives in a world where time is forever running out. On his inner clock it is always two minutes to midnight and the work only half done, maybe not even started yet, and he absolutely must have it ready for the printer before the bell tolls, whether he has anything to write or not.

It's not a work that suits everybody. High blood pressure goes with the territory, alcohol is an occupational hazard, and anyone too proud to confess cheerfully to a steady flow of errors and bad judgments will not be happy at it. When you are playing to a large public and there is no time for second thought you may as well get used to looking foolish, for error and misjudgment are your destiny.

I first submitted to this discipline in 1947, served fifteen years as a reporter, and became a columnist in 1962. Columnist sounds easier than reporter, but the deadline problem is even worse. This came as a shock to me at the start. Notified that I was now free to write three columns a week about almost any subject on earth, I was exultant. After fifteen years of living under reporter's constraints, I was at last free to disgorge the entire content of my brain.

Somewhere between the third and fourth weeks, having written fewer than a dozen columns, I made a terrifying discovery: I had now disgorged the entire content of my brain, yet another column was due at once. Worse, three more columns would be due in the next week, and three more in the week after that, and in the week after that . . . three more.

11

All the joy oozed out of the thing as I stared down an end-less vista of weeks, each a gaping maw demanding its three columns, every column to be delivered on schedule with metro-nomic regularity, no defections from duty allowed, no excuses accepted. The column quickly turned into a tyrant. It was not interested in hearing that I didn't feel like writing that day, that I had influenza with fever and hallucinations, or that I hadn't a single idea in my head. It demanded to be written before its deadline passed.

In those first few months it often seemed that the column would be the end of me. It was impossible to think of anything but the next deadline. I worried about the next column while riding home on the bus, while eating meals, while helping with the children's homework, while driving through the corn belt and down the Mississippi, while watching movies, while standing around at smoky parties, while lying in bed at night. Often I woke in the middle of the night simply to worry about the next column. I began to pester my wife by asking, "What would you like to read a nice column about?"

I realized that only ruthless measures could save me. What I did was simply refuse to think about the thing until the mo-ment I had to write it. Writing one took about four hours. Most of this was spent deciding what to write about and what tone to use in writing it, in finding the right voice, as I thought of it, to speak this particular piece. This usually involved a lot of false starts on the typewriter. Sometimes twenty or thirty opening sentences went into the trash before a useful one popped out of the typewriter. After that, because I am a touch typist and facile with words, the rest of the column usually fell together easily. Then I put columns out of mind until it was time to write the next.

Minds have their own ways of defeating tyrants, of course, and mine was not so easily pushed around that it automatically stopped thinking column thoughts just because I told it to. Its refusal to obey orders was a blessing. A lot of the material in this book exists because between columns my mind had sneakily stored away something valuable. Afterward, while I sat in ag-ony, without an idea in the world and deadline getting closer and closer, thinking, "This is the end, this is the day I finally can't write the thing before deadline, this is the day I go out the window"—always at that moment of ultimate desperation my mind turned over something it had filed away when it should have been idling.

On one peculiarly desperate day the paper was still blank though I had been four hours at the typewriter. I had passed beyond panic into resignation. It felt like doomsday. I was going to miss the deadline. I was through, washed up, kaput. It was the end of the world. Very calmly I typed out the bad news: "The world was coming to an end."

Taking this as its cue, my mind sent down something it had tucked away when it should have been loafing; to wit, that nothing interesting could happen anymore without being trivialized by public-relations overkill. The process was invariable:

First, news of Great Event; second, excessive hype of Great Event by media desperate for material to fill paper and air time; third, exploitation of Great Event by everybody with something to sell; finally, utter public fatigue with Great Event.

And so, after I wrote, "The world was coming to an end," the column began to write itself. Somebody would blame it on "pseudo-intellectuals," somebody would offer a fourteen-point plan, the stock market would post huge gains, sportswriters would argue whether it was good for baseball, soap-opera fans would protest TV plans to interrupt their favorite shows for live coverage of the terminal event. Finally, the end of the world was canceled on account of public boredom. I had survived another deadline.

I go on about these deadline agonies not because I crave sympathy for having one of the best jobs in the world, but to justify any undertone of desperation the reader may detect in this book. It is a newspaperman's book, and it is a rare newspaperman who doesn't fear heavy pummeling when he ventures into bookwriter society. The kindest of critics is likely to say, well, we have to make allowances for the poor devil because he is only a newspaperman. The cruel ones home in like vultures on a fresh carcass, flailing their wings at the shoddiness of the project and pecking away at the vulgarity of the journalistic soul.

Professors, historians, scientists, poets, biographers, novel-

ists—all writers of finer goods than journalism feel duty-bound
to abuse the deadline brotherhood for our inelegant prose, passion for banality and empty heads. A journalist, goes a typical
wisecrack, is a person with nothing on his mind and the power
to express it.

But so is the typical United States Senator. So are the representatives of hundreds of arts, crafts, businesses, professions,
trades and criminal conspiracies writing to editors and telephoning radio stations to give the world a piece of their minds. So,
much of the time, is the typical President of the United States. I
do not denounce these people for their shameless hot-air emis-
sions. I simply note that of all the people insistently expressing
their mental vacuity, none has a better excuse for an empty head
than the newspaperman: If he pauses to restock his brain, he
invites onrushing deadlines to trample him flat.

Broadcasting the content of empty minds is what most of us
do most of the time, and nobody more relentlessly than I. The
one thing we ought to ask of such people is that they do it grace-
fully. If you want to afflict the world with the contents of an
empty skull, common courtesy requires that you at least try to
do it with a little polish.

This is the rule I tried to observe from the start after realizing that mine would have to be a casual column without anything urgent to tell humanity. It might be only a casual column,
I thought, but at least people should be able to read it without
getting a headache.

Why casual? Because The New York Times editorial page
was already full up with columns that trafficked in heavy matter.
John Oakes, who ran the editorial page, said of course I was
free to write what I wished but he already had columns on
Washington, national affairs and foreign affairs and didn't need
another on any of those themes.

At The Times in those days the world was pretty much confined to Washington news, national news and foreign news.
Being ruled off these turfs seemed to leave nothing very vital to
write about, and I started calling myself The Times's "nothing
columnist." I didn't realize at first that it was a wonderful opportunity to do a star turn. Freed from the duty to dilate on the
global predicament of the day, I could build a grateful audience

among readers desperate for relief from The Times's famous gravity.

The first column appeared on July 16, 1962. This book puts the best possible face on what happened next. Since then there have been some 3,800 columns, give or take a hundred. My original idea was to publish the best of these and hope the reader would gape in wonder. The flaw in this conception became apparent when the selection process began.

This required reading 3,800 columns, give or take a hundred. At a conservative estimate these columns averaged 775 words each, which meant there were 2,945,000 words to be read. Marcel Proust's gigantic seven-volume "Remembrance of Things Past" contains a mere 1,300,000 words. In columns alone I had more than doubled the wordage of Proust's mighty mountain.

Reader, until you have tried it, you cannot imagine the stupor that results from reading 2,945,000 words spread through 3,800 newspaper columns. First you lose the power to tell good from bad, then to tell what time it is. Somewhere around Column Number 600 you start hating everything this man writes. By Column Number 1,500 you hate the man who writes it. Never mind that this man is you, because the horror has scarcely begun: You have another 2,300 columns yet to read, give or take a hundred.

The mental distress produced by this exercise quickly destroys all judgment, making it impossible to tell best from worst. It seemed more interesting to treat all these words as a history of sorts. From 1962 to 1990 the column had reflected the main themes of American life in the second half of the century. It might be interesting to look at the development of these themes as they had looked to an uncertain writer when he had no idea what direction they might take.

It was fascinating, for example, to follow the column's account of the evolution of the American child after World War II. The progress chart went from sweet newborn babe, to beloved "kid," to 1960's firebrand, to Early Reagan yuppie, to today's middle-aged fogy. The column recorded this evolution live, eyewitness from the scene as it was happening. Like the people who lived through it, the column was taken by surprise at every bend in the road.

Here in 1990, rereading those dispatches from the front line, I marvel at how innocent all moms and dads are when they bring baby home from the hospital and how unprepared all of us are for life's inevitable jokes. I mean, come on now, can you believe what those forty years did to us? Turning those sweet kids of ours into rebels, rockers, druggies, yuppies, fogies and lawyers! Lawyers!

The political history of these years was almost unremittingly bleak: assassinations, Vietnam, the decline of American power and wealth, public loss of faith in democratic process, the failure of what once was called "corporate statesmanship." This was not my turf, and though I sometimes sneaked onto it anyhow, I leave it to more sober historians, except for a few glances at the bleakness of 1968, that bleakest of years.

Another kind of history is told here. It tells of the change in what was needed to keep Americans entertained. It reports how a passion for newness produced an era of exemplary shabbiness. It is about the loss of Americans' ability to make sense when they talk. It is about a time when we had a bizarre affair with fancy eating, when the good guys died at the end, when greed was the stuff of heroes.

It is the tale of the age when America quit chatting with the neighbors while watching the passing scene from the stoop and went into the house, locked the door, turned the lights low and sat down in front of the television set. It's about that time of transformation when Americans ceased going forth to challenge the world and went inside to watch it on a picture tube. It's about a time when the country turned into television and when, if you wanted to be in communion with the country, you had to settle down with your set.

For a long time I kept my set in the cellar. I often went there to be part of the country. There I knew I was communing with the millions watching Perry Mason solve another case, or one of our state funerals for the assassinated, or a war, or the Academy Awards, the Miss American contest, the Super Bowl, the World Series, the moon landings, the elections, the creation and self-destructions of Presidents, soap operas, sitcoms, weather fronts, people becoming famous by being on television. . . .

Sitting down in the cellar enjoying America made me think of Walt Whitman who wrote that he heard America singing. Nowadays, I thought, Whitman's opening line for a poem about America would be, "There's a country in my cellar."

It was also a time when Americans were haunted by a sense of breakdown. This sense of breakdown was in some ways more demoralizing than the failure of all that firepower in Vietnam had been. It gnawed your confidence away day by day, relentlessly, bit by bit. The breakdown was happening in small, everyday things we once took for granted. It made you feel that foundations were rotting away down in the dark. Quality was eroding. Workmanship was becoming slapdash. Service with a smile was becoming service with a sneer when you were lucky enough to get any service at all.

The first section of this book is a chronicle of American life at the breakdown point. I place it first not because it is more dangerous than many other perils here described, but because it makes my blood boil. As somebody should have said, but apparently hasn't, "It's a doomed country that spends the Fourth of July boasting about the pursuit of happiness when it can't even get the roof fixed right."

WHY JAPAN IS AHEAD

Bulmer Strikes Back

Roger the roofer couldn't believe it was happening. "Be serious, Mr. Bulmer," he said.

"Toss your roofing tools into the back of my car, then get in there and lie face down on the seat," said Mr. Bulmer, pressing the gun against the roofer's ribs to emphasize his seriousness. "We're going for a little ride."

Climbing into the car, the roofer saw a body face down on the floor. "Ye gods and leaky shingles!" he cried. "You've got a body in here."

"That's not a body," said Mr. Bulmer. "That's Palumbo the plumber."

The prostrate plumber said, "Careful what you say to him, roofer. He's insane."

"Precisely," cackled Mr. Bulmer, slamming car doors, sliding behind the wheel and starting the getaway. Feeling thoroughly kidnapped, the roofer and plumber could only lie silent, listening to the pounding of each other's hearts as well as the pounding of a third heart, which seemed to come from behind the back seat.

"It's me, Milton the mason," said a muffled voice. "He's got me locked in the trunk with my mason's tools."

"He's going to kill us all," said Roger.

"Worse than that," said the plumber. "I've got a feeling he's going to make us finish the jobs we started at his house."

This dread sentence drew groans of despair from the roofer and the mason. Roger's entire life passed before his eyes, and he could not choke back a sob as he remembered his youthful triumphs at Roofing A. and M., where he had taken honors in Leaving the Job Unfinished 101.

He thought too of his wife, Reba, and of how proud she was when someone asked, "Just who do you think you are?" to reply, "I am Reba, wife to Roger the roofer."

He thought of the awe in the voices of strangers when they gasped, "Not that Roger the roofer who has roofed these twenty years past without once finishing a roof job?"

Yes, that was he. "Always leave enough of the job unfinished to drive the customer up the wall," his professors had taught. He was proud of never having let down the old school. Of course he couldn't have done it without Reba.

Theirs had not been a love match. He had needed a wife to answer the telephone when people called about some roof work. The need for such a wife had been impressed upon him in his early education, just as it had been impressed upon Palumbo the plumber at the United States Plumbing Academy and upon Milton the mason at historic old Mortarboard Institute.

His marriage proposal had not sounded romantic. "Reba," he had said, "don't get the idea I love you."

"I feel the same way, Roger," she had said, "but I've just got to have a man I can answer the telephone for when people call up mad as hornets to ask if he's ever going to come and finish that roofing job, or the plumbing, or the concrete mixing . . ."

"So you promise you'll always tell them I'll call them back?"

"Only when you've got no intention of calling them back."

Yes, Reba had been well educated at Slithery Eel Finagling School. They had been made for each other. And now—

Now, captured by this madman Bulmer and borne relentlessly toward the Bulmer household, Roger the roofer saw no way to escape the ignominy of being forced to finish repairing Bulmer's leaky chimney flashing, a job he had started eight months ago. Could Reba have betrayed him?

Yesterday Bulmer would have phoned, as usual, in a rage, demanding as usual to know if Roger was "afraid to stand up and roof like a man."

Reba was supposed to reply, "He had to go to Washington, Mr. Bulmer, for a big reroofing job on the Capitol dome." But suppose there had been treachery in her heart. Might she not have told Bulmer the truth? "The only way you're ever going to get that flashing fixed is if you get over here at dawn and take him at gunpoint."

Reba wouldn't have done that. Couldn't have. It was unlikely that Reba and Melva, the wife of Milton the mason, and Pearl, the wife of Palumbo the plumber, had all sold their husbands out at the same time.

The truth was known that evening after the three workmen were forced to finish their jobs at Bulmer's, and then were tarred, feathered and ridden home on a rail by fellow workmen who felt their trades had been disgraced. At home, the three found the notes their wives had left.

Reba's note, like the other two, said, "After that crazy Bulmer threatened to get me convicted for telephone perjury, I figured the fun was all over, so why not go someplace new and start looking for love?"

Outrageous Claims

There was a notice in the mail. It came from the automobile insurance company. It said that the cost of automobile insurance had gone up again. This time the increase was 80 percent. It would cost $715 to insure the car for one year.

That was only slightly less than $2 a day for auto insurance, but the notice from the insurance company did not bother to point that out. The insurance company figures people can do their own arithmetic.

The auto insurance man was not sure he wanted to talk to anybody today, said his secretary. He had had a hard week.

"Raising rates?"

The secretary said the auto insurance company had started canceling policies of customers who thought they were witty. She made a memo for the investigation department. It instructed agents to cross-examine customer's associates and de-termine if he had ever made anti-insurance-company remarks. Also to inspect his whitewalls for evidence of dirt which would justify another rate increase.

Suddenly the insurance man stormed out of his office. He had on his hat. "Someone has made a claim," he told his secretary.

"The dirty rat!" said the secretary.

"Don't you worry," said the insurance man. "It's the last claim that guy will ever make."

The insurance man dashed for his car. It was no time to be polite. "I'm a customer. Can I ride along with you to the scene of the claim?"

"I don't need customers," the insurance man said. "I'm in the auto insurance business."

Still he didn't object to having a front-seat passenger. He needed someone to talk to, he said. The customer who was making the claim was a dangerous risk. "Take a look at that file," the insurance man said, sliding a folder across the seat.

The file said the customer's name was Herman Furman. The insurance man said the name alone made him such a grave risk that no company would have insured his car if insurance companies had been smarter during the 1950's when Furman was sold a com-prehensive liability and collision ($100 deductible) policy.

Show business ran in the blood of families in which names like Herman Furman were used, the insurance man said. That meant risk.

Furman had paid the insurance company $11,783.91 in pre-miums since taking out his policy. The insurance man said that was all right. Furman had a right to pay the company that sum. What irritated the company was a claim for $210 Furman had made in 1959 for a new windshield. He had parked his car under an oak tree that autumn. Several squirrels gathering acorns got into a fight and dropped their acorns on Furman's windshield. It broke.

The insurance man said the insurance company should have dropped Furman's insurance at that time. People who lived near oak trees were high acorn risks.

We were at Furman's house.

"You're through, Furman!" the insurance man bellowed. He was using a bullhorn. His .38-caliber policy canceler was cra-dled in the bend of his right arm.

"I want $267.85 for that crumpled fender, and I'm going to get it," called a terrified voice from within Furman's house. "I'm going to get it if I have to take the whole automobile insurance industry down with me."

Afterward, the insurance man seemed shaken by what he had done. "It was for his own good," he insisted, again and again. "Listen, suppose every customer who has paid the insurance company $11,783.91 gets the idea that he's entitled to $267.85 every time he wrecks a fender. Why, we'd have no recourse except to raise rates."

"Speaking of raising rates . . ."

The auto insurance man listened. He said he had no sympathy for people who objected to an 80 percent rate increase now and then. How else, after all, could insurance companies raise the capital to invest in the vast real-estate operations which increased their assets so impressively?

Those assets would be mighty comforting to the customer, the auto insurance man said, if a real emergency stretched the company's resources to the limit.

What might be a real emergency? Atomic attack, the insurance man said. Think of the claims for wrecked fenders!

"Incidentally," the auto insurance man said, "people who object to eighty percent rate increases are usually considered pretty poor risks"—he was fingering the canceler in his armpit—"unless they are planning to remember their auto insurance company in their wills."

Not at Your Service

Let's get back to this question of pumping your own gasoline. Axel Fitzgerald of Shucker, Wis., writes that it shows a spendthrift attitude on my part to refuse to learn how to work the self-service pump when the oil companies are charging extra for gas at the full-service pump.

"Before long the full-service pump is going to disappear from the face of the land, and you're going to be as antique as an antimacassar on the parlor sofa," he writes. "You're setting a terrible example to your children by resisting change while squandering the wealth you could amass if you took a cheap night-school course in gas pumping."

I take it from this letter that Axel Fitzgerald is a very young man, too young probably to remember the day of the full-service grocery. I was young and foolish myself in those days, which is why I heartily embraced the advent of the self-service grocery. With youth's innocence, I couldn't foresee that the self-service grocery was going to turn into the supermarket, and then into the superdupermarket.

Have you ever got to the checkout counter at the supermarket—one of those twenty-acre warehouses containing everything from Peruvian rutabagas to cut-rate encyclopedias—and discovered that you'd forgotten to get the jar of capers on your shopping list? Have you ever tried to find a jar of capers in a twenty-acre warehouse while the people backed up behind your cart in the checkout line are hating you for having a palate that fancies capers?

This is what self-service gets you in the end: the hatred of your fellow humans. Exhaustion from walking infinite distances in search of provender. Self-hatred for being a person who eats capers.

Before the self-service grocery begat the superdupermarket, all you had to do was belly up to the counter, slice a snack of cheddar off the cheese wheel, tell the clerk you wanted a half pound of gingersnaps, a can of string beans and a jar of capers, and he brought everything to you.

You didn't have to work for the grocery industry: the grocery industry worked for you. Industry's discovery that the buyer could be made to do its work for it promises to blight the lives of those generations to come, whose welfare so concerns Axel Fitzgerald.

Already half the restaurants in the country make the customers get up from the table, make their own salads and carry them back, thus performing the work of both chefs and waiters. In New York department stores, finding someone to sell you the merchandise is so difficult that some stores supply fancier customers with special telephone numbers through which they can make an appointment to meet a sales clerk.

It's easy to see where this is going to end unless we start rebelling, and the gasoline pump is a good place to begin. The oil companies are the leaders of industry; if they succeed in making us all get out of the car in a driving rain to pump our own gas, then carry the money to an oil man sitting dry and snug in his glass booth, the rest of industry will quickly follow.

Am I worried about setting a terrible example to my children? No, Axel Fitzgerald. I am worried about the terrible future my children will face unless self-service is stopped dead in its tracks.

Speaking of dead, how do you, Axel Fitzgerald, feel about the coming of the self-service funeral station? Far-fetched, you say? Don't bet on it. Those of us who cheered the coming of the self-service grocery also thought it far-fetched that we would some day exhaust ourselves in a twenty-acre quest for capers.

Those of us who remember filthy, grease-soaked old Pete rushing gratefully out of his filling station in a hurricane to pump us a tank of gas thought it farfetched that Pete would some day sit in a glass booth and sneer while we got drenched at the gas pumps.

You, Axel Fitzgerald, speak of the future of beloved children. How are you going to feel when you've just died and the only listings in the Yellow Pages are for self-service funeral stations? You are going to feel incapable, that's what. Incapable of handling the self-service for yourself.

It will probably be up to your children to do the job. Is that the kind of economy you want your children to inherit? An economy in which bereaved children, exhausted from prowling twenty acres in search of funeral capers, have to rush off to excavate six feet of earth?

Put that hose back on the self-service tank and join me at

the full-service island, Axel, and together we shall start a movement for which our children will bless us.

Letter to a Waitress

Dear Madam:

I am now at the Chinese restaurant across the street from your place of employment, eating a large platter of General Tso's chicken. It is delicious, but a bad conscience keeps me from enjoying it. I fear I hurt your feelings by leaving your table without explanation and coming across the street to eat.

True, I heard you tell the people at the next table that they could come over here to eat if they were unhappy with your service. This, you'll recall, is what you told them when they complained they'd been waiting twenty minutes to order and wondered if you could attend to them.

Their rudeness was properly chastened when you told them, "I don't have to serve you if I don't want to." Aware that they had behaved swinishly, they did not take your advice to eat across the street but waited meekly another ten minutes until you were ready to take their orders.

I am quite clear on the timing because I had been waiting at my own table long enough to read The New York Times from front to back and finish the crossword puzzle when they came in. Having finished The Times, I had nothing left to read but my watch, and I was deeply absorbed in it when you gave them the tongue-lashing.

In fact, I had read my watch thoroughly and was pondering my chances of sneaking out without being thrashed when I overheard you tell those louts about the labor shortage: how you were one of only two waitresses who had shown up for work.

Here was a new face on matters. The exploitation of labor. Only two waitresses to cope with tables where nine people now sat.

When you brought those two complainers their hamburgers and beer, I had a moment's panic. Yes, I was afraid you might notice me sitting there in my vast pile of thoroughly read newspaper. If so, you would surely feel obliged to approach and say, "What's yours?"

Fortunately, you did not, for if you had I would probably have mumbled something heartless and unfeeling, like, "A cheeseburger and cup of coffee."

I doubt you would have understood in the distraught state of mind under which you were then laboring, but if I had said, "A cheeseburger and cup of coffee," it would not have been a gloating sneer at the cruelty of your life. It would have been a stumbling, inarticulate substitute for the gentle words that swelled my heart but could not take shape on my tongue.

Would you believe that I cannot speak truly brusquely to salespeople of any sort, including waiters and waitresses, when they make it clear they hate me for wanting to buy something?

With you, as with all of them, my only desire is for forgiveness. Had you come to my table and said, "What's yours?" my shyness would have permitted me only to say, "A cheeseburger and cup of coffee," but in my heart I would have wanted to fall to my knees and apologize. Let me do it now, sitting here at the restaurant across the street in front of General Tso's chicken:

I am sorry. Sorry I came in so thoughtlessly anticipating a cheeseburger and cup of coffee on the day only two waitresses showed up for work. If I had known there were only two waitresses, I would never have done it.

This, of course, doesn't excuse me. I should have phoned ahead. Should have asked, "How many waitresses have come to work today?" But I didn't. I am too thoughtless of others.

Otherwise, I might have had the good grace to ask the manager before taking a seat: "Tell me, my good man, do you have sufficient waitresses working today, or are you mercilessly sweating an undersized staff?"

Once I learned the harsh facts, I might still have done the proper thing. I could have stormed off to the manager. Could have said, "Look here: You have only two poor waitresses on duty, and they are furious with you for overworking them."

The manager couldn't otherwise know about your anger, could he? As a waitress, are you going to go to the manager and rage at him? He might tell you to try to get a job at the restaurant across the street. Of course. But somebody has to pay for all the grief you are suffering. Who? The insensitive, thoughtless, cruel, demanding customers.

Sitting here across the street, I want you to know that I understand. Understand that you don't truly hate me, but that it's economically sounder to hate me than it is to hate the boss. Please believe that I would have stayed and tried to apologize for even thinking of a cheeseburger and coffee, if only I hadn't felt a heartless urge to get lunch eaten before dinnertime set in.

I am tempted to show good faith by bringing you a snack of this delicious General Tso's chicken, but refrain from doing so, knowing I would feel like a terrible human being if the gesture compelled you to throw it on my necktie.

I am, Madam, yours apologetically, . . .

The Man in the Red Coat

At Miami the car rental company failed to deliver. "Your car is at the airport," said the computerized woman on the phone. We were at the railroad station.

"I was told a man in a red coat would meet me with a car at the railroad station." It sounded unbelievable, like explanations you give to policemen who have heard it all.

The computerized woman did not believe in railroad stations except as she believed in stagecoach stops and the Titanic. "Your car is at the airport," she said. She believed in airports as she believed in drugstores.

The airport was located at a distance of $10 and looked like a drugstore that had gotten out of hand. "I have had to pay an extortionist ten dollars to bring me from the railroad station," I told the rental clerk.

"Railroad station," she murmured. Caution was in her eye.

"There are still railroad stations."

"I see."

"I was told a man in a red coat would meet me with a car at the railroad station." To establish credibility I showed her the notes I had made in New York while dealing with the car rental company. The notes were on red paper.

"Ah," she said, "red paper."

She surrendered the car keys anyhow, intimidated no doubt by the sight of my magnificent credit card. She did not believe in railroad stations, but she believed in credit cards, all right. I wanted to tell her I didn't believe in Baretta, but, realizing that the situation was delicate, thought better of it.

The episode set off a long period of brooding about what people believed in and didn't believe in and how the differences in people's beliefs led to these systemic breakdowns. It is a fact that car rental companies do not believe in railroad stations, and, so, when you telephone and ask to pick up a car at a railroad station, they assume you are having your little joke and say, "Sure, we'll have a man in a red coat meet you there with a car," and then arrange to have your car at the airport.

My problem had arisen from ignoring my own lack of faith in toll-free telephone numbers attached to Area Code 800. It was an Area Code 800 number that had promised the man in the red coat, and as a nonbeliever in dialing 800 I should have ignored the promise and taken a plane.

At about the same time Jimmy Carter was being badly translated in Warsaw and talking private business into an open microphone in New Delhi, and both incidents were being extensively reported as news. Obviously, the people operating the great engines of communication, called "the media," believed anything a President did while traveling was news, whereas these two events confirmed my own belief that a President in global transit is almost utterly incapable of producing any news worth interrupting a reader's swift passage to the sports page.

"The media" can no more imagine a newsless President than a car rental company can imagine a railroad station. This is because they do not believe in Calvin Coolidge. We should not be too hard on the media about this. It is, admittedly, hard to believe in Calvin Coolidge, yet many persons who find it impossible to believe in Coolidge have no trouble at all believing in the Fonz.

I don't believe in the Fonz or Charlie's Angels, but millions of people obviously do. It is even harder to believe in policemen with $35 blow-dry hair stylings who toil in the spaces between the Fonz and the Angels; and sometimes it is harder to believe in Jimmy Carter than in Calvin Coolidge.

All these people seem to live in Area Code 800, a place that must look very much like an enormous drugstore under fluorescent light, sealed off perhaps inside one of Buckminster Fuller's geodesic domes. Everything is up-to-date, from slang to dental caps. On silent winking telephones and dazzling computer printouts, data from the outside world flow through to sustain the illusion of dynamism. Jimmy trip socko in Philly, floppo in West Europe. "Soap" takes 42 percent of audience. Carson inks $15 million contract.

I don't know where Area Code 800 is located. It probably floats at very high altitude between Kansas City and Moline, Ill. Wherever it is, everything there is new until it is three weeks old, at which time it is officially declared never to have existed. Thus, nobody believes anymore in the New Left, the New Politics, or the New Journalism, and everybody talks about the New Sex.

Once in a while a phone blinks and it is some joker trying to rent a car at a railroad station. The talk between dispatchers must be like this: "A railroad station?"

"Maybe I should ask him if he'd prefer a suite on the Titanic."

"The system doesn't like gags, Charlie. Give the customer what he wants."

"The old man-in-the-red-coat arrangement?"

"Sure. And be certain his car's ready at the airport when he gets off the plane."

Postscript

If Baretta, the Fonz, Charlie's Angels and "Soap" seem as mysterious to you as the whereabouts of Area Code 800, chances are you were dozing when you should have been watching television in 1978. I was dozing myself so can tell you very little about them. Baretta was a sawed-off tough guy, and the Fonz was supposed to be an adolescent male, but looked as if he'd been shaving for fifteen years. Charlie's Angels were female private detectives with stately breasts and stunningly beautiful teeth and hair stylings. I seem to recall them solving a case while on roller skates. "Soap" was a situation comedy that hoped to ridicule the idiocies of soap operas. It failed so totally in its mission that hour-long soap operas like "Dallas" started turning up in prime time and soon became the nation's favorite entertainment.

Flying with a Heavy Heart

Economists say airline deregulation is the best thing to happen to customers since the invention of the electric salami slicer, and they have figures to prove it.

Economists always have figures to prove what they say, and figures don't lie, so three cheers for free marketing in the sky, say I.

Yet why does my heart grow heavy when I arrive at the airport?

Is it because there are twenty-nine customers ahead of me in line, and the flight for which I need a ticket is scheduled to leave in thirty-five minutes, and the man at the head of the line has already spent fifteen minutes buying tickets to everywhere and will need another twenty minutes to search his luggage for his checkbook, and there isn't another ticket seller on duty because having two working on the same day would run up labor costs?

No, that is not why my heart grows heavy, for I know I can leave this line and race with my suitcases to the faraway gate where the airplane awaits and, there, find other authorities who will put me aboard before it leaves.

Then maybe my heart grows heavy because I realize I am not so young as I used to be and, therefore, while racing through the airport with my suitcases will probably trip over one of the family groups, college sorority chapters or sleeping (possibly dead) individuals who camp on airport floors because flying is so cheap they can't afford to go by bus.

No, that is not what makes my heart grow heavy, for I know that even if I trip on several such people and fracture them, they will not become cross because they realize that to benefit from the low cost of flying they must be willing to put up with a lot of inconvenience.

Perhaps, then, the reason my heart grows heavy is fear that I will arrive at the faraway gate exhausted by my luggage-laden race and the exertions of picking myself up from fellow travelers on whose sleeping bags I have fallen, only to find that there is no plane there because the flight has been canceled.

No, that is not what makes my heart grow heavy, for a flight is never canceled unless there are too few passengers to make it profitable, and this flight, as indicated by the line of 29 persons and the presence of 163 others who will be waiting at the gate to board, is going to be so packed that passengers will need treaty arrangements among themselves to determine whose turn it is to breathe.

Perhaps my heart grows heavy because a loathsome elitism makes me dislike being squashed haunch-to-haunch against so much steamy humanity after the last seat is filled, the last knap-sack placed in the overhead luggage racks or under our seats in obedience to F.A.A. command, and we all sit contained, elbows to ribs, worrying about being caught by our flight attendants with our seats not in the upright position for taxiing.

No, it is not loathsome elitism that makes my heart grow heavy, for if my loathsome elitism took that outlet why did it never make my heart grow heavy in bus-riding days long ago, when I enjoyed being packed closely into the human comedy because it seemed to create among us bus travelers a cama-raderie in which we swapped fried chicken and apples for ham sandwiches and cookies and occasionally even passed the time in group singing?

Then maybe my heart grows heavy because I know almost everyone on the plane will be too tense, too drugged, too angry, too lonely, too devoted to misery chic, too sophisticated or too sick-of-it-all to dispel the misery inside this deregulated human-transport device by offering grapes in trade for some cheese or by joining in a sing-along.

No, it is not knowing that the plane's cargo will be sodden with misery that makes my heart grow heavy, for what does that tell us except that my fellow passengers will be my spiritual brothers and sisters, or, to put it otherwise, that their hearts too have grown heavy upon arriving at the airport.

Could it be that my heart is made heavy by suspicion that these incredibly cheap prices can be made possible only by dan-gerous economies in the maintenance shop?

No, this does not make my heart heavy, for though I have heard that the law of life requires that every person must even-tually leave it, I believe an exception will be made for me.

If this be so, then why does my heart become leaden when I look up the aisle to where the pilot—O Captain, our Cap-tain!—is entering the plane and see that he is not the reas-suringly grizzled gray veteran of the TV commercials who has been flying since Errol Flynn sent his men up in those old crates held together with nothing but baling wire and chewing gum, but a stripling who can't possibly be a day older than seventeen?

Let's not think about that. Let's think about how lucky we are to have these fruits of deregulation.

Have You Noticed?

We stand at the outermost frontier. Human enlightenment is far advanced. We can now say "chairperson" without feeling absurd. Technological progress is miraculous. We have the digital wristwatch.

Yet things are breaking down.

Three weeks after I bought a roll of 22-cent stamps from the postal authorities, the stickum had dampened sufficiently to glue the entire roll tightly together. Stamps ripped apart in my hands when I struggled to salvage enough of one to pass the Postal Service's rigorous inspection. In a temper, I hurled them out the window.

"Things are breaking down," I shouted.

The splendor of our science tells us everything about breakdown. Old folks had to get by with only appendicitis, shingles and boils, but we have a stunning array of medical terrors. We have stress. We have Type A behavior. We have stroke induced by insertion of artificial hearts. Thanks to the electronic picture miracle, we have doctors available at breakfast to inform us about the newest bodily plagues.

Yet things are breaking down.

"Speaking of the Postal Service," said a woman who had seen me throw the useless stamps out the window, "what about the time the mailman threatened not to deliver any more mail unless you shoveled the snow off the steps?" Yes, I recalled that and recalled speaking to the mailman:

"Shame! Now as we stand at the outermost frontier, are we to have couriers whom snow can stay from the swift completion of their appointed rounds?" Too late, I realized he was drunk.

"Things are breaking down," I told him.

We have psychiatrists, and politicians to give comfort or warning. We have pills to distract one's mind from the break-down. The young can be placed in front of miraculous boxes producing incredibly fast-changing pictures, which leave their minds too incapable of sustained thought to realize that things are breaking down. Persons unwilling to risk chemical or elec-tronic help can be persuaded to think happier thoughts if cau-tioned that it is unpatriotic to notice that things are breaking down.

Yet things are breaking down.

Two months after ordering a washing machine for his new house, my friend Bob came by to weep. He had been to the huge national mail-order retail-house outlet that had taken his order. Why hadn't the machine been delivered? The human robot manning the inquiry booth checked his electronic miracle box and said, "Because you never ordered one." Bob said the miracle box was an imbecile. The robot said, "You can reorder with me now if you want, or buy one someplace else."

"Things are breaking down," Bob said.

Yet the machinery of efficiency has never been more com-plete. Police squads and ingenious barricades at transportation centers and public buildings, combined with seat belts and inge-niously designed highways, insure an all-time standard of safety. We have the most advanced weapons ever built. We have the car burglar alarm.

Yet things are breaking down.

A relative of mine, ticketed by highway police for driving ten miles an hour over the speed limit, recently had her insur-ance canceled, though she had fourteen years of driving experi-ence without ever being previously ticketed for a moving violation. The police miracle box had reported her ticket to the insurance industry, which had not been turning a profit in her part of the country. Because she shared ownership of the car with her husband, for good measure the insurance company can-celed his insurance, too.

He phoned me long distance, wanting me to tell him, "Things are breaking down, boy, and the best thing for you to do is set your brain down in front of that miracle box with the fast-changing pictures or else take a pill."

He could not reach me. I had thrown the telephone out the window in a fury at a mechanical voice that had been constantly telling me to dial my miracle calling-card number again because the miracle number I had just dialed was "not valid."

It had got so that I had to dial the "not valid" number three or four times before the mechanical voice would say "thank you" and let the call go through. So during a marathon session when the voice had told me for the fifth time running that my perfectly valid card number was "not valid," I told the voice, "Things are breaking down," and threw the phone out the window.

That was childish, because we stand at the outermost frontier where human enlightenment, far advanced, permits us to say "chairperson" without feeling absurd. We have the digital wristwatch, we have stress—not just boils and shingles—and we have the artificial heart that can induce strokes. We have the car burglar alarm, the human robot, the miracle box. We have couriers threatening to be stayed from the swift completion of their appointed rounds by snow.

Yet things are breaking down.

FAMILY MATTERS

I was married in 1950 at the age of twenty-four, which was not young for marriage in those days. My wife was twenty-two. It was no secret to her that I came to the altar with less than unabated enthusiasm. Being a realist, she didn't much care. Men of that era were supposed to approach marriage with abated enthusiasm, and usually did so. Maybe they still do, though the typical male nowadays puts off marrying until he's so old you might think he'd be delighted to have a companion to enliven his dotage.

The reason I did not bristle with zeal for marriage had to do with the story teller's tradition of ending all good tales with the depressing announcement that after the fascinating couple were wed they lived happily ever after. This tradition was embedded not just in fairy tales and women's magazine fiction, but in Hollywood movies. And it was movies that taught people of my generation half of what we knew about life.

The lesson of the movies was sad: When the excitement ended, man and woman headed for the church. Usually the movies didn't even show the final ceremony. It was too predictable, too depressing. Anyhow, everybody knew what was coming. The man and the woman who had shared such a wonderful story were now doomed to live happily ever after.

No wonder men who had been marinated for twenty years in such movies looked forward to marriage as a doom. Being in love with all its furies and farces and sweats and unhappiness was a delicious experience. Who would sacrifice such rapturous misery for the bland contentment of living happily ever after? Living happily ever after was not so bad as dying, but the limitless prospect of dull, uneventful happiness was so bleak that marriage seemed more an end than a beginning.

In this, as in everything else, Hollywood proved to be a terrible teacher. There was no such thing, you discovered, as living happily ever after. Entering into marriage was walking into turmoil. Next thing you knew there was a family, and life had become more complicated, more fascinating, more exasperating, more dangerous than you ever dreamed possible when you were an innocent unmarried lover with a mind full of Hollywood nonsense.

My wife and I have been married forty years. Except that we did not divorce, it was a fairly typical marriage of its time. In the 1950's we had three children, which was only half a child more than the average per family. They were destined to be known far in the future as "baby boomers" and "yuppies," but for us the future was an abstract speculation, like the edge of the universe. We heard about it, talked about it, agreed it was out there, but didn't really expect the future to happen to us. Not to us and ours. Certainly not to our lovely, innocent little children.

When it started to happen we were, naturally, unprepared. I doubt anybody was prepared for the parent-and-child adventures of the 1960's: those drugs in the schoolyard, the onset of rock music, the hair explosion, the whole family clustered around the television following the latest assassination news and watching our state funerals . . .

Talk about happily ever after! One day we looked closely and found Lyndon Johnson had followed Jack Kennedy's lead into Vietnam and was in up to his waist, people dying everywhere out there, and the statesmen haranguing us to show resolution by sending them more sons. With Johnson giving way to Nixon and four more years of the same, I noticed disturbing signs that the future was arriving. The first gray hairs appeared, and our sons were approaching draft age.

Of course it was also the great age of draft dodging. Get into college and get out of the war: That was the law of the draft until Nixon finally evened things up a little better. So naturally you wanted the draftable ones to go to college whether they wanted to go to college or not, which a lot of them didn't, including ours, my wife's and mine. Ours didn't go to college. Instead, they went to work. Then they got married. Then they had children.

That's how fast it all happened as the years clicked past.

One day I had stood at the altar, young and unhappy about the prospect of living happily ever after. The next I was walking around the block with granddaughters. It had all gone by so fast, and my wife and I were living in a new world governed by people whose diapers we used to change.

The pieces that follow are artifacts from various epochs in this family history. Some, like the plea for young Welby Stitch, were written out of my own family experience. Most, however, resulted from watching what seemed like the universal family experience during these years. The young fogies who appear near the end of these pieces bear no relationship whatever to my own children, who haven't an ounce of fogy in them, thank heaven. Young fogies, like yuppies, are other people's children, dear reader, not yours any more than mine.

Bride and Groom

It's June-bride time again, the society pages remind us, as we sit in the shade of the horse chestnut tree and read happily, half asleep. Through our half-doze, we are smiling pleasurably. Who says the newspapers have to lead to suicide? Just close your eyes and read, as follows:

Miss Abigail Concannon Buttress, daughter of Mr. and Mrs. Walter Osgood Buttress 4th of Pale Vale, Pa., and Sweetgum Bay, Me., was married to Robert Victor Scott Epsom Bent Brigham, son of Mr. and Mrs. Brant Brock Brigham of Brisk Breeches, Minn.

The bride was given in marriage by her father, who realized, too late, alas, that he loved her with an inexplicable tenderness, despite her numerous bad habits, not the least of which had been her absolute refusal for many years during her adolescence to clean up the mess in her room. The father had admitted to a number of associates on the previous evening, while under the influence of alcohol, that he regarded the groom as a lout.

Mrs. Buttress, the mother of the bride, wore a fortune in recently purchased gowning, acquired through the assistance of a revolving charge account.

After cutting their wedding cake with the traditional Brigham family sword, on which the groom's great-grandfather, Colonel "Bat" Brigham, had been fatally impaled by a Comanche brave at the Battle of Branded Bend, the happy couple threw the first slice of cake into the eagerly cowering throng of guests.

A slight incident threatened to mar the joy of the occasion when the man upon whom the first slice of cake splattered—and who is traditionally, therefore, supposed to be the next man in the room who will get divorced—proved to be an utter stranger.

Fortunately, he was able to identify himself as a Pinkerton agent who had been hired by the caterer to make sure that none of the guests, should one of them try, would succeed in making off with the crystal punchbowl.

After the festivities had ended and the honeymoon was over, the bride and groom took up residence in a small apartment conveniently close to a delicatessen, where they entertained their many friends, became deeply immersed in debt and had their first baby. Their second baby and their first mortgage followed in rapid succession, as well as a series of increasingly larger automobiles.

The groom mowed the lawn and washed his expanding cars while the radiant bride reared their two lovely children to school age, never failing for one day, however, to fulfill herself as a human being by working as the manager of a brokerage office, acting as batting coach for her Little League baseball team and becoming the first member of the happy couple to develop both stomach ulcers and high blood pressure.

After the bride, in obedience to doctor's orders to slow down, reduced the level of her activity, the slack was taken up by the groom, who, despite a hard day at washing the car and mowing the lawn, never once hesitated to assist the couple's two charming children with their homework.

In this fashion, Mr. Brigham was enabled to become extremely well-self-educated in arithmetic, Latin, advanced algebra, fifth-year French, qualitative analysis, biochemistry, the history of Byzantine art and playwriting.

In their many long conversations which followed the wedding the couple dwelt at length upon familiar subjects, such as comparisons of the relatively vast amounts spent in department stores and the more niggling sums spent in Paris and Venice. They frequently discussed their parents, their children, the astounding incompetence of their children's teachers, the piratical proclivities of colleges, the difficulty of finding a competent automobile repairman and the periodic failure of their many, many machines.

Once or twice, on very bad nights, they inquired aloud, in speculative terms, whether their many, many machines had indeed, as they had been led to anticipate, brought happiness and meaning into their lives. More often, they watched television, read bad news in the paper and, on occasion, went to the seashore.

A number of years after the wedding ceremony their daughter, Miss Agatha "Bat" Brigham of Broken Appliance, U.S.A., and Credit Card Lagoon, was married to the son of a couple who had had the same experience themselves. He came from a recently paved wheat field and had shaped his hair to protest against a society that covered its wheat fields with drive-in hamburger stands and houses with swimming pools for cultivating and growing people like him.

The father of the bride, Robert Victor Scott Epsom Bent Brigham, drank too much the night before the wedding and, in a forceful talk with his imminent son-in-law, told him he ought to learn something about the history of Byzantine art, as life would not be all peaches and cream and protest after the children came.

Advise, and So What?

A mother stood on a bridge over a narrow stream watching her young son playing below at the water's edge. After watching a moment she decided that the boy required advice and, raising her voice, she shouted it down to him.

"Don't fall in!" she cried.

It is hard to imagine a more parental piece of advice. Most parents dispense similar wisdom day in and day out for years and get away with it. They are fortunate parents indeed.

Harry's parents are not fortunate, for Harry, though he is not quite six years old, seems to have been born with a middle-aged intolerance for the well-intentioned fatuities which issue regularly from moms and dads.

Harry was only three when he was first advised by his mother not to fall into the stream beside which he was playing. As the idea of falling in had never crossed Harry's mind, he was puzzled, naturally, about why his mother felt obliged to advise him against it.

Did she regard him as an imbecile incapable of approaching a body of water without knowing whether or not he ought to fall in?

A few weeks later while Harry was sitting in an apple tree, his father advised him not to fall out.

Again, the uselessness of the advice irritated Harry. "That's all very well, telling me not to fall out," Harry said, "but if you wanted to give me some useful advice you would tell me how."

"How what?" asked his father.

"How not to fall out," Harry explained.

His father smiled because he was very proud to have a son with an inquiring mind, and he said, "Don't get stung by any bees while you're up there, Harry."

"Where would you advise me to be when I get stung by some bees?" Harry asked. His father smiled, and frowned.

Harry's patience snapped again recently toward the end of a dinner when, eating an unusually large portion of dessert, he heard himself being advised by his mother not to get sick.

"Did you say, 'Don't get sick, Harry'?" Harry asked.

His mother frowned.

"Because," Harry went on, "I have been looking forward to getting sick for weeks. Why can't I have a little violent nausea once in a while and shooting pains—?"

"Go over in the park, and play, Harry dear," his mother said.

"And don't get hit crossing the street," his father advised.

Harry is regularly advised, whenever it rains and he has to leave the house, not to catch cold. If he stays inside to cut out pictures for his scrapbook, the invariable advice is, "Don't cut yourself, Harry."

Once, last summer when his father let Harry help push the power lawn mower for a few minutes, his father advised Harry not to cut off his toes.

At about the same time, when Harry had to open the front door momentarily during a severe thunderstorm one day to let in the cat, his mother strongly advised him against getting hit by lightning. Whenever it is cold and icy, of course, the advice is, "Don't fall and break a leg."

The other day when Harry's father was painting the kitchen, Harry came in and said he would like to ask a question. "Sure, Harry," said his father. "Don't step in the paint."

"What kind of advice are you going to give me when I grow up?" Harry asked.

"Don't lose your money, Harry. When you're listening to the radio and taking a bath, don't get electrocuted. When you go up to see if there are loose bricks in the chimney, don't fall off the roof and break your neck."

"How do I know I can trust your advice?" Harry asked.

"Harry," said his father, and stepped in the paint can, which twisted his ankle, throwing him off balance and propelling him toward the floor at a graceless angle.

"Don't break your wrist," Harry advised, just an instant too late.

"As this incident has illustrated," Harry's father explained later as his cast was hardening, "nobody ever really takes advice. That's why parents don't waste their time giving you any worth trusting."

After 36 Years School Is Out

All across America this month persons creaky with middle age will be saying their last farewells to elementary school, and the words will go more or less like this:

Farewell, Ben W. Murch Elementary School. Our paths now part forever after twelve long years of struggle and trial. Let our names be stricken from the rolls of the P.T.A., for we have done our duty and would rest.

Twelve years ago we came to you, Ben W. Murch Elementary School, with Barbara, our eldest, and you helped us to teach her the multiplication tables; to awaken her to the excitement of the world of Dick, Jane, Sally and Spot; and with the splendid assistance of Officer Kelly to persuade her of the wisdom of crossing streets at guarded intersections.

As the years passed and we sent you young Carlos, you put us in touch with the school psychologist, and in time we stood proud in the June sunlight and saw you send them both forth into the great world of the Alice Deal Junior High School.

And now, little Hans, our last, prepares to go forth in their footsteps. As we stand proud in the June sunlight to see you consign him to the future, our sense of sadness—evoked by this evidence that after thirty-six years our elementary-school days are finally ended—will be tempered with exhilaration.

No longer will the call for lunch mothers be heard on the phone. Never again will we be called upon to man the penny-pitch concession at the annual school fair. No more shall we be summoned to conference with Miss Plimpton to justify our failure to produce offspring capable of mastering the nine-times table.

Farewell, Miss Kaufman, princess among principals. How we will miss your speeches of gratitude on behalf of the boys and girls for our annual appearance in the audience at the Ben W. Murch school play!

Farewell, Mrs. Wechsler, Mrs. Rose, Mrs. Rich, Mrs. Bode, Miss Cotter, Miss Vail, Mrs. Grieb, and all the others, some retired, some dead perhaps, with whom we have toiled a dozen years in uneasy partnership. When our patience seemed strained by your tight-fisted ways with the "A's," it was not because we were angry with your inability to perceive the brilliance of Barbara, Carlos and little Hans.

No. It was because, having told the children that education was not a business of getting grades, our patience was exhausted by the labor of trying to get good grades for them. Teachers of the Ben W. Murch Elementary School, have you ever at the age of thirty-nine, written a book report on "Mike and Pete Visit the Zoo" and had it sent home by a second-grade teacher with a C-minus?

These have been years full of the exciting discovery that we are never too old to learn. Thanks to you, Ben W. Murch, we have learned in the high afternoon of life to subtract in base eight, to recognize an adverbial phrase and to distinguish the subject of a sentence from the predicate. (The predicate has two lines drawn under it; the subject, only one.)

After twelve years with the Weekly Reader, we have learned who Moise Tshombe is, and Kwame Nkrumah, Bao Dai, Nuri es Said, Erich Ollenhauer and Khrishna Menon. Some day, perhaps when Barbara, Carlos and little Hans have all finished college, they will come for a family reunion and we will amuse ourselves by trying to guess what became of these men whose identity we spent our youths trying to master.

As we part forever, Ben W. Murch Elementary School, the sense of relief on your part is understandable, and so it is only fair that you should indulge us in a small display of sentimentality.

We, who are now getting on toward the ultimate abyss, have been in elementary school for more than one third of our lives. The smell of chalk dust, the sound of dodge ball, the memory of Fire Prevention Week, the sight of school-patrol badges, the passion of class elections and the excitement of the fifth-grade play have become part of our lives.

From Miss Broadbent, back in 1931, to Miss Kaufman, the pillar of strength at Ben W. Murch, there have been more schoolmarms than lovers in our lives. Now it is all over, and it is a little sad and quite a bit shocking. Sad to discover that after all these years we have finally graduated; shocking to discover that by the time you at last get out of elementary school, you are too thick of waist, short of wind, weak of eye and faint of heart to enjoy the new freedom. Wherefore, let us satisfy ourselves with a tear.

Farewell, Ben W. Murch Elementary School.

Farewell, childhood.

On Helping Youth to Help Itself

Instructions for teen-agers:

1. Always leave the shoes in the center of the living-room floor, where the parents will be certain to notice them. Let the parents call you three times to come pick up the shoes before you hear them. Then say, "Were you calling *me*?"

After a few months the parents will pick up the shoes themselves, reasoning that this is easier than shouting your name three times. Once the parent is conditioned to picking up the shoes without making a scene, he will naturally take on other housekeeping chores connected with your presence and cease harassing you to pick up skirts left under your bed, soda pop bottles left in the shower stall, bicycle chains left on the refrigerator, etc.

2. Use the record player at all times while in the house. Acquire no more than six records and play them at peak volume, starting immediately after entering the house and leaving the shoes in the living room.

In a short while the parents will stop saying, "No!" when you ask permission to go out. If dealing with unusually obdurate parents, have three or four friends drop by and bring their records just before the hour when the parents normally sit down to watch Lawrence Welk or to read "The Decline and Fall of the Roman Empire."

3. Arrange to have fifteen or twenty friends telephone you at five-minute intervals at all times while you are out of the house. The parents will eventually tire of answering the phone and come to realize that the phone belongs to you. Thereafter they will be apologetic about asking to use the phone when you are using it to play your record collection to your best friend.

4. When ordered to bathe, always take the best towels. Do not bathe too thoroughly, but merely wet the body enough to produce muddy rivulets in its creases. Use the best towels to remove the streaks. Then splash water over the bathroom floor and mop it with the towels. Throw the towels under your bed. In due time, the parents will become less insistent about forcing you to bathe when you would prefer to listen to the top forty.

5. Never hide the cigarettes in the kind of places parents use to hide things. You will know from experience what places these are.

6. When using the parents' car, never practice a racing getaway until you are two blocks from the house.

7. After using the parents necktie or hosiery, remove it and leave it in the dog's or the cat's favorite sleeping place. This will assure you a fashionable wardrobe turnover to keep you in the style forefront of your group.

8. When in need of money, be helpful around the house. Insist upon making breakfast, taking pains to burn the bacon and overcook the coffee. Go off without fanfare and clean your room, being certain to splash the floor wax over the bedspread. When the parents tax you with incompetence, assume an expression of contrite misery while explaining that they have never

given you the opportunity to assume the responsibility of being self-reliant.

If they obtusely miss the point and withhold the money, make the parents feel guilty by reminding them that it was their generation that produced the atomic bomb.

9. Invent another set of parents. Attribute them to Joe or Angela. When the parents are intolerable, tell them things such as, "Angela's parents are letting *her* stay out until midnight," and "Gosh, Joe's parents don't care if *he* has a beer once in a while."

In all cases, the invented set of parents must be shown to have the teen-age spirit. At dinner, for example, it is effective to say, "Gee, Angela's parents listen to the Beatles all day long!" Being compared to Angela's parents will eventually make other parents feel very old and broken in spirit.

In this condition, it is a small task to reduce them to complete surrender.

Youth as a Tiresome Old Windbag

In one of his early songs Bob Dylan taunts the middle-class parent by insisting that "something is going on" among his children and that the parent doesn't know what it is, "do you, mr. jones?"

For a long while, Dylan's question was a poser. Indeed, something did seem to be "going on," and indeed, if you were over the mystic age of thirty, it was extremely hard to guess what it was. The answer can now be supplied. Like most mysteries, its solution was right under our noses—or in this case, right inside our eardrums—all the time.

Quite simply, we have produced a generation of garrulous

young windbags. If "Hamlet" were a contemporary play, the Polonius character representing life's tendency to burden mankind with tedious, moralizing bores would be drawn as a young man.

Shakespeare had Polonius edging up on senility, of course, and quite reasonably so. Until the present generation, garrulity had always been a distinguishing vice of the aged. It would never have crossed Shakespeare's mind that a man still warm with the blood of youth might afflict humanity with such meaningless prattle as, "To thine own self be true."

Today, however, it is an unusual household that does not have two or three young Poloniuses catechizing Father and Mother on the mysteries of life with such vapid advice as, "To thine own thing be true." When Father is trying to decide these days whether to be or not to be by taking arms against seas of trouble, it is his common fate to be distracted by ridiculous advice from a beardless youngster to be true to his own "thing." It is doubtful that any generation of young people before this one wanted to, dared to, or thought it worth while to burden Father with such pompous vapidities.

The answer to Dylan's riddle burst in the mind with depressing clarity during a reading of the "dialogue" between generations in Harper's Magazine. It consists of several statements by distinguished elders like Walter Lippmann and of replies by several young persons.

The burden of the youthful replies is that contemporary youth either has in hand or is about to produce the solution to the mystery of life and that Mr. Lippmann and his aging associates, while well-meaning codgers, do not know the score.

Now there is nothing unnatural or wrong about youth's believing that it has the answers and that grown-ups do not know the score. What is odd, however, is contemporary youth's passion for wasting good answers and energy on grown-ups.

Until now, youth has instinctively known that adults are not going to take its advice anyhow, has gone peaceably about life in its own way and, when the time came, has nudged the old people aside and done things the way they should have been done all along.

Not any longer. Something is going on here, Mr. Jones.

The kids are becoming as much of a nuisance as their grand-parents.

Once upon a time a couple who decided to take too much alcohol before dinner could do so knowing that they would have only Grandmother's silent disapproval to daunt them. Nowadays they are trapped between Grandmother on one side and, on the other, an eighty-year-old son sermonizing about why they should take marijuana instead of alcohol.

Once upon a time they had only Grandfather to talk on into the night about the corruption of their way of life. Now they are trapped between Grandfather's wheezing and the homiletic tedium of two or three young fogies denouncing the shallowness of their goals.

Once they could turn on the radio and risk nothing worse than the network news report that their world was flying to pieces. Nowadays they are ground between doomsday pronouncements on the one hand and, on the other, youthful old gasbags whining through guitar chords about how not being true to thine own self is what built the atom bomb.

Once upon a time they could talk politics and risk nothing more than a row with the neighbors. Nowadays they invite not only bad blood with the people next door but a barrage of deadly moral precepts ("Love is good, hate is bad. War is evil, peace is sweet, etc.") from some nineteen-year-old nonagenarian.

Like the old, old folks they emulate, our young windbags seem unaware that they are telling us what we already know. Civility compels us to listen respectfully to the aged. What social convention constrains us from saying, "Youth of America, just tell us the things we don't know, please"?

The Excellence of
Welby Stitch Jr.

Dear Harvard,

Welby Stitch Jr., age seventeen, of 174 Hemlock Terrace, has asked me to write you a letter of recommendation supporting his application for admission to your college next fall. No one else, it seems, is willing to recommend Welby, which just goes to show how few people recognize excellence when they see it.

I am not going to resort to the usual perjury, which you probably expect in letters of recommendation, and tell you that Welby's mastery of Greek irregular verbs, impeccable table manners and singular dedication to extracurricular activities mark him for a future of dazzling eminence. Welby's peculiar excellences are so rare among today's college applicants that it would be criminal not to tell you quite candidly about them.

Frankly, about Greek verbs Welby knows from nothing. Even his English verbs tend to buckle under the pressure of formal composition. A glance at his academic record—monotonous battalions of C's, broken here and there by a forlorn D—will give you a clear idea of how Welby feels about verbs, as well as quadratic equations, the laws of thermodynamics and "The Scarlet Letter."

It is clear enough from the record that Welby has protected himself with great cunning against tyrants who tried to litter his mind with the sort of knowledge most adults spend years struggling to forget. Thanks to his successful resistance, he brings you the finest gift it is possible to present to a university—a pure

mind, unused, untouched and unscarred by the educational production line. A mind ripe for wakening.

This is not all. You should note particularly Welby's ex-
traordinarily healthy lack of interest in extracurricular activities.
Through twelve long years of schooling, he has never joined the
stamp club, never maimed fact or taste for the school newspaper, never tormented his elders by taking part in "The Desert
Song" on the school stage, never ranted through megaphones to
packed grandstands.

After school one day I ran into him as he was about to
enter a burlesque house. "Welby," I asked him, "why don't you
spend your afternoons at the high-school government club learning Robert's Rules of Order? You know how Harvard likes its
applicants to show an early interest in public life."

"To do that," Welby explained, "I'd have to take time out
from my education," and he went into the burlesque house to
observe, if memory serves me, Ima Peach perform an ancient
dance.

Despite many obstacles placed in his way by schools, Welby
has achieved a well-rounded education. Aside from familiarity
with ancient dance, he has become expert in the care of tropical
fish and has assisted competently at the birth of three litters of
cats. He drives with confidence, spends with ease and does a
devastating imitation of his father throwing a scene at the dinner
table.

Welby has learned something more valuable than the distinction between the indicative and subjunctive moods (of which
he is totally unaware). He has learned that it is ridiculous to
decide at seventeen what he will do when he becomes an adult.

"When I'm forty years old," he asked me recently, "why
should I have to spend my days sitting around courtrooms because some kid decided at the age of seventeen that I'd have to
be a lawyer?"

I mention this, Harvard, only because if you ask him what
he plans to do with his life he is likely to tell you he wants to be
a Beatle. Do not assume that he is being juvenile. This is merely
Welby's polite way—he is exceedingly polite to old people—of
reminding you that people who ask juvenile questions usually
get juvenile answers.

Of all Welby's excellences, the most commendable is his indifference to proving his excellence. "If you want to get into Harvard, Welby," his father told him at the age of six, "you'll have to get straight A's for the rest of your life."

Young and pliable, Welby pursued A's for a few weeks. Then he observed that many of his fellow first-graders were pursuing A's with such intensity that they were coming down with gastric ulcers. And he saw others being led away for psychiatric treatment. After that, Welby never pursued an A again.

"The way I look at it," he told me recently, "if I make a big deal out of proving my excellence in order to get into Harvard, I'll either be a physical wreck or a very unpleasant person by the time I get there, and I won't enjoy it."

Today, at seventeen, Welby is a fine physical specimen, notably free of neurosis. He is full of good humor, gentle intentions, affection for life, and indulgence for his less fortunate schoolmates who have shattered duodenum and psyche in the pursuit of A's. He is capable of feeling humble about not understanding the subjunctive mood. If he did understand it, however, he would be incapable of feeling arrogant about the accomplishment.

Can Harvard fulfill its obligation to the nation if it denies Welby the privilege of higher education and consigns him, instead, to feed cannon? I think not. Consider, Harvard, the contributions that Welby will almost certainly make to humanity.

Indifferent to pedagogy, he will never take up scholarship and start producing those incredibly dreary scholastic books written to win professorial tenure. With Welby Stitch Jr., Harvard will lighten humanity's burdens by at least six unnecessary books.

Indifferent to the flaunting of excellence, Welby will surely never enter politics. And so, with Welby, Harvard will assure itself of at least one graduate who can be relied upon not to visit yet more taxes and wars upon mankind.

Welby's admirable lack of brilliance makes it certain that he will make immense contributions to human happiness by never becoming a Wall Street lawyer, an advertising executive, a Secretary of State or a world-renowned psychiatrist.

Welby's absolute incompetence at science argues its own

case. Thanks to Welby, Harvard will produce at least one graduate who can be counted upon to make life better by never building a bigger computer or synthesizing a deadlier nerve gas.

Not accept Welby Stitch Jr.? Harvard cannot refuse him. In years to come when the class of '73 reunites at Cambridge, Harvard will feel mighty bad as the old grads get up one by one and boast that it was Harvard that made it possible for them to inflict unreadable books, taxes, wars, lawsuits, bigger computers and deadlier nerve gas upon humanity.

On that grim day, Harvard will feel proud of itself when, at last, Welby's turn comes to speak, and he rises, and says, "I guess I'm the only fellow here who hasn't made the world just a little more unbearable. I might have, with proper encouragement, but thanks to Harvard I learned early that there's a place in life for everybody, even for a few who refuse to do their worst."

Sincerely yours,
WELBY STITCH SR.

Of Course It Does

Dear Buck, Harry, Cal and Jimbo:

During the World Series I have been watching you fish and look self-satisfied about beer, and possibly because it was a long Series I seem to know and care about you.

I can tell, for instance, that the beautifully cooked fish which Jimbo held up to the camera wasn't really prepared by Jimbo. You've got too much of the showboat in your makeup, Jimbo, to be the reflective philosopher it takes to cook a fish as imaginatively as that. That's why they chose you to ogle the camera behind the fish.

Cal couldn't have done that persuasively. He's too objec-

tive about himself, too quick to realize when he is looking foolish. That's why they didn't ask him to do the big display scene
with the cooked fish. Cal couldn't play a supporting role to a
cooked fish without looking sardonic, and sardonic looks do not
sell beer. Harry is shy, isn't he? I wondered at first how Harry
got into the quartet. Then I realized that the lakeside lodge
where the fishing and beer-drinking occur belongs to Harry's
dad. Harry's dad probably earns and loses several million dollars
a week in the commodities market. He's uneasy about Harry.

I may even have met Harry's dad. At any rate I recall a
powerful god of money telling me once over a lunch of salad and
no-cal seltzer about a son, "a nice boy, too nice, no instinct for
the jugular, the kid buys records of people playing the cello, the
cello, can you believe the cello!"

That dad had plenty of lodges. He probably cut a deal with
the televised-beer-film industry. "Use my kid with some he-man
guys fishing and praising beer, anything but cellos, and you can
keep the lodge."

Harry, I think your dad, if the man I'm thinking of really is
your dad, has a small point. Do you have to listen to cello records whenever he visits? He probably doesn't expect much now.
You're through college, couldn't earn $75 a week if your life
depended on it; your father is resigned to that. Probably all he
wants is a little make-believe of the father-and-son type. Ask
him to take you to lunch, ask him to tell you about the price of
pork bellies. Make him happy.

But it's not Harry, or Cal, or Jimbo who worries me.
It's you, Buck. I've listened to you speak that line too many
times now:

"It doesn't get any better than this."

Each time is more depressing than the time before, because Buck says that line so beautifully that it's obvious he
really believes it. Ponder that for a moment, Buck:

You're at Harry's dad's lodge with an actor who is too
self-conscious to play straight man to a fish, another who's so
tough he would play the fish if the pay was right, and an ama-
teur who would rather be listening to a cello recording.

Day in, day out, between innings of baseball, the four of
you catch the fish, cook the fish, display the fish for the cam-

era, then sit out on a porch being satisfied about beer. And you, Buck, have to say, "It doesn't get any better than this."

They wouldn't let Jimbo, Cal or Harry speak that line, would they? Do you think it's because the people who planned this fish-and-beer trip have looked at Jimbo, Cal and Harry and said, "Those three have too much sense to believe that line; they will make a mockery of it"?

Buck, let me speak as an older friend who has seen much of the world, including lodges, fishing, cooked fish and beer:

It gets better than that, Buck. Fishing and drinking beer at lodges—all right, there are worse ways to spend a World Series. But it's going to get better, Buck, much better.

When you are a little older and sufficiently self-confident to talk to mature women, you will no longer find much pleasure in fleeing from girls to spend weeks in the woods with young men whose idea of life's ultimate experience is drinking beer after a fish dinner.

It gets a lot better than that, Buck. There are marvels of delight awaiting you. A sip of pure water by the Taj Mahal in the moonlight, coffee at Florian's in · Venice, a bottle of Montrachet at the Connaught in London, a dry martini in Manhattan's December dusk with a piano tinkling in the hotel bar, and all this with a woman at least slightly gray, who remembers the old days in Vienna, Beirut, Chicago and—oh, why not—Casablanca.

It's going to get a lot better, Buck, once you ask yourself why, if the fish-and-beer life is so good at the lodge, Harry's dad hasn't moved in to stay.

You Can't Lose 'Em All

Now that it's over I have to admit it was a pretty good holiday around our place. Our son Duke and his wife Louise came and spent several days and brought their dog, Biff.

Biff is a big fellow. Real big. But he has settled down a lot since last year when he ate the Christmas tree. I had been looking forward to having Biff again this year, but only halfheartedly, to tell you the truth. It is a lot easier having a dog eat the Christmas tree than it is to dismantle the thing yourself, but on the other hand it upsets Duke and Louise.

Last year they wanted to rush out right in the middle of the turkey and find a veterinarian to pump Biff's stomach, and that left a gaping hole in the middle of the day, and of course Biff stayed up all night howling with a stomach ache and belching pine needles all over the parlor rug.

Anyhow, Biff had settled down this year, which made for a pretty good holiday. So had our son Parker who came with his wife Sybil and stayed several days, though we always think of Parker's visits in terms of nights, since he likes to sleep until sundown, then have breakfast and settle down for six or seven hours of listening to old Rolling Stones records just about the time everybody else is going to bed.

Last year Parker and Biff had a terrible row. After three or four nights of tossing sleeplessly on account of the blasts from the Stones, Biff lost his temper and threatened to eat Parker's records. Fact is, I threatened to eat a few myself, but Parker is a big fellow now. It's been a long time since I could spank him with any success.

The long and short of it was that Parker faked out Biff by throwing him my Bing Crosby records and warned me that if I ate his Rolling Stones records he would never again get my car started for me. Parker, you see, is sort of a magician with carburetors and distributors as well as automobiles in general, all of which treat me with contempt.

Well, that's the kind of holiday we used to have, but not this year. This year was a pretty good one. Under Sybil's influence Parker settled down and played nothing at night but high-stakes poker with a group of beer guzzlers he has known since high school.

For a while we didn't think our daughter Glenda would join us on account of not being able to find a cat sitter to look after her four cats, but she did. We were over at Jim and Harriet's when she phoned from the airport. Jim and Harriet have a new dog named Prince and he had eaten their Christmas tree just before we arrived, and they were near tears, and I was comforting them, telling them they ought to be thankful they didn't have to listen to the Rolling Stones until 5 A.M., when Glenda phoned and said could we pick her up at the airport because no taxi driver was willing to transport four cats.

Well, I went out to the car and naturally it wouldn't start, so I had to walk home and get Parker out of bed—it was still only 4 P.M.—and bring him back to speak to the carburetor, then drive him back to our place so he could have breakfast before his poker cronies arrived, then drive to the airport and collect Glenda and her four cats, which I did without having a major accident. It was a pretty good holiday.

We were afraid maybe Glenda's cats and Biff would not get along and possibly destroy the couch in a fight, but not so. After stalking each other for a while, cats and dog came to a fair settlement of territorial rights under which the cats took the parlor and left the rest of the house to Biff.

The cats marked off their territory with the assistance of Glenda's male cat, Max Bialystock, who sprayed the couch, the wing chairs, the carpet and curtains with aromatic cat perfume. It was a pretty good holiday. I am told the parlor will be almost entirely inoffensive to the human nose by late July.

After Glenda arrived, Grandmother surprised us all by showing up from her home in the North. It was pretty cold that day—about two degrees below zero—and of course the furnace had quit work on the theory that the end of December is holiday time for furnaces as well as people, and the house was so cool that you could chill your eggnog by putting your own finger in it when Grandmother arrived from the North and said we didn't know what cold was. For real cold, she said, we ought to go north where she lived.

Usually Grandmother spends the whole week telling us how much colder it is up north where she lives than it is where we live, but this week she let up after only two days of boasting. This may have been because Biff threatened to bite her, or maybe because Biff really did bite her. As cold as it was, she wouldn't have been able to feel a bite and the toothmarks wouldn't have shown until the spring thaw.

In any case, her boasting stopped after only two days. It

was a pretty good holiday. By New Year's Day everybody had left us, and Jim and Harriet came over and brought Prince, and Prince ate our Christmas tree, saving us an awful job since he also finished off the ornaments for dessert. It was a pretty good holiday.

The Disposable Idea

When the thirty-year-old masses became inflamed by Gary Hart's "new ideas" campaign, I was suddenly overwhelmed with sadness. Partly, I suppose, this was brought on by discovery that the country would soon be run by the people I used to spank.

Down deep, of course, I always knew this time would come. That's probably why I took so much trouble to bring them up right. When riding the merry-go-round with them as a reward for passing arithmetic, and even when I was spanking them, what I was really telling them was, "Someday you're going to have to run this place, and I want you to do it better than I'm doing."

But it was their passion for "new ideas" that was more depressing. What was wrong with the old ideas? Taking a kid on the merry-go-round when the arithmetic grade was solid—that was an old idea. Spanking a kid for kicking Aunt Molly in the shins—another old idea. But weren't both of them still as sound as the day they first dawned in the human brain?

These were ideas that had passed the test of time, whereas most of the new ideas that have come along since I first rode the merry-go-round leave a lot to be desired. The atom bomb is a case in point. So are instant coffee, instant gratification and going to the movies seven nights a week right in your own parlor.

The sad reality about most new ideas is that they create new problems that are often worse than the problems they were intended to solve. I recall the early 1950's when everybody suddenly became rich enough to buy a car and somebody had a new idea: Let's everybody move to the suburbs and enjoy the green, pastoral life.

Here was the new idea at its absolute worst. It destroyed the cities. It buried the green, pastoral countryside under concrete and asphalt. It enslaved the country to the automobile, which poisoned the air, turned mothers into taxi drivers and finally made the whole economy hostage to the whims of Arabian politics.

Well, you can't expect thirty-year-olds to shun a new idea the way they'd skirt a swamp at midnight. I was thirty years old once myself and was in love with new ideas. Thus I came home inspired one night and shattered every Rolling Stones record in the house. It was a new idea for achieving peace and quiet.

The resulting uproar was so fierce that the next day I had to replace every record to keep the family from flying apart. When you look back like this, you can sympathize with those heartbroken kids who have since grown little worry lines around their eyes and believe that new ideas can erase them.

Despite all we have done for them, we have left so few really good old ideas that you can't help feeling sorry for them. When I think of them now, it is with a pang of guilt. If I had done a better job with them, I would not have let so many wonderful old ideas go out of American life.

Because I did, we have an entire generation that has never tasted dumplings and gravy, an entire generation that thinks chicken has to be made in a factory, an entire generation that thinks a tomato is basically a red baseball, only with less taste.

For such people, it is easy to sneer at old ideas, for they cannot know that these old ideas were new ideas just thirty years ago—new ideas that destroyed perfectly splendid old ideas.

They are a generation that has never known travel, an idea older than Moses, an idea that still thrived until thirty years ago when travel was abolished and replaced by the new idea of transportation. For most of their lives, these poor people have suffered the dreary discomfort of transportation when the memory of their blood cried out for the glories of travel.

Packed like hoofed beef into sealed cylinders and rocketed hither and yon through the air for a two-day trip to here and a fourteen-day vacation to there, they have never known the soothing throb of an ocean liner carrying them on a seven-day journey to Naples or the delight of waking in a Pullman berth and breakfasting on white linen in a California-bound train.

Travel was a good old idea, which was killed by the new idea of transportation. And why? Because travel was not economical. It's the same reason dumplings and gravy vanished, and chickens were made in factories, and tomatoes turned into baseballs. A new idea had infected America: Quality didn't pay, therefore make everything disposable and forgettable.

We did a disservice in not preserving those good old ideas for the kids we spanked thirty years ago. We left them with lives in which too much was disposable and forgettable. No wonder they are hungry for new ideas.

The Day of the Young Fogy

A good place to see Young Fogies is on the "MacNeil/Lehrer NewsHour." When you tune in, look for the young man disagreeing with everything the young man from the American Civil Liberties Union just said. He will be the Young Fogy.

If you don't like listening to arguments that get nowhere, turn off the sound and look at their eyeglasses. The fellow wearing horn rims is the A.C.L.U. man; the one with the wire rims is the Young Fogy.

Wire rims are worn by ninety-seven Young Fogies out of one hundred. This is their way of showing respect for Assistant Attorney-General William Bradford Reynolds, whom they always refer to as "Brad," whether they know him or not, just as newspaper reporters Henry Kissinger never heard of always call him "Henry." Brad wears wire rims.

Brad is known as "the dean of Young Fogies" and is a hero of the Young Fogy Youth Cadres. These accolades result from his civil-rights work at the Justice Department, where he wages the struggle to restore civil rights to white males oppressed by women and blacks with the connivance of the Supreme Court.

Brad's discovery that white men are victims of racial and sexual discrimination galvanized the oppressed masses of young white men packed into Harvard, Stanford and Yale, not to mention those on "hold" at Hotchkiss, Exeter and Andover, and led to the formation of the first Young Fogy Youth Cadres.

The question those pioneer young white males asked was destined to restore dignity to the word "fogy":

Why should young white men have to toil through incredibly elegant schools in order to become Wall Street law partners and investment bankers when women and blacks can get first crack at jobs in the fire department despite attending inferior schools?

The Young Fogy Youth Cadres foresaw that, as oppressed people, they would be lost in the general human mass called "yuppies" unless they developed pride in their youthful fogyism. They had no intention of becoming yuppies, a human category that included A.C.L.U. sympathizers as well as women and blacks insensitive to their role as oppressors.

And so was formed the Young Fogy Finishing School where white male youth was taught the fogyfied graces: how to wear the Brad wire rims, for example; the importance of wearing suits with vests; the slovenliness of wearing a necktie loosened in the manner of young A.C.L.U. men.

Yes, deep down, the Young Fogy is just as regular a guy as the young A.C.L.U. man with his loosened necktie, but he will never adopt vulgar "regular-guy" tricks, like loosening his necktie, just to please the crowd.

His mind honed to steel-trap sharpness by incessant intellectual combat with young A.C.L.U. men, the Young Fogy disposes of the regular-guy question by asking, "If God meant regular guys to wear their neckties loosened, why did He put collar buttons on shirts?"

The Young Fogy's natural habitat is an "Institute." The word "Institute" suggests great seriousness, but any Institute worth the name is also an encampment of potential TV stars.

Washington, being the home office of Young Fogies, naturally teems with Institutes. In these Institutes, hundreds of Young Fogies are on constant duty awaiting the call of the "MacNeil/Lehrer NewsHour," where they will disagree with everything that young men from the A.C.L.U. will say.

Do Messrs. MacNeil and Lehrer occasionally tire of presenting arguments that illuminate nothing but the disagreement between young A.C.L.U. men and Young Fogies? If so, Young Fogies need not feel discouraged, because the Institute has probably got itself an hour or two on the C-Span cable for a seminar on the network TV news shows' dangerous lack of respect for Hamiltonian economic theory, and one of the Sunday interview shows may phone for a Young Fogy to come and dilate on the intellectual shabbiness of the Supreme Court.

As all this suggests, it is not easy being a Young Fogy. Of course, it's not easy being a young A.C.L.U. man either, unless you're a masochist who enjoys being constantly disagreed with on the "MacNeil/Lehrer NewsHour."

Young Fogies, however, are quick to point out that constantly disagreeing is no picnic either, especially when you can't even loosen your necktie. Naturally, they would much rather have exciting jobs in the fire department, but oppressive women and blacks make those jobs inaccessible.

What else can they do but sit around the Institute waiting for MacNeil or Lehrer to phone for a Young Fogey. No, it is not easy being a Young Fogy.

It can't be so easy being MacNeil and Lehrer either; they have to listen.

A Young Fogy's Guide

The recent report in this space on the rise of the Young Fogies has elicited barrels of inquiries from readers. Here are a few, and their answers.

Can a gay be a Young Fogy?

Yes, but only if he quits calling himself "gay" and starts saying "homosexual." Being a Young Fogy is serious. Homosexuality is no excuse for using frivolous language.

Your report suggested that only a male lawyer could qualify to become a Young Fogy. Is there no hope for persons of the feminine gender, like me?

Absolutely none. If, however, you are willing to quit being a person of the feminine gender and to start referring to yourself as a lady, you may qualify for membership in The Lovely Spouse Society. To anticipate your next question: No, you will not be allowed to eat lunch there, but will be admitted for cocktails and dinner.

I am 51 years old. Would I have to lie about my age if I wanted to become a Young Fogy?

The worst thing you can do is lie, because Young Fogies are very sincere about their desire to put more people in prison. However, if you have held your waistline down so you still look trim in a three-piece suit, and if you have never abandoned your faith in capital punishment, the Young Fogies may be willing to overlook your age.

I have bought the three-piece suit and the wire-rimmed eyeglasses. I have written letters to the editor abusing the American Civil Liberties Union for subverting the Constitution. Nothing helps. The Young Fogies still ignore me. How can I win their respect?

Publish a revisionist history of the Constitution proving that the Emancipation Proclamation was illegal.

A distinguished Young Fogy invited me to lunch in an expensive restaurant. I knew why. He was on the Admissions Committee and wanted to check out my three-piece suit and wire-rimmed glasses and hear me denounce the American Civil Liberties Union. After picking up the lunch tab, he said I was "not Young Fogy timber." What did I do wrong?

By letting him pay the lunch bill, you outraged the Young Fogies' most sacred principle: There is no free lunch.

I have heard it said that Young Fogies never ride in limousines. Why?

This is not true, although no Young Fogy would be caught

dead wearing his identifying three-piece suit and wire-rimmed specs in a limousine, for fear that the Eastern, A.C.L.U.-dominated press would make jokes about his becoming a limousine liberal. To preserve his reputation as a four-door-sedan conservative, the Young Fogy disguises himself in horn rims, faded jeans and a magenta-tinted punk wig before stepping out limousine-style.

What is it like being married to a Young Fogy?

Women who have had the experience say it is very gratifying if you enjoy lectures on constitutional law and the illegality of the Emancipation Proclamation, but disappointing if you're hoping to get out of washing the dishes.

I have heard that Young Fogies are marvelous lovers. Is this true?

Marvelous lovers? You're talking about people who, given a lovemaking situation, won't make a move that hasn't been approved by the Supreme Court. Really now!

What's it like being a Young Fogy's child?

The bedtime stories are pretty dull unless you're the kind of child whose blood runs cold at mention of Earl Warren and the American Civil Liberties Union. Also, no permissiveness. First time you're caught with a copy of Playboy under the mattress, you have to read and write an 800-word book report on "The Ed Meese Story; or, The Rediscovery of the Lost American Constitution." Second offense: You have to help your mother do the dishes for six months, even though you're a boy.

As a lady who wants to save America from the American Civil Liberties Union before it's too late, I resent being sidetracked into the ineffectual Lovely Spouse Society. My idea is, we could have thousands of women fighting for the Young Fogified philosophy if I could only think of the perfect name to attract them. What do you think of a name like Young Fogyesses?

It could set the Young Fogy movement back twenty years. Fogyesses is one of those words that gives you a headache just to look at. And think of all the people who are going to say you're too dumb to know how to spell "four guesses." You don't want people associating lady Young Fogies with dumbness. The sensible name for your movement is The Young Fogypersons. I give you the name free. Yes, though there is no free lunch, there is free naming. Trust me. I am not a member of the American Civil Liberties Union.

Giving Till It Hurts

When I was a tot there was only Christmas to worry about, but then I aged, and along came Valentine's Day. I couldn't believe it.

"It was just two months ago that I went out and bought a Christmas card and a Christmas gift for Mommy," I said. "And now you're telling me I have to buy a valentine for somebody I love?"

"That's the way life is, sonny," said the voice of American civilization. That year I bought the Christmas card, the Christmas gift and the valentine, and I aged some more.

And learned about Mother's Day.

"This is incredible," I said. "I buy the Christmas card. I buy the Christmas gift. I buy the valentine. And it still isn't enough?"

"You're a big boy now," said the voice. "Quit whining and buy the Mother's Day card and the Mother's Day gift."

It was getting hard to keep track of all the dates that had to be celebrated with cards and gifts. When my mother gave me a card that said "Happy Birthday" and baked me a cake and invited my friends in to eat it and bring cards and gifts, I was—I'll admit it—suspicious.

"What does it mean when people give me cards and gifts on my birthday?" I asked.

"It means they love you," my mother said.

"Sure, but doesn't it also mean—?"

That was exactly what it meant. I was now old enough to remember other people's birthdays—at least Mother's and Baby Sister's—with cards and gifts.

I was in high school now. While other boys were learning to drive cars and jitterbug the girls right out of their bobby socks, I was struggling with the calendar. As youth faded, I faithfully bought the Christmas card, the Christmas gift, the valentine, the Mother's Day card, the Mother's Day gift, the birthday card and birthday gift for my mother, and the birthday card and birthday gift for my sister.

It kept me so occupied I didn't get around to learning about girls. Naturally, then, I was puzzled when a girl proposed marriage.

"What does marriage mean?" I asked her.

"It means you'll have to remember our wedding anniversary every year with a card, a gift and an expensive restaurant meal with champagne," she explained.

Well, why not? Getting married—at least it would provide somebody worth giving the valentine to. Before it was time to give her the anniversary card, the anniversary gift and the anniversary champagne dinner, though, she spoke to me sadly.

"You forgot my birthday," she said.

"The anniversary card, the anniversary gift and the anniversary champagne dinner aren't adequate?" I inquired, knowing what the answer would be. The following year kept me busier than I had dreamed possible.

I bought the Christmas card, the Christmas gift, the valentine, the Mother's Day card, the Mother's Day gift, the anniversary card, the anniversary gift, the anniversary champagne dinner and the birthday cards and the birthday gifts for my mother, my sister and my wife.

Other men were becoming captains of industry and flying their personal jets to Switzerland, but I was not envious. I was too grateful to calendar science for not creating a year with 600 days.

When my wife and I decided to have three children, I knew what it meant. As all of us aged, life became more complex. I bought the Christmas card, the Christmas gift, the valentine, the Mother's Day card, the Mother's Day gift, the anniversary card, the anniversary gift, the anniversary champagne dinner and the birthday cards and birthday gifts not only for my mother, my sister and my wife, but also for the three children born to my wife and me.

The children rapidly aged and married, bringing us three new children-in-law with birthdays not to be forgotten. The thing was growing. Scarcely a day passed that did not require a card, a gift, flowers, a bottle of champagne—especially after the four grandchildren arrived.

Now we were coping with fourteen birthdays, four wedding anniversaries, three generations of valentines and Mother's Days and a fresh nuisance—Father's Day—that somebody sneaked in years ago while I wasn't looking, presumably on the assumption that anyone who bought as many greeting cards as I deserved to receive many more unspeakable neckties than Christmas can provide.

Am I complaining? Far from it. I am boasting proudly: I have done my duty. This is more than can be said for certain family ingrates whose identities were silently recorded at my recent birthday party.

Baby Boomers

It was inevitable that the baby-boom generation of the 1950's would eventually come to power in America, and it did. Life was bound to be different when they took over, but I was ready to adjust. "Youth must be served," they say. I was prepared to serve it cravenly.

I had known the baby-boom generation from its cradle and, so, knew it had terrible scores to settle with its forefathers, not to mention its foremothers. I also knew its unique capacity for peevishness, especially when automobiles were discussed.

For this reason, I had my strategy ready when the company announced that Giles Conway, twenty-nine-year-old corporate genius, was the new boss of my department. Being familiar with the frustrations of his generation, I reasoned that he would immediately look for a reason to fire me.

It was obvious how he would do it:

"Can I ask a big favor of you?" he would inquire.

"What is it, Giles?"

"Can I use the car on Saturday night?"

Naturally, he would expect me to say, "No," after which he would chew the rug, whine that I didn't love him, and tell me I was fired.

"We'll see about that, Giles Conway," I muttered as I prepared counterstrategy. It was uncomplicated. When he asked to use the car, I planned to say, "Of course you can. And what's more, when you bring it back at 3 A.M. be sure to see if I'm sleeping soundly and, if I am, play some Rolling Stones records at maximum volume on my stereo."

Such was the scheme for holding on to my meal ticket, but they didn't call Giles Conway a twenty-nine-year-old corporate genius for nothing. He had studied plot twists for years by watching Rod Serling's "Twilight Zone," I suppose.

Pausing at my desk, he said, "Could you do me a big favor, old-timer?"

"Anything, sir. Anything at all."

"Ask me if you can use the company car Saturday night," he said.

Here was a surprise. I asked anyhow: "Can I use the company car Saturday night?"

"Absolutely not!" he roared and, beaming with diabolical satisfaction, studied me for symptoms of anguish. Too slow-witted to realize that he might raise my salary if I chewed the rug and cried that he didn't love me, I could only gasp, "Why not?"

"Because I'm the boss around here, and what I say goes," he thundered, and stalked off a happy man.

It was soon apparent that he needed me. He invited me for dinner with five other people who had worn diapers in 1955 and started the discussion by saying, "You're too old ever to have watched 'Ding Dong School' with Miss Frances, I suppose."

Suppressing a suicidal urge to gloat that he was too young ever to have heard "Chandu the Magician" and "Buck Rogers in the Twenty-fifth Century" back-to-back on radio, I said, "Television must have really been exciting in your days. Tell me about Captain Kangaroo and the Pharaohs."

"Don't you know anything at all?" his date said. "Captain Kangaroo had Mr. Moose and Mr. Greenjeans."

"And the Pharaohs," said Conway, "sang with Sam the Sham."

"Tell him about Herman's Hermits," somebody said.

"The trouble with people your age is that you don't know any history," said Giles Conway.

I asked to be excused to go listen to some Benny Goodman records, but he refused. "Sit here and listen to us, and maybe you'll learn something," he said.

By 11 P.M. they were reminiscing about adventures in the gasoline lines in the good old days of 1973 when Conway interrupted.

"It's past your bedtime, mister," he said. "Go home and get into bed right away. And don't leave your light on."

I obeyed gratefully. He's ordered me to come to his place next week and take a bath. I know why. He wants to be able to yell at me for making a mess of the bathroom. I'll leave a wet towel on his sofa and a pair of gym shoes on his dining table. After he blows up about that, he'll probably feel good enough to give me that raise.

Don't I worry he might read this? Come on, this is the baby-boom generation. If it's not on television, it doesn't exist.

Prescript

By 1969 those wonderful kids born to the victors of World War II had met the future and decided it was theirs. Parents were resisting all across the landscape. The result was a monumental battle for turf. A new age was at hand, but who was going to own it— parents or those once wonderful kids?

Once such wonderful little darlings that all decent parents wanted to build them a better world, the kids (always called "kids" in those days) were now revealed to be people. Not un-wrinkled replicas of Mom and Dad eager to relive Mom's and Dad's lives, but individual, idiosyncratic, irritating, infuriating, maddening human beings. People with minds of their own, just like the ornery people Mom and Dad had to contend with every day out in the world.

The kids attacked Mom and Dad and everything they stood for at the most sensitive point: the state of the world. It wasn't the better world the old-timers had promised. It was a dreadful world, said the kids. Mom and Dad were failures. It was time to move them offstage and let the kids make a truly better world.

So we had "the generation gap" with every cherished belief of the old folks under attack by the new. On campuses this produced what were called, in the overheated newspaper prose of the era, "student rebellions." Some were indeed violent and bloody, though most consisted of thumbing the nose at authority by walking out of classes and holding the dean prisoner in his office until he acceded to whatever "unconditional demands" the students were making that week.

Graduation ceremonies posed terrible threats for authority. Every graduate of real character was expected to do something humiliating to the college if subjected to platform appearances by representatives of the hated "Establishment," by anyone who could possibly be branded a "war criminal," by people who spoke well of the government, or by anyone else who was thought to be on the wrong side of "the generation gap."

Colleges, anxious to avoid dreadful incidents that might alienate rich potential contributors to the endowment fund, suddenly became desperate for commencement speakers who wouldn't infuriate the students. That's why I happened to find myself at Hamilton College in the spring of 1969 looking out over the all-male graduating class and talking very much like a preacher.

The Becoming Looseness
of Doom

When I was asked to address the graduating class here today, I naturally leaped at the opportunity. The impulse was probably similar to the one that impels men to leap from the Empire State Building.

These days, when any man over thirty is offered an audience that was born in the Truman Administration, he is irresistibly impelled to rise from his chair, take a running start and leap at it. There is no accounting for this. It probably indicates the rising strength of the death wish that accompanies hardening of the arteries.

When my first elation subsided and sanity returned, however, it occurred to me that I had not the slightest notion of what one was supposed to *say* in a commencement speech. So I went to the library and spent many hours reading old commencement speeches, hoping to learn the secret of how the thing was done. It was grim reading. The typical commencement speech, I discovered, is given by a hanging judge on his day off. Feeling relaxed, no doubt, and therefore full of mercy, he lets the graduates off lightly by sentencing them to a lifetime at hard labor on a global rockpile. Tradition among these fellows has them urging the graduates to *go forth* into the world and do their utmost. But what a world!

After reading six or seven descriptions of the world painted by skilled commencement orators, I was terribly sorry that I had ever gone forth into it in the first place. If my knowledge of the world were limited to what I had read in commencement speeches, I should stand up here today and tell you: "To those of you about to go forth into the world, heed my advice. Don't do it!"

My studies showed that you cannot do this. There are only two set conventions for a commencement speech, but both absolutely must be observed. First, the graduates must be advised to *go forth*. Second, they must also be congratulated upon their commencement. This second makes no sense. Nothing could be sillier than to congratulate the young on such occasions. If we are to behave sensibly, the persons to be congratulated today are your parents, for they are the people who are truly, at this hour, commencing.

For them, life is at last about to begin. They are the people who have conquered the diapers, beaten the multiplication tables, hoodwinked the bankers and staved off the undertakers. For them, freedom can finally commence.

And so, I congratulate them upon *their* commencement, and invite you to join me. In a less youth-struck society, this address would be devoted to advising them what to do with their new freedom, but this would violate the rules. As James Thurber observed, "Youth must be served—frequently stuffed with chestnuts."

Therefore, let us begin.

I do not share the traditional commencement orator's view of the world as global rockpile and, therefore, I shall not urge you not to go forth into it. I believe that the joy of living can never be tasted until a man cuts himself loose from the last ties of youthful dependence and swims free in that big turbulent ocean out there. For this reason I would say to those of you sitting here today, with both feet still on dry land, what e. e. cummings said to all those reluctant to wade into life: "Hey, there's a hell of a good universe next door—let's go!"

I also have one piece of cautionary advice I hope you will keep in mind when you get out there. It is this: My generation has worked hard and done a remarkable job of building a world we can all be proud of. When you get out there, please don't mess it up. My generation, you see, was not as lucky as yours. When *we* graduated from college, the world we inherited from *our* parents was a dreadful place.

The older generation of that day had been a disastrous failure. Politically, their corrupt system of values had given us not one, but two world wars in twenty years. Economically, they had produced the most devastating depression in history. Their aspirations for the future were beautifully summed up in the immortal campaign slogan of Herbert Hoover—"a chicken in every pot." Whole continents were dominated and exploited by a system of white colonial imperialism.

Culturally, they were still in the Dark Ages. Fanny Hill and her old friend, Henry Miller, were officially banned from the United States. Their cultural heroes were Rin Tin Tin—Rin Tin Tin was Lassie's grandfather—and Bing Crosby, a sort of prehistoric Wayne Newton.

In short, the world was in dreadful shape in those days, but, fortunately for you, my generation was more than adequate to the task of cleaning up the mess.

Consider just a few of our achievements:

We have eliminated the insane cycle of world war every twenty years—a cycle which had resulted in the deaths of more than twenty-five million men in our parents' lifetime.

We have rebuilt Europe, raising out of rubble and ash a new state even more congested than the Emperor Augustus created on the ruins of the Roman Republic.

We have outlawed racial segregation in the United States. We have eliminated such human scourges as tuberculosis, poliomyelitis and buck teeth. We have put Shakespeare in the drugstore, Coca-Cola in the Piazza San Marco, Matt Dillon in the living rooms of Tokyo, and X-rated movies in your neighborhood theater.

We have abolished the scrub board, the shaving brush and the hand crank. We have invented the automatic hair dryer, the contraceptive pill and the telegenic statesmen. We have unleashed Norman Mailer. We have put whipped cream in an aerosol bomb, Lawrence Welk on stereo tape under the dashboard, and the pop-top can in the refrigerator.

We have abolished the teaching of Latin—not to mention the teaching of English. We have developed and perfected the instant skyscraper, the electronic narcotic and the workless job.

What we have accomplished is, I submit, a revolution of heroic proportion.

Admittedly, the mess we inherited from our parents has not been reshaped to perfection, but if you look at the record from a detached viewpoint, I think you will have to concede that we have done an impressive job, particularly when you reflect that we had to work with a world we never made.

In fact, we are even about to give you an unusually detached viewpoint to view it from—the most detached viewpoint ever afforded to man.

In a few weeks we will place a human being on the moon. Others of you will follow him there. For the first time in human history even the densest clod will be able to stand there and partake of the vision of the philosophers.

To some we will seem tiny prisoners on a lonely rock adrift in the void. Others will look out across the ocean of space to the blue globe of home and ask, "Is it not a marvelous thing to be a man and have a universe to know?"

Many of my generation are angry with what they take to be your generation's lack of appreciation for all this. If I interpret them correctly, you are charged with being, at best, a generation of ingrates; at worst, a conspiracy of well-poisoners.

I will tell you confidentially that this charge is fraudulent and should not trouble you. What we have done with the society, we did not do with you foremost in mind. As you are now, so once were we. We, too, were determined to take the world and shape it to our desires.

We, too, regarded society as deplorable. Society *was* deplorable. Society still *is* deplorable. Society will *always* be deplorable.

When we thought of improving it, it was not with the purpose of making it a shining gift to the next generation, but of making it more tolerable for ourselves.

You will soon discover that the next generation is not planned for with any exactitude. When you are young and remaking worlds, the next generation is not even anticipated.

You talk a great deal about building a better world for your children, but when you are young you can no more envision a world inherited by your children than you can conceive of dying. The society you mold, you mold for yourself.

It was this way with my generation. We were unhappy with what we inherited and we tried to reshape it in ways that would make it more tolerable to us. *You* were not uppermost in our thoughts.

Now, in middle age, some of us are trying to rewrite history. Some of us tell you, "We labored and dared and sacrificed—all for you—yet we hear no thanks."

You will not be unduly moved, I hope, by these laments. They are sentimental cries from persons so attached to the society they have rebuilt that they cannot bear the thought of seeing it overhauled by the new proprietors.

I urge you not to feel guilty about rejecting a great deal of the legacy left you by the former owners. It is, after all, your property now, this society, and you will have to re-do a lot of it if you are to live comfortably in it.

I would suggest, however, that you not reject it all out of hand, for we are giving you much that is priceless.

I do not refer to the notorious material affluence, which we also hand you. This material comfort was a luxury to my generation. Sociologists who have pummeled your brains, studied you and graphed you, tell us that most of you take it for granted— rather as we took for granted indoor plumbing—and that some of you regard it with contempt.

This is all right. Indoor plumbing is nice, but past civilizations flourished without it. What was luxury to us, however, has yielded quite a different luxury for you. This is one of the most precious luxuries available to man—the luxury of being able to apply rigorous moral principle to the conduct of society.

My generation never planned to set you up in such high moral style. Not at all. It was an incidental by-product of affluence which we did not foresee.

What we did, quite accidentally with our affluence, you see, was to create a whole new stage of man. Until quite recently in this country, people went from adolescence directly into adulthood, with all the unpleasantness which that ugly word connotes.

Before a man could mature, he was confronted with the nuisance of earning a living. His first adult years were spent learning how to shape himself to fit successfully into a social structure which he had had no influence in building.

He learned the value of compromise and cunning, learned

not to stand too boldly on principle, learned to conform to the standards of neighbors and colleagues without raising the kind of questions that might label him "oddball" among the persons who could control his destiny.

The coming of affluence changed all that. Suddenly, youth no longer ended with adolescence. Suddenly, great masses of adolescents were required to prolong youth into their adult years, and as this happened we began to develop a new stage of mankind.

You are the beneficiaries of this development. You have not been forced to spend your early adult years mastering the arts of compromise, cunning, hypocrisy and conforming. The affluence created by my generation has spared you that.

Instead, you have enjoyed the luxury of becoming adult while retaining the sense of moral principle and the capacity for moral outrage which are youth's.

This has made for an explosive new element in society. For the first time in our history we have a large mass of adult Americans who have not been required to jettison the purity of youth in order to keep body and soul together.

In consequence, we are now seeing, in the so-called "student rebellion," the tremendous power that moral principle can generate when fused with adult sensitivity.

This event is characterized by an inordinate amount of moral self-righteousness among the young. We are all familiar with youth's clichés about adult hypocrisy. We have all heard about the moral bankruptcy of the Establishment and about the immorality of the old men who run the government.

Though the rhetoric is facile, there is a good deal of truth behind it. There *is* hypocrisy in the organization of society. There *is* compromise. There *is* immorality.

There is also sharp irony in the fact that the students for whom the campus Savonarolas speak have not, in the mass, hesitated to accept the fruits of these vices.

You, sitting here today, for example, are members of the most comfortable class in the world. This is what might be called the educated American youthocracy.

The degree you receive today is only incidentally a certificate of your intellectual attainment. Its primary function, you will find, is as your visa to the sweet land of full employment, fancy wives, high-rent town houses and private schools for your children.

It admits you to the full privileges of American society, with all its hypocrisies and compromises and immorality. And this, you will find, is a society governed *by* you and *for* you—the privileged agents of established thought, order and income.

Some of these privileges you have already tasted, such as an educational system organized on the principle of the greatest good for the moneyed class.

You have been sheltered by an Army drafted largely from persons for whom the educational system was designed *not* to work. You are aware that young men of the youthocracy have been for years excluded, by virtue of their affluence, from the obligation to be shot at by illiterates in unpleasant latitudes.

You will find later that it will not be as easy to dismantle this system as it now seems. Shortly you will become more intimately involved with Government, and you will see that Government in the United States, as now constituted, has been built to work for *you.*

Though the poor will be taxed to compensate for the revenue loss caused by tax loopholes created for *your* benefit, it is *you* who will be the chief beneficiary of Government activity, and not the poor.

The best schools will not be in *their* neighborhoods, but in *yours.*

The great ugly highways needed to ease your way from home to office will not go through *your* neighborhoods, but through *theirs.*

The function of the police will be to protect *you* from *them.*

When war is necessary to protect this society of yours, and money is needed to pay for it, it will not be obtained by raising *your* taxes, but by reducing expenditures on programs for *their* benefit.

Now I trust that all of you are as capable as I am of deploring this organization of society, and more capable than I have proven of doing something to change it.

We have granted you the luxury of sitting in judgment on society, and you have indulged it with a vengeance, though not,

I might note, without accepting the fruits of the vices you con-
demn.

I doubt that you can be indicted for that. In this court
youth is a mitigating circumstance. The serious question, however, is, What policy will you adopt toward a society you have
judged and found guilty? Where does the judgment lead?

There is considerable evidence that for some it leads into
curiously distraught attitudes.

I am thinking particularly of those who would substitute
love for national policy—and think Joan Baez would make a
perfectly satisfactory Secretary of State.

The dream of love as the universal panacea is a dangerous
delusion. The truth is that love is one of the world's most violent
phenomena. In its more exalted forms it is the historic justification for the holy war. In its physical manifestation it is responsible for half the Saturday-night shootings in America.

Others seem to despair so intensely for society that they
want to destroy the whole thing and start over again. Their idea
is to build a world where humanity can be permitted to come to
its senses.

This is perfectly all right with me. My business is satire. I
cannot think of a richer source of material to preserve satire into
my old age than a serious movement to bring humanity to its
senses. Whether it will amuse *you*, however, is doubtful.

History suggests that twentieth-century man is unsurpassed
at destroying things, but peculiarly inept at improving what he
builds on the ruins.

I suggest that before you join the "Let's-tear-it-all-down-
and-rebuild-it-right-movement," you look at the results of such
movements in the past.

To start you might consider the construction of the Third
Reich on the ruins of the Weimar Republic. Then you might
consider the construction of the Interstate Highway System on
the ruins of our cities. Finally, you might consider the construction of the thermonuclear balance of terror on the ruins of the
balance of power.

The destruction policy and the love policy both lead to
dead ends, but I doubt that either has much following here or on
any other American campus.

The more widespread attraction, I suspect, is the drop-out policy. It is terribly easy to drop out from life, far easier than it is to drop out from school. This is because the life dropout has become a fashionable community figure.

We find him in all age groups—blotto in the Haight-Ashbury and sodden on the Riviera.

Some use narcotics to tune the world out permanently and some use alcohol. Some use television. Television narcosis, in fact, probably accounts for far more social inertness than all the chemical narcotics combined. Others disappear into their jobs and find their work a socially acceptable pretext for refusing to live.

It is not hard to account for the impulse to drop out. It is a natural outgrowth of despair, and in the last twenty years despair seems to have replaced optimism as the American mood.

It is not quite so easy to say why this has happened, but the evidence is persuasive. You find it expressed in our literature, in our films and in our religion—or lack of it. Our humor is of the gallows variety; our music a discord. Our moralists' attitude is one of revulsion, and their message, fire and brimstone.

Our artists constantly confront us with a contrast between material plenty and spiritual death. In a world of fantastic wealth and excitement, they tell us, humanity is imprisoned in joylessness.

Our young shun commitment to the great institutions of American society, fearing that they will reduce their identities to cyphers in the superorganization.

In such an atmosphere despair is to be expected. We are urged to believe that this extraordinary world we have built is a people trap—a world in which values have ceased to exist, where everything is relative and nothing is what it appears.

If we accept this vision of life, then life itself becomes a pointless joke, and man can only retaliate by withdrawing from it into a totally self-centered existence devoted to the hedonistic pursuit of momentary pleasures.

To those who accept this view, the world is suffused with a sense of doom. Its people have been the victims of a dirty trick—life.

Being born was, for them, a disaster, and in a mindless

seizure of self-pity they spite themselves by working at destroying themselves moment by moment.

The destruction, you will find if you accept this vision of the world, does not proceed by violence. On this path, destruction has become more thorough, more insidious than a destruction of the body. Here, it is man's humanity that is destroyed.

You will all recognize the death symptoms, perhaps in some persons you know, perhaps already sprouting in yourselves. They are such things as boredom, hedonism, resignation, the inability to sustain the most primitive human relationships, such as sexual love, interpersonal loyalty and even simple communication.

It is very difficult to prevail against this contemporary mood of despair and the accompanying decision to drop out. Indeed, there are important elements of truth behind the vision that impels the dropout. In a world of such unutterable complexity as ours, some sense of human entrapment is inevitable. When old codes and value systems are being rendered irrelevant by scientific and technological revolution, some sense of disorientation is a natural human response.

When we are forced to accept the possibility of the instant atomization of all society as part of the price we must pay for living here, it is natural that there should be a tendency to dwell on our mortality.

Where we must all balk, however, is at the assumption that being born into a world in flux was a dirty trick played on us by life.

The exciting times to be born have always been during moments when old orders were tumbling down. This is why the Athenians and the Renaissance men still stir memories in our blood. In the midst of cataclysm, they exulted in having been born.

I do not know whether this is such a golden time, but there is no doubt in my mind that any time is a better time to be born than no time. Fate's dirtiest trick is played on those who are never born at all.

And so I urge only this upon you, and nothing more: that you not be lured by the easy temptation to yield to the fashionable life of un-birth avenged by living death.

e. e. cummings once put it like this: The world, he said, is made up of two groups—"We and mostpeople." "Mostpeople," he wrote, regard life as "catastrophe unmitigated."

But We—"We," he said, "can never be born enough. We are human beings; for whom birth is a supremely welcome mystery, the mystery of growing; the mystery which happens only and whenever we are faithful to ourselves. You and I wear the dangerous looseness of doom and find it becoming. Life, for eternal us, is *now*—

"And *now* is much too busy being a little more than everything to seem anything—catastrophic included."

BLACK HAT
VICTORIOUS

I was going to title this section "Culture" until I remembered the deadening thud with which that word fell on my mind in high-school days. The instant some well-meaning teacher said "culture," I groaned inwardly and thought of everything dull: Wagner's operatic "Ring," Milton's "Paradise Lost," Renaissance art, classical ballet, Shakespearean theater, ancient mythology . . .

It is embarrassing now to list all the miracles of human creation that once seemed to me only tedious, mind-numbing "culture." Still, what's to be expected of a high-school student who had been mired too long in pulp fiction, swing music, gangster movies and the journalism of William Randolph Hearst? Hearst was supposed to have said that the typical newspaper reader cared about only three subjects—blood, money and sexual intercourse. Whether Hearst said it or not, his newspapers dealt lavishly in all three commodities, and I read them avidly.

I was resolutely lowbrow, which was what Joe Sixpacks and rednecks were called in those days. Not that I wore the label proudly, as the dumber lowbrows did. Being adolescent, I simply wanted to be like most people. In southwest Baltimore this meant being a lowbrow. The boys who hung out on the street corner were not dumb by any means, but neither did they pass the hours listening to Wagner, arguing about Shakespeare, or doing anything else that could be called highbrow. The proper form was to be contemptuous of highbrows. We all groaned when the teacher said "culture."

That seems silly now, because what is culture, after all, but a word that speaks of growth—of things grown and of the soil, or laboratory, or society providing the nourishment that makes things grow and determines what they will grow into. The pieces that follow are about the intellectual nutrients that make the American mind whatever it may be. For most of us the important nutrients are anything but highbrow. They are not symphonic music, history, poetry, opera, ballet or theater, but movies, best-sellers, popular music, television, newspapers and magazines.

In the past thirty years the nature of all these has changed radically, and the nature of Americans has changed with them. Television, for instance, has changed the way Americans keep up with what's going on in the world. The citizenry used to get its information from newspapers and radio. Now the majority relies on television as its chief source of supply. Instead of being nourished on words, our minds are stuffed with such pictures as cameras can make.

The question is whether we are any better informed under the new dispensation than we were back when Mr. Hearst was marinating us in blood, money and sex. My answer is, who knows? Or, to borrow the favorite sign-off line of all television reporters who feel obliged to seem as wise as Solomon: "Only time will tell."

The XI P.M. Report

"Good evening. I am Gaius Fulvius. My colleague is Marcus Fluvius and this is the XI P.M. Fulvius-Fluvius Report brought to you on WSPQR Channel XVI, where the big story tonight is still that strange star hovering over the troubled Middle East. What do you make of that star, Marcus?"

"It sounds like the kind of star you see after one of those five-day orgies down at Capri, Gaius."

"Funny you should mention that, Marcus, because we also have a special film report tonight on how inflation is cutting into the orgy budget of the typical Roman family. And from faraway, fog-shrouded Britain, a new idea in how to dress for an orgy at practically no cost at all. Our cameramen have found some Englishmen up there—they call themselves Druids—who run around in the woods with nothing on but blue paint."

"When in Rome, do as the Druids do, eh, Gaius?"

"All these stories and others when the Fulvius-Fluvius Report continues, right after these messages."

Commercial interlude. The excellence of Cicero Chariot Springs illustrated. Also the superiority of Caracalla Bath Soap and Vestal Talcum Powder for relieving the itch of toga irritation. A paid plea for the election of Quintus Cunctator as quaestor of Rome. A public-service commercial urging Romans not to drop litter in the Forum, and a demonstration of a new wax that lasts twice as long on the atrium floor.

"And now, our top story tonight, that mysterious star over the oil-rich Middle East. A party of three Wise Men has been on the road for several days now, traveling eastward in the direction of the star, and they have attracted a large number of media representatives."

"Fascinating, Gaius. I saw one report that over 1,500 news people are already accredited to the Wise Men, and more applications for credentials pouring in by the hour."

"Exactly right, Marcus, and tonight that huge crowd of newsmen rioted in a small town south of Jericho when the local innkeeper was unable to put most of them up in the tiny six-room inn where the Wise Men had stopped for the night. There are rumors that King Herod, who doesn't like mysterious stars much anyhow, may crack down on the Wise Men for creating a public nuisance."

"Haven't we spent a lot of time on this story, Gaius, old pal? I want to see these blue Druids."

"One last item, Marcus. It was learned today that the Wise Men are carrying three gifts with them, and one of the gifts is frankincense."

"What are the other two?"

"We don't have time to go into detail, Marcus, but we'll be right back for a report on Emperor Augustus's reading of the chicken entrails right after these messages."

Commercial interlude promoting Mark Antony Sword Steel Razor Blades, Praetorian Guard Belt Buckles, snow rims for chariot wheels, sacrificial altars marked down 30 percent and reconditioned Greek slaves.

"Well, we seem to have lost that film we promised you of the Emperor's annual reading of the chicken entrails, Marcus. Do you have a report on what omens he found in them?"

"I do indeed, Gaius. He found a deformity in the gizzard that means there will definitely be an upswing in the economy during the second quarter of next year."

"How does that check with what your gizzard tells you, Marcus?"

"My gizzard isn't speaking to me these days, Gaius, but my corns sure are, and they tell me it's going to rain all over the Seven Hills any minute now. To find out if those corns are right, we'll hear from WSPQR's meteorologist, Cincinnatus Emptor, right after these messages."

Commercial interlude. Longer-burning torches, banquet lounges, vacations to all three parts of Gaul, Egyptian obelisks for the lawn, artificial laurel wreaths, U-Sail-It Trireme Rentals and condominiums in Sicily.

"And now, Cincinnatus, what about that rain?"

"As we look at the weather map, Gaius, we have this funny frontal pattern over the eastern Mediterranean—"

"It sure looks bad for Egypt, Cincinnatus."

"Yes, Marcus, this front is full of hail, and I wouldn't be surprised if Egypt doesn't get a pretty good onset of locusts and boils, too. But more about that after these messages."

Commercial interlude is interrupted by Goths and Huns who have seized Rome and WSPQR. Rome falls with loud bang.

"We should have had an item on these people, Marcus."

"We did, old buddy, but the film was no good. Good night for the Fulvius-Fluvius Report."

Saturdays on Planet Libido

Far away on the gray planet Uxor the Emperor Zung, with evil incarnate written all over his goatee, is confronting the luscious Velma Suttee, U.S. space-traveling sex object. Yes, space fans, it is 1937 and we are watching a Saturday-afternoon movie serial, and we know what is about to happen now, do we not?

Emperor Zung's dilated nostrils leave no eleven-year-old in doubt about what is on his mind, but Velma, apparently unaware of the effect a miniskirt and tight silk can have on an imperial libido, has to inquire. "What do you want of me, you swine?"

At this point, let us interrupt the action for a nostalgia quiz. What, in fact, does Emperor Zung want of luscious Velma Suttee, space fans of 1937?

To help you toward the answer, here are some additional facts. Velma is not only bound in chains but also surrounded by four Nubian slaves. Velma obviously thinks Zung wants her to ask why he imports slaves all the way from Nubia, especially when he has such a surplus of chains, but she is determined not to give him the satisfaction.

Moreover, Aces Norton, U.S. space hero with whom Velma travels from galaxy to galaxy to make the universe safe for democracy, is at this very moment drugged and shackled in an impenetrable dungeon crawling with man-eating bill collectors. Zung has just explained to Velma that she is completely in his power and that Aces Norton will not live to see the dawn.

In "Star Wars," which does a creditable job of re-creating the feel of these Saturday-afternoon thrillers, Velma's plight is recapitulated in the character of the captured princess, but what

93

happens to the princess is odd and disturbing. The evil powers which have her at their mercy have no desire to do anything but pick her brain for secrets and then kill her.

The people who made "Star Wars" are very young, and so, while they have otherwise done a fine job of re-creating Saturday afternoons in 1937, they have failed to include one ingredient that made those afternoons so delicious. They have left out the sex.

This may result from the natural tendency of the very young of all generations to assume that sex was not invented until they came to puberty. In fact, however, sex already existed, even in children's entertainments in 1937, having been invented during the previous year. And, of course, it was a prime ingredient of such space thrillers as "Flash Gordon," "Buck Rogers" and all the other films in which square-jawed heroes wandered the cosmos in form-fitting union suits in company with ladies of ample bosom and graceful calf.

When the Emperor Zung leered at the helpless Velma we all knew all too well what he wanted. He wanted to get married. This news invariably produced pandemonium in Velma's breast, signified by enchanting heavings of same, and all over the theater eleven-year-olds briefly forgot to chew their Jujubes.

Nowadays it will strike eleven-year-olds as odd that anyone could have regarded getting married as the equivalent of a fate worse than death. The contemporary moviegoer, accustomed to more directness in libidinal transactions, could understand Emperor Zung indulging in a brisk bout of rape, but would be flabbergasted if the old rascal ordered Velma to prepare to get married at once.

In 1937, however, nobody in the audience was in any doubt about what was going on. By threatening to marry the poor girl, Zung was—in the movie code of the time—declaring his intention to have his way with her.

Dale Arden, who traveled with Flash Gordon, seemed forever to be threatened with marriage, as did Wilma Deering, Buck Rogers's spaceship companion. Curiously, although Buck and Wilma presumably lived together constantly in their travels, as did Flash and Dale, no one ever suspected them of being up to anything for the simple reason that they were *not* married. It wasn't until late in life when Dick Tracy finally married Tess Truehart that it even occurred to any of Dick's fans that he might be capable of a sex life.

On occasion, space emperors had luscious daughters—always brunettes—who were intent on marrying the captive hero. Though memory may trick me here, I seem to recall one instance when Emperor Ming threatened to marry Dale Arden and his daughter threatened to marry Flash Gordon in the same adventure.

One reason marriage may have seemed such a dreadful fate to audiences of that day may have been the clean-movie code, which specified that once a movie character got married, she or he could never get divorced, or, if they did, that they would have to die at the end of the show.

Whatever the reason, the moment when marriage threatened the helpless female lead was indispensable to a well-rounded Saturday-afternoon adventure thriller, and "Star Wars" would have been even better than it was if its makers had realized that even to the kiddies the prospect of sex is almost as interesting as a talking robot.

World War II Revisited in the Parlor

An insomniac's history of World War II, synthesized from fifteen years of watching TV at midnight:

Fortunately, when the Japanese bombed Pearl Harbor on December 7, 1941, Gary Cooper was at sea on the aircraft Enterprise and, hence, survived to win the Battle of Midway, with Walter Brennan and Bruce Bennett fighting strong supporting roles.

The Japanese failure to time their attack so as to catch

Cooper, Brennan and Bennett in drydock typified the ineptitude of the Axis powers. Neither Berlin nor Tokyo ever clearly saw the importance of destroying such vital elements of the Allied force as Errol Flynn, Humphrey Bogart, Gregory Peck, Cary Grant, Robert Taylor and James Cagney.

This miscalculation cost them dearly. By mid-1942, the Axis was up against the most awesome concentration of box-office power ever assembled. The only enemy who seems to have understood the hopelessness of his situation was Sir Cedric Hardwicke, to whom the Nazis assigned the impossible task of preventing Errol Flynn and Ann Sheridan from throwing the German Army out of Norway.

"It will do no good to hang them," Sir Cedric said at one point when his inferiors were preparing to execute a dozen supporting players in retaliation for the killing of Helmut Dantine.

At the peak of Axis strength their first-line forces were limited to Dantine, Erich von Stroheim, Conrad Veidt, Abner Biberman and Philip Ahn. Ahn had been recruited from the "Charley Chan" family and Biberman was drafted from the supporting cast of "Gunga Din."

J. Carroll Naish, though serving under Mussolini, was a weak reed. Constantly explaining that he had relatives in the United States, he was always out of sympathy with the Nazis. In fact, Naish, more than any other actor, may have been responsible for the Axis's easy defeat through saving Bogart's life with water during the Sahara campaign.

Had Bogart not survived, von Stroheim would have won the Battle of El Alamein. Moreover, without Bogart, the Allied powers would never have kept the North Atlantic route open to Murmansk, and the devastating roundup of Nazi spies in New York (which put Peter Lorre out of action) would never have been pulled off by Bogey's gangster pals.

Worst of all, Ingrid Bergman would probably have fallen in love at Casablanca with Claude Rains, who—hedonist that he was—would not have sent her to Lisbon with Paul Henreid, as Bogart did. It is difficult to believe that Henreid, without Ingrid Bergman at his side, could have masterminded the anti-Nazi resistance inside Europe.

Even with Bogart out of action, of course, the Axis would

have had its hands full. Flynn, after liberating Norway, moved east and retook Burma from the Japanese in ninety minutes.

Cagney, having received the Medal of Honor for writing "Over There," had joined the O.S.S. and was undermining the German occupation of France. Pat O'Brien and Van Johnson had bombed Tokyo, wiping out Ahn and Biberman twice, while Cary Grant had taken his submarine into Tokyo Bay and torpedoed the Imperial Fleet.

While all this was going on, Brian Donlevy made the first atomic bomb. Thanks to Walter Pidgeon's rescue of the British Army at Dunkirk and Greer Garson's capture of Helmut Dantine, Britain had been secured as a base from which Van Johnson could lunge into Fortress Europa and win the Battle of the Bulge.

It is apparent today that the Axis had challenged an unconquerable force—a battalion of leading men who could never be wounded except inconsequentially in the shoulder and an audience that demanded happy endings for every battle.

From Bing to Elvis

The grieving for Elvis Presley and the commercial exploitation of his death was still not ended when we heard of Bing Crosby's death. Here is a generational puzzle. Those of an age to mourn Elvis must marvel that their elders could really have cared about Bing, just as the Crosby generation a few weeks ago wondered what all the to-do was about when Elvis died.

Each man was a mass culture hero to his generation, but it tells us something of the difference between generations that each man's admirers would be hard-pressed to understand why the other could mean very much to his devotees.

There were similarities that ought to tell us something.

Both came from obscurity to national recognition while quite young and became very rich. Both lacked formal music education and went on to movie careers despite lack of acting skills. Both developed distinctive musical styles which were originally scorned by critics and subsequently studied as pioneer developments in the art of popular song.

In short, each man's career followed the mythic rags-to-triumph pattern in which adversity is conquered, detractors are given their comeuppance, and estates, fancy cars and world tours become the reward of perseverance. Traditionally this was supposed to be the history of the American business striver, but in our era of committee capitalism it occurs most often in the mass entertainment field, and so we look less and less to the boardroom for our heroes and more and more to the microphone.

Both Crosby and Presley were creations of the microphone. It made it possible for people with frail voices not only to be heard beyond the third row, but also to caress millions. Crosby was among the first to understand that the microphone made it possible to sing to multitudes by singing to a single person in a small room.

Presley cuddled his microphone like a lover. With Crosby the microphone was usually concealed, but Presley brought it out onstage, detached it from its fitting, stroked it, pressed it to his mouth. It was a surrogate for his listener, and he made love to it unashamedly.

The difference between Presley and Crosby, however, reflected generational differences which spoke of changing values in American life. Crosby's music was soothing. Presley's was disturbing. It is too easy to be glib about this, to say that Crosby was singing to, first, Depression America and, then, to wartime America, and that his audiences had all the disturbance they could handle in their daily lives without buying more at the record shop and movie theater.

Crosby's fans talk about how "relaxed" he was, how "natural," how "casual and easygoing." By the time Presley began causing sensations, the entire country had become relaxed, casual and easygoing, and its younger people seemed to be tired of it, for Elvis's act was anything but soothing and scarcely what a parent of that placid age would have called "natural" for a young man.

Elvis was unseemly, loud, gaudy, sexual—that gyrating pelvis!—in short, disturbing. He not only disturbed parents who thought music was a soothing by Crosby, but also reminded their young that they were full of the turmoil of youth and an appetite for excitement. At a time when the country had a population coming of age with no memory of troubled times, Presley spoke to a yearning for disturbance.

It probably helped that Elvis's music made Mom and Dad climb the wall. In any case, people who admired Elvis never talk about how relaxed and easygoing he made them feel. They are more likely to tell you he introduced them to something new and exciting.

To explain each man in terms of changes in economic and political life probably oversimplifies the matter. Something in the culture was also changing. Crosby's music, for example, paid great attention to the importance of lyrics. The "message" of the song was as essential to the audience as the tune. The words were usually inane and witless, but Crosby—like Sinatra a little later—made them vital. People remembered them, sang them. Words still had meaning.

Thus a group like the Rolling Stones, whose lyrics are often elaborate, seem to the Crosby-tuned ear to be shouting only gibberish, a sort of accompanying background noise in a "sound" experience. The Crosby generation has trouble hearing rock because it makes the mistake of trying to understand the words. The Presley generation has trouble with Crosby because it finds the sound unstimulating and cannot be touched by the inanity of the words. The mutual deafness may be a measure of how far we have come from really troubled times and of how deeply we have come to mistrust the value of words.

Although many of Presley's songs were highly lyrical, in most it wasn't the words that moved audiences; it was the "sound." Rock 'n' roll, of which he was the great popularizer, was a "sound" event. Song stopped being song and turned into "sound," at least until the Beatles came along and solved the problem of making words sing to the new beat.

A Dying Breed

The movie scene is pure bliss these days if you're a gangster fan. Not since Warner Brothers packed Barton MacLane away in mothballs have there been so many tough cookies looking daggers at each other, so much mayhem and snarling, so many guys named Vito and Red pumping so many Tommy-gun bullets into sound-stage reproductions of the old Warner Brothers Edward G. Robinson set.

I write the name—Edward G. Robinson—with reverence, for I am a connoisseur of gangster dying styles, and Edward G. Robinson set the standard by which all others must be measured. What Einstein was to physics, what Babe Ruth was to home runs, what Emily Post was to table manners—that's what Edward G. Robinson was to dying like a lousy rat.

In August, to check up on how the new crowd compared with the old master, I spent a week watching up-to-date gangster movies. They are all in color now. The two "Godfather" movies started that trend, which I consider unhappy for two reasons.

One, esthetically speaking, dying ought to be done in black and white; it is simply not a colorful activity. Two, filming in color tempts movie people to cover the dead and dying with a bright photogenic red sauce, which I take to be ketchup. It's hard to be awed by the death of a lousy rat when he's covered with ketchup. You keep thinking irrelevant thoughts such as, Why don't they throw on some onions and pickle?

Edward G. Robinson didn't have to be gussied up like a barbecue to die impressively. When the bullets went into him he didn't have to spurt all over the camera to make you realize he was hurting. He just winced, and you knew that those bullets

100

had gone through the incredible densities of his overcoat and those huge lapels on his suit and had lodged right there where he was clutching the midriff with his cigar hand, and the wince told you everything so he never had to say, "Them bullets hurt me so. . . ."

Robinson never toppled like an axed tree. Although he was full of lead, he kept moving. If they shot him at the foot of the church steps, he kept fighting his way up the church steps despite unbearable pain so he could die at the church door. If they shot him at the top of the church steps, he always made it all the way to the bottom so he could die in the gutter.

People who say James Cagney was the better man when gunned by the law are doubtless too young to remember Robinson. Cagney could dance rings around Robinson—I'll give you that—but he couldn't die in the same league.

Remember "The Godfather"? They had to resort to ketchup to help those kid actors persuade you they were really dead, didn't they? And what about Marlon Brando? The great Brando—I concede he is great—no argument there—but you noticed, I hope, that he chose not to try to outdie Edward G. Robinson.

When Brando's time came, how did he go? Did he choose to get shot at the top of the church steps? Or at the bottom of the church steps? Either choice would have given him a great chance to make gangster fandom forget Edward G. Robinson forever.

And he could have done it any way he wanted. He is Brando. Brando dies the way Brando wants to die. If Brando says, "Build me some church steps—I am going to show the world what a ham-and-egger Eddie Robinson was," they will build the church steps.

So how did Brando choose to die? A heart attack in a vegetable garden. I couldn't believe I was seeing it. The great Brando playing his greatest gangster, and he dies of a coronary thrombosis under a tomato plant.

Well, what can you expect of a gangster movie they have to photograph in color? You do Donald Duck in color. "The Wizard of Oz." And now all the gangster flicks. It's sad, but it can produce some good moments, as in "Prizzi's Honor," a really elegant sendup of gangster shows. If you're going to do gangsters in color, what do they deserve except sendups?

After "Prizzi's Honor," though, the week I spent watching gangster movies was very mediocre. In movie after movie I saw nobody die with style. In "The Pope of Greenwich Village" one hood killed another by putting lye in his coffee, thus producing some thrashing around on the coffee-house floor and a dash through a cardboard wall.

That is a no-class way for a gangster to go. The same obtains for Dutch Schultz's demise in "The Cotton Club." Machine-gunned at a saloon urinal, Dutch seems for a moment in the mood to stagger out in search of a church with a long flight of steps, but he barely gets out of the men's room before folding on a back-room table.

The most disgusting dying I saw was in "Once Upon a Time in America"; Edward G. Robinson would never have died disgustingly. Cagney either. Not even Barton MacLane. I couldn't take it. Walked out. Gangsters shouldn't put you off your feed, even though they have to do it to each other.

Getting on with It

Nobody knows how to get on with it anymore. Henry Kissinger, for example. For years people have been calling Kissinger "brilliant," and maybe he is, but if so why does his latest book of memoirs run on for 1,283 pages?

If you're brilliant you ought to be able to get on with it, shouldn't you? I don't call 1,283 pages getting on with it, especially since Kissinger's book covers only a year and a half of his career. His first volume, covering four years, was just as long, and there are more years to come. Many more. It reminds me of the author of the windy letter who ended by saying he was sorry about writing such a long letter but he didn't have time to write a short one.

Nowadays though, people don't apologize for being unable to turn themselves off. Inflicting tedium is the modern habit and, brilliant or not, Kissinger has been infected with it. Gibbon's "Decline and Fall of the Roman Empire" is my idea of a truly monumental book, a genuine soul crusher not to be undertaken until you have a year or two with nothing else to do. Checking my edition, I find that Gibbon covered more than 1,000 years of territory in 1,170 pages, or 113 fewer pages than it takes Kissinger to cover a year and a half.

I doubt there are a hundred people in the whole country right now who are reading "The Decline and Fall of the Roman Empire," and why should there be? There are only twenty-four hours in the day. Yet the bookshops on Fifth Avenue are stocking the Kissinger memoir in warehouse lots, and it is selling by the ton.

Are all these buyers really going to read it?

Does the day have 2,400 hours?

I don't want to sound unduly sour about Kissinger's windiness because there is nothing singular about his inability to leave a little something out and get on with his tale so we can finish before senility sets in. Hardly anybody knows how to leave anything out anymore.

The new idea is that if it doesn't take forever it can't be much good. The old notion that brevity is the essence of wit has succumbed to the modern idea that tedium is the essence of quality.

When television films a book it goes on and on until the audience is too groggy to beg for mercy. Not long ago we had the TV version of "Brideshead Revisited," a very good small book which could be read in two evenings.

It's the sort of book David O. Selznick used to condense into a two-hour movie, on the humane assumption that life was too short to expect audiences to spend two nights of it in the Bijou watching a small show. On television it ran twelve hours and was drawn out over eleven weekly installments.

If Selznick had produced "Gone With the Wind" at this pace, you would have had to sit in the Bijou from the time

Hitler invaded Poland until the election of Lyndon Johnson to see it all. It was considered remarkable that Selznick actually let it run three hours and forty-five minutes, since few Americans were thought sufficiently torpid to spend that much of their lives on a single film.

You could name a lot of other good ninety-minute shows that have been turned into eight-hour "miniseries" or "docudramas" under the new theory that while less may be more, obesity is even better. When Americans liked to get on with things most of these eight-hour blockbusters would have been reduced to "selected short subjects" jammed in between Betty Boop and Charlie Chan.

You keep hearing how life is so much fuller and more complicated than it used to be and how nobody has enough time to keep up with it these days. If so, why do network news shows take thirty minutes every night to broadcast a collection of headlines we could absorb by scanning a front page in twenty seconds? For the same reason Kissinger takes 1,283 pages to deal with material Gibbon would have disposed of in three pages. Because nobody knows how to get on with it anymore, that's why.

One of the worst cases is the Government's war division. Can you imagine any Government of the present age getting itself in shape to win the Battle of Midway six months after Pearl Harbor and to land an army of invasion in North Africa five months later?

I can't. Nowadays, I suspect, we'd need at least a year just to decide how big a tax break to give corporations for converting to ship and tank construction, and another five years to find out why the ships and tanks weren't quite ready yet for battle.

I don't think you'd really have to offer the enlisted men tax incentives for agreeing to take part in the Battle of Midway, but there'd probably be a lot of pressure for it on the home front, and everything would probably be slowed down while Presidential candidates tested public sentiment in the next New Hampshire primary.

Meanwhile, of course, the Government would be scolding the public for impatience, and reminding it that Rome wasn't built in a day, and telling it to remain hard-nosed toward the enemy, and show plenty of will, and be prepared for great tests of endurance.

I think the Japanese would set up shop in Detroit forty years ahead of schedule. I think when Kissinger took 1,283 pages to Mitsubishi, Little & Brown, they would tell him, "Sorry, Professor, but we have never been interested in gas guzzlers."

Tote That Ball; Smell That Ether

It was not until early December that one sensed he might be seeing something historic. It was December 14, in fact, and Junius Loftlubber, fabled interior lineman for the McKeesport Duckbill Platypuses, had just been assisted from the field by his colleagues.

Chuck Sturdy, who was doing the color commentary for the network that day, said, "Junius probably has a hamstring pull, judging from the way he moved when they got him on his feet there."

Suddenly it seemed that there had been more hamstring pulls than touchdowns on television this year. The sports pages for months had carried news of little else except pulled hamstrings, and whenever television switched abruptly from an interesting fist fight on the playing field, as it invariably does, it was invariably to show us some poor devil out of action on the bench because of a pulled hamstring.

Could it be that we were seeing a new record established for pulled hamstrings in a single season? We now have the answer, and it is an exciting, "Yes!"

The Medico-Sports Writers of America have just finished the arithmetic and pronounced 1969 the year of the pulled hamstring. They will give a special award—a three-hour supply of ether—to Ron Volponik of Creek State College for pulling the first hamstring of 1969 in the Cactus Pot last January 1.

To Sherman Wenga, tight tackle for the Lubbock Daws, the Medico-Sports Writers will present the coveted Doctor Kildare Trophy, a lead loving cup made from a full set of traction weights. Wenga sustained more pulled hamstrings—eighty-seven—than any other player in televised network games.

With cloying modesty (he is a member of the old, square, insincere, gee-whiz, Joe Palooka school of perspirant heroes), Wenga says, "Shucks, anybody could have done it who had eighty-seven hamstrings and somebody to pull 'em for him."

Modest as Sherm Wenga is, perhaps he is not modest enough. He might have added, "and a full complement of medico-sports writers to keep the score," for until the advent of the medico-sports writer in the mid-1960's very little attention had been paid to the medical aspects of the nation's favorite games.

The old-time sports writers could tell you what the score was, but it is doubtful if most of them even knew that athletes had hamstrings, much less how to go about pulling one. One reads through the old sports pages in vain to learn whether Napoleon Lajoie had bone chips in his elbow, how many shoulder separations Bronco Nagurski suffered, and how much cartilage Albie Booth had left in his knees at retirement.

Nowadays, by contrast, a browse through the sports pages is like attending the morning conference in the accident ward.

"Coach Kidneystomper began the week in a black mood and no wonder," begins the typical medico-sports story. "His injured list includes eight pulled hamstrings, two impacted wisdom teeth, an ingrown toenail, three cases of lesions of the scapula, six separated shoulders and a duodenal ulcer. Assorted pimples and shingles added to the coach's woe."

Relatively little time is spent with Coach Kidneystomper, however. The modern medico-sports writer spends the greater part of his time talking to Dr. Scalpel. ("We had to take all the cartilage out of Sam Pete's right knee and use it to sew the shoulder together. It may be as long as six weeks before we know—.")

The pre-game stories have changed for the better with the

advent of medico-sports reporting. The old-fashioned pre-game story had the reporter asking the coach, fighter or manager how well he would do in the forthcoming battle.

We all knew the answers by heart. Football coach: "I've got a fine bunch of boys, but I don't see how we can possibly hope to beat the Hoop Snakes, who are the greatest team I've seen in forty years of football." Fighter: "I'll murder the bum." Baseball manager: "This year I think we've got the material to win it all." Etcetera.

Now the pre-game story is all medical contingencies. "If Joe's knees hold up, Vince's shoulder separation stays united, the bone spur on Sam's heel responds to cortisone, and the Asian flu doesn't spread to Ron, the Jackrabbits are even money against the Squids, provided that Squid ace Jackie Muntzak does not recover from his esophagus resection before game time." Etcetera.

Anesthesia, anyone?

Postscript

Since 1970 when this piece was written, pulled hamstring is no longer the sports media's medical darling. Shattered knee—cartilage, caps and/or joints—now gets the lion's share of the sports pages during football and basketball seasons. In the baseball season it's all torn rotator cuff.

Have baseball pitchers always had rotator cuffs? I had never heard of rotator cuffs until recent times. This suggests either that rotator cuffs are new equipment on pitchers or that they didn't tear in the old days. Is this plausible? People who believe in the Good Old Days will say it's because they don't make pitchers like they used to. People who believe the Good Old Days were terrible but there's A Great Day coming will say it's because they still

*haven't worked the bugs out of the rotator cuff, but when they do
pitchers will be better than ever.*

*More likely, the Japanese will hit the market any day now
with a pitcher that doesn't need a rotator cuff.*

Is That All There Is?

Cable TV came to our house last month. Now I can get the
Weather Channel. It tells me of the climate in faraway places:
Very hot in Dallas. Severe thunderstorm warnings for three
counties in Kansas.

I struggle to get interested, but fail. It is hard getting interested in weather that is 1,500 miles away. Great distance from
the scene of hardship makes it easy to be indifferent to suffering. Generals always knew that. Now, thanks to the Weather
Channel, everybody with a TV set knows it, too.

And anyhow, what is cable TV for if you don't keep changing the channel?

I get the Inescapable Sports Channel. Some men are playing soccer on the far side of the earth.

It is a game that was played last week. Hungarians are involved. I am not. Watching televised sports events that were
held last week, last month, last year or last night makes me
weep with boredom.

Especially soccer.

A voice begs me not to tune out. As soon as last week's
soccer game is over, says the voice, I will see a long-awaited
welterweight prizefight held last week in Las Vegas.

I get the Eternal News Channel from Atlanta. Some narcotics dealers have been arrested. They are the same narcotics
dealers who used to get arrested every night on the ABC, CBS
and NBC network news shows before we got cable TV.

The same policeman puts the same improbable value on their narcotics cache: hundreds of millions of dollars.

Improbable. But I don't know. I am so excited about discovering that this familiar old gang is also available on cable that I don't care what figures he is using tonight.

A woman is pleading: Please don't tune out because after these advertisements you will see people with bombs and guns bombing and shooting each other in the Middle East.

"Sorry, sweetheart," I growl, "but the only reason I've been watching those birds shoot each other for years was because I didn't have forty-five other channels to tune to, many of which now offer 1932 movies starring Kay Francis and Lyle Talbot."

I get the College Antique Movie Channel. Rats! No Kay Francis tonight. Not even any Lyle Talbot, Victor McLaglen, Edmund Lowe, or Anna May Wong. Instead, highbrow moviegoers are having a symposium.

A brilliant seventeen-year-old campus newspaper movie critic is talking about the great horse stars. The greatest, he says, was Roy Rogers's nag, Trigger. The kid doesn't even mention Tom Mix's oatburner, Tony, because he's obviously never heard of either Tony or Tom.

I get the Perpetual Prayer Channel. A man in Messina, Italy, has written a letter. It is being read aloud over the Perpetual Prayer Channel. It states that prayer has had salutary effects on his life in Messina.

I get the Endless Social Security Channel. A deceptively genial man urges me to enroll in a lobby that will apply thumbscrews and bastinado to politicians who don't redistribute the wealth in my direction once I hit The Golden Years.

I get the Utter Success Channel. A man in a suspiciously cheap-looking suit assures me that easy wealth awaits once I set up my own corporation.

"Out!" I cry, tuning him in that direction. Well do I remember what happened the only time I had wealth, which wasn't even Mercedes-Benz-class wealth either. Tax men took it all. They'll never trick me into getting wealthy again.

I skim the Baseball Channels. The Chicago Cubs, a team I

never think of, is playing the San Diego Padres, a team I never heard of.

The Atlanta Braves and New York Mets are taking up two entire channels. This is terrible. Baseball is fine, but enough is enough, and cable TV threatens to make it as tiresome as network TV made the Statue of Liberty.

I tune out the Braves, tune out the Mets, pause at the Nashville Network to catch a little Championship Rodeo, then flip to Nickelodeon for a few minutes of the "Mister Ed" rerun while I decide which way to tune next.

HBO, perhaps? Not yet. A few years ago we rented a summer place that had cable with HBO. It was a solid month of Burt Reynolds. Burt's all right in moderation, but in his movies he always has to have all the girls in love with him, which is depressing if you stop to think about it, though I'm not sure which is more depressing: not having all the girls in the world in love with you, or never having them give you a moment free from love to watch the Weather Channel.

Speaking of which, the jet stream is cooling off North Dakota.

Outside I can hear my garden dying of drought. It's the same kind of sound I hear in my head.

Fry, Fry Again

The present heat wave reminds me of my Uncle Henry who once fried chicken on the sidewalk. It was Uncle Henry's way of showing his contempt for newspapers.

At that time, as soon as a heat wave started going well the newspapers sent out photographers to take pictures of somebody frying an egg on the sidewalk. "Hot enough to fry an egg," was the invariable picture caption.

After fifty or sixty summers of looking at the same old egg-frying picture in his newspapers, Uncle Henry phoned his local papers one steamy July day and said he was going to give them something new to photograph.

"I am going to fry a chicken on the sidewalk," he said.

"Are you crazy? You can't fry a chicken on the sidewalk," is more or less what all of the newspaper editors replied.

"But even if I fail," Uncle Henry said, "you'll have a new kind of picture for your heat-wave story. You can caption it, 'Not hot enough to fry a chicken.'"

Naturally the editors didn't send their photographers.

This pleased Uncle Henry, since it confirmed his suspicion that newspapers had no interest in anything that was new.

Aunt Jenny, who was practical, said he was acting like a fool.

"If you'd told those editors you were going to fry an egg on the sidewalk, you could have got your picture in the papers," she said.

"You don't understand," Uncle Henry told her. "I'm not interested in giving a fried food demonstration. I am dramatizing the press's enslavement to clichés."

"If you told them you were going to fry both the chicken and an egg side by side out there on the cement, you could have got them interested in a nice heat-wave feature story. Think of the headline possibilities: 'Man answers age-old question—Which fried first? The chicken or the egg?'"

Uncle Henry ignored her, as he usually did.

When he brought the chicken in from the sidewalk, of course, none of us wanted to eat it, but as Uncle Henry pointed out, "If I'd fried an egg out there in all those dog tracks, you wouldn't want to eat that either."

At this stage of his life Uncle Henry's distaste for newspaper clichés was drawing him toward eccentricity.

Much as he hated heat waves because of the inevitability of the fried-egg-on-the-sidewalk picture, he detested the autumnal change of foliage color even more.

Uncle Henry had nothing against tree leaves changing their color, but he dreaded the same old annual newspaper stories about forests "ablaze in russet, gold and brilliant scarlet."

When he came into a sum of money from Great-Aunt Martha's will, he bought a wooded tract and a considerable amount of spray painting equipment.

His plan was to spray his trees with navy blue paint, thus challenging reporters covering the annual fall foliage story to shed their clichés and write something fresh.

He knew, of course, that they wouldn't. "I'll bet when they see it, they'll write about 'a forest ablaze in navy blue,'" he said.

Unfortunately, Uncle Henry was unable to carry out this ambitious demonstration of the press's passion for the trite, for his paint and spraying equipment were destroyed in a four-alarm fire, which also destroyed his house.

Uncle Henry escaped uninjured, except by the newspaper report, which said that the fire had "roared through" his house.

After reading the account, he turned to Aunt Jenny with tears in his eyes.

"Roar for me, Jenny," he said. Aunt Jenny gave a passable imitation of a lion in a testy mood.

"Did you hear that?" he asked the editor, after he had Aunt Jenny roar a second time into the telephone. "Does that sound to you, Mr. Editor, like the noise a fire makes?"

Though a mere adolescent in those days, I tried to comfort him. "Fires always roar in newspapers, Uncle Henry. They've roared since I began reading newspapers seven years ago at the age of six, and they'll probably still be roaring when I'm an old coot of thirty-three."

"That's not good enough, boy," he told me. "There's supposed to be progress in this old world of ours. It's time newspapers quit misleading people about fires roaring and started telling us something accurate about fires."

"I know what you're saying, Henry," said Aunt Jenny. "It would be so much more graphic if, when a house burned down, the papers sent somebody around and you put an egg in a skillet and held it in the fire and they could write, 'It was hot enough to fry an egg.'"

If there hadn't been oppression of women in those days, Uncle Henry always said, Aunt Jenny would have made a great editor.

The Well-bred Mummy

As always when "The Mummy" is shown on television, I was riveted to my armchair the other night when the rotting casket containing the Scroll of Thoth was excavated from the sands of Egypt, along with a linen-wrapped object that looked suspiciously like Boris Karloff.

What has always fetched me to "The Mummy," a film which dates from the Administration of Herbert Hoover, is the high-society poise maintained by the principal characters in situations that might make even the Duke of Edinburgh forget to shave.

On first encountering the film, as a shabby but ambitious lad eager to learn how the swells lived, I marveled at the cool savoir-faire with which, despite murder, hypnotic spells and an ambulatory mummy in their midst, the leading characters always found time to don evening gowns or tuxedos for dinner and dancing. In recent viewings, however, my attention has centered on the truly exquisite manners of the mummy.

Somehow in spite of 3,000 years or so of lying buried out of touch with Emily Post, the mummy has become a master of the social graces, and where once I watched to learn how the upper classes did things, now I watch to learn from the mummy.

Coming back to it the other night, I hoped to discover how the mummy had dealt with a social problem that has stumped me for years; namely, how to get respect in a snooty haberdashery when you go in dressed like a bum.

After being exhumed, you will recall, the mummy comes out of his sarcophagus looking perfectly dreadful, what with dust and cobwebs all over his linen wrappings, and stumbles off

113

toward Cairo with what looked like filthy ragged bandages dangling from his heels and elbows.

From previous viewings I know the mummy is going to turn up a bit later looking like something off the cover of The Islamic Gentlemen's Quarterly in a stunning tarboosh, silk shirt and gorgeously tailored knee-length coat, suitable for indoor wear on cooler evenings.

How did the mummy, with not a thing on his back but those odious old mummy rags, manage to walk into the fanciest haberdashery in Cairo and persuade the salesman to give him threads like those? When I walk into such places, though my wardrobe is several cuts superior to 3,000-year-old mummy wrappings, salesmen always take one glance and suggest I'd be happier shopping the vendors' stands on Canal Street.

Obviously the mummy knows the right thing to say, and when I tuned him in the other night the purpose was to learn the secret words. Unfortunately, the confrontation with tailors and salesmen was omitted from this night's screening, which reminded me that I didn't recall it in any of the versions seen since my attention had shifted to the mummy's social conduct. Perhaps the director cut it out of the film in the 1930's. If so, what a loss.

In any case, no night with "The Mummy" is ever a total educational loss, so swallowing my disappointment, I viewed on. Reward was soon forthcoming in a scene I had never before noticed.

In this scene the mummy is strolling about a museum in his smashing new haberdashery when he encounters the archeologist who has dug him up. Naturally the archeologist doesn't recognize the mummy in those elegant clothes, nor does he notice anything odd about him although we, the audience, have noticed that the mummy's eyeballs tend to glow like the high beams on automobile headlights now and then.

What does the archeologist do? Being a real toff, what can he do but invite the mummy to come to dinner sometime? Suddenly I am totally engaged in the mummy's social problem. I can see that the mummy, like me, really doesn't like to go out to dinner very much. I can see that the mummy, as I do in similar predicaments, has sized up the archeologist as a colossal bore. But how does he escape the dinner without seeming rude?

Can he say, "Thanks, but I much prefer to sit home alone

and read the Scroll of Thoth?" I don't think so. I know I am never able to say, "Thanks, but I'd rather stay home and watch television." All I can ever think of to do is lie, which is terrible.

If you say, "Unfortunately, I am tied up every night this week," you are confronted with, "Well, how about next week?" If you say, "Thanks, but I'm planning to be in Europe for the next year or two," you don't dare show your face publicly for a year or two for fear of being exposed as a liar.

I watch the mummy in total absorption as he contends with this most trying of social problems, and the mummy does not fail me. Without blinking an eye, he replies suavely, conclusively, with the only response that brooks no argument.

"I regret," says the mummy, "I am too occupied to accept invitations."

Too occupied to accept invitations. It is magnificent. It is perfect. Why didn't Amy Vanderbilt feed us these lines?

Full Ketchup Nelson

Professional wrestling suffers from superb television camera work. If it were not so good, the fraud would not be so distressingly obvious to the audience, and the entertainment would be better.

I speak as an authority on wrestling audiences. I was once a regular weekly patron of Carlin's Arena in northwest Baltimore and there studied with wonder and admiration such historic performers as Jim Londos ("The Golden Greek") and the French Angel.

Though intellectually persuaded that the show was pure theater and that nobody was getting hurt, I could never silence the primitive sucker within (there's one born every minute, after all) who kept saying, "Sure, but this time they're really mad at each other and something terrible could happen."

I had unimpeachable testimony that it was all fakery. This came from my Uncle Jim, a gorgeous physical specimen who in the 1920's kept body and soul together in a variety of jobs that included used-car salesman, bodyguard to minor bootleggers, and occasional wrestler.

When I was only ten years old, Uncle Jim disillusioned me by explaining that wrestlers who were supposed to be suffering unbearable agony got part of their effect by keeping wax capsules of ketchup tucked under the tongue and, at the crucial moment, biting through the wax and spraying the ring with tomato gore.

I later heard that it is wrong to expose children of ten to such truths, for it will only make cynics of them, but I have always been grateful to Uncle Jim for not heeding these bleeding hearts. Without such instruction early in life, I would never have been fit to cover politics and government for a newspaper.

But note that the truth was not a total defense against deception, for I was still a faithful wrestling customer even after I started college and should have been foolproof.

At about this time "The Golden Terror" appeared on the wrestling scene, and I was soon whipped into frenzies of passion against his arrogant brutality. (Why the word "Golden" was so popular in such a shabby business is a mystery I leave to students of press agentry.)

The Terror was one of the first wrestlers to wear a mask. This was an exciting development at the time. The Lone Ranger, who was already established as an important American, had made the mask a symbol of heroism. The Golden Terror, on the other hand, turned it into the mark of the cad.

No blow was too foul for him to strike, and the cruelties to which he subjected his victims were agonizing to witness. One of his favorite grips involved putting an opponent flat on the canvas, then, from a standing position, twisting the poor devil's leg until it seemed certain to come off in his brutish paws.

Yes, I knew it was mostly fraud, but I was pretty sure it hurt something awful, nevertheless.

Who was this masked man? Would I be in the lucky audience that finally saw him pinned, his mask removed, and his identity exposed at last? Yes, we were promised that when he was finally defeated, his mask would be torn off, and he would stand exposed for all to know.

My passion for wrestling reached its apex in the months that followed. I couldn't bear to miss a week of it. I came to my senses one morning while riding the trackless trolley to college and wondering if the Terror might be unmasked that very night.

Some wise old inner voice, possibly Uncle Jim's, spoke loud enough to silence the primitive sucker within. It said:

"So what if the Terror is unmasked? He will be somebody nobody ever heard of. Or do you think it's really Wendell Willkie behind that mask?"

That was the end of my career as a wrestling fan, though I have always retained a decent opinion of the business, out of fond memory of happy youth and respect for Uncle Jim, who helped wise me up enough to understand politics before I fell into the hands of civics teachers.

It is sad to see what has happened to this wonderfully fraudulent old pastime since modern television with its beautiful camera work has moved in on it. The cameras prove unmistakably that the performers are missing by miles with their killer head butts, death dives and flying squat leaps. It's enough to make a toddler hold his nose and cry, "Fraud!"

Even worse are the interviews held with these hambones between grunts. They howl and bay at each other with a ridiculous lack of conviction reminiscent of Presidential candidates in those "debates" designed to gull the rubes. So many people don't even try anymore.

Breakfast Visitors

Here are the newspaper movie ads on a typical May morning in New York.

An expensively groomed young woman stands beside a casually attired young man holding a pistol. Both stare me straight in the eye with cold deadpan expressions. These babies are mean, and they're looking at me as if they've just caught me cheating at Trivial Pursuit.

I wouldn't mind except for the young man's pistol. While giving me that psychopathic stare, he dangles his pistol in his left hand, business end down toward the name of the movie ("Blue City") printed just below his hip.

Though this is only a photograph glaring across the breakfast table, I sense it would take no effort at all for him to tilt the gun upward and blow me away right in front of my oatmeal.

All right, maybe I'm a nervous Nelly. Maybe these are the nicest folks in any movie in town. Their ad gives no clue. Some print over the photo says, "It's the coolest heat you'll ever feel," which is incomprehensible, and some under the photo says, "It's below Miami, and above the law," which doesn't help either. They look too blow-dried to be crooked judges in the Dry Tortugas.

What in the world is this!

To escape from that pistol I turn the page to find a party of four, two armed with machine guns, knee-deep in a swamp. Both armed parties, a young woman and a young man, are blazing away, but not straight at my head. His machine gun is aimed at my coffee cup and hers 90 degrees to starboard.

Behind them stand another man and woman.

Neither of these persons has a gun.

It is outrageous. I want to call the people who designed this ad.

"What is the idea of letting two people appear unarmed in a movie ad?" I want to ask them.

Because right behind them, unnoticed—though why they didn't notice a giant splashing through that swamp, I can't guess—right behind them, unnoticed, is a giant with a shaved skull raising a sword to behead the unarmed pair before I can burn the toast.

The movie is "Cut and Run." The ad says, "It's the one story you won't see on the 6 o'clock news."

To which I say, "Thank goodness." Having to look at all those body bags on the 6 o'clock news is harrowing enough;

thank goodness my local TV team never gets to the scene of the gore in time to see the guns flash, the swords swish and the heads fall.

Now, here, right beside those blazing machine guns. . . . This is my kind of movie: two people in the ad, and only one of them armed, and he (Jeff Bridges) is equipped only with a pistol, and that pistol is clutched in his right hand while his right arm is wrapped around the bare shoulder of Rosanna Arquette.

This is a pistol that will not be aimed at me for putting butter on the toast. ("So it's cholesterol suicide you're up to, is it, Toastburner? Well here's a message for weak-willed dairy gobblers like you." Bang Bang Bang.) No, this is a pistol that will be used only to protect Rosanna Arquette from all 8 million of "8 Million Ways to Die," rated R.

Feeling reassured, I let the eye roam, and what does it see? A man is running through what appears to be a dark alley. A young woman runs slightly behind, but she has no gun. Sexism is still not totally crushed. This is the third ad of the morning in which no woman has a gun.

Only the man in this ad has a gun. As he runs through the alley he holds the gun, a mere pistol, in his right hand. Though he is Charles Bronson, I am not worried, because the course he is on will carry him off to my left, where any firing will hit nothing more than the remnant of my breakfast cantaloupe.

"The movie ads can't scare me," I mutter and, turning the page, recoil in horror. Glaring holes right through me stands a man with an immense gun supported on his right shoulder.

This weapon must be part elephant gun and part .50-caliber machine gun, because that's a belt of .50-caliber bullets festooning its bearer. Now I know what the gun lobby means about bearing arms; this baby is so big it surely can't be carried, but only borne, like the trials of Job.

The mustachioed young man carrying it looks demented (whites showing all the way round in the eyeballs), making me wonder if he has the strength of the mad. If so, he can probably get Big Bertha off his shoulder and play havoc with my expensive new jar of Trappist cherry preserves, because I can count forty-eight bullets in that ammo belt slung over his chest.

The movie is titled "Getting Even," and the ad says, "No matter who you are . . . there comes a time."

Comes a time? They mean, comes a gun. Bang Bang Bang. Poor Trappist cherry preserves.

A Sadness of Team and Pants

As usual, it failed to snow for Christmas in our neighborhood despite the local radio stations' tireless efforts to butter up the snow god by ceaselessly playing "White Christmas."

The song is one of the few World War II relics that Americans cling to. In 1942, when Bing Crosby first sang it in the movie "Holiday Inn," its sentimental expression of yearnings for home, old times and better days was ideally suited to the mood of an innocent country at war.

The makers of "Holiday Inn," failing to realize what gold Irving Berlin had given them, let it get lost in a batch of less moving Berlin songs, which gave Warner Brothers an excuse to cash in a second time with an inferior movie titled "White Christmas." That one had snow galore.

By then, Frank Capra had used the Hollywood equivalent of a Russian winter to gussy up "It's a Wonderful Life," his Christmas Eve tale about James Stewart's discovery that money doesn't matter if you have friends. That was in 1946, and the movie was not very successful, probably because the hokum of Capra's message was too much to be swallowed by an America that still remembered the Depression.

Nowadays, in one of greed's great ages, when people are esteemed for saying "I want it all, and I want it now," Capra's movie is so admired that it is almost inescapable on December television. Maybe you have to be filthy rich before you can enjoy the happiness that poverty affords others.

Movie snow seems to make hokum go down smoother. The secret may be that movie snow is rarely cold and seldom falls at inconvenient times, such as during the afternoon rush hour on days when 100,000 suburbanites have driven into town in cars without snow tires.

A movie Christmas without just the right amount of beautiful, warm snow is almost as rare as Sylvester Stallone letting anybody get out alive. One of the nicest of all movie Christmas snows falls in London in the 1935 version of "A Tale of Two Cities." It is a magnificent movie marred only by the implausibly lovely Christmas snow that falls on Ronald Colman outside Lucie Manette's house.

Note the year, 1935, and the story locale, London. Note that the film was made in America. In 1935 Americans firmly believed that England was blessed with gorgeous snowfalls every Christmas. Actually, Christmas snow in London is even rarer than it is in the eastern United States south of Boston, where it is a long-odds proposition.

In 1935 few Americans in the Middle Atlantic states expected snow before January. There was a wide-spread faith, however, in Christmas snow in Britain. This was reinforced by movies and greeting cards depicting snow falling on ye olde British types in British-looking surroundings.

It has been written, though not authoritatively, that Charles Dickens is to blame for the myth about snowy old English Christmases, and that he got the idea because the only Christmas snow to fall on London in the entire nineteenth century occurred when he was an impressionable boy.

I have seen that written, but forget where, and do not submit it under oath, though it will seem plausible to anybody who has experienced an English winter or two, when the climate rains, fogs, sulks and lies around feeling sorry for itself and making everybody else miserable, but never seems to snow.

Unrealistic American expectations of Christmas snow reached peak intensity in World War II, thanks to "White Christmas," which filled a powerful wartime need for separated family members to express melancholy yearnings at holiday time. These expectations seem to have subsided hardly at all, despite overwhelming statistical evidence that outside the snow belt, though you dream of a White Christmas through forty-five Decembers, you're not going to see much snow before January.

The durability of the song and the unreal hope it excites—that Christmas will produce snow and it will not be rotten and miserable like all other snows—is remarkable when we reflect how far behind us we have put most of World War II.

You probably forgot, or never knew, but we fought that war to save the Brooklyn Dodgers and the two-pants suit. Captured movie actors always told it to Gestapo torturers. "You rats will never break America because America's fighting to save the things we love and believe in, things like the Brooklyn Dodgers and the two-pants suit."

What kind of people would let the Brooklyn Dodgers and the two-pants suit go down the drain and mope because they didn't get snowed on?

Badlands

For many years Luke rode the range in a white hat. When he saw a man in a black hat, Luke chased him and shot him. Men in black hats were always trying to prevent the cattle from getting to Abilene or stealing the widow's ranch. Luke was fearless and kind. He never drank anything stronger than sarsaparilla and never tried to kiss the schoolmarm.

One day the studio stopped Luke just as he was about to shoot his 27,613th man in a black hat. The studio boss told Luke that Americans were growing up. Audiences wanted their cowboys to be more human. "You want me to stop shooting black hats?" asked Luke.

"Of course not," said the studio head, "but we want you to stop shooting them so fearlessly. Gunfighting is scary business. Before you shoot the next one, we want you to sweat a lot to show you're afraid."

Luke sweated and showed fear through several years of shooting, as he had seen Gary Cooper do in "High Noon." One day he rode into a strange town, where he was scheduled to shoot a man in a black hat, and was stopped outside the saloon by the director.

The director gave Luke a black hat and told him to put it on. Luke blanched. The director told him not to worry. He was not going to be shot. But American audiences were growing up. They wanted Luke to look a little more sinister, the way heroes in real life were beginning to look.

Luke started wearing a black hat. It made him feel ornery nights at home when he was into the gin, and one night he took a real pistol out of the bedside table and shot at Mrs. Luke, but missed her, never having fired a real pistol before.

Sometime later, wearing his black hat and sweating with fear, he was just about to stride into the saloon in Dodge City when the script girl handed him new directions. They said he was to step up to the bar and drink two shots of whiskey fast.

"America's growing up," she said. "Audiences no longer believe in cowboys who drink sarsaparilla."

About that time, Mrs. Luke started forbidding Luke's children to go see their father perform his famous shootings because she didn't want them to grow up thinking good men drank whiskey neat.

A few years afterward, the producer called Luke to his swimming pool. "Luke," he said, "America is growing up. Audiences will no longer believe that rugged cowboys who wear black hats and toss back the hootch would draw the line at a little hanky-panky with the schoolmarm."

"You want me to kiss her?" asked Luke.

"Don't talk like a Boy Scout," said the producer. "We want you to live with her out of wedlock."

"Sort of like Redford in 'Butch Cassidy and the Sundance Kid,'" said Luke. "But Redford was no good. He was holding up trains and stealing from decent folks."

The producer said America was growing up. Cowboys had to grow with the audience. For several years, Luke lived illicitly with schoolmarms, drank straight whiskey, did a lot of fearful sweating under his black hat, and stole the cattle of widows' herds which were being driven to Abilene.

One day Luke was rustling a herd of longhorns down in Texas when he fell from his faithful horse. The director rushed over shouting, "Shoot him!"

"Shoot my faithful horse?" asked Luke.

The director told Luke America was growing up. Audiences knew that cowboys who spent long lonely weeks rustling cattle and drinking straight whiskey far from the schoolmarms with whom they lived illicitly were turned into vengeful sadists likely to shoot any horse that threw them.

So Luke shot his faithful horse. That was when Mrs. Luke divorced him. She had been devoted to his faithful horse. As long as his horse was faithful, she had thought, there was still a chance that Luke would go back to his white hat and sarsaparilla and stop spending steamy nights with schoolmarms. She had failed to grow with America.

Her divorce suit made Luke so furious he wanted to horse-whip her, an idea he had picked up from the script of his forth-coming relationship with a schoolmarm in Tombstone. His director had a better idea. America was growing up, he told Luke. Audiences were now aware that in every hero lurked a sadistic killer trying to get out.

He assigned Luke to lead a murderous band of cowboys to a Mexican town where they would pillage the church, hang the priests, rape the schoolgirls and dump poisonous scorpions in the hospital beds. While Luke was doing all this, a man in a white hat rode up, fearlessly ordered some sarsaparilla and told Luke he would have to shoot him if he didn't behave better. Luke put six bullet holes in him and laughed when the sarsaparilla ran out.

"Things aren't supposed to end like this," gasped the dying stranger. "That shows how out of touch you are with the audience," explained Luke before dashing off to burn the orphanage.

Postscript

Sarsaparilla was a soda pop that tasted something like root beer. Movie cowboys pronounced it sasspuh-rilla. I distinctly remember seeing it ordered in tough movie saloons by both Buck Jones and Ken Maynard during the early 1930's. Both Buck and Ken had to administer severe beatings to gangs of sneering black-hatted booze guzzlers who thought sarsaparilla drinkers were sissies and made the mistake of saying so.

In early Westerns the black hats were always making that mistake. I used to wonder why saloonkeepers bothered to stock sarsaparilla, since selling it led inevitably to so much destruction of their chairs, tables and glassware.

Seeing sarsaparilla drinkers like Buck Jones and Ken Maynard whale the tar out of whiskey drinkers should have been good for the sarsaparilla industry, the way Popeye was good for spinach, but it didn't work out that way. It's been years since I've seen a bottle of sarsaparilla for sale anywhere. The rest of America's youth must have been just like me in the carbonated beverage department. After seeing what sarsaparilla did for men like Buck and Ken, I never bought it if Dr. Pepper, Royal Crown Cola, Coke, Pepsi, Nehi Orange, root beer or ginger ale was available. Maybe I was afraid it would tempt street-corner toughs to think they could whip me in bare-knuckle combat. Since I was sure every street-corner tough in the neighborhood could easily do so, I may have thought a long draft of sarsaparilla wasn't worth a bloody nose, black eye and loosened teeth.

After winning so many movie-saloon battles for temperance, Ken Maynard died broke, forgotten by moviegoers, and alcoholic. Buck Jones died in 1942 in a Boston nightclub fire. I like to think he had just dropped in for a sarsaparilla, but the stories didn't say.

ROOTS

Late in the 1970's Americans became root conscious. The country was full up with people talking about their roots and trying to find their roots so they could cleave to their roots, and draw nourishment from their roots, and boast about the depth of their roots.

Alex Haley's book, "Roots," was to blame for this foolish fad, as I thought it. I knew exactly where my roots were and had spent a lifetime trying to get as far from them as possible. Most Americans, I thought, would tell the same story if strapped down and pumped full of truth serum. What was America, after all, if not a refuge from roots?

My own roots were in a rustic Virginia backwater so remote from the twentieth century that long after Lindbergh had flown the ocean my people still read by the coal-oil lamp. My mother took me to the bright lights of town for good when I was five, and I grew up in cities. I counted myself lucky in having escaped the primitive country life and never for a moment thought about going back. My goal in life was to live in an apartment over a movie house next door to a delicatessen, and that pretty much describes where I was living in New York by the 1970's.

The roots people made me laugh. It was useless telling them of the miseries they would have to endure back at their roots. You had to have been there. I had been there, friend. No roots for me, thank you.

So pretty soon where was I?

Headed back to my roots. The trip had many phases and took several years, but at the end it had moved me out of New

York's gaudy squalors and delights and carried me back to Virginia.

The journey began in 1978 on a summer day in Nantucket when I had to write a Fourth of July column. I was only slightly desperate about it, for so few people looked at a newspaper on the Fourth of July that low-quality goods would do to fill the space. I could interview Thomas Jefferson or eavesdrop while the Founding Fathers told Button Gwinnett he couldn't be the father of his country because it would be silly to have the nation's capital called Button, D.C. Something like that. It didn't matter.

The first few efforts turned out hopelessly sophomoric and went into the trash. The Fourth of July deserved better. I went to the window and gazed out into that soft, pastel sunlight which sometimes makes Nantucket in high summer look like everybody's dream of earthly paradise. How different this northern Atlantic light was from the hot and brilliant glare of the Julys of my childhood. As I stood at the window a scene of nearly fifty years ago unfolded in my mind.

I had just awakened in the back bedroom of my grandmother's house in Morrisonville, Virginia. It was an early morning in June, the sun not yet high, mist still on the fields visible through the window beside my bed. The morning day was sweet now, but I knew that my aunt or one of my uncles, when I went down for breakfast, would say, "It's going to be a scorcher today." And it would be.

Bounding out of bed with childhood's joy in simply being awake on a summer morning, I went to the other window and looked down into the dirt road that ran in front of my grandmother's house to see who was playing catch. That was what had wakened me, the sound of a baseball smacking into the pockets of leather gloves. There were two big farm boys in clodhopper shoes playing catch while waiting for somebody to come give them a ride to work.

Standing at the window, I watched them with a pleasure so deep it would stay alive inside me for nearly fifty years. Nantucket's misty summer light had brought back to life that soft June light of the Morrisonville morning, soon to become a scorcher, and I could again hear the heavy thump of the baseball in the leather gloves, see the grace with which the farm boys moved, and feel the pure pleasure of being alive in a world where everything was beautiful.

Under the spell of the memory, I started to write a piece that was different from the usual column but might, I thought, be O.K. for the Fourth of July since practically nobody would read it anyhow. Reading it long afterward, I realized it was the first sure clue that those old roots had me in their tentacles, or whatever roots grab with.

Summer Beyond Wish

A long time ago I lived in a crossroads village of northern Virginia and during its summer enjoyed innocence and never knew boredom, although nothing of consequence happened there.

Seven houses of varying lack of distinction constituted the community. A dirt road meandered off toward the mountain where a bootleg still supplied whiskey to the men of the countryside, and another dirt road ran down to the creek. My cousin Kenneth and I would sit on the bank and fish with earthworms. One day we killed a copperhead which was basking on a rock nearby. That was unusual.

The heat of the summer was mellow and produced sweet scents which lay in the air so damp and rich you could almost taste them. Mornings smelled of purple wisteria, afternoons of the wild roses which tumbled over stone fences, and evenings of honeysuckle.

Even by standards of that time it was a primitive place. There was no electricity. Roads were unpaved. In our house there was no plumbing. The routine of summer days was shaped by these deficiencies. Lacking electric lights, one went early to bed and rose while the dew was still in the grass. Kerosene lamps were cleaned and polished in an early-morning hubbub of women, and children were sent to the spring for fresh water.

This afforded a chance to see whether the crayfish population had multiplied. Later, a trip to the outhouse would afford a chance to daydream in the Sears, Roebuck catalog, mostly about shotguns and bicycles.

With no electricity, radio was not available for pacifying the young. One or two people did have radios that operated on mail-order batteries about the size of a present-day car battery, but these were not for children, though occasionally you might be invited in to hear "Amos 'n' Andy."

All I remember about "Amos 'n' Andy" at that time is that it was strange hearing voices come out of furniture. Much later I was advised that listening to "Amos 'n' Andy" was racist and was grateful that I hadn't heard much.

In the summer no pleasures were to be had indoors. Everything of delight occurred in the world outside. In the flowers there were hummingbirds to be seen, tiny wings fluttering so fast that the birds seemed to have no wings at all.

In the heat of midafternoon the women would draw the blinds, spread blankets on the floor for coolness and nap, while in the fields the cattle herded together in the shade of spreading trees to escape the sun. Afternoons were absolutely still, yet filled with sounds.

Bees buzzed in the clover. Far away over the fields the chug of an ancient steam-powered threshing machine could be faintly heard. Birds rustled under the tin of the porch roof.

Rising dust along the road from the mountains signaled an approaching event. A car coming. "Car's coming," someone would say. People emerged from houses. The approaching dust was studied. Guesses were hazarded about whom it might contain.

Then—a big moment in the day—the car would cruise past.

"Who was it?"

"I didn't get a good look."

"It looked like Packy Painter to me."

"Couldn't have been Packy. Wasn't his car."

The stillness resettled itself as gently as the dust, and you could wander past the henhouse and watch a hen settle herself to perform the mystery of laying an egg. For livelier adventure there was the field that contained the bull. There, one could test his courage by seeing how far he dared venture before running back through the fence.

The men drifted back with the falling sun, streaming with heat and fatigue, and washed in tin basins with water hauled in buckets from the spring. I knew a few of their secrets, such as who kept his whiskey hidden in a Mason jar behind the lime barrel, and what they were really doing when they excused themselves from the kitchen and stepped out into the orchard and stayed out there laughing too hard.

I also knew what the women felt about it, though not what they thought. Even then I could see that matters between women and men could become very difficult and, sometimes, so difficult that they spoiled the air of summer.

At sunset people sat on the porches. As dusk deepened, the lightning bugs came out to be caught and bottled. As twilight edged into night, a bat swooped across the road. I was not afraid of bats then, although I feared ghosts, which made the approach of bedtime in a room where even the kerosene lamp would quickly be doused seem terrifying.

I was even more afraid of toads and specifically of the toad which lived under the porch steps and which everyone assured me would, if touched, give me warts. One night I was allowed to stay up until the stars were in full command of the sky. A woman of great age was dying in the village and it was considered fit to let the children stay abroad into the night. As four of us sat there we saw a shooting star and someone said, "Make a wish."

I did not know what that meant. I didn't know anything to wish for.

Meanwhile, back in New York a real-estate frenzy was destroying everything in its path.
    I was in its path.

The Incredible
Shrinking Life

When we moved to New York we had to get rid of the children. Landlords didn't like them and, in any case, rents were so high. Who could afford an apartment big enough to contain children?

Naturally, we all wept. What made it doubly hard was that we had to get rid of the dining-room furniture too. It made you feel sad. It was like being whittled away.

When the apartment rent went up, we had to settle for something with one room less, which meant getting rid of the trunk with Grandmother's old snapshots and 1899 letters to her grandfather, as well as our favorite easy chair, locks of the children's baby hair and the urn containing Uncle Mark's ashes.

"All that junk," said the real-estate agent, "belongs in an attic, and New Yorkers can't afford attics." Attics were the past and New York was now. "To hell with the past, and three cheers for now!" we cried, as we got rid of it all.

And yet it made you feel sad. It was like being whittled away.

The rent went up again, and we had to get rid of the guest bedroom. Everybody said we were crazy for keeping a guest bedroom anyhow. It was an invitation for impoverished relatives, deadbeat acquaintances and children to bilk you of a free night's sleep. So we got rid of the guest bed and the sampler that said, "Welcome to our happy home," and we settled into a one-bedroom place with a doormat outside in the hallway that said, "Scram."

The doormat came from one of the chic new doormat boutiques in SoHo and looked so up-to-date that it made us feel almost as trendy as Jackie O. Still, when you got inside, you couldn't help feeling sad. You felt you were being whittled away.

The next rent increase presented hard choices by driving us into a one-room place with a windowless kitchen. The old sofa on which we had sat to watch the Super Bowl of 1964 had to go. So did the old lamps by which we had struggled to read Marcel Proust's "Remembrance of Things Past." The old bed went, too, and the old rugs, the old mirror and the spare toothbrush.

When we first approached this new, lean shelter, scarcely larger than a procurer's automobile, we felt inexplicably sad until I cried, "Come now, it was just such a cubbyhole as this in which we first set out on the great American adventure of marriage and success."

With that, I scooped my companion into my arms and bore her over the threshold. How thrilling it was to recapture the euphoria of better days and to be young again. And, this time, in New York! And yet, it made you feel sad. It was like being whittled away.

The next rent increase was brutal. We refused to pay, refused to be whittled again.

"You don't want to pay, suit yourself," said the landlord. "This town's crawling with saps who'd give an eye and their front teeth for a place like this." He was apparently right. Entering and leaving the building, we saw half-blind, toothless saps staring at us with slavering apartment lust.

Out we went. Moving down again.

"Why are we always moving down?" I asked friends. "In the old days everybody used to move up. I remember the year I moved up to Kents. That same year I moved up to a three-bedroom house for only $22,000."

Friends assured me that moving down was what you did in New York. Why didn't any of us ever consider moving out? I asked. "You crazy?" they explained. "New York is where it's at."

I moved down. To fit into the smaller space I had to get rid of my companion. "It's just a closet," I said. "You wouldn't really like it." Anyhow, I pointed out, landlords didn't like women in their closets.

Naturally we both wept. It really did make you feel sad. It was like being whittled away.

One night the landlord opened the closet door and showed the hooks to a German with a favorable rate of exchange, a millionaire Italian playboy, an oil-rich Arab and two highly skilled American tax evaders.

There was no doubt what that meant. I called real-estate agents. They took me all over Manhattan, looking at warehouse shelves. Not one of them could accommodate anybody more than four feet tall.

The surgeon was reassuring. "I have done hundreds of such operations," he said, "since the real-estate boom began. My patients inhabit some of the most expensive shelves in Manhattan."

"Will I regret it afterward?" I asked.

"A touch of sadness is only to be expected," he said, "after you've been whittled away."

The day the above piece was published James Reston, an old friend and colleague, wired me two words of advice: "Get out."

I couldn't. New York was too wonderful. Still, I couldn't shake the vision of Morrisonville which had come to me in Nan-

tucket. The first stage of roots fever was in my bones. I began wondering what it was like down there in Virginia so far from rich, exciting New York. Why not go down and look around?

At breakfast time one spring morning my wife and I pulled into Leesburg. Morrisonville lies about twelve miles west over a small mountain. This is Loudoun County. Leesburg is the county seat. It is infested with lawyers and real-estate saleswomen, but an innocent from New York, finding the streets so quiet, would never guess they were there.

Alert on Dangerous Turf

My eyes are New York eyes. They are wary, wise, cunning eyes. They are eyes trained in swarming streets and fetid subways to identify menace and maniacs at fifty paces and signal the brain to order the feet to change to a safer course.

They are eyes that know how to see everybody while looking at nobody, to notice everything without glancing at anything. They are veteran eyes, hardened by years of New York survival.

Last week I brought my New York eyes to Leesburg, Va., where they instantly spotted a parking place at the curb on the main thoroughfare. They were astounded. They hadn't seen an unoccupied curb parking space in years.

Sweeping the battlefield, they reported even more amazing information: There wasn't a single enemy car anywhere in traffic seizing position to do battle for this parking space. I moved into it without being threatened by sidearms or even cursed.

"This is weird," the eyes said. "This town gives us the creeps. Let's vamoose out of here."

I am not one to be terrified by a suspicious parking situation. What's more, I was hungry and determined upon lunch, but after leaving the car I reminded the eyes not to make contact with anyone on the sidewalk. They began scanning with their New York cunning and immediately swept across an approaching couple—a man of about sixty and a woman, possibly his wife, about the same age.

The eyes looked through them to a point 500 miles away, noticed no suspicious bulges and reported, "They may be traveling without weapons."

Judging them safe, I let the distance close between us when the eyes reported that both woman and man were not only struggling to make eye contact, but also smiling. "Don't let them make eye contact!" I shouted to the eyes.

Too late. My cunning New York eyes, fatigued perhaps by too much driving, maybe lulled to a false sense of security by the absence of Mayor Koch on the corner crying, "Have you heard how well my book's doing?"—my marvelous New York eyes succumbed and locked in eye-to-eye embrace, first with the man, then with the woman.

The contact lasted only a thousandth of a second, but that, I knew, was long enough for disaster.

Then an eerie sequence of events failed to take place:

1. The man failed to ask me for a cigarette while the woman failed to maneuver behind me and produce a knife to cut off my retreat route.

2. Simultaneously, the woman failed to seize my lapel, shriek that her babies had all been kidnapped by pygmy tribesmen and implore me to go to their rescue.

3. The man, holding his smile firmly in place, failed to pinion my hands, stuff my pockets with pamphlets and threaten to pursue me through the streets until I came to Jesus, subscribed to the Manichaean heresy or gave him money for the propagation of Zoroastrianism.

4. A millionth of a second later, despite having me locked in eye contact, the woman failed to insist I sign a petition demanding unilateral disarmament, bilingual education or a Federal program for the spaying of stray cats.

5. This failure by the woman was followed almost instantly by the man's failure to lean into my ear and chant either, "Acid and grass, acid and grass— What'll it be? Acid or grass?" or, "I've got the butyl, I've got the amyl; I've got the amyl, I've got the butyl."

As I say, all these things failed to occur in the fraction of a second that my New York eyes failed in their duty. Brief though that instant was, I experienced an eternity of anxiety, and although amazed at what had not happened, I realized that something worse might be coming.

This, after all, was not New York, but Leesburg, Va. Leesburg had probably developed tricks still undreamed of in Manhattan. If there had been time, I would have broken out in a cold sweat, for they were now abreast of me, close enough to reach out and do their worst.

The man struck first. "Good morning," he said.

Then the woman: "Nice day, isn't it?" she said.

Before I could recoil they were beyond me and walking away. "Check 'em out," I told my New York eyes.

The eyes reported both man and woman proceeding unmenacingly away from us. "I told you this town was weird," said the eyes.

"Weird, schmeird," I said. "This place is crazy."

We got out of town fast.

Not fast enough, though.

A real-estate saleswoman must have seen roots fever in my eyes because in no time at all she had me back in Morrisonville, and in less time than that my wife and I had a mortgage on a dilapidation and seventeen acres located within shouting distance of the house in which I was born.

That wasn't too alarming, though. We were still New Yorkers. New Yorkers were supposed to buy funny real estate in the sticks. They say nobody can survive in New York without having a quiet, faraway place where he can soothe his frenzied soul and forget the mayhem he has seen.

Moseying Around

We went to the country and acquired seventeen acres of farm-land. My respect for farmers has been increasing ever since.

"What are you planning to grow on that land?" an official person inquired at the time of the transaction. "Chickens," I said, without knowing why. A few days earlier in Manhattan I had been walking through Abingdon Square and saw a man washing a plucked chicken in a drinking fountain. This had left a powerful impression. It seemed like something you could build a musical comedy on, and I had chickens on the mind, though actually I haven't the foggiest idea of how to grow chickens.

"Chickens aren't grown on seventeen acres anymore," said the official person. "Nowadays chickens are manufactured in broiler factories."

I must have looked too stunned to go on because my inter-rogator glanced up impatiently and said, "I'll put down hay," and filled in the blank where the crop was to be specified with the single word "Hay."

Freed to survey my domain, I strolled over the field envisioning amber waves of hay rippling in the summer breeze. The neighboring farmer moseyed over to pass the time of day. I had already noticed that when you're a farmer you have to do a lot of moseying, and I tried to mosey over toward him, but made a mess of it, and I could tell he knew I had a lot to learn about moseying.

After neighborly greetings he asked, "What kind of crop you thinking of putting in?"

"Hay," I said. "This time next summer this whole field will be rippling with amber waves of hay."

"You want amber waves, you'd better put in wheat," he

said. "With wheat you get those amber waves of grain. With hay, about all you're going to get is grasshoppers."

I didn't let on that he was telling me anything I didn't know, but he had given me quite a start. I suddenly realized I knew absolutely nothing about hay, except that you have to make it while the sun shines.

Now this, if you have just turned your hand to farming, is a depressing realization. How can you call yourself a farmer if you know nothing about hay? I have heard about hay all my life, of course, and have often been called a hayseed. But while farmers all over the world knew hay as well as I knew the New York subway system, I hadn't the slightest notion of how to make the stuff.

If you are the new farmer on the block, this is not the kind of confession you make publicly. It's out of the question to walk around among the neighbors, even if you're good at moseying, and say, "Tell me a little something about hay. Do you have to plant hay or does hay just come if you leave the field alone?"

Not wanting to be the joke of the community, I decided to study up on hay at the library when I got back to town, which I was mighty eager to get back to after talking with the man who had agreed to make livable quarters out of the old cabin on the property.

I had entertained fine rustic fantasies about life in that old cabin, rising at dawn to the rooster's crowing, enjoying an invigorating shower and a robust pot of black coffee before moseying out in my hip boots to start the day's making of the hay.

"How are you planning to get the water for the shower and the coffee?" asked the builder.

"We'll put in one of those tin shower stalls and a sink," I explained.

"So what kind of water are you going to use?"

"Whatever kind of water comes out when we turn on the faucet."

"Look," he said, "we put in the shower, we put in the sink, we turn the faucet, and you know what? No water is going to come out unless you've dug a well and tied into it."

"You mean the water doesn't just come?"

"I never heard of the water just coming," he said. "The well will cost you a pile, but maybe you can save a few thousand by installing a pump that will get water up from a spring, if you've got a spring, but of course it can always go dry on you."

"In New York," I said, "if you want to wash a plucked chicken you just take it to a public park, hold it over a drinking fountain, step on the pedal, and the water just comes."

"Speaking of New York," he said, "you'll have to spring for a bundle to put in a septic field for your sewage."

"You mean, when you flush, the sewage doesn't just go?"

"Not without a septic field. The only thing that just goes down here is money."

I am back in New York, not in defeat, but only to make enough hay to pay for the realization of my dream and to take moseying lessons at Lincoln Center. Any tips on hay of the vegetable variety will be gratefully received if mailed in plain brown wrapper.

Making It

When I go back to my hometown with my world-weary New York eyes and my expensive New York teeth the folks always look at me in that sly superior country way. That's partly because they're country people and my hometown—Morrisonville, Va.—is a country town, nestled as it is three miles south of metropolitan Lovettsville and two miles north of Wheatland, which is not a town at all but just a sign on the side of the road.

Partly though, it's also because of Frank Sinatra, whose voice reaches everywhere, even to Morrisonville, with his musical paean to New York City, a song that says if a person can "make it there" he can "make it anywhere."

I've noticed that dyed-in-the-wool New Yorkers—maybe I should call them spray-painted-in-the-subway New Yorkers—always look as if they're having a hard time keeping from patting themselves on the back when Frank sings this song. It seems to make them feel like heroic achievers, especially the way Frank phrases it with those big notes on the "make it" lines.

Morrisonville people don't seem to respond the same way. Truth is, if they weren't such sweet people, I'd say their response is an inner sneer. I first detected this a few weeks ago when Lester, with the big house down by the creek, asked if I was "making it up there in New York."

Since my idea of "making it" in New York is not getting run down by a bicyclist or a car running a red light, I said, "Guess so, Lester."

"Just what is it you're making?" he asked.

"Well, you know, day by day—getting by—I'm making it O.K."

"Sure, but making what?"

Was Lester pulling my beautifully tailored New York leg?

"I heard the man sing that if you can make it in New York you can make it anywhere," he said. "And Morrisonville is just about as close to anywhere as you can get. Whatever it is you're making in New York, I'd sort of like to see you make some right here."

"It's just a song, Lester. You know songs are silly."

He went off to make hay, after pointing out that though he could make hay right there in Morrisonville nobody had ever claimed that if you could make hay there you could make it anywhere, for the simple reason that though hay was very easy to make in much of the country, even those who made it best wouldn't be able to make it in downtown Los Angeles, if there was such a place.

In this I detected a gentle rustic contempt for my suave New York worldliness. True, I couldn't make hay in Morrisonville because I didn't know the recipe, but on the other hand Lester probably couldn't navigate the Union Square subway station without getting lost. I let it pass.

On the next visit, however, I encountered the ghost of my Uncle Bruce outside the ruins of my grandmother's house in the very spot where he used to hide his moonshine behind the lime barrel and he, too, had been listening to Frank Sinatra.

Uncle Bruce, who had lived and died in Morrisonville, was

in an uncharacteristically melancholy mood. "Guess you're making it up there in New York, boy," he said.

"Getting along. Day by day. Paying the rent. Keeping the spray paint off my Sunday suit," I said.

"I did that much right here in Morrisonville," he said, "and it was hard toil. Of course, I wouldn't say I was making it. Then, on the other hand, it wasn't easy to make it in Morrisonville. That's what grinds me every time I hear Sinatra sing that song."

"How does a ghost hear, Uncle Bruce?"

"What that song should say, if the writer knew anything," he said, ignoring my question, "is that making it in New York is a lark beside trying to make it in Morrisonville."

"I always thought it ought to be about Baltimore," I said. "Compared to Baltimore, New York is a piece of cake. If you can make it in Baltimore, you can make it anywhere."

"Lord o'mercy, boy, I used to think that just getting to Baltimore would be making it. But Mama always told me, 'Bruce, you stay right here in Morrisonville and test yourself, because if you can make it in Morrisonville you can make it anywhere.'"

"Why are you talking to yourself?" asked my cousin Ruth Lee, who had wandered around from across the road. "Is that the way you make it?"

"Don't make fun of us New Yorkers, Ruth Lee," I said. "I understand how you feel, what with it being so hard for you to make it here in Morrisonville."

"Goodness gracious," she said. "Morrisonville is a picnic compared to Wheatland. If you can make it in Wheatland you can make it anywhere."

Meanwhile, back in New York the landlord announced another rent increase. He was a good landlord, and I liked him, but I knew he would talk. Soon everybody would know how much rent

I was paying, and I would be mobbed by people trying to sell me the Brooklyn Bridge.

There were three places I could go: bankrupt, New Jersey or back to my roots.

My wife pointed out that she had not come to New York to live in New Jersey, so roots it was. She also pointed out that I could forget Morrisonville since she didn't drive and the nearest supermarket was a six-mile journey over hilly, cow-infested terrain. For the rent we paid in New York, I said, maybe we could buy the whole town of Leesburg.

Instead we settled for a house that would have gone for about $4 million if it had been an apartment in Manhattan. Naturally it needed work. About a year's worth. We went down to disturb the workmen occasionally.

"Looks like you're spending a barrel of money on that house," one of the neighbors told me one day.

"After New York," I explained, "it seems like just a cup."

Eventually it was habitable, but even though I was going back to my roots it was sad leaving New York. As time ran out I no longer cursed the real-estate frenzy, because what would New York be without frenzy? Just Podunk with a million potholes on every street corner. It had been a privilege to live there. There were so many amazing things to do there at any hour of the day or night.

Who Wouldn't Love New York?

Things to do on Saturday in New York:

1. Put on five suits of clothes and walk crosstown talking out loud to yourself in Esperanto.

2. Put on a pair of brushed-suede trousers and get a $35 haircut.

3. Burn down a building in the Bronx.

4. Get together with two other women on Twelfth Street and argue about who has the best Cuisinart.

5. Get rained on for twenty minutes while waiting for a bus on York Avenue.

6. Diet until you look like you are made of sticks. Then put on an elegant fur coat and find a girl in an elegant fur coat who also looks like she is made of sticks. Go together to a pet shop and buy a dog that looks like it is made of sticks and then all three of you take a walk in the East Sixties.

7. Wait for the telephone to ring and then don't answer it. Afterward, hide under the bed until your neighborhood burglar arrives for your television set. Introduce yourself.

8. Buy some antiques and frozen bagels.

9. Argue with your wife, husband or lover about whose turn it is to go outside to find out whether the sun is shining.

10. Get together with several people from the Upper West Side and display the keenness of your sensibility by deploring the banality of Italian opera, contemporary architecture and The New York Review of Books.

11. Get stuck for two hours in an elevator with somebody holding advanced views on calendar reform.

12. Telephone several acquaintances and ask if they have heard of any interesting new liberation movements worth joining. If they haven't ask if they have heard of any interesting new opinions worth declaring truculently to liven up dull parties.

13. Go to Ninth Avenue and look at the groceries. Go to Eighth Avenue and look at the pimps. Go to Seventh Avenue and smell the grease. Go to Sixth Avenue and cringe under the architecture.

14. Think of the futility of life. Then ponder the certainty of doom. Reflect at length on the fact that nothing good has ever happened to you and that nothing ever will. Think on the certainty of rising taxes, deteriorating arteries, dandruff and disappointment in love. Then take a ride on the subway.

15. Meet with some really decent people in Central Park and have a really serious talk about ecology, good writing and social injustice.

16. Get into your own head, or into art or leather.

17. Buy the loudest transistor radio in midtown, tune in a rock station, turn it to maximum volume and carry it around the streets so everybody can admire your taste in music.

18. Discover an incredibly fantastic new restaurant in the Village that nobody has ever heard of and which would be ruined if everybody did. Then telephone several people and feel superior by not telling them about it.

19. Write a letter to the editor deploring the middle class's persecution by the poor, or demanding to know why the editor permits so much unmitigated trash to be published in his newspaper.

20. Get a job in a snooty delicatessen or a snooty Italian boutique on Fifth Avenue and assure customers that you do not regard them as people of sufficient quality to deserve your lox or Florentine toothpicks.

21. Stand in a Third Avenue movie line for an hour and have a really deep talk about cinema and existentialism while eating a pretzel.

22. Buy a house on Sutton Place and lie in bed until 3 P.M. thinking how rich you are, yet unloved for all your wealth. Telephone an old school friend out in Brooklyn and tell him how you have envied his poverty since discovering that money can't buy happiness. Afterward book a Concorde flight to Paris for Sunday brunch.

23. Have a friend over for lunch and make her respect you by explaining the correlation between the Manichaean heresy and hot pastrami.

24. Walk around the East Side until you see Jackie Onassis, Greta Garbo and Woody Allen or develop blisters. If unsuccessful on all four counts, buy some blisters on Madison Avenue so you will have something to talk about Saturday night.

Prescript

I had been back at my roots practically no time at all before discovering that mine were not the only roots embedded thereabouts. A lifetime lived in cities had left me unprepared for the excesses of which Nature is capable when you let a little soil and sunshine into a community. When you are thinking how grand it will be to get back to your roots, you are too full of romance to reflect that while your begetters were perfectly at home with plow and shears, you are better at telling a potential mugger from a harmless weirdo than at distinguishing a boxwood from a tulip poplar.

Dangerous to the Last Drop

The house in which we live sits under a coffee-bean tree. Had we known about coffee-bean trees before buying the house, we probably would have told the real-estate agent to show us the next place. Because we lived previously in the city, however, we knew almost nothing about the personalities of trees, so we said we would take the house.

On first seeing the house, we did notice huge shade-casting vegetation overhanging it and recognized the stuff as trees. To make conversation with the woman who was about to become the previous owner, I pointed to one and said, "What kind of tree is that?"

"A Kentucky coffee-bean tree," she said.

Yes, she was honest about it. She could have lied, but she didn't. Neither, though, did she come right out and say, "Nobody sensible wants a house located under a coffee-bean tree."

Since she didn't, the only reply I could think of was: "A coffee-bean tree, eh? Imagine that."

A curious thing about trees, which urban people are apt to forget even if they once knew it, is that trees have distinctive personalities. Hemlocks, for instance, like to stand around drooping with melancholy.

Ginkgo trees become discontented with humdrum sex lives

that require them to bring forth fruit monotonously every spring. To show their resentment, they bring forth fruit so foul to smell that one whiff would be enough to kill the romantic impulses of all other ginkgo trees for miles around, if ginkgo trees were like people.

The coffee-bean tree is more like people than most trees, and the people it is like are the people we call adolescents, though with an important difference. Adolescents are adolescents for only a few years. Coffee-bean trees stay adolescents until they are eighty or ninety, which is the age of the coffee-bean tree overhanging our house, according to the tree man.

When you live in the city you don't think of the tree man. We certainly never did. In the city we thought of the exterminator. The tree man never crossed our minds until the day a coffee bean came within inches of killing me.

Have I described the fruit of the coffee-bean tree? It is a brown leathery pod six to nine inches long, shaped somewhat like an airplane propeller, with a stiletto point on one end. The botanical point of the point is to enable the plummeting coffee bean to plunge daggerlike into the earth, or any skulls that may be passing below. I told you this tree was like an adolescent; as the adolescent drives, so the coffee-bean tree disseminates its fruit.

The coffee-bean pod is slightly lighter than a piece of granite of comparable size. This is because the pod contains several roundish, black seeds somewhat bigger and a good bit heavier than marbles. You can see how easily one could be killed by a falling coffee bean just by stepping out of the house in the shedding season.

Anyhow. So we called a tree man. Pointing way, way up, we said, "We'd like that big branch up there cut off before this tree kills somebody down here."

That branch was really way up there. From the way the tree man looked way up there at it, I could tell that he thought this was a job that would require the balance as well as the nerves of a flying-trapeze artist. "It's the wrong time of year to prune," he said, and promised to come back when the pruning season came in.

We never heard from that tree man again. Talk about ingrates. Adolescent ingratitude is nil compared to a coffee-bean tree's. As soon as the chicken tree man departed, the tree began dropping coffee beans by the thousand. I do not hyperbolize. By the thousand. It was not all done in a few days, as civilized trees do their dirty work. It went on for months. Coffee beans fell from September to May, making the roof thunder all night in the windy times.

On windless days, wearing hard hats, we shoveled coffee beans into trash containers. Their weight was prodigious. The pods were dreadful if they broke in your hands: full of a hideous, green, viscous substance suggesting sci-fi tales of things from nasty galaxies.

Did I mention the tough, thick, eighteen-inch-long leaf stems that fall to the earth and clog gutters and downspouts from autumn to spring, leaving the property always looking as though angry giants had thrashed it with giant brooms that disintegrated as they thrashed?

Another tree man has just left. He will be back next pruning season, he said lyingly. Meantime, I count at least 500,000 coffee beans still up there. Way, way up there.

Justice in the Grass

In the mornings I go to the garden. The garden shudders when it hears the back door slam and recognizes my footsteps on the porch. By now it knows the man it is dealing with: a harsh but just master who brooks no nonsense from flora or weed.

The wisteria on the back porch is the first stop on the morning tour. I know what is in its pulpy heart: hatred and murder. During the night, when it thinks me asleep, it grows deadly new tentacles and flexes them in the dark.

Lying awake in the bedroom I have heard it down there, practicing strangulation techniques and cursing quixotic Nature for making it a wisteria vine.

Oh yes, I know its dreams. It dreams of being a boa constrictor looped around the porch post so that when the back door slams some morning it might fling its deadly coils and slowly mash me.

This is the nature of wisteria. It yearns to crush all things. Given its freedom, it would slowly crush the back-porch posts and, when the roof had collapsed, would strangle it, meanwhile reaching tentacles into the house to crush refrigerators, velocipedes, television sets, beds, bathtubs and overnight guests.

To survive wisteria, you have to remind it constantly who the boss is. This is why I always begin the garden tour by giving the wisteria a kick in the trunk. In Maytime it sprouts a dozen new tentacles overnight, each a foot long. Letting it get away with this can be fatal. I attack the entire plant with dull pruning shears to keep it humble.

Gardening, as someone smart once said—possibly Voltaire—is the only sensible thing to do after you become wise enough to know there is no use trying to do anything about people. How true this is, yet how disorderly and people-like is the behavior that takes place in a garden.

The wisteria, for example, is the botanical equivalent of those Wall Street people who want to have everything wrapped in their crushing embrace. Like them, the wisteria is forever saying, "I want it all and as fast as I can get it."

Would it not be a better society if every morning you could slam the back door, walk into Wall Street and give these want-it-alls a hearty kick in their trunks before pruning them with a dull blade?

Alas, this cannot be done without inviting a lot of legal brouhaha about the rights of these human wisteria. No wonder the wise man retreats to the garden. There he can give wisteria the treatment it needs to make it behave harmoniously with the rest of botanical society, yet not be hounded as an abuser of wisterias' rights.

The morning tour brings me next to the peonies. Beautiful flowers they are, but the blooms are so short-lived. They are the garden equivalents of the stars, the famous stars of stage, screen and television whose stardom, sad to say, so often results only from a brief moment of physical bloom.

Afterward these poor stars, threatened with income and audience decline as the dew evaporates from their bloom, must suffer surgical mutilation of faces, bosoms, buttocks and who knows what else in a macabre struggle to look forever as fresh as a peony on a May morning.

By retreating to your garden you will never have to witness the degrading spectacle of a peony going under anesthetic for a bloom tuck. The peony is content with a week of glory. Afterward it mellows into adult dignity and plays subtle but vital supporting roles, now as a lovely green leafy setting for the lilies and roses that succeed it, now as a sinister hiding place for the cat stalking the bluebirds.

But what is this with its vicious, entwining, strangling grip on the beautiful peony? It is bindweed. I am amazed that there is any here in the peony patch. Didn't it see how ruthlessly I destroyed the tulips across the way to get every last bit of bindweed root torn out of that bed?

Bindweed is the lawyer of the garden. Its aim is to entwine the entire garden in exquisitely delicate wire until nothing can breathe and nothing can grow. Against the human bindweed mankind is hopeless, but in the garden satisfaction can be had, though at a price.

As with the wisteria, I attack, muttering to the bindweed: "Aha, my good bindweed, you have made a fatal error by going into my peony bed instead of corporate law."

A trowel gouged deep into the soil is needed to deal with these devils, for like lawyers, they are deeply rooted. Removing them usually kills the peonies, but I have more serious worries. Like sneaking into position to kick that cat stalking the bluebird.

Well, you finally get back to your roots only to find that back isn't where you are at all. Not at all. You're right up front, and there's a bulldozer coming right at you, and a developer pulling up all the roots in sight so he can lay down asphalt.

I got back to my roots in the nick of time. If I'd tarried much longer there wouldn't have been any roots left to get back to. Something there is in America that hates a root.

Burgville Marches On

Too poor for New York, we moved to Burgville. It is not a suburb. It is not an exurb. Despite its name, it is not even a burg. It used to be a burg, but since it was attacked a few years ago by earth-moving equipment and occupied by squadrons of $30,000 German cars, its burgness has died.

I call it an urboid. Whatever it's called, Burgville is now held up as a sad example of what can happen to a burg that sells its burgright for a mess of asphalt. People in Round Hill, an unruined town on the mountain to the west, now have bumper stickers that say, "Don't Let Them Burgville Round Hill."

That's Round Hill's way of saying it likes being undevastated, unasphalted and unaccustomed to the throaty "Achtung" of high-class Teutonic exhaust pipes, and would like to remain so.

Round Hill's chances don't look good. I base this judgment on the phenomenon of "bumper-sticker lag." If my observations are correct, bumper stickers run about two years behind the bankers, lawyers, contractors and land speculators whose income depends on turning rustic America into a land of urboids.

For instance, just last year Burgville cars were bearing bumper stickers that said, "Don't Let Them Fairfax Burgville." Fairfax was a whole county east of here, down near Washington, which the earth-movers and asphalters were then finishing off.

Toward the end, Burgville people could see the results on the eastern horizon, the scariest being a superurboid called Tyson's Corner: all automobiles, bad air, dehumanized people containers, asphalt, Moloch worship, treelessness, humdrum stores galore and spiritual boredom, not to mention 117 restaurants serving thawed food.

Looking down the highway on a clear day toward the awful Fairfaxed ruins, you saw Tyson's Corner on the horizon and thought of Godzilla headed straight up the pike for beautiful, charming, lovely, old Burgville.

That's when the bumper stickers appeared that said, "Don't Let Them Fairfax Burgville."

This should have been the signal to all who knew about bumper-sticker lag that the jig was up, that the groundwork for Fairfaxing Burgville was too far advanced to be stopped, even by a citizenry inflamed enough to resort to bumper stickers.

So it's funny and sad now to see bumper stickers pleading, "Don't Let Them Burgville Round Hill." It can only mean that it's all over for poor old Round Hill.

Out beyond Round Hill lie West Virginia, Pittsburgh and the great state of Ohio. It is easy to imagine the fall of the dominoes being recorded in a western march of bumper stickers:

"Don't Let Them Round Hill West Virginia,"

"Don't Let Them West Virginia Pittsburgh,"

"Don't Let Them Pittsburgh The Great State of Ohio."

Why is the game always over by the time bumper stickers go on? Because urboid dwellers have faulty intelligence networks, underpaid lawyers and no instinct for the whereabouts of a politician's jugular.

What urboid dwellers do best is go to public meetings and scowl angrily. In Burgville we spend most of our lives in public meetings, scowling. We scowl in meetings of the Planning Commission, the Zoning Commission, the Preservation Commission, the Devastation Commission, the Buildability Commission, the Inevitability Commission and the Commission on Commissions, to cite just a few.

Upon learning that the Eternal Greenery Development Corporation has not only quietly made a deal to cut down Birnam Wood, level the surrounding mountain and on the resulting plain of mud erect 637 units of tract housing, each with its private personalized cesspool, we paste "Don't Let Them Fairfax Birnam Wood" on our bumpers and go to scowl en masse at platoons of commissioners.

Only to find that it's all over but the scowling. The lawyer for Eternal Greenery produces the crusher. Papers. Everything in order. All in conformity with this and that. Bureaucratic niceties and necessities all settled months and months ago. The law, the law, good urboid dwellers, above all the sanctity of law, government of laws, you know. Not of scowlers.

After lifetimes of Fairfaxing poor old Fairfax, these lawyers have seen so many scowlers, read so many pathetic bumper stickers, filed so many right papers so often, explained the law to so many commissions. Thinking that mere urboid scowlers can ever deflect these veteran champions of Eternal Greenery from the swift completion of their appointed Fairfaxings—it is to weep at one's own foolishness.

Today Burgville, tomorrow the world.

SERIOUS
NONSENSE

Washington where I lived for twenty years swarmed with people who despised nonsense. This was odd because I had never seen a place that was more nonsensical. In Washington nonsense ran ankle-deep in the gutters. People spoke it to you in parlors, restaurants and big offices, between TV commercials, and over the backyard fence.

Hordes of humanity there earned a living by concocting and spreading nonsense. And yet you constantly heard people being praised as "a no-nonsense" judge, or committee chairman, or White House flunkey, or chef, or decorator, or tree pruner.

This was one of Washington's most dangerous weaknesses because, of course, nonsense makes up a very high percentage of all human endeavor. To hold nonsense in contempt is to distance yourself from the human condition. You don't want to make that mistake if you think you're the most important city on this or any other planet.

I am a lover of nonsense. This may be explained genetically or by the fact that it is easier to succumb to it than to carry on the Herculean labor of trying to make sense of a universe like the one in which we strut. I don't know. What I do know is that periodically I have the irresistible urge to write something that will make the entire city of Washington rise up crying, "What absolute nonsense!"

The following pieces were born of that impulse. In each case I was saying. "To hell with it all, I'll be as silly as the world deserves."

To help the reader through this foolishness, I should offer a few clarifications:

The murder trial reported in the piece about inflated wine prices may seem impenetrable to anyone unfamiliar with the Perry Mason television series. I include it, nevertheless, because I believe every American should be encouraged to learn the sad tale of Hamilton (Ham) Burger, the only district attorney in history who never won a case.

The first of these pieces was written in 1979 in anticipation of the coming Eighties decade. Everything in it seems as valid today as it did ten years ago, so I have taken an artistic liberty by adding ten years to all the original dates.

Stranger Than Orwell

A no-nonsense letter from the National Academy of National Academies put the question crisply: "The 1990's will be here before you know it. What should America do about it?"

They have asked the right man. If there is one thing I have firm convictions about, it is what this country should do in the 1990's. The first thing it should do is reduce output of no-nonsense letters, as well as no-nonsense executives and no-nonsense politicians. Look where all this no-nonsense nonsense has got us in the 1980's. In a nonsensical pickle, that's where.

I say let's cut out the no-nonsense in the 1990's. While we're at it we should also cut out the habit of letting computers and desks write letters to living human beings.

Just yesterday I had a letter from the desk of Wilmer Bainbridge urging me to subscribe to a twelve-month course in home insulation. This letter was written by a computer, which apparently serves as amanuensis for Bainbridge's desk. Why can't Bainbridge's desk write its own letters? Why doesn't Bainbridge's desk fire Bainbridge and cut expenses?

Better yet, why don't we fire all three of them in the 1990's and restore the peace of mind that my grandmother, rest her soul, knew in the halcyon days of William Howard Taft? She lived to a splendid old age, my grandmother, in large part because she never absorbed the shock of receiving a letter written by a machine at the behest of furniture.

Let's also cut out the inefficient business of taking two aspirin tablets every time a cold or headache comes along. One aspirin tablet can do the job with half the swallowing if American science will quit playing with mice long enough to invent the king-size aspirin tablet.

The secret of the king-size aspirin tablet is already well known to the Germans and Japanese. You double the volume of the present aspirin tablet. Let's have a crash program in the 1990's and beat the Germans and Japanese to something for a change.

We also need eyeglass defoggers. The 1980's gave us windshield defoggers but left the bespectacled driver just as blind as before by failing to extend the principle to his eyeglasses. What is the usc of a clear windshield if you can't see the steering wheel?

While the 1990's are about it, they ought to give us a tomato shaped like a hamburger. In the 1970's, tomato science produced the square tomato, which can not only be easily packed in a cardboard box but also tastes like one. If hamburgers are going to be too expensive for the hamburger classes, let's at least give them a tomato that looks like a hamburger. A little laboratory work might even make it possible to produce it in six flavors—strawberry, raspberry, cherry, orange, fish stick and fried chicken.

And what about the car? Is fuel efficiency really what we need most desperately? I say what we really need is a car that can be shot when it breaks down.

Grandmother didn't make it to ninety-seven by having her horse towed in for $267 worth of repairs every time it broke down. She called one of her sons, who shot it, then had him get into the traces and haul her home in the buggy. As she passed Locomobile owners waiting to have their ailing cars towed to the garage, she had a good laugh and stayed young-at-heart by shouting, "Next time get a son!"

There is plenty medicine can do in the 1990's, but nothing would help more than moving ahead with head transplants. The possibilities here are revolutionary. The sex-change operation, so commonplace in the 1980's, would become obsolete, since males who wanted to become females could simply arrange to exchange heads with females who wanted to be males.

If it turned out they didn't like it, each could return the other's head with no harm done and both parties a little wiser.

It would also end many of the present inconveniences of the Presidential system. By exchanging heads with his predecessor, a newly elected President would no longer have to wait for the outgoing President to clear out his clothes closets before moving into the White House.

Finally, let's use the miracle of the computer to solve the crime problem and end violence on the streets. Nothing is easier. Every law-abiding citizen would be required to register for victimization, much as young men used to register for military drafts.

Every ten days the computer would select at random victims required to be robbed by legalized criminals registered with a Federal Bureau of Thugs, Burglars and Knuckle-Duster Artists. When your number came up, you would receive notification as follows: "Greetings. You have been selected to be robbed by Maxwell Abercrombie of $37 in cash and your wristwatch. Please forward this loot to the Bureau for nonviolent transfer to your assailant within three days, or Abercrombie will be authorized to use his own methods of collection."

The Government, of course, would tax Abercrombie's revenue, and also charge him an annual license fee. Some things will not change in the 1990's.

The Case of Vinous Inflation

News item: The price of European wine is rising so fast that people with money to invest are no longer putting it into waterfront property and pork bellies but into Château Ducru-Beaucaillou and Chambertin Clos de Beze.

Any number of persons had ample motive for murdering Harry Dudd. There was his son Fuddy, for one, who hated his father for the macabre sense of humor which had resulted in his having to go through life bearing the name Fuddy Dudd.

The famous overweight woman lawyer, Merry Payson, had reduced Fuddy Dudd to blubbering suds on the witness stand but had not been carried away by his confession. Merry Payson had seen too many innocent people confess to murder.

"Very touching, Mr. Dudd," she said, "but not convincing. You knew that the decedent had specified in a codicil—"

"I object to counselor's unwarranted suggestion that the decedent was the kind of man who would even go into a codicil, much less specify in one," said Hamilton Burr, the district objector.

"Your Honor," said Merry, "Fuddy Dudd could never have murdered his father. He knew the old gentleman's will provided that if he died violently, his son, Fuddy, was to be cut off without a bottle of muscatel. He is covering up for the real killer."

Merry summoned Harry Dudd's business partner, F. Gore Galore, to the stand and adroitly forced Galore to admit that he had threatened to kill Dudd unless he paid a gambling debt— two bottles of Schloss Johannisberger Trockenbeerenauslese, Von Metternich, which the two had bet on the 1972 World Series.

Under Merry's brutally logical examination, Galore cracked and confessed. "No, Mr. Galore," said Merry. "You would never have killed Dudd for the Schloss Johannisberger. You knew all too well that without a Brink's truck no man would have a chance of carrying those two bottles of wine from his house to yours and living to watch their market price triple and quadruple."

Hamilton Burr objected to counselor's forcing all the witnesses to confess. He was sustained.

Merry said Galore was covering up for the real killer and called Selem Short, Dudd's broker. Short said he would confess only if Merry would not humiliate him on the witness stand.

"You're covering up for the real killer, Mr. Short," said

Merry. "Tell us about the telephone call you received two minutes before the decedent's decease."

Short said it was dinner time, the usual time of Harry Dudd's calls. Dudd always telephoned his broker to ask if the wine he was planning to have with his dinner had dropped in price that day.

"And if it had not dropped?" asked Merry.

"Naturally he wouldn't drink it," Short said.

"Why not?"

"If you owned an acre of sea-front land on Cape Cod, with land prices going up the way they are, would you drink it?" explained Short.

"When was the last time you were able to tell Mr. Dudd that the price of the dinner wine he was phoning about had gone down?"

"Never," said Short. "At least not since my firm abandoned stocks and bonds and went into wine."

"And what was the wine Mr. Dudd inquired about on the lethal evening?"

"Vosne-Romanée la Grande Rue, H. LaMarche, 1966," said Short.

"This is ridiculous, Your Honor," objected Hamilton Burr. "Nobody can even pronounce that wine."

"Sustained," said the judge.

Merry called Mrs. Dudd to the stand. She was beautiful. "All right," she cried. "I did it. And I'm glad."

Merry asked her to get on with it quickly because they were running out of space. Mrs. Dudd said it had been months since she had had a decent glass of wine with dinner. Even an indecent glass. Once her husband had found a half pint of cooking sherry under her pillow and asked her cuttingly whether if he owned an acre of Cape Cod seashore she would drink it behind his back.

She had determined to kill him and did so shortly before he arrived home for dinner. He saw the weapon in her hand. It was a freshly emptied bottle of Vosne-Romanée la Grande Rue, H. LaMarche, 1966. Dudd staggered to phone his broker to learn how much of his fortune had been wiped out. The broker's market quotation finished him.

"I object," cried Hamilton Burr.

"Sustained," said the judge. "Ms. Payson," he said to Merry, "this court reminds you once again that you must always serve a good Bordeaux with a murder confession. Case dismissed."

So You're Thinking of Cloning

Reports that the first human clone is now in existence and well on his way to becoming a taxpayer have raised many questions about cloning. Here are some of the answers:

1. If I get cloned, would my relationship with the resulting child still be parenthood?

No. The relationship is called clonehood. When your clone enters school you will be required to attend meetings of the Clone-Teacher Association.

2. I'd like to be cloned, but am afraid. Is it painful?

Not at all. You simply peel off one tiny little cell from your person, place it in a female human egg cell and place the mixture in the reproductive housing of an obliging woman. In nine months she will convert it into a clone and send it to you.

3. What are the advantages of cloning compared to old-fashioned reproduction methods?

It eliminates the necessity for sex, which means you never have to interrupt your television viewing, and also cuts your outlays for movie tickets and wine.

4. I have heard that people are already beginning to tell clone jokes. Isn't this a disgusting example of ignorance and prejudice?

That reminds me of the Ku Klux Klansman who had himself cloned so often he became known as the Ku Klux Klone.

Cyrus, his first clone, became so tired of hearing the local people call him Cyclone that he moved to the land of the midnight sun, had himself cloned and gave his son the name of Ike. The boy became known as Kloned Ike of the Klondike, but he took it well until his teeth went bad and his jaw became heavy with gold inlays, the weight of which made his mouth hang open. He became so exasperated at hearing passing pedestrians shout, "There's gold in the Kloned Ike!" that one day he drew a BB gun and shot a tormentor harmlessly. "Why did you buy such a cheap little gun?" the police asked him. "Because it was all my personal eclonomy could afford," he said.

5. I hear it is very expensive to get cloned. How long will it be before the price comes down to a level the average person can afford?

There is already talk of a Clone-It-Yourself Kit, which could be sold at hardware stores for a nominal sum. This would include a small cell peeler, one human female egg, a pair of tongs for placing the cell in the egg and an obliging woman willing to house the mixture until it turns into a fully developed clone. The problem is to develop an adequate supply of obliging women small enough to fit into the kit.

6. From the tax viewpoint, is it better to have to clone or a three-martini lunch?

Under present tax law, deductions for clones will not be allowed. However, the full cost of the three-martini lunch is still entirely deductible. This means that a person who can afford to have himself cloned a dozen times or more can still deduct the full cost of taking all his clones to lunch, which could make for considerable tax savings. Warning: They must, however, discuss business.

7. If a clone comes to my house for dinner, how should I treat him?

Do not open the conversation with some graceless remark such as, "I hear you're a clone." Many clones do not know they are clones and might be disturbed to learn it from a stranger. If they have been told, they may introduce the subject themselves with some offhand remark such as, "You know, of course, I'm a clone." Some self-disparaging remark, such as, "You're lucky. I'm a clod," might put the clone at ease. Under no circumstances should you tell a clone joke.

8. I hear they are now perfecting a clone so smart that he will soon be able to beat the grand masters at chess. Won't this take all the fun out of life?

Only for the grand masters, if it were true. Actually, it is not a clone that is now playing winning chess, but a computer. Do not confuse the two or you will end in deep trouble with Internal Revenue. Computers cannot deductibly talk business at lunch.

9. What will it be like when everybody is a clone?

Very much as it is today, except of course that there will never be any interruptions to television viewing, and outlays for movie tickets and wine will be practically zero.

Looking Up Trouble

The first time I went to England, George told me to look up a baron. Let us call him Lord Flutter. "When you get down around the Cotswolds, nip over to the castle and look up Lord Flutter," George urged.

I did so, for I was very young then and totally inexperienced in looking up people. This was because I had never traveled to any of the places inhabited by people worth looking up. Now and then I might travel from southwest Baltimore to Ellicott City, but news that I was planning such a trip never stirred the world's Georges who invariably want you to look people up.

"Ellicott City, eh?" George would say, dismissing me from further consideration so he could focus on Bill or Leo, who were always traveling to romantic places.

"When you get to Rome," he once told Bill, "nip up to Florence and look up Bernard Berenson for me." Leo once got into a tight spot in Moscow during the Stalin era for looking up a remote cousin of George's named Trotsky.

Stalin is said to have halted the execution himself on grounds that anyone dense enough to go to the police for directions on how to find Leon Trotsky was probably the mere butt of some joke played by a certain American buffoon named, according to his spies, George. I doubt this story, because George never plays jokes. The people he wants looked up are people he knows or, at least, has met.

Elizabeth Taylor, for example. An uncle of George's in the film industry once bribed a union leader to get George a summer job as a caterer's aide during the shooting of an Elizabeth Taylor film. One day, George served Miss Taylor a cup of tea.

"Thank you," Miss Taylor said.

Twenty-five years later George told Bill, "When you get out to California, nip down to Hollywood and look up my old friend Liz Taylor."

But back to Lord Flutter those many years ago. . . .

I finally got down around the Cotswolds and, remembering George's request, nipped over to the castle to look up Lord Flutter.

He was civil, as only the English can be civil.

"So you are looking me up, are you?"

"Exactly."

We stood there in long silence. It was in Lord Flutter's garden. He was watering the geraniums. He obviously knew nothing about geraniums, because his were being overwatered to death.

He finally interrupted the silence to ask, "How long will it take?"

". . . will what take?"

"Looking me up," he said. "How long will it take to look me up?"

"It was George's idea," I said. Realizing that Lord Flutter did not like being looked up, I yielded to a craven urge to shift the blame.

Later the police explained that Lord Flutter, unfamiliar with the American habit of looking people up, thought that I was either a blackmailer, a kidnapper, or a bounder who had come to seduce his ward. And, after all, as the constable noted, his Lordship had called off the dogs before they could maul me beyond surgical repair, hadn't he? I did not press charges. With his English civility, neither did Lord Flutter.

I can laugh now that I am rich and famous, with a touch of distinguished gray at the temples and a private humidor that is the envy of belted earls and royal dukes, but the experience left a psychic scar.

After the Lord Flutter humiliation, naturally I was never able to look up anybody again. It became a famous case for psychologists. They diagnose a disgusting timidity that left me powerless to intrude on the privacy of persons who had no desire to meet a thundering bore.

In a sense, my inactivity was un-American, as Senator Jenner declared when they hauled me before the committee; but as Senator McCarthy, who could sometimes be sweet, pointed out in my defense, "It's a waste of time rooting out America's party poopers until we get rid of all the pinkos."

Naturally, a person with my problem is no more at ease when being looked up than when he is looking up somebody. The crux of the neurosis, you see, is fear of being recognized by strangers as the world's most tiresome human.

When you are rich, famous and distinguished, with an enviable humidor, the world mistakes such fear for snobbishness. Winston Churchill once libeled me by telling Queen Elizabeth, "Well, go ahead if you must, Ma'am, and look him up when you get to America, but you are inviting a snub from an insufferable boor."

The Queen's note said: "Dear George, I am so sorry that I shall be unable to look up your friend this trip."

Count Your Miseries

Here is a postcard from Sheila and Dick. They are in Athens, having a wonderful time. They saw the moon over the Acropolis. It was fantastic. I should have seen it.

Of course I should have seen it, but I couldn't, could I? It's impossible to see the moon over the Acropolis if you're stuck in Manhattan with an air-conditioner blocking the only window in the room. Sheila and Dick know that, so why did they bother to send a postcard?

Why does anybody bother to send a postcard?

Here's one from Belle and Ollie. Judging from the picture, they are renting the Rocky Mountains for the summer. It's really cool there. Have to wear sweaters every night. They bet I'm really suffering in fetid, steamy New York.

That's Belle and Ollie for you. They only bet on sure things. They know for an absolute fact that I'm really suffering in fetid, steamy New York. But do they care? Really care?

If you really care about somebody who is suffering, you don't send him a gloating postcard. You send him a letter to cheer him up. With people who send postcards, having a wonderful time isn't enough; they have to remind you that you are not having a wonderful time.

Here's a postcard from Sam, who goes around on yachts. Every summer he manages to ingratiate himself into becoming the yachting guest of somebody who has beaten the income tax. This summer he is guesting on the bracing water off Maine.

Sam warned me that he would send a postcard. "I'll send you a card," he said.

"I don't want a card," I said. "I want your tax-chiseler friend to send me an envelope stuffed with enough cash to get me to Athens. I want to see the moon over the Acropolis."

Sam sent the card anyhow. After four weeks on yachtboard, he hasn't been mugged once, he says. "Hah hah."

Anyone who didn't know Sam well might think his "Hah hah" was a subtle way of expressing satisfaction at the thought of his friends back in New York being mugged twice a night. This is not the case. Sam is just one of those people who develop writer's block when they see all that blank space to be filled on the back of postcards. So he writes "Hah hah" a lot to get his money's worth out of the stamp.

I once had a postcard from Sam in Jamaica. It was February. He was yachtguesting around the Caribbean and paused at Jamaica to read the papers reporting a blizzard in New York.

His card said, "Don't get sunburned," followed by fourteen "Hah hah's."

It's strange about postcards: People only feel the urge to send them from elegant surroundings. Take Sheila, for instance, who is in Athens seeing what I should have seen; to wit, the moon over the Acropolis. Sheila goes down to Trenton three or four times a year, but she never sends a postcard from Trenton.

The moon shines on the Amtrak station at Trenton just as it shines on the Acropolis, but I have yet to receive a card from Sheila announcing that she has seen the moon over the Trenton Amtrak station.

Another curiosity is that nobody ever sends a postcard to let you know when the vacation is a disaster. Two years ago Belle hauled Ollie out to India to see the moon over the Taj Mahal. Belle's aim was to lay the groundwork for a postcard from Agra stating that the moon over the Taj Mahal was fantastic and I should have seen it.

She failed to reckon with Ollie's terror of snakes. On arrival in Agra, their car was approached by a roving snake showman wearing some twenty feet of python around his waist and thrusting the other eight feet proudly in front of him.

The man's only purpose was to cadge a rupee or two from Ollie by letting him admire and stroke the snake, but as he approached the car, obviously intending to thrust six feet of serpent through the open window for Ollie's admiration, Ollie screamed, "For God's sake, close the window!"

The snake man, thinking Belle and Ollie were being coy and wanted to be coaxed out of the sealed machine, spent what seemed to Ollie like years thrusting his pet against the glass and grinning proudly at its muscularity. Since the temperature that night was 120 degrees in the moonlight, Ollie and Sheila finally had to be removed by stretcher bearers. On leaving the hospital Ollie insisted on flying at once to Ireland, where, he had heard, Saint Patrick had rid the landscape of reptiles.

Did Ollie or Belle send a card from Agra saying that they were having a miserable time and telling me I was lucky to be in fetid, steamy New York? "Hah hah," as Sam would write. The only card I had from them came from Ireland. They had seen the mist over Galway Bay. It was fantastic. I should have seen it.

Boneless Sunday

More tales for bright kids only:

As long as Old Mother Hubbard kept a bone-filled cupboard for her poor dog the two lived so happily that the dog often said, "Surely we are living happily ever after, just as fairytale characters do, and our lives must therefore be a fairy tale."

"Don't deceive yourself," Old Mother Hubbard said. "Life is earnest, life is real." The dog, who had never known anything but good times with plenty of bones, sneered when she talked in this vein, for he was confident that the bones would go on forever.

One day, the King announced that there was a great bone crisis. "The bones are running out," he said. To conserve bones, he created boneless Sunday and doubled bone prices for the other six days of the week. "Always remember," the King said, "that life is earnest, life is real."

"Nuts to the King," said the dog. "The crisis is just a conspiracy by the bone cartel to gouge the bonesumer."

One Saturday, while trying to cut into a long line of waiting bone buyers, Old Mother Hubbard was shot by an angry man who had been waiting two hours to buy a half pound of chicken-wing bones. "Life is earnest, life is real," he told her after pulling the trigger.

The last bone shops had closed for the weekend when the old lady was released from the hospital. At home a bill collector awaited her. "All your bills have been doubled due to the bone crisis," he explained, cleaning out her purse, $10 hidden under the mattress and some Indian-head pennies stashed in the sugar bowl, while showing her a legal document which stated, "Life is earnest, life is real."

Sunday night, Old Mother Hubbard went to the cupboard to get her poor dog a bone, but when she got there the cupboard was bare, and so the poor dog left home to go to Acapulco with a Texas bone millionaire who loved the idea of having a dog who could say, "Nuts to the King."

"You're leaving me all alone, shot, destitute and boneless," cried the old woman.

"Life is earnest, life is real," replied the dog, more to amuse his new master than to justify himself to Mother Hubbard.

Moral: If you want to be one of the people-eating people you must always describe life as a dog-eat-dog proposition.

When the King was told birds had been baked into the pie just set before him, he was alarmed. "The cook must be losing his mind," he said. "Only a very sick man would try to make a pie out of something as stringy, tasteless and lice-infested as a blackbird."

Then the pie was opened, and the birds began to sing. The King was revolted. "Ugh!" he whispered to the Queen. "Pastry that chirps." "Shut up and eat a slice," said the Queen, "or you'll hurt the cook's feelings." So the King did. Two nights later, on his way home from the palace at the dark of the moon, the cook was attacked by two armored figures and his body thrown into a ravine.

Moral: If you must engage in gourmet cooking, don't try out brand-new recipes on people who can have bodies dumped in ravines.

At the top of a steep hill they had climbed to fetch a pail of water, Jack and Jill began quarreling about who would carry it down. Angered at Jack's insistence that she, being "just a woman," must let Jack carry the pail, Jill called him "a male chauvinist pig" and gave him such a push that he fell down and broke his crown.

The hospital was unable to repair Jack's crown correctly, and he was permanently incapacitated. He retained lawyers to sue Jill, who had taken over Jack's old job as a hogshead roller and had done it so well that she was rolling hogsheads twice as fast as Jack had ever done.

A jury ruled that she would have to pay Jack most of her salary for the rest of her life and she died in early middle age of wondering where the next dollar was going to come from to pay the gas bill. The King sent a wire at her death but, having misunderstood his press secretary, he referred to her as "a great hedgehog rider."

Moral: The fruit of victory in the good struggle is usually coronary thrombosis.

While eating curds and whey on a tuffet, Little Miss Muffet was so startled to see a spider amble along and sit down beside her that her first impulse was to run. Instead, she inspected the spider closely and saw that it was actually a new eavesdropping device designed to look like an ambulatory spider.

Placing her mouth close against the electronic spider, she shouted in her loudest voice, "Nuts to the King!" Both the King's eardrums were broken and, so, while he was in the gorse hunting wild boar next day, he did not hear the warning screams of his court, and succumbed to a charging boar.

Moral: Security will yet be the death of us all, especially Kings.

Bearing a Burden

Some people in Tennessee want Goldilocks out of the classroom. They say she undermines standards of Christian morality.

Hers is the story of a young girl entering a strange house while the tenants, who happen to be bears, are out for a stroll. She takes advantage of their absence to test their furniture for comfort and eat some of their porridge.

Inexplicably fatigued by these small exertions, she falls asleep in one of their beds where she is found snoozing when the bears return. Goldilocks jumps up and runs away.

This limp anticlimax ends the story. The Tennesseans object that since Goldilocks isn't punished for invading private property, children may conclude that poking around in other people's houses is morally O.K.

In the library I find another version which ends with Goldilocks being scolded by her mother and instructed that it's wrong to enter other people's houses uninvited.

I suspect this is of recent vintage, concocted to satisfy the modern demand for textbooks with milksop morality. Whether it might satisfy the objections of Tennessee Christians to Goldilocks I don't know, but it certainly doesn't satisfy mine.

Before plunging into the sticky issue of morality, let's look at the artistic problems in Goldilocks. These are considerable.

Are we really to believe, as the author obviously wants us to, that Goldilocks left home not knowing there was a house in the vicinity occupied by bears? Nonsense. When bears move into a neighborhood, everybody for miles around knows it.

Goldilocks has surely heard groans of despair from the grown-ups. If she was too innocent to know about bears, her playmates would have been happy to tell her. Can we doubt that a rogue like Tom the piper's son, capable of stealing a pig, would hesitate to poison a little girl's ears with nasty talk about how bears ruin a neighborhood?

And these are not ordinary bears lumbering off to fish with their paws or steal the bees' honey, are they? These are porridge-eating bears. These are bears that have chairs and beds custom built so each bear can enjoy perfect chair and bed fit.

In short, these are bears that bear watching.

The author's story ignores their extraordinary behavior. He wants us all, Christian and infidel alike, to believe Goldilocks entered that house utterly ignorant of a situation so amazing that everyone else in the country could talk of nothing else.

Consider those bears. Porridge eaters. Custom-built furniture. Ostensibly a family composed of father, mother and child bear. But are they?

In a neighborhood like Goldilocks's, where people don't normally see bears that eat porridge and buy custom-built furniture, it would be easy for three very cunning, very tough male bears to fool everybody. Suppose one bear wore father clothes, another went around in drag and the runt bear wore short pants with a slingshot sticking out of the hip pocket.

But, you ask, why would three cunning, tough male bears want to do something that weird?

That, I submit, is the same question that was asked by a mysterious man for whom Goldilocks was secretly working inside that ursine household. I do not know who her mysterious boss was. Suppose, however, that it was G. Gordon Liddy.

Liddy doubtless feared the security of the free world was endangered by whatever those housekeeping bears were up to. He needed somebody to get in there while the bears were out and have a look-see.

Liddy didn't dare. Though a brave man, he knew that if caught, he might be sealed in a diplomatic pouch and shipped to Bearland where, imprisoned in deepest Sibearia, he would be powerless to foil whatever the plot might be.

Who was the one person sure not to arouse the bears' suspicions if caught poking through their house? A sweet, innocent, golden-haired tyke. Of course Liddy didn't dare tell her his suspicions. He didn't know her well enough. She might be a weakling who broke down under torture. But there was no need to tell her. It was enough to say, "Honey, did you know the three bears all take a long walk just before breakfast every day and leave the house wide open?"

Adding, "While you're in there, keep an eye peeled for anything funny."

Oh yes, there's an exciting story here, but it is buried by the author's clumsiness. Goldilocks's sudden slumber obviously resulted from a sleeping potion the bears put in the porridge. Her escape, possible only because the bears couldn't believe such a lovable little dear capable of working for Liddy, creates a happy ending, not an immoral lesson on invading privacy and getting away with it.

Morality demands that Goldilocks escape, uneaten by the bears and unscolded by her mother. However unwittingly, she has risked her life in the struggle against hanky-panky. Possibly even bear-panky. And they call that immoral! Shame!

Little Red Riding Hood Revisited

In an effort to make the classics accessible to contemporary readers, I am translating them into the modern American language. Here is the translation of "Little Red Riding Hood":

Once upon a point in time, a small person named Little Red Riding Hood initiated plans for the preparation, delivery and transportation of foodstuffs to her grandmother, a senior citizen residing at a place of residence in a forest of indeterminate dimension.

In the process of implementing this program, her incursion into the forest was in midtransportation process when it attained interface with an alleged perpetrator. This individual, a wolf, made inquiry as to the whereabouts of Little Red Riding Hood's goal as well as inferring that he was desirous of ascertaining the contents of Little Red Riding Hood's foodstuffs basket, and all that.

"It would be inappropriate to lie to me," the wolf said, displaying his huge jaw capability. Sensing that he was a mass of repressed hostility intertwined with acute alienation, she indicated.

"I see you indicating," the wolf said, "but what I don't see is whatever it is you're indicating at, you dig?"

Little Red Riding Hood indicated more fully, making one thing perfectly clear—to wit, that it was to her grandmother's residence and with a consignment of foodstuffs that her mission consisted of taking her to and with.

At this point in time the wolf moderated his rhetoric and proceeded to Grandmother's residence. The elderly person was then subjected to the disadvantages of total consumption and transferred to residence in the perpetrator's stomach.

"That will raise the old woman's consciousness," the wolf said to himself. He was not a bad wolf, but only a victim of an oppressive society, a society that not only denied wolves' rights, but actually boasted of its capacity for keeping the wolf from the door. An interior malaise made itself manifest inside the wolf.

"Is that the national malaise I sense within my digestive tract?" wondered the wolf. "Or is it the old person seeking to retaliate for her consumption by telling wolf jokes to my duodenum?" It was time to make a judgment. The time was now, the hour had struck, the body lupine cried out for decision. The wolf was up to the challenge. He took two stomach powders right away and got into bed.

The wolf had adopted the abdominal-distress recovery posture when Little Red Riding Hood achieved his presence.

"Grandmother," she said, "your ocular implements are of an extraordinary order of magnitude."

"The purpose of this enlarged viewing capability," said the wolf, "is to enable your image to register a more precise impression upon my sight systems."

"In reference to your ears," said Little Red Riding Hood, "it is noted with the deepest respect that far from being underprivileged, their elongation and enlargement appear to qualify you for unparalleled distinction."

"I hear you loud and clear, kid," said the wolf, "but what about these new choppers?"

"If it is not inappropriate," said Little Red Riding Hood, "it might be observed that with your new miracle masticating products you may even be able to chew taffy again."

This observation was followed by the adoption of an aggressive posture on the part of the wolf and the assertion that it was also possible for him, due to the high efficiency ratio of his jaw, to consume little persons, plus, as he stated, his firm determination to do so at once without delay and with all due process and propriety, notwithstanding the fact that the ingestion of one entire grandmother had already provided twice his daily recommended cholesterol intake.

There ensued flight by Little Red Riding Hood accompanied by pursuit in respect to the wolf and a subsequent intervention on the part of a third party, heretofore unnoted in the record.

Due to the firmness of the intervention, the wolf's stomach underwent ax-assisted aperture with the result that Red Riding Hood's grandmother was enabled to be removed with only minor discomfort.

The wolf's indigestion was immediately alleviated with such effectiveness that he signed a contract with the intervening third party to perform with Grandmother in a television commercial demonstrating the swiftness of this dramatic relief for stomach discontent.

"I'm going to be on television," cried Grandmother.

And they all joined her happily in crying, "What a phenomena!"

Lawn Treason

In this radio commercial being used in the termite belt two termites are overheard discussing the dumbness of the man whose floor they are eating. While they gorge on white pine boards and oriental rug, they speculate whether it will ever occur to the poor boob to call the exterminator for whom they are shilling, and to make it harder for him they eat his telephone directory.

There is something disturbing in the idea of these freeloaders abusing their host in earshot of a wide radio audience. Once a man's termites begin holding him up to public ridicule, there is no telling where this sort of thing may end.

First thing you know the houseflies will be telling everybody on the East Coast you don't have enough sense to buy flypaper and the cockroaches will be making a fortune broadcasting your ignorance of roach poisons.

There's a Country in My Cellar

When a man's dependents start behaving like this, harsh repression is called for. Some years ago a Washington man, whom we will call Jones, had a lawn that began sneering at him when his back was turned, and his response, once he discovered what was up, had a wholesome effect on all the lawns in his neighborhood.

Jones's lawn had always been an ugly customer, being composed largely of dandelions, goose grass, chickweed and brown spot. Whenever any grass threatened to root, the lawn would get in touch with some moles it knew and have them eat all the roots and leave big tunnels in the ground.

One day after Jones had crossed over this eyesore after a hard day at the office and entered his house, one of the dandelions said to the goose grass, "Look at old Moose Jaw walk right over us without looking. Do you think the poor half-wit even knows we're out here making a mess of his lawn?"

"That numskull?" the goose grass asked. "By the time it dawns on him that there's such a thing as Madame Orloff's three-application weed killer, we'll have this lawn looking so hideous that Jones's name will be mud in this neighborhood."

Now, passing Jones's lawn at this very moment there chanced to be an advertising man. Let us call him Whipple. "Say," Whipple said, addressing the lawn, "did somebody in that eyesore say something?"

"We were just having one of our periodic chats about the poor sap who takes care of us," said the brown spot.

"Yeah," said the chickweed, "while he's toiling all day in a hot office, we lie here living off the fat of the land because he's so dumb he doesn't even know enough to zap us with weed killer."

Whipple asked the lawn if it would be willing to talk this way in a series of radio commercials for Madame Orloff's three-application weed killer.

"What's in it for us?" asked the goose grass. Whipple explained about residuals and public recognition. The lawn, which had visions of making enough money to move to a climate where it could look hideous all year round, signed a contract to do six one-minute commercials.

Jones, who automatically shut his mind off whenever commercials interrupted his radio listening, did not hear his lawn abusing him up to thirty-five times a day on most of the local stations, but his neighbors did. And so did his neighbors' lawns.

At first all the neighbors laughed to hear Jones's goose grass and chickweed and brown spot calling him "a chump" and "a dumbbell" on the radio. Soon, however, the neighbors' lawns began to envy Jones's lawn its fame and reputation for wit. The azaleas on the lawn next-door to Jones signed a contract to slander their owner, Ed O'Toole, because of his ignorance of azalea foods.

Several other lawns got in touch with Whipple about the possibility of ridiculing their providers. The upshot was a meeting of the neighbors with Jones, a meeting at which they invited him to listen to his lawn on the radio.

That very evening Jones had his lawn plowed by a team of horses and punched Whipple's nose. The following week, he had the lawn covered with cement. It has been mighty quiet ever since. So have the other lawns in the neighborhood.

Crashing into Crosswordland

One recent Sunday, wearied by my efforts to determine whether Dr. Dolittle's duck was named Dabbab, Dabnab or Dabrab, I fell into a doze and crashed through the paper into Crosswordland.

I recognized it immediately, for admis were grazing under a dhava and an ai hung from a tondo in one of the salas. I was delighted, for I had never believed in the existence of the admi, the dhava or the ai, and had never expected to see a tondo or a sala.

I had always assumed that these were simply words created

by tormented puzzle makers to help them escape their hopeless traps, but there was no mistaking them. The admis were definitely admis (African gazelles). The dhava was unmistakably an East Indian gum tree, and I could tell from the way the ai hung from the tondo (circular painting) that he was indeed a sloth.

The salas (reception rooms) in which I found myself (ego) contained three other persons. They were Ava (Miss Gardner), Evita (——— Perón), and Monk (Jazzman Thelonious). They were ired (angry) about being trite (overworked). Ava averred (stated) that she had to appear in every puzzle ever created. Evita and Monk expounded (delineated) in like (similar) vein (circulatory aid).

"Estop (stop) delineating in similar circulatory aid," I told them (No. I stated others), "and show me this strange place." "Eerie locus," Ava corrected. "Or more properly, since this is many places, eerie loci."

"Egad," said Monk. "Bah," said Evita. "Hah," said Ava. (Exclamations.) They would not abet (help), but fortunately Etta (Miss Kett) entered just then with Como (Perry or Lake) and took me to see the ort and ana.

The ort (scrap) was in an ugly mood and kept trying to pick a clash (fight) with the ana (miscellany). They made such a clang (loud noise) that both Arcas (Zeus's son) and Irus ("Odyssey" beggar) admitted (entered) to perceive (see) what was errant (wrong).

Arcas warned (threatened) to break the ort's ulna (arm bone) and Irus told the ana he would take him on a Hadj (trek to Mecca) and leave him with an emeer (Sheik of Araby) or emir (Sheik of Araby: var.), or possibly an amah (Eastern nurse) nisi (Caesar's "unless") he kept quiet.

"There must be an inexhaustible supply of emeers, emirs and amahs in Crosswordland," I observed to Etta.

"Aye," she said. (Affirmative.) "We have a rare (unusual) population mass (density). There are almost as many emeers and emirs as Utes and Otoes. Onondagas, Portuguese, Ukrainians and Ghanaians are unknown here, but we have more Celts than Eire (Ireland)."

The zoology of Crosswordland is equally bizarre. The woods are filled with beasts such as the admi, the ai, the zebu, the kudu and the ibex, although the elephant, the bullfrog, the tomcat, the cockroach and most other zoological forms common in the outer world are unknown.

Etta and I entered a new time span. "Here," she said, "is a genuine Apap (Egyptian month)." I did not like the Apap. It reminded me too painfully of the Sunday a puzzle had defeated me because I could not produce the word for "Of bronze: Latin" (aen) because the crossed word for "Egyptian month" was Apap instead of Epup, as any sensible person would naturally have expected Egyptians to name a month.

I told Etta I should prefer to see Meton (moon plain) if it was convenient.

To my delight, nothing was more facile (easier). In Crosswordland, Meton lies between Adano (bell town) and the vast vale (valley) of prefixes and suffixes. Thus was I able to glimpse it over ences (noun suffixes), dento (tooth: prefix), itol (chemical suffix), endo (within: prefix), exo (outer: prefix), ano (upward: prefix) and acu (prefix for puncture).

I felt emotionally anolifted by the spectacle, for there on Meton was my familiar old Otsu (Honshu town), and on the outskirts of Otsu an aani (dog-headed ape) stood under a nabo (P.I. shrub: var.) eating an awn (barley beard).

"If you're going to sleep," said my roommate, "let me have the puzzle. What's the name of Dolittle's duck?"

"I forgot to ask," I wept.

Fanchismo

Mike was a fan. He cared deeply about the hometown in any sport that happened to be played by a team in his hometown in any given year.

When the hometown team won, Mike's digestion improved

and he looked upon other people with fondness and good humor.

When the hometown team lost, Mike became depressed. His work suffered. He became surly toward his wife and kicked the cat.

It was no lark being a fan at that time because of the great mobility which had become characteristic of the sports industry. Players were bought and sold or traded like horses, sometimes singly or in small lots, but increasingly in Mike's time, in large herds.

One day Mike was badly shaken when he went to the baseball park and found that the whole hometown team had just been sold to a shopping mall in Texas. It was almost, but not quite, the worst baseball team in America, and, therefore, in the world.

As a good fan, Mike did not mind that. Ever since the team had acquired Kip Bimbelhoff the year before, in a trade for a lawnmower and an eight-year-old mare, Mike felt that the team was "building."

He had had the same feeling about the team every year since 1937, the last year in which the hometown team had finished higher than fifteenth place. "If we can come up with three twenty-game winners, a first baseman who can hit .240, a good double-play combination around second base and a decent catcher to go with Kip Bimbelhoff," he told his wife, "we could be in contention next year."

Upon hearing that the whole team had been sold into Texas, Mike's fan mettle temporarily failed. "Baseball," he roared through tears of rage, "is a racket run by money-grubbing con men who exploit suckers like me!"

"And what's more," said another enraged fan, "Kip Bimbelhoff was just another bum who couldn't hit the curve ball."

This remark brought Mike back from the brink of sanity. "You can't say that about Kip Bimbelhoff," he objected. "Kip Bimbelhoff really loved this hometown."

With his fanhood intact, Mike turned to the hometown football team. It had won only two games since the Truman Administration. This dismal record was blamed on the terrible Herman Piano, coach of the relentlessly victorious Medicine Hat Backbreakers.

Whenever Mike's hometown football team approached a level of competence that threatened to win it a victory, its schedule brought it into demoralizing conflict with the Piano-coached Backbreakers and it was crushed for the rest of the year in spirit and body.

Mike hated Herman Piano. He wrote letters to the authorities urging that Herman Piano be removed from football for foul character and bad sportsmanship.

Then, one year, Mike's hometown football team announced that it had hired coach Herman Piano from the Backbreakers. Mike was ecstatic. He wrote letters to the editor stating that Herman Piano was the greatest football coach since Bernie Bierman and the greatest spiritual force for manly goodness since the founding of the Y.M.C.A.

Under the shrewd Piano eye, Mike told his wife, the wonderful hometown team players he had cheered for so many years—Steve Sapparoonian, B. D. Higglesworthovich, Merton Mims and Bruno ("The Beast") Peruna—would become the terrors of the league.

Being a fan, of course, Mike did not wince when Herman Piano immediately traded Sapparoonian, Higglesworthovich and Mims to the Chicago police force and sold Bruno Peruna to a soap factory.

He even went to the game the next week and booed Sapparoonian when the Chicago Police played the hometown team. He called Higglesworthovich a "bum" and told everybody around him that the best thing that had ever happened to the hometown team was getting rid of Merton Mims. At half time he went to the washroom and washed his hands with a cake of Bruno Peruna.

The following week Herman Piano imported the eight players Mike had always hated most from the Medicine Hat Backbreakers. They were Marley, Cotts, Wye, Utz, Surd, Uncas, Goering and O'Tolstoy.

"With players like Marley, Cotts, Wye, Utz, Surd, Uncas, Goering and O'Tolstoy on your hometown team," Mike told his wife, "you feel terrific all over just knowing you come from this hometown."

The following week Herman Piano traded all of the remaining hometown team for a set of used goal posts and a hundred pounds of sideline paint, and brought in 32 players from 21 other cities, none of which was located closer than 800 miles to Mike's home town.

That week the hometown team won its first game since the Korean War. Mike kissed the cat and took his wife to dinner. "It's great to be part of a city that can produce a winner," he told his wife.

She started to say something sensible to Mike, but stifled the impulse in the nick of time. After all, he hadn't taken her out to dinner since the year the whole hometown hockey team was sold to Grand Rapids for a truckload of furniture and a beautiful money-saving tax loss.

Murder Most Foul

A strange story was buried in the "Whatever Happened To" column of last month's Executive's Digest. It concerned one Pringle Sideshaft who had been quietly let go by a large eastern corporation after shooting his desk. What made this remarkable was that Sideshaft just eighteen months earlier had led the list in Executive Digest's "Young Men to Watch" column, in which he was called "dynamic, hard-driving and a demon memo writer."

Why Sideshaft shot his desk and destroyed a promising career was not explained. My hunch, based on personal experience, is that he made the mistake of eating lunch at his desk instead of going to the company cafeteria. Young men on the way to the top often make this mistake. They believe that lunching at their desks will gain them promotion points with their bosses.

This is a dangerous notion, as Sideshaft's experience indicates. No corporation can afford to have an executive walking around shooting desks. At a certain stage in my life, however, I believed, as Sideshaft must have, that lunching at the desk was the way to get ahead, and made the mistake of doing so.

Trouble was not long developing. After three weeks or so of being lunched at, the desk began to act oddly. After shoving the dirty lunch dishes aside, I noticed that the desk was reluctant to be worked at. This puzzled me so deeply I could not concentrate on my job for trying to deduce what had got into the desk to make it behave so.

While pondering the mystery I would order in some coffee and pie to assist the thought process and very shortly the desk would perk up. It seemed to enjoy having coffee and pie eaten at it. This prompted me to test a theory, which I did by staying in the office through the dinner hour one evening and eating a full three-course dinner at the desk.

Need I labor the point? The desk had undergone a personality change. Those three weeks of being lunched at had given it a glimpse of a jollier life. Apparently, it was no happier about being a corporate tool than I was, but it had not realized that there was a more pleasant side to life until it began to serve as dining furniture.

In this role it was able to provide pleasure and satiety to the troubled spirit; it was no longer a brutal instrument over which that spirit was stretched as upon the rack. The desk wanted to be a dining table.

I imagine that Pringle Sideshaft's desk developed the same complication. If his experience was like mine, matters between him and his desk became increasingly tense. It is easy to guess at their deteriorating relationship, at Sideshaft's desperate efforts to work producing nothing from the desk but surlier and surlier behavior.

Sideshaft probably realized that his desk felt frustrated and unfulfilled. No dialogue occurred, of course; at least it did not, in my case. In my case there was only angry monologue uttered at the eloquent silence of this insolent, inanimate quadruped.

The desk's silences were more eloquent than my monologues. "I have the right to be a total piece of furniture," they said. "I have the right to hold more than these gritty little memos and this squalid out basket and this nagging telephone. I have the right to bear steak au poivre and hummingbirds' tongues in aspic, to know the sweet weight of pork chops, candied yams, Chincoteagues on the half shell and chocolate soufflés.''

You may imagine how difficult it was to get any memos written or enjoy a dynamic romp through the out basket while this infuriating desk filled my head with whinings about lemon meringue pies, baked Alaska, hothouse grapes, roast rack of delicately pink lamb set off with a rare Montrachet, and similar distracting comestibles.

In brief, I yielded to its importunings. Desks have rights, too, as I told the delivery boy when he would arrive bearing roast prime rib of beef, a succulent scallopine of veal or whole roast chickens slowly basted on an open spit. By leaving these great spreads on the desk where I could partake of them throughout the afternoon, I found I could not only satisfy the desk but also get off a few letters and take a phone call or two.

Very little fuss was made the day the company let me go. "You are infecting the morale of every desk throughout the company," said the manager, carving himself a slice of duck à l'orange and pocketing a chunk of Cheshire cheese. By that time, I didn't care, since I had decided to get off the executive ladder and take up journalism, hoping to work myself up to restaurant criticism.

I don't suppose it was my old desk that Pringle Sideshaft shot. If it was, I hope he ate some tender filet mignon with fried zucchini at its last meal. These were its favorites.

How Shall I Dear Thee?

A friend, as Lyndon Johnson used to say, is "somebody you can go to the well with." Not for an instant would I consider going to the well with Times Square. I certainly wouldn't invite Times

Square home to meet the folks. Truth is, whenever I see Times Square on the sidewalk I cross the street to avoid it.

Why then do I receive mail addressed to "Dear Friend of Times Square"? For the same reason I get mail addressed to "Dear Fellow Angler" and "Dear Decisionmaker." Because America is undergoing a salutation crisis, that's why.

The severity of this crisis is indicated by that "Dear Fellow Angler." I was flattered by this form of address at first, thinking it embraced me in the brotherhood of sharpsters who know how to work the angles. It has long been my hope to be greeted as "Dear Fellow Finagler," thus winning membership in that class for which the income tax laws are written. "Dear Fellow Angler" seemed like a step toward this goal.

Closer reading, however, showed I was being addressed by the Izaak Walton League, whose idea of a "dear fellow angler" is someone who hooks fish. As one who has not fished since the age of eight and plans never to fish again, I was puzzled.

Being addressed as "Dear Decisionmaker" was downright nerve-racking, since my paralysis at decision time is notorious on six continents. Could this letter be from some cruel master of sarcasm who knew I sat home biting my nails all weekend because I couldn't decide whether I preferred to see "Stir Crazy" or "The Devil and Max Devlin"?

No. It came from a complete stranger, in fact a large corporation ("our sales now exceed $500 million"), which wanted to sell me its payroll, accounting and financial expertise.

Each of these letters had three things in common. All were from complete strangers, all wanted me to pass some money their way and none of the letter writers knew my name. Examination of a two-week accumulation of money-seeking mail revealed a fourth characteristic. The people sending these pleas don't even know whether I am male or female.

"Dear Sir or Madam," several of them begin. One greets me as "Dear Sir or Madam of the Press." This is a plea for publicity for a new book. "Be a columnist and report facts!" it commands. The fact I want to report right now is that I am not a madam of the press.

While I'm at it, let me advise a certain charity that lusts after my bank account that I am not "Dear Friend of the Arts" either. Lord knows, I have tried to be a friend of art, but art has snubbed me for years as a common drudge who sold out to Grub Street. It's too late to extend the hand of friendship into my wallet now, arts. I know who my real friends are.

They do not include a certain large institution in Utah that hails me as "Dear Business Friend."

I never make business friends. Years ago Uncle Charlie advised me, "Never mix business and friendship, boy. That way you'll never have to cut a friend's heart out."

Uncle Charlie also warned me about becoming an investor. "If you become an investor," he said, "sooner or later you're going to be wiped out like all those buzzards in 1929, and while you're waiting to go broke you're going to have to put up with a lot of mail addressed to 'Dear Investor.'"

Now I get the mail even though I followed Uncle Charlie's advice. "Dear Investor," says a letter from Wall Street trying to lure me into the gold business. I am concerned about these ill-informed salutations. Naturally there is a letter that catches my eye.

"Dear Concerned American," it begins. But no, it is not about the salutation crisis. It comes from a complete stranger who wants me to buy his novel about the red menace. Apparently he cares not a whit about the salutation menace, though it infects the highest levels of Government.

For evidence, I submit Senator Moynihan's newsletter. It begins, "Dear Yorker." Does Moynihan believe he now represents York, Pa.? More likely, I think, he has an acute case of salutationitis, which produces severe inflammation of the prose style when the sufferer attempts to compose a mass mailing.

It is everywhere and spreading. An insurance company scribe writes, "Dear Policy Holder." Can anyone imagine a policy holder being dear to an insurance company in any but the crassest sense of the word? "Dear Collector," begins a vendor of small statuary to a man who has never collected anything in his life but matchbook covers.

A wordsmith for a magazine publisher begins with "Dear Civilized Friend" (my idea of civilization's finest achievement is the 1969 Buick Electra), and a letter from a public-television station starts out with "Dear Viewer." Why not "Dear Moneybags"? The gun-control lobby that addresses me as "Dear Potential Handgun Victim" at least knows that I am still alive, which is more than can be said for New York magazine wondering why a subscription hasn't been renewed.

Its author begins, "Dear Silent One." I have received two copies of this letter. They will be forwarded to my late grandfathers.

The Great Whale's Mistake

A mother whale and a father whale were swimming along the coast with their adolescent son whale when the mother sighted a school of people on the beach.

"Thar they boil," she sang out in her eerie whale voice.

"What's that?" asked the son whale, who had never seen a school of people before, or even a stray person.

"That's people, son," said the father whale. "You see them all up and down this coast at this time of year. They cover themselves with oil and lie up there on the sand and boil themselves until they sizzle."

"But they're such little things," said the son whale. "I'll bet I could swallow one whole and have him live in my stomach."

His mother said she would not want her stomach filled with anything that had been boiled in oil and had sand all over it. Moreover, she said, it would be very unhealthy because people were filled with smoke and hot dogs.

"What do people do?" asked the young whale.

"They sit on the beach and stare at the ocean," the father whale said. "And they eat hot dogs."

The mother whale said they also walked into the ocean now and then and flopped around in the water for brief periods and made such clumsy splashes that the fish had to get out of their way.

"They seem to be useless," said the son whale. "Why did the Great Whale make people anyhow?"

"Son," said the father whale, "no creature in the Great Whale's universe exists without a purpose. If the Great Whale made people it was for a good reason."

"Maybe people are the Great Whale's way of keeping down the hot-dog population," the young whale suggested.

"There are some things," said the mother whale, "that even whales can't understand. We must accept the world as it is and live in harmony with it."

The father whale called their attention to a small group of people who had detached themselves from the school and were getting into a metal box mounted on wheels. When they were all inside, the metal box moved along the beach throwing up a great cloud of sand and destroying vegetation and birds' nests.

"What are they doing now?" asked the son whale.

"Making garbage," said the father whale. "People make almost all the garbage in the world, and they use those little moving boxes to do the job."

He showed his son the dark gases which spewed out of the box and pointed out the efficiency with which the beach grasses and the birds' eggs were quickly converted into garbage.

"And inside the box," he said, "they are also preparing more garbage."

At that moment six beer cans came flying out of the box, followed by a bag containing a half-eaten hot dog, a mustard jar, some banana peels and an empty plastic body-oil container.

"Maybe that's the reason the Great Whale made people," said the young whale. "To make garbage."

"The world doesn't need garbage," growled the father whale.

"Now, now," said the mother whale, who was always uneasy in the presence of religious speculation, "we must accept the world as it is and learn to live in harmony with it."

"Sometimes," said the father whale, "I think the Great Whale doesn't know what he's doing."

"Your father has been very sensitive about garbage," the

mother whale explained, "ever since he dived into 800 tons of fresh sludge that had just been dumped off the New Jersey coast. He smelled like a sewer for weeks."

"Eight hundred tons of sludge!" cried the young whale. "Wow! That's what I call garbage production!"

The young whale was so excited that he spouted, and the people on shore saw it and cried, "Whales!" and somebody threw a beer bottle at them. The whales made for deep distant water and later that night as they drifted off the Gulf Stream admiring the stars a large ship passed by and spilled oil over them, but they remained in harmony with the world as it was, and afterward dreamed of the unfortunate people far behind them making garbage through the sweet summer night.

1968

Reader, if you love the smell of doomsday on a gray wind, return with me now to 1968, and we shall revisit those scenes of riot and murder that made 1968 the worst of times, and listen for echoes of the screaming and cursing that were the melody of 1968, and recall the fatigue and hatred that were the very soul of 1968.

What a monstrous year it was. People who romanticize the 1960's overlook 1968, and for good reason. It was surely the most unromantic year of the twentieth century. Nineteen sixty-eight was the end of the road for the romance of exuberant, sassy, rebellious young America. It was the end of the road, too, for the old political romancers whose roots went back to the New Deal. At times it seemed it might be the end of the road for the whole country.

At the heart of the catastrophe was Vietnam. Washington had casually double-crossed the Vietnamese twenty years earlier by letting France reclaim it after World War II and make it French colonial property once again. This betrayal had now come back to haunt a new American generation too ignorant of the past to understand why the Vietnamese should be angry with us, thus forcing us, good folk though we were, to kill so many of them for the good of all mankind, much as it pained us of course to do so.

Almost all of us were pained, but many were also outraged. There arose a fiercely bitter struggle across America between the pained and the outraged, and it culminated in riot, madness and murder, which is to say, 1968. Lyndon Johnson's Presidency was the first casualty. His insistent prosecution of the war so

197

swelled the ranks of the outraged that he chose to pass up his doubtful chances for a second term and put the Presidency up for grabs, as it were.

The impassioned power struggle that followed took part on a landscape where emotions bordered on the murderous. Disturbed people armed themselves and began stalking celebrated public men and headlines. Martin Luther King was shot to death that spring. Robert Kennedy was shot to death soon afterward.

Summer brought the party nominating conventions. Republicans held theirs in Miami Beach because, with a watery moat between them and the mainland, it seemed a relatively easy position to defend against assault.

Democrats, bold and, as it turned out, foolish, met in Chicago. Disaster ensued when Chicago's police, licensed by Mayor Daley to bust impudent skulls in defense of America, civilization and the Democratic party, ran amok. I survived Chicago unscathed, thanks to my old police-reporter skills at mollifying cops, but the Democratic party was mortally wounded.

The Republican Nixon won the Presidency that November, and Republicans have ruled almost constantly ever since. Thus ended the romance of the 1960's, very much as romance always ends, with staid gray heads turning youth from its folly and bringing the household back to its senses. Which in this case meant four more years of the Vietnam War and complete triumph for a gospel which preaches that there is nothing, absolutely nothing, more important than money.

The fragments of 1968 resurrected here are eyewitness reports from the field. I did a lot of reporting that year, but covered only one of the funerals. All the pieces I wrote about that one are included. Do not object, reader, that this is too much. We are talking about 1968. It was a time of coffins.

Let's Keep This Show off the Road

How tired they all seemed, the clutch of Senators and the Secretary of State there on the television set struggling hour after hour with the enigma of Vietnam.

A melodrama had been anticipated. The Senators had tried for a year to lure Secretary of State Rusk into public confrontation, and now that they had him pinned in the camera's eye, one expected climactic events. But there was only fatigue. It was a disappointment at first, and then, gradually, it became clear that N.B.C.'s cameras were showing us something far more interesting than any slanging match between Senators and bureaucrats could have been.

The tiredness of a whole Government—Congress and Executive, Democrat and Republican—was being anatomized on a twenty-one-inch tube. Once you understood what you were watching it became hypnotic—an entire Government, represented by some of its very best minds, was sleepwalking right in the living room.

The Foreign Relations Committee, with its large contingent of doves, had exhausted its ammunition months before Mr. Rusk took the witness chair. Its members hadn't a single question that he had not long ago answered again and again. For his part, Rusk hadn't a single answer that we all hadn't already learned by heart.

It was morbidly fascinating: all those splendid minds, utterly incapable in their fatigue of producing a single new thought, or new question, or new answer; with nothing really

199

worth saying to each other at so much expense; yet driven by
the same hope that animates an insomniac on a Benzadrine
jag—if you fight exhaustion long enough something is bound to
happen.

Before the show was two hours old Monday morning it was
obvious that there was nothing left to be said between the
Administration and its critics about Vietnam. Indeed, there
probably hadn't been anything left to be said for several months.
The only remaining possibility of excitement was for Mr. Rusk
and Senator Fulbright to start swinging at each other with the
chairs.

Mr. Rusk's performance has been well reviewed by the
political critics, but it is hard to see why. His patience has
grown under the batterings of years until it seems oriental but
his familiar lines are now delivered almost by rote. He can probably recite them in his sleep and, in fact, often seemed to be
doing so.

His eyes, which used to twinkle when he first became Secretary, now have a burned-out look, like a racer who has gone
twenty-four hours at Le Mans, like a prisoner who has been
beaten too many times with the knout. As a man he compels
sympathy, which may be why his performance was so favorably
reviewed, but as a symbol of the Government he is a study in
Vietnam fatigue.

The Senators are no less so. Most of them ignored the
country's entry into the war when the voter attitude was indifference. Now, with the voters aroused, they were trying to develop political attitudes toward the war that could be usefully
exploited in elections.

Faced with a situation for which there was no parallel in the
past, many fell back on the familiar old lines that had served
them for the past ten, twenty years.

The world's mightiest military, naval and air power had
been fought to a standstill in a country which, in a less humble
day, would have been dismissed as a banana republic. Surely
something new is going on, Mr. Mundt.

Yet there was Senator Karl Mundt, just as though it were
still 1951 and Stalin were still under the bed, expatiating on the
Communist "monolith." And there was Stuart Symington, the

voice of airpower, still urging the unleashing of the Air Force, as though it were still 1942. Some reminded us for the third and fourth year that enemy atrocities could not be ignored, and once more Wayne Morse reminded us that, as often happens, he was the only man who was right four years ago.

Frank Lausche took us all the way back to the Lyndon Johnson era of the Senate by urging something for everyone— an end of killing for the doves, an end of debate for the hawks, and a fresh vat of patriotism for all the other birds in the indeterminate middle.

They were all so tired that it made you yawn to watch them. Senators Mansfield and Fulbright, obviously hopeful that the President was awake, urged him to consult more with the Senate, and as the Tuesday session dragged to its end, a new truth gleamed on the screen. It isn't Communism anymore that is on the march against democracy, it's fatigue.

Nightmare out of the Attic

This morning it was waking up to another installment in the American nightmare. There it was again, out in the open, first on the radio and then, because we have already acquired the habit of sharing it communally through pictures, on television.

It is strange how quickly we have become familiar with the rituals that accompany its recurrence. The shocked expressions of the TV newsmen. The distraught faces of those who have touched it. The clergymen offering prayer. Utter strangers in faraway cities electronically transfixed near tears in the streets. Exhausted commentators struggling for explanations because there are none and yet there is time to be filled and it is their duty to fill it.

The President issues his statement. Congressmen expound.

Someone assesses the political significance. Legislation is proposed. Gradually, grouped together around the social center of the TV screen with its humdrum evocation of the shared boredom of idle evenings and endless Sunday afternoons, we struggle to suppress the horror.

National explanation is the best defense, of course. Push back the dark with light and terror hasn't a chance. And so we listen, eager to believe, to the explanations. Someone suggests it is merely an isolated case of madness, but that is small comfort. A Congressman insists that a crime bill with teeth in it will put things right quickly enough. It would be comforting to believe that, but instinct argues that the case is not quite so simple.

These incidents of public violence, says a sociologically minded commentator, are, after all, only to be expected in periods when public policy and opposition to it both place unusual reliance on violence as a political instrument. Throughout history it can be well documented that . . .

Well, perhaps.

Still, one has the uneasy suspicion that there is some new quality in American life which is not explained by any of the assurances oozing from the box. The fact is that the nightmare has acquired a permanence in this decade, and we manage to live with it by keeping it suppressed, like the mad brother of Gothic novels who is kept sealed in the attic.

For us the attic has become the deep interior of the newspapers. When the nightmare escapes and someone like President Kennedy or his brother or Martin Luther King is touched by it, it must temporarily be faced on page one, but the fact is that even after it is rationalized back into the attic it remains a constant presence in American life.

Here in Washington, for example, Tommy Williams was buried today. He was eighteen and would have been graduated next week from high school. Saturday night he had gone to Georgetown with some friends. One of his friends seems to have started a quarrel with another group. A casual passerby, a stranger to both groups, decided to restore order. He produced a pistol and shot Tommy four times.

For Tommy Williams's classmates the nightmare was in the open again, but for most of Washington the event was a short item to be mused over in the evening paper while waiting for the baseball game to begin, and the nightmare was kept securely in the attic. Such incidents are buried daily in every large newspaper in the country. What has happened is that murder has become the substitute of the 1960's for the old-fashioned punch in the nose. And, even more alarming, it may be becoming a form of self-expression.

It does not really help understanding to say that we are seeing a modern evolution of the frontier tradition of gun law. The old gunmen wore their pistols in plain view on their hips or cradled their rifles out where everybody could see them. Today's gunmen are men who shoot their victims in the back, and their victims are usually the unarmed and the unwary.

And knowing this, all of us who are unarmed and unwary live with the condition as best we can by keeping the nightmare locked in the attic until it strikes someone of such eminence that we are forced to admit aloud that we have reached a pass where the bullet is now widely regarded as an instrument of political discourse, the perfect squelch in the petty quarrel, a device for gratifying the ego or a substitute for movies on Saturday night.

Some disarmament would help, of course, but the National Rifle Association blocks that in Congress. Guns do not kill people, they say; people do. Marshall McLuhan has the answer to this. Human behavior, he says, is altered by the technological innovations that extend man's power. In a gun technology, the opportunity and the power to kill are extended to everyone with the ambition to send an order blank to a mail-order house.

Mourners

People had always needed to touch him—it was part of what the commentators liked to call "the Kennedy magic"—and yesterday they came for the last time with hands outstretched and reaching.

Now, however, the touch was timidly, tenderly proffered, with fingers resting just barely a moment on the foot of the closed coffin in a gesture of gentle farewell. All day long they filed past the bier, lifting their hands, letting the fingers flicker momentarily on the dark mahogany, and then passed from the cathedral into the heat of East Fiftieth Street.

The funeral today will be the occasion for the austere, the official and the eminent, but yesterday was the people's day, and for all its solemnity there was much of the mass excitement about it that his political campaigns had engendered.

It was in pointed contrast to the bleak November Sunday in 1963 when his brother's body had lain in state in the rotunda of the Capitol. There, too, the crowds queued for a mile and more to pass the coffin, but they were gray crowds bundled against the cold in a city as silent as a mausoleum. Also, in the Capitol rotunda they were able to look but not approach near enough to reach out. Very few probably would have wished to, for that was a high occasion of state in which grief was suffused with awe.

Yesterday, the coffin rested on a low bier with the top only waist high for the throngs, making it possible for them to brush it with a hand in passing. Once, an elderly woman in deep mourning began quivering with sobs as she passed and had to be saved by a policeman from collapsing over the coffin.

The ubiquitous television lights, which turn even the most solemn moments into theater, beat down ceaselessly from the steps approaching the altar, illuminating for the home viewer the faces of the famous who stood vigil beside the coffin.

Andy Williams, the popular singer, took his turn there, and so, briefly, did Leonard Bernstein in white suit and white shoes. Robert S. McNamara, the former Secretary of Defense, and Douglas Dillon, the former Secretary of the Treasury, served their vigils together in somber gray, and Sugar Ray Robinson, the boxer, came in green slacks and a white sport shirt open at the collar.

Just beyond the glare of the floodlights newsmen clustered to exchange notes, broadcast technicians worked on their equipment; workmen toiled to prepare the cathedral for the funeral ceremony; walkie-talkie radios squawked, and a priest celebrated mass at a small altar just off the north transept.

Outside, Fifty-first Street was choked with the huge mobile television vans used for remote color pickups. The west side of Fifth Avenue, abutting Rockefeller Center, was packed all day with the curious who, all over the world, are capable of standing for hours for no reward more substantial than the chance to catch a glimpse of a celebrity.

The people who waited in a line twenty-five blocks long, eight abreast at many points, were neither shattered nor awed for the most part. They were a cross-section of everybody, including the shouters and jumpers and touchers who had been attracted by every campaign of all three Kennedys. A few wore mourning. Some had obviously put on their Sunday best. But most were dressed "sensibly" for hot weather, as a crowd might dress for an outdoor political rally in midsummer.

It was steam heat, mixed with choking exhaust fumes, in which the people waited for periods up to five hours. Many of them fainted.

"They're turning it into a festival," a policeman complained at Park Avenue and Forty-seventh Street. "They're bringing babies and children, and they're dropping over like flies."

Five blocks from the cathedral the line moved with agonizing slowness. At times it took an hour to move a single block. The reason may have had something to do with the business of cutting into the line that was going on up near the cathedral.

One woman from the Bronx, who seemed to reflect the general absence of awe for the occasion, boasted, "I just snuck across the street and cut the line. I've got guts like he had."

The policeman who called it a "festival" probably overstated the case. The crowds were good-humored, even about the line cutters, but not by any means gay. They waited with patience, fainted and returned to the line, took what sustenance the soft-drink vendors could manage to offer against the opposition of the police lines, and littered Park Avenue with soft-drink tins and food wrappers.

Theirs was the mood of the people whom Robert Kennedy had often kept waiting because of falling far behind schedule in his campaigns for the Senate and White House. In death, as in life, Bobby Kennedy was an event, and some quality about him made people want to be there.

They Line the Tracks to Say Good-by

Robert F. Kennedy's family brought him back to Washington for the last time today by train, and megalopolitan America lined the rails to say good-by.

The journey, slowed by accidents along the way and great crowds that often forced the train to slow almost to a stop, lasted from 1:02 P.M. to 9:08 P.M.—more than twice as long as had been expected.

Drawn by two black electric locomotives of the Penn Central Railroad, the funeral train traveled the 226 miles from New York through an almost unbroken succession of station throngs, urban street crowds and clusters of small-town mourners.

In the rural stretches separating the great eastern cities, girls came to the railroad on horseback. Boys sat in the trees. In a desolate swampy section of New Jersey, a lone man knelt in prayer by the trackside. In the loneliest sections, family groups clustered around cars parked in the woods to hold up flags, to wave, or to salute.

It would be idle to guess at how many saw the train bearing the Senator's body. The train's route took it through the greatest concentrations of population on the continent, and in many places it seemed as if whole towns had turned out.

In many places the crowds ignored undermanned police lines, and swarmed dangerously onto adjacent tracks to be closer to the train.

The train cortege has been part of the American legend since

Walt Whitman immortalized Abraham Lincoln's funeral train back to Illinois in "When Lilacs Last in the Dooryard Bloomed."

There has probably been nothing quite like today's, however, since President Warren G. Harding was buried about forty-five years ago.

Senator Kennedy's coffin rested on chairs at window level in the last of twenty-two cars. It was a private car with an old-fashioned observation platform on the rear end, and in the old tradition, was draped with black bunting.

From time to time as the train passed through large clusters of people, Mr. Kennedy's widow, Ethel, and his brother, Senator Edward M. Kennedy, appeared on the platform to acknowledge the salute of the crowds.

What they saw as they looked out was a picture of America pausing in its Saturday-afternoon pastimes and wearing the casual dress that America wears on its day off. The majority of the women seemed to be in shorts or slacks. Thousands had their hair up in curlers, obviously preparing to look beautiful after sundown.

The men wore T-shirts or Bermudas, as if interrupted at their lawn work or the shopping. Because it was hot, many of the men stood bare-chested, though without neglecting to place hand over heart as the train glided by.

In many places Little League teams stood beside the tracks, sometimes saluting, other times with baseball caps held solemnly over their chests.

At New Brunswick, N.J., a long bugler on the station platform sounded taps at the passing train. Farther down, in a Philadelphia suburb, a brass marching band played an air that was impossible to identify from the rapidly moving train.

There were a few homemade signs. At Newark, four women on the platform wore cardboard placards around their necks. Each said "Farewell Robert."

At Linden, N.J., two tots, a boy and a girl in sunsuits, held a piece of hand-painted cardboard that said "Good-by Bobby."

"Good-by Bobby" seemed to be the favorite. It appeared perhaps two dozen times between Newark and Washington. Despite the Saturday-afternoon informality of the crowds there was no lack of emotion.

In the big cities—Newark, Trenton, Philadelphia, Wilmington and Baltimore—the train slowed to a funereal ten miles an hour. Leaning out the doors, its passengers could hear women sobbing on the platforms and see girls struggling to hold back the tears.

At the North Philadelphia station, a woman cried over and over again, "Poor Bobby! Poor Bobby! Poor Bobby!"

"We love you, Bobby," said a piece of crudely hand-lettered canvas held by a man and a woman at Middle River, Md. The casual informality of the multitudes, the picture of America interrupted in the middle of its easygoing summer Saturday pastimes, seemed appropriate homage to a man who had never stood on form, but the odd thing was that so few brought flowers.

Here and there a girl held up a rose or a small bouquet of wildflowers to throw as the last car passed. But these were rare. Many brought flags and many, many more brought cameras. But virtually no one brought flowers.

"Americans have gotten too sophisticated for that," one member of the train party suggested. "We have come a long way from Lincoln."

In Maryland, of course, there were nature's offerings, wild roses pink along the tracks, and honeysuckle, but for the people it was not a day for flowers.

On the Southbound Train

All stories purporting to reveal the "mood" aboard the Kennedy funeral train during that remarkable eight-hour journey from New York Saturday are to be read with skepticism.

The funeral party—some 1,100 persons scattered through twenty-two passenger cars—was too big and too fragmented to be susceptible to a single "mood." Moreover, the extraordinary duration of the journey, the heat that increased as the air-conditioning buckled under the demand of too many over-crowded coaches, and the difficulty of obtaining food in densely packed diners—all tended to wilt emotion down to mere fatigue long before the train arrived at Union Station.

In consequence, no sustained unity of emotion was possible. Those who saw the accident at Elizabeth, and they were many, experienced a special horror; one woman was still white and speechless four hours after the event. As word of the accident passed through the train, however, the first cries of horror ("Oh, my God, no!") gave way to the normal human urge for information. ("Did you see it?" "How many were killed?" "Do you know if Ethel knows about it?")

At Baltimore in the dusk the day's most solemn crowd massed on the station platform singing "The Battle Hymn of the Republic" as the train glided past, going so terribly slow. And as that noble old hymn floated across the tracks, for the first time all day not a single face in the crowd smiled, not a single child waved in gaiety, and the awful dignity of all those grave faces on the edge of night seemed to embrace the entire train with awe and pity.

Such moments were the exception. For most of the journey the crowds outside, pressing dangerously close to the track, transmitted not so much a sense of mourning as a sense of excitement at being part of an American event. Many persons wept, of course; some prayed, and a few, very few, held flowers.

Still, the obvious shows of grief were relatively few among these Americans in their Saturday-afternoon summer play clothes—jeans, T-shirts, gaily colored blouses, hair curlers, Bermudas, baseball caps. From inside the train they looked much more like crowds turned out to hear a candidate make his pitch than like crowds come to stand in the presence of death.

Life inside the train, sealed off for hours from the outside, began to flow in many paths. A young woman in mourning dress and veil warmly kissed a young man on a coach platform. The bars in the diners became jammed with long, sweating lines of the thirsty. Walter Reuther and Sam Huff, in shirtsleeves against the heat, chatted idly with old friends.

For a while there was a passable effort to turn the journey into an Irish wake. Old friends who had not seen each other in months embraced and exchanged notes on what they had been doing lately. It was a time of reminiscence and quiet jokes, and because most of these people had for years lived lives entwined with politics there were the postmortem analyses of how events might have turned had Bob done this or that instead of that and this.

They were also, nearly all, people who had loved him with that singular loyalty the best politicians inspire.

Riding aboard this train, with its distillate of everyone and everything associated with the Kennedys over the years, one often had an eerie sense of being merely on another leg of an endless campaign. From time to time through the day, the Kennedys—Ethel, Teddy, Bobby's oldest son, Joe—would appear in the most remote coach to shake hands with every soul in the car. At other times they went to the rear observation platform to return the salutes of the station throngs.

Frank Mankiewicz, the Senator's press secretary, seemed to be living still in the campaign world when, groggy with fatigue, he inadvertently referred to "our advance man" for the trip, using the campaign term for the man in charge of getting out the crowds and buttons and handling arrangements for the next stop.

Among those who were the Senator's very closest friends, there seems to have been something of the same sense. No one said it, of course, but among them there must have been a poignant awareness that when the train reached Washington it was unlikely that they would ever all gather together again in common enterprise, and that this, aside from being a funeral train, was also their last hurrah.

One of the men who had been closest to President Kennedy in the old days may have voiced it for them all near the end of the day. When people farther forward in the train were wishing the train would hurry faster to Washington, he said, "I wish this trip would never end."

Postscript

In the accident at Elizabeth two persons were killed and six injured when some of the spectators at the station edged onto tracks carrying a northbound passenger express moving at high speed.

That Time When Minutes Last Hours

MIAMI BEACH, Thursday, Aug. 8—The atmosphere was crackling with tedium when the Republican party assembled in the Miami Beach Convention Hall last night to pick itself a President.

It had been building relentlessly all week, the boredom, and at 5 P.M., when Chairman Gerald Ford called the faithful to order, it had reached an intensity that was scarcely bearable.

It was not so much due to the pervasive assumption, which prevailed at the cocktail hour, that Richard Milhous Nixon had actually been nominated several weeks ago and that this evening's rites were merely a charade. Not at all. As "Casablanca" and Humphrey Bogart have demonstrated, there is nothing an American enjoys more than a good show with a familiar ending.

The American nominating process, however, is a vestigial leftover from the baroque era of nineteenth-century politics. It is capable of producing melodrama when the outcome is uncertain, but when uncertainty is minimal it becomes a vehicle for brutal and agonizing punishment of human spirit and flesh.

Hour upon hour of thundering cliché, of enervating restatement of the obvious, of prancing up and down the hall in exhaustively planned "demonstrations"—the whole soggy business relieved only by an occasional burst of asininity—this is the way it has been done for a century or more and, unless politicians change more in the next hundred years than they have in the last, the way it will doubtless be done for a century to come.

Typically, last evening's performance began with a bout of inspirational song by the "Up With People" chorus, a group of very attractive but nonetheless very square young people whose musical message is a hymn to the good old American values. They are the politician's answer to soul music. Lee Bowman, the actor, certified them orthodox with the cry, "And not a hippie among them!"

The resounding cheer suggested that hippies were not a major force in this convention, and that being established, the roll-call of states began for the purpose of ascertaining how many nominating speeches the convention would subject itself to. The result would have been dispiriting to an elephant.

Alabama—"We love our state," its spokesmen bellowed across the hall, and probably across the continent—said it was yielding to California for the nomination of "a man who stands foremost for the love of God and country." (Political code meaning "Ronald Reagan.")

Arkansas announced its determination to nominate Governor Winthrop Rockefeller, and Michigan gave fair warning that it intended to do the same to George Romney. Kansas insisted upon nominating its retiring Senator, Frank Carlson. Pennsylvania, Maryland, Minnesota, New Jersey, Ohio and South Carolina also had men to put in nomination, some of such grandeur as Richard Nixon and Nelson Rockefeller, others mere stalking horses like Senator Strom Thurmond, the ageless hero of the grits belt who last ran for President in 1948 on the States' Rights ticket.

The Hawaii delegation stood up and said something about "aloha." From the press platform, where it was difficult to hear the proceedings without benefit of a radio, it sounded as if Hawaii were threatening to nominate "aloha."

Even without "aloha," this program confronted the delegates with the prospect of having to endure fifty speeches and ten "spontaneous demonstrations." (Every nominee was entitled to one nominating and four seconding speeches plus one demonstration.)

To aid the digestion of this news, Chairman Ford called up a three-minute organ recital. When this ended, the somber news spread that two more men—one Harold Stassen and Governor Walter J. Hickel of Alaska—would be added to the list. Endless night loomed.

And so, at 5:48 P.M., twelve minutes before the hotels on Miami Beach close the ocean for the night, Mrs. Ivy Baker Priest Stevens strode into the camera's eye to nominate Governor Reagan.

She is without doubt the most merciful woman ever to nominate a man who has been marked by destiny, and with an altogether becoming disdain for the grosser oratorical abuses she spent precisely fifteen minutes explaining that "destiny has marked this man." And the demonstration began.

The reason for demonstrations is lost in the mud of primeval time. Why they survive today and what purpose, if any, they serve are questions that have never been answered. One is like another. Balloons cascade from the ceiling. Sober men who earn their bread at the law, at the bank, at embalming, trot through the aisles in party hats, expressions of joy frozen rigidly on sweating faces, shouting and whooping like freshmen being hazed by the sophomores during hell week.

Let a curtain be mercifully drawn about the drearier details of their humiliations. Suffice it to say that the Reagan demonstration produced the spectacle of United States Senator George Murphy hoofing through the aisles with considerable less dignity than Shirley Temple's producers used to accord him when he was in show biz.

After the demonstration cometh the seconding speeches, and Governor Reagan undoubtedly picked up support in the galleries, if not on the floor, by contenting himself with a mere three instead of claiming the four to which he was entitled.

Even with this concession it took fifty-two minutes to get him nominated in proper style and to clear the way for the nomination of Governor Hickel. ("In 1966 Walter J. Hickel gave up a comfortable position. . . . Hardly anyone gave him much of a chance. . . .")

Mercifully, Governor Hickel's proved to be nothing more than a "Hi mom!" candidacy—a case of capitalizing on the presence of television to wave at all America—and after a one-minute demonstration he smiled into the camera "with deep humility" and withdrew.

Governor Winthrop Rockefeller, Nelson's brother "Bubba," was not granting mercy, however. Not content with a nominating speech and an eight-minute demonstration, he insisted upon not one, but two seconding speeches. Considering the modesty of "Bubba's" chances, this put him in the position of a man who had been invited to tea and decided to stay for the weekend.

At 7:19 it was Governor Romney's turn. Senator Robert Griffin of Michigan spoke for twelve minutes and demonstrators demonstrated for fourteen minutes with a zeal that was all the more remarkable because the Governor had told the world last February that he was out of the contest.

Actually, of course, the Romney candidacy, like "Bubba's," was not a candidacy at all, but part of a desperate holding operation being staged by an odd assortment of Governors who agreed on nothing except the desirability of preventing Mr. Nixon's nomination.

Nelson Rockefeller, for example, lent his band to the Romney demonstration and the New York delegation joined it in response to one New Yorker's cry, "He's going for us; let's go for him!"

By 8 P.M., lull had given way to torpor and Kansas was nominating Senator Carlson ("this man of the soil," "a man who will rise above partisanship to act for the good of the nation," etc.). From the floor came word that New Jersey, thus far committed to the favorite-son candidacy of Senator Clifford Case, was suffering a seizure of Nixonism and might destroy the entire holding operation.

On the floor, Rockefeller demonstrators were being smuggled into the auditorium to swell the Governor's demonstration beyond licit limits. In the Ohio delegation, Governor James Rhodes, linchpin of the holding operation, insisted that Ohio would not even caucus until the first ballot was over, and on the press platform the smart-money boys were saying, "In that case they won't caucus until the next convention."

"Will the convention please be in order!" Chairman Ford barked as Edward E. Johnson of Hawaii came forward to nominate Senator Hiram L. Fong. The convention would not be in order, of course. It was going out for hot dogs and being interviewed by men with small cameras and scratching its ribs and comparing notes on the quality of the pastrami at various poolside restaurants, and no power on earth could have brought it to order for Hiram Fong.

Mr. Fong had tried the patience of the convention once too often. He had been put in nomination at the 1964 convention, promptly to withdraw. That is permissible. Every politician is entitled to one nomination, but by insisting upon a second tonight, the honorable gentleman from Hawaii raised among the delegates the disturbing spectre of years of Fongism to come, with the likelihood that they will never again be able to attend a convention without suffering through a Fong nomination.

By 9:05, with the session precisely four hours old, Mr. Fong's nomination had been seconded, and still six names remained to put in nomination. Now it was Mr. Rockefeller's turn. The chairman recognized Governor Raymond Shafer of Pennsylvania. Disorder in the rear of the hall. Rockefeller demonstrators, eager perhaps to earn their pay and go home, began to do their stuff. Governor Shafer silenced them with a gesture—Toscanini muting the brass—and began.

As nominating speeches go, Shafer's was a model of understatement. The moment, he said, was "great." The opportunity was one "to preserve and perhaps save the nation." Mr. Rockefeller, like Lincoln of course, was "a man for his time." After these bows to floridity, however, his theme became somber, also cautionary.

He reminded them that they had elected only one President in the last four decades; that they were, in fact, a party of losers; that they had not been quick to nominate even the one successful candidate they had chosen since 1932—General Eisenhower. "A victory is what this party needs," he said. And Mr. Rockefeller, he urged, was the one candidate likely to assure it.

For a nominating speech, this was tough talk. The message was implicit. A party representing "only 27 percent of the electorate" could not afford the luxury of a candidate popular in the party but incapable of appealing to millions whom the party would need to win the election.

Mr. Shafer did not state that Mr. Nixon was the luxury candidate, but the hint could not have been misunderstood even by the cops in the aisles when he said of Mr. Rockefeller, leaning on every word, "He has never lost an election." Richard Nixon cannot make that claim.

The Rockefeller demonstration, lasting twenty-eight minutes, was notable for a group of gentlemen dressed more or less as butterflies. They bounced through the aisles fluttering their spread wings at the delegates, thereby proving something about American politics; to wit, that nothing, absolutely nothing, is completely irrelevant when the Republic's salvation is at stake.

Placing Mr. Nixon in nomination required the fifth and part of the session's sixth hour. A few wheezing cheers came from the gallery when Governor Spiro T. Agnew of Maryland promised that his would be "a very short nominating speech." Running sixteen minutes, it proved to be one of the longest.

One can only speculate why Mr. Agnew was chosen for the job. He was a Rockefeller man during the winter snows, but was left stranded when the Governor's blundering spring campaign took Mr. Rockefeller temporarily out of competition.

Perhaps Mr. Nixon made the choice out of pure superstition. The last Republican Presidential candidate to be nominated by a Maryland Governor was Dwight D. Eisenhower in 1952. That year the nominator was Theodore McKeldin, the man of a thousand voices as he is known on the Irish-Italian-Israeli banquet circuit, and McKeldin launched the party for the White House.

Governor Agnew, sad to relate, is no McKeldin at the spellbinding art. His clichés are impeccable—"a man not only to match this moment, but to master it," "a man of warmth and wit," and so on—but his fires are banked low.

He raised the one animal shriek of the endless night when he reminded everybody that Mr. Nixon had "stood by the party and its candidate in their darkest hour." It was a twist of the knife in the Rockefeller campaign, reopening momentarily the old wounds created by the Governor's refusal to fight on the barricades for Barry Goldwater in the catastrophe of 1964.

It was only a momentary flicker of passion, however, and a moment later Mr. Agnew ended with a return to the peristaltic prose which has characterized most of this convention's oratory.

Of Mr. Nixon, he declared, "You don't create such a man. You don't discover such a man. You recognize such a man."

Came the demonstration. And the Nixon seconding speeches. And the night crept on.

At 11:16 of the clock, Harold Stassen is nominated. Reality seems far away. The demonstration lasts sixteen seconds. The seconding speech, by Paul Walters of Ohio, produces a rare moment of candor when Mr. Walter concludes with "Thank you for your inattention."

Let history record that as the clock told midnight the nomination of Senator Clifford P. Case of New Jersey to be President of the United States was being seconded. Thus, too, began the new day.

The first man to be put in nomination today was Governor Rhodes, the Ohio Robespierre who had resolutely refused to the twelfth hour to endorse Mr. Nixon and had just as resolutely refused for months to join battle openly on anyone else's behalf. Rationalists might conclude that Mr. Rhodes wanted the Presidency for himself; a whimsical man, on the other hand, might suspect that he enjoyed his own mystery more than he enjoyed power.

Overheard on the floor at 12:43 this morning, during the fourth seconding speech for Governor Rhodes: "Oh, shut up!"

Last to be nominated was Senator Thurmond. This anticlimactic moment completed one of the most mobile careers in the history of American politics. In 1948, he bolted the Democratic convention at Philadelphia to lead the Dixiecrats against Harry Truman and Thomas E. Dewey. He then returned to the Democratic bosom until 1964, when he bolted to the Republicans to support Mr. Goldwater. "A great American," his fourth and final seconder declared. By that time, of course, everyone

else was pretty tired too. And of course, Mr. Thurmond immediately withdrew.

It had taken the Republicans eight hours and seven minutes
simply to tell each other who was available to vote for.

And yet "War and Peace" was cut to six hours for fear of
losing the American audience.

Beleaguered in
the Mainstream

CHICAGO, Aug. 26—Scratch a Democrat and nine chances out
of ten you will find a masochist. There is no other explanation
for the party's decision first to hold its 1968 convention in Chicago and then, despite ample excuse for going elsewhere, refusing to change its mind.

Every nightmare that besets the party—race, antipathy to
war, urban breakdown, alienation of youth, disaffection of the
blue-collar vote and ethnic blocs—all flourish here with peculiar
virulence. The Republicans, aware of all this, elected to transact
this year's business in the detached isolation of Miami Beach.
The Democrats, being Democrats, chose to immerse themselves
in their own miseries.

They are trying to make a virtue of their taste for mas-
ochism by boasting that it proves they do not fear contact with
"the mainstream" of American life. At the same time they are
meeting in a hall with virtually no seating for the public but
enough firepower to repulse a battalion of Vietcong.

The fact is that they are not in "the mainstream" here, but
beleaguered by it. Or, worse, perhaps only by their own fear of
it. Policemen in riot helmets of robin's-egg blue work twelve-
hour shifts in the central city and troops of the National Guard
and regular Army wait on the edge of the city against the possibility of mayhem.

In the convention area around the Conrad Hilton and Blackstone Hotels, surrounded by legions of good-natured cops, life seems safely remote from the dreaded "mainstream." There are the transportation and telephone strikes, of course, and they provide unpleasant reminders that city life is breaking down, but the inconvenience of having to walk and conduct political business face-to-face is negligible compared to the terrors that Mayor Daley has concentrated so much firepower to prevent.

In an age when politicians would rather wear lipstick than risk projecting a "bad image," the Democrats' decision to convene in a "mainstream" dammed by barbed wire must cost them more sleep than the conventional roar of jollity in the Conrad Hilton Hotel.

In no convention of the past twenty years has the jollity been less convincing. The central corridors of the Conrad Hilton are as packed, as usual, as the Times Square subway station during the rush hour. Women in funny dresses are swept along in the mob, and Robert Lowell and William Styron and Arthur Miller and, now and then, Abraham Lincoln. A band tootles last year's rock in the Huberét, Hubert Humphrey's idea of a discotheque. Flying wedges of armed men conduct candidates here and there. Politicians cluster to make limp jokes.

It goes on all day and half the night, that ceaseless shuffling through the lobby, and by midmorning the place has a sour, damp smell compounded of worried politicians, ten thousand cigarettes, last week's dirty laundry and angry men who have perspired in television floodlights.

All convention hoopla is essentially phoney, of course; a contrived farce to persuade the delegates that they are having a fine time, rather as canned laughter is used by television to goose a laugh from the comatose home viewer. Here, however, there is not even a halfhearted effort to lighten the atmosphere.

It may be because "the mainstream" is too close for comfort here. It keeps leaking in through the sealed perimeter. In Miami Beach it seemed remote and unreal. Here the delegates have to breathe it, and it makes them edgy and irritable and uncertain about the wisdom of what they came here to do, which was to participate in the Roman triumph of Hubert Humphrey.

Committed to still more of the status quo, they are constantly being reminded that the status quo has brought them to Mayor Daley's armed perimeter, to control of their own convention by the Federal Secret Service, to the angry young men dodging billy clubs on the North Side. And when not occupied with these more somber thoughts, they are reminded that the status quo is also telephones that don't work, taxis that don't run, not being able to get a bus and being told that you can't get your shirt washed.

There were rumors here today suggesting that discontent with the status quo was reaching such heights that the Democrats might go wild, scrap their plans for the Roman triumph and hold a convention after all. Wisdom suggests that this is improbable, but if it should happen, Hubert Humphrey can probably blame not only his threadbare showing in the polls, but also the Democratic party's insistence on convening in "the mainstream."

A Macabre Atmosphere Pervades the Convention

CHICAGO, Aug. 27—The only people who can possibly feel at ease at this convention are those who have been to a hanging.

All the macabre trappings are here except the rope and the condemned, and a case might even be made for these by accepting the political coroners' verdict that the Democratic party is giving itself the business by letting this particular spectacle go out over the miles of communications cable, strung through Mayor Richard J. Daley's chambered fortress.

For the rest, the analogies are uncomfortably clear. Battalions of nervous cops gallop through the streets in squadrons of menace calculated to intimidate any unrest that might deter society in the collection of its debt.

Keepers of the vigil—in this case mostly young people—try to sleep on the park grass and, for this impertinence, get their skulls cracked and their ribs kicked by the gentlemen whom Mayor Daley calls "the finest police force in the country."

Using the public grass after midnight can be a dangerous provocation to a policeman bent upon keeping the masses docile while grim business is being conducted.

The grimmest of Democratic business is conducted, of course, in the grim hours between midnight and dawn. Hangmen and politicians work best when the spirit is at its lowest ebb.

As at executions, public witnesses are rigorously limited at the convention hall and, as usual at such affairs, there is a complex system of security checkpoints at which the witnesses are subjected to hostile police scrutiny, credentials examination and possible frisking.

The International Amphitheatre sits, appropriately, adjacent to an abattoir. It is white—the true color of evil in Herman Melville's view and the favorite color of death-chamber decorators. It has the architectural sprawl and stolidity of a prison.

To arrive at the site one travels with a suitcase full of credentials past factories, under railroad tracks and down "respectable" streets lined with small bungalows and respectable people waving American flags; passes along six or seven blocks of police barricades behind which all evidence of unpoliced humanity has disappeared, and at length penetrates a high wire fence topped with barbed wire.

Electronic credential scanners control admission to the hall's antechambers. They are usually out of order, but the guards here tend to be merciful and rarely turn anyone over to the Chicago police.

All these things, of course, are physical superficialities which, by themselves, would scarcely account for the unnatural mood here.

In the view of Lester G. Maddox, the Democratic party's most distinguished fried-chicken salesman, all this simply represents what a southern fried-chicken entrepreneur yearns for when he calls for "law and order."

What puts iron into the analogy, however, is the behavior

of the Democrats themselves. They are, most of them, a bare breath from panic, the panic of men who sense that something utterly unpleasant and perhaps terribly final is about to be done to them down by the abattoir.

You see them at their noontime breakfasts talking about the chance that Ted Kennedy can be drafted for the Presidency. This seems fantasy in a class with the Queen's Coronation Day pardon for Mack the Knife, and the fact that so many pass the time dreaming of it speaks of the general state of mind.

In such an atmosphere, sellout and double-cross become the standard ethic. Senator George S. McGovern, whose candidacy was manufactured by the Kennedy forces, discovers suddenly that his creators have fled back to Kennedy.

Hubert Humphrey, who tried to please everybody, harvests hisses and boos by the bushel, but never a cheer.

Eugene McCarthy, whose candidacy disclosed the depth of Lyndon Johnson's weakness, finds himself a pariah for telling the party the truth it did not want to hear.

Some of the older hands went through all this in 1948, lived to see Harry Truman pass a miracle and now comfort themselves with the assurance that it can be done again with Hubert Humphrey.

This is death-row talk, and the question is why the mood of this convention dwells so uncharacteristically on thoughts of the great beyond.

Just a few weeks ago these very Democrats were chortling in their soup about the prospects of waging one more campaign against Richard Nixon. Even then they conceded that a campaign in defense of the Johnson Administration would be hard, but now, in three days at Chicago, they have persuaded themselves that it will be hopeless.

It is not easy to account for the lightning transition from courage to despair. Not many of them, surely, can ever have been to a hanging. Chicago can hardly have stirred memories of old nightmares.

It is possible, of course, that they sensed at first sight of Mayor Daley's arrangements the pattern that was developing here and merely reacted as normal men would. After all, a man's first hanging is the hardest, particularly if he suspects it may be his own.

Postscript

Lester Maddox was a Georgian who became a small-bore politi-cal figure among segregationists in the 1960's. Operator of an Atlanta restaurant specializing in chicken, Maddox had become famous among racists and infamous elsewhere by threatening to assault black persons with pickax handles if they sought service at his restaurant. This won him such fame that he was elected Gov-ernor of Georgia in 1967.

The City That Fascinated Itself

CHICAGO, Aug. 31—Carl Sandburg has deceived us all these years about Chicago. All that hair-on-the-chest talk about hog butcher to the world and city of the big shoulders—well, it may be poetry, but it doesn't go to the heart of Chicago.

The shoulders may be broad—the policemen's beams cer-tainly are—and the town may butcher even more hogs than Democrats, but underneath it all there beats a heart of pure mush. Quite simply, Chicago wants desperately to be loved.

The Democratic disaster held here this week has left the city as desolated as the girl in her first evening gown who went to the dance and fell in the punch bowl. It was not the shattering of the Democratic party that obsessed Chicago during those days of charnel, but the embarrassment caused by having it happen in Chicago.

In fact, it would surely have happened in any American city which the Democrats chose to afflict this year. The Democrats were bent upon it as surely as the lemming is bent upon the sea. It is the measure of Chicago's innocence that it believed it could never happen in Chicago.

When it inevitably did, Chicago responded in a variety of ways, all of them typical of the socially insecure matron caught in a social gaffe. Some took it out in recriminations against Mayor Daley or the police; Mayor Daley took it out on television and the press; and The Chicago Tribune took it out on the New Left, "professional agitators," Berkeley and New York.

Chicagoans with a taste for the hair shirt winced and apologized for what they embarrassingly insisted was the native barbarism. It doesn't seem to have occurred to anybody that Chicago had nothing to be embarrassed about. In the self-consciousness and insecurity of its civic pride, the city seemed incapable of interpreting an act of God as anything but a humiliation for Chicago.

The art of confrontation and provocation perfected by the New Left this spring at Columbia University in New York produced the predictable brutalization of the police force, just as it did on Morningside Heights. Here, of course, there was television coverage for the mass audience. The Mayor's response was typically Chicago. He immediately smelled a television plot to besmirch Chicago with electronic propaganda.

New York was admittedly not subjected to the burden of having the Morningside Heights skull crackings televised around the world, but even had it been it is inconceivable that New Yorkers would have transformed the issue at Columbia into a television plot against their city.

Mayor Daley's ham-handed management of the convention has also embarrassed many of the higher-browed citizenry, who find his turn-of-the-century gasworks political style too old-fashioned to suit the cool, dynamic, cultivated picture of Chicago which they would like to project abroad.

Yet in a sense, Daley is the perfect symbol of Chicago. He has the small-town chauvinist's love of hometown that characterizes the most sophisticated Chicagoan. The cut of his jaw and his lapel and his rhetoric are all wrong for the Playboy Club set on the North Side, and he lacks the fashionably blasé attitude about Chicago's being "The Second City"—to Daley, Chicago is the only city—but for all that he remains the symbol of Chicago's sentimental self-esteem.

Some have called him a *gauleiter* here this week, but that is an emotional glamorization of the reality. He is at worst only a bush-league de Gaulle, persuaded that he is the hope and salvation of Chicago.

One feels the need, watching Chicago in its humiliation, to reassure it that everything is really all right. It is, just as it boasts daily through television and press, an excellent city of fine parks, good restaurants, elevated culture and, particularly along the lakefront, extraordinary beauty. At its best, it makes Manhattan look like a slum, and at its worst it is no worse than any of a dozen other American cities.

These words, of course, would probably be read in Chicago as a patronizing sneer. Such are the reflexes of the insecure that praise's motives are suspect while criticism produces depression. Chicago, being romantic as well as insecure, defends itself in myths about hog butchers, big shoulders, Al Capone reflexes and all the rest of the Warner Brothers Chicago Story.

James Morris, the English writer, relates a story about a stranger arriving here for the first time by train and gawking at the skyline and asking a fellow passenger what sort of city he was entering. And the man replied, "Mister, Chicago ain't no sissy town."

Maybe it ain't, but just "maybe."

Just the Varnished Truth, Please

It is not surprising that public opinion has thoroughly endorsed the behavior of the Chicago constabulary during the Democratic National Convention, nor that it has condemned press and television on grounds that they gave false accounts of the affair.

There are few things more odious to men than truths they do not want to hear, and those who tell them usually have to take the consequences. In Galileo's time the Church did not want to hear that the earth moved around the sun, even if it did. It became very angry with Galileo and threatened him with unpleasant consequences until he recanted.

"And yet it moves," Galileo said afterward. And indeed it did.

Eugene McCarthy during his campaign used to cite the ancient practice of killing the messenger who brought bad news to the King as the reason why he would not get the Democratic nomination. With his victory against President Johnson in New Hampshire, he reasoned, he was the messenger who had brought the bad news to the party.

Like the Church suddenly challenged by the revolving-earth news with the necessity of re-ordering its thought, the party, challenged with the difficulty of reorganizing itself, preferred to pretend that nothing bad had happened. And so it crushed McCarthy and, by nominating a Johnson surrogate, asserted that the news wasn't bad at all.

"The truth will set you free," goes the old maxim. The trouble, as a modern philosopher has noted, is that "the truth that sets men free is usually the very truth they do not want to hear."

History is full of examples of angry human reaction to unwelcome truth. The French, so emotionally committed to Dreyfus's guilt that they refused to act against Esterhazy even after he was shown to have been the fellow who committed the crimes Dreyfus was convicted for, jailed Emile Zola for irritating them with the facts.

President Kennedy in 1963 did not want to hear that the South Vietnamese were losing the war. Reporters who wrote that they were felt the weight of the Presidential anger. When finally the South Vietnamese Government collapsed, the men who had brought the bad news were blamed in some quarters of Government for causing it.

The Johnson Administration's distaste for hearing the truth about Vietnam is, of course, largely the story of its own self-destruction. It is all terribly human. As every civilized man realizes, there are some truths that no one wants to hear.

Consider the matter of love. A Frenchman, Raoul de-Roussy de Sales, warned Americans years ago in his essay "Love in America" that they were toying with dynamite in pursuing the theory that successful marriage required a policy of brutal candor at all times.

"A fine theory," he observed, "but it has seldom been practiced without disastrous results. . . . Truth is an explosive, and it should be handled with care, especially in marital life. It is not necessary to lie, but there is little profit in juggling with hand grenades just to show how brave one is."

In the case of marriage, as de Sales pointed out, excessive zeal for truth will almost invariably set you free, but only "to find someone else to be recklessly frank with."

The same argument against truth can probably be made in certain public affairs. Conceivably, this may be a very dangerous period for the public to believe what was reported about the Chicago gendarmerie. It is arguable that a vote of public no-confidence in constabularies might be dangerously demoralizing just now.

What is curious is not that part of the public that approves of the bully-boy tactics, but that large portion of it that insists that it didn't happen or that press and television did not tell it truly. The argument, usually made by people who weren't there, is that the newshawks either created it or distorted it.

Logically, people who believe the press capable of such falsification might be expected to question the same press's accounts of Soviet behavior in Czechoslovakia. They do not, of course. There is no mental or emotional discomfort required to swallow the truth when it is about Russians behaving abominably.

In Chicago, on the other hand, something happened that many persons did not want to know happened. Press and TV are under pressure to recant.

And yet it happened.

AGE OF GOLD

When fashion turned against smoking I undertook to give it up, for I have the adolescent's terror of being different from the crowd. I had then been smoking two packs of cigarettes daily for nearly forty years. From earlier failed attempts to break the habit, I knew what agony lay ahead, so prepared for a hard struggle and probable defeat.

This time, however, I was victorious. What brought the triumph was my love of money. The key to victory was a plain white envelope stowed in a desk drawer. Into this envelope, at the end of each day during which I had not smoked, went $2.30 in cash. This was what two packs of cigarettes would have cost had I smoked them. Not smoking put money in my envelope. I began to love it more than any wallet, purse or bank account that had ever been mine.

I was enchanted to watch the envelope fatten nightly. Soon I could scarcely wait for the end of another day of smoke deprivation. During the day I would pause from time to time to contemplate the pleasure ahead that night when I would put another $2.30 into the envelope. As the coins piled up, I converted them into dollar bills. Soon it was necessary to convert the stack of one-dollar bills into fives, and then to convert the fives into tens, and then the tens into twenties.

One or two nights a week I would close the door so as to be alone with the money. Then, taking out the envelope, now dirty from too much handling, I would stroke the thickening wad and, with sensuous pleasure and probably an erotic smile on my face, would count the money and marvel at what a lovely pile of money it was. There came a day when I converted a stack of it

231

into a $100 bill. Then there was a second $100 bill, and then another. What delight it was, lovingly counting the money and writing the total on a piece of paper on which to feast my eyes, what joy to realize the envelope would soon be packed with dozens of $100 bills.

Nothing could have tempted me to destroy this pleasure by lighting a cigarette. Before the third $100 bill joined the others I was permanently cured of the need for smoke.

What had happened was a variation on the psychologist's trick of curing one neurosis by substituting another. My passion for nicotine had been replaced by a passion for money. I was carrying on like the classical comic miser.

There was more than $1,500 in the envelope before I finally recovered from the money madness. By then I was completely indifferent to tobacco's charms. What was strange about all this was the importance of having the cash constantly at hand in the envelope, so my treasure could be felt, clutched, stroked, counted, admired.

Putting it in the bank would have destroyed everything. I had never really believed that money in the bank was really money. I was, and am, you see, a true peasant about money. Money under the mattress is money. So is money buried in a kettle behind the woodshed. Money in an envelope in a desk drawer is money. Any money you can run through your fingers is money. Exposed to the sight and feel of such stuff, I am as money-mad as the greediest money king on Wall Street and the sleaziest finagler in Washington.

I differ only by being a small-time, bush-league, penny-ante, rinky-dink, nickel-and-dime-size money lover. I can go so far off my head about $300 that I forsake the joys of tobacco forever, yet I care little for the billions of the junk-bond king. Billions are just paper. Probably not even paper nowadays, but just electronic blips in a computer. Blips lack the magic to make my mouth water, no matter how many digits they represent. On money, I am resolutely small-bore.

I tell you all this so you will not be deceived by the pieces that follow. All are about money in the richest country there ever was at a moment when it was so stupendously rich that it was almost obscene. The tone of many of these pieces borders on disapproval. The writer sometimes seems so down on money that he appears primed for a hellfire sermon against the stuff and all who lust for it.

America was operating at this time on the belief that there was nothing, absolutely nothing, more important than money, and so what? The newspaper columnist has traditionally been a moralist, and true to that tradition I naturally try to take a very starchy attitude toward this theory and toward money's tendency to breed nastiness.

Before condemning me on charges of depressing moral rectitude, remember the low-budget peasant so greedy for money that he gave up one of life's large pleasures for a few squalid $100 bills in a dirty envelope.

The Golden Spouse

Everybody is buying gold by the ounce. It is the biggest thing since disco and, since the price is now $400 an ounce, much more expensive.

Once again I have bet on the wrong horse. In this case, the wrong metal. For years I have been buying aluminum. The kitchen is full of it and it is worthless, absolutely worthless. A man who buys gold every time he can get away from his desk came in to look at it the other day.

I had heard of his vast metallic acquisitions and lured him in with tales of my own, but he became churlish when he saw it was all aluminum. The entire hoard, he told me, wasn't worth a single ounce of gold.

He will sing another tune some day when he wants to warm a can of beans, but I didn't say so out loud. Instead, I tried to get some respect by telling of hundreds and hundreds of ounces of chrome which I had secreted in far away New England to keep the parking-garage gnomes of Manhattan from taxing it at the rate of $100 a month.

He sneered. Everybody had chrome, he said. At least everybody who owned a decrepit American automobile.

"How about rust?" I asked. I have rust galore.

"Bah!" he said and stormed out. I stormed along with him, reasoning that he probably meant to calm his nerves by buying some gold. I wanted to see how he did it.

The truth, which I was ashamed to tell him, was that I didn't know how to buy gold by the ounce. Not knowing commonplace things like that always makes you feel stupid and ashamed.

It was obvious that you didn't walk into a bar and ask for a shot glass of gold. With gold at $400 a shot, few bars would be able to stay in business.

What's more, it was pretty clear that you didn't walk into the confectionary and say, "Give me a pack of chewing gum, a lottery ticket and fifty cents' worth of gold."

"Nobody buys fifty cents' worth of gold," said my metals friend. It would be so small that the cockroaches would eat it if you left it on the kitchen sink overnight.

"That's one thing you never have to worry about when you're buying cast-iron," I told him, but he wasn't interested in getting out of gold and into my skillets. The gold heat was on him. He went into a drugstore and emerged two minutes later flushed with pleasure, relaxed and talkative.

"That was splendid," he said.

"You had a quick bromide?"

"I just bought gold," he confided.

"They sell it in drugstores?"

"On the telephone," he said. "I order it by telephone."

"Do they deliver?"

"You have been stockpiling rust too long," he said.

"When are the big-metal boys going to dump gold and get into brass?" I asked. I have invested heavily in brass.

"In Zurich," he said, "we refer to brass as 'the metal equivalent of the American dollar—fit only to rest your feet on when you go to the bar to celebrate your daily gold.'"

In good spirits produced by his purchase, he invited me

home to meet his wife. She had a heart of gold. And not only a heart, but also lungs, kidneys, head, hair and liver—all of pure gold. "Yes," he said, "I have a solid gold wife. I had her cast when gold was only $100 an ounce. Do you know what that means?"

"That she makes a cool, quiet and rigid helpmate," I suggested.

"That, of course," he said. "But the principal point is that she has appreciated four hundred percent during a period in which the dollar has lost fifty percent of its value."

"Then you recommend a solid gold wife as the perfect hedge against inflation?"

"Oh, I could have had a papier-mâché wife of Swiss francs and German marks and done well enough," he said, "but she'd be harder to keep dusted than a gold wife."

On the other hand, I pointed out, an aluminum wife would be much lighter to move around.

"Not interested," he said.

"With a cast-iron wife you wouldn't have to worry about cockroach nibbles."

"Nonsense," he said.

"A wife made of rust would enchant you with constant changes of complexion."

"You need a drink," he said, producing a bottle worth one fortieth of an ounce of gold. The liquid was dark amber. I declined the stuff and left. You couldn't be sure what this man kept in his bottles. Quite possibly, I thought, he had a brew that would convert me into 170 pounds of copper.

Ermine, Skin and Bones

It is still unclear whether we are supposed to shout "Whoopee!" or "Shame!" about the new elegance the Reagans are bringing to Washington. I speak of the new elegance cautiously. Not hav-

ing made an on-site inspection as yet of Washington's Rea-
ganized salons, I am dependent on the Washington reporters for
information about social conditions down there, and "the new
elegance" runs through their copy like melted butter through
popcorn.

Sometimes it is called "the new opulence," but not by
those who want us to be pleased by the high-toned ambiance
that the Reagans are said to have brought to town. "Opulence"
has nasty connotations of oriental splendor, whereas "elegance"
sounds much more austere and Republican, though in a snooty
uptown way.

I classify reporters who refer to "the new opulence" as Jacobins and their colleagues who prefer "the new elegance" as
royalists, but terminology aside, they are all talking about the
same thing: rich people who like life on a lavish scale.

The display of wealth during the inauguration festivities
was either exhilarating or loathsome, depending upon whether
you read the Jacobins or the royalists. One of Washington's
most distinguished literary curmudgeons, Henry Fairlie, was so
irritated by the spectacle that he gave the celebrating rich several whacks with his typewriter and, in a Washington Post essay,
ended by strangling them with pity.

This was surprising coming from Fairlie, who boasts of his
shameless Toryism. Not that Tories in their time were any more
devoted to the rich than the Republicans are today, but on the
other hand they were not any more opposed to pearls and sables
either.

Fairlie's attack on the wretchedness of the rich he saw
flocking to the Reagans was so unremitting in its ferocity that I
wanted to cry out in their defense.

It is the nature of rich people to wrap themselves in animal
fur, attach stones to their flesh and ride around in large machinery. They do it all the time in Manhattan, regardless of who is
President. It is one of the things rich people do.

You do not expect them to put on tennis shoes and motorcycle jackets and ride the subway any more than you expect a
subway rider to wrap up in ermine, trim the ears with diamonds
and ride through town in the back seat of an eighty-foot limousine. People can't help it if life imprisons them in a certain

shade of skin or a certain income bracket. Why abuse the rich
for being wrapped in animal fur if we do not abuse the subway
classes for being shod in tennis shoes?

Fairlie goes beyond the Jacobin critics of Reagan's rich to
insult the entire moneyed class for its inability to wear clothes
well. The rich, says he, look ugly in their clothes, and here, I am
embarrassed to tell you, ladies, he is talking about rich women.

It shows how too many limousines impeding a man's progress to the office can sour the milk of human kindness in his
veins. A few moments of peaceful reflection would, I am sure,
have brought the good Fairlie to the fore and led him to muse
sympathetically upon the plight of rich women.

Wearing clothes well is not easy for rich women, since,
being rich, they must be exceedingly thin. The richer a woman
is, the thinner she becomes. Why great wealth afflicts women
with emaciation is a question I leave to medical science, but
there, nevertheless, is the fact.

It is easy for women of moderate means to look beautiful in
clothes. In their income bracket, flesh tends to cover the skeletal
frame. When clothes are draped upon it, the flesh exerts subtle,
charming little pressures on the fabric and makes it undulate
beautifully. One notices not the dress so much as the woman
who is turning it into a marvelous liquefaction.

Rich women are not so blessed. Their poor sparse frames
become merely bony supports for the dressmaker's gewgaws.
Rich women's dresses, like expensive coffins, are not intended
to make their residents look beautiful. They are built to conceal a sad state of physical affairs under the dazzle of the crafts-
man's art.

To a dress designer a rich woman is a mannequin on which
he can display his workmanship without danger of the audience's being distracted by a fleshed torso. The fanciest design-
ers, those who whip up $25,000 tea gowns, for example, refuse
to concoct anything large enough to be worn by women with
meat on their bones. Who wastes time admiring the container if
the contents make the mouth water?

The humane attitude toward rich women dictates sympathy
rather than abuse, as Fairlie will doubtless see once he becomes
accustomed to these poor gaunt creatures inside their unrippling

garments during the coming days of the new elegance. Remember, Fairlie, they cannot help being rich and unfleshed, and they are, bless them, women. Mothers. Daughters. Loved ones, just like the women of the subway classes, only richer.

The Common Touch

Returning home after a month's absence during which the mail had piled up, I was astonished by the number of requests for money. Everyone in the United States seemed to want money. Mobil Oil, for example. You wouldn't think Mobil Oil would want for money, would you? You would be wrong. Mobil Oil wanted money sent immediately to one of its heating-oil divisions.

The John Hancock Company, which must be wallowing in money, was not satisfied either. Its mail was explicit. John Hancock wanted money.

The governments of the United States, the State of New York and New York City are all notorious spendthrifts, forever spending more money than they earn, and I anticipated that they would all be waiting for me at home, babbling. "We want money." I was not disappointed. They were all there waiting. They all wanted money.

Among them was a private trash collector, and he wanted money, but the sum was so small—only $15—that I was tempted after giving it to him to upbraid him for failing to want on the noble scale. No such complaint could be lodged against Bloomingdale's, which wanted money, or Macy's, which wanted money. Those outfits know how to want big when the hounds pick up the scent of a purse.

The landlord wanted money. The bank wanted money. It also wanted to notify me that it was going to want even more money next month. If I understood the bank rightly, it was going to want this additional money next month to calm the Federal Reserve people who are furious.

Federal Reserve people, it seems, have deep respect for money. They do not approve of people having so much money that they can hand money over to everybody who wants it. They prefer people to hold their money, stroke it and admire it, as they do. They want people to appreciate money and treat it with respect, like motherhood. They want people to cherish money, not give it away to everybody who says, "How about coming across with some money, pal?"

They are well on their way to realizing their ambition, judging from the evidence in my mail, because almost every envelope testified to how widely money is cherished.

The window-shade maker on Hudson Street, for example. He cherishes money, and yearns to have $62.95 of mine to esteem and admire. It is good to see that the small artisan shares the mighty Federal Reserve's respect for money, and so I was not distressed that the window-shade maker wanted money. I noted with approval that the lowly picture framer on West Forty-fifth Street also wanted money.

The mighty were equally devoted to the cause. Like statesmen who walk with kings but keep the common touch, the great corporations were not too snooty to put the common touch on me. Consider the Consolidated Edison Company of New York, father and mother of electric power to earth's most electric metropolis. It is hard to believe that such a grandee would have time for the likes of me, but there was the envelope containing the evidence. Yes, Con Ed wanted money.

And the mighty New York Telephone Company—it, too, wanted money. American Express wanted money. Time-Life Books wanted money. All I need do to satisfy its urge for money is accept an astounding new publication in next month's mail.

There was a plumber who wanted money. There was a man who cuts grass; he wanted money. There was even a man who restores broken tombstones. What did he want? Money. And who was this? Of course. The man who works on the automobile. I knew what he wanted, all right. Money.

The doctor who is so knowledgeable about livers and arteries wanted money. The doctor who understands eyes, he wanted money. Same with the doctor who is good with teeth. But where was the foot doctor, skilled in bunion relief, wise to the quirks of thousands of delicate little pedal bones and gristly tendons? There he was, hiding behind the man who sells frying pans, who also wanted money. The good old foot doctor. Wanted money.

Four colleges wanted money.

The New York Public Library wanted money.

People who assist unmoneyed black youths to go to college wanted money, and people who want to cure respiratory problems, arterial disease, mental and emotional ailments, a variety of wasting diseases—all wanted money.

Pausing for relief, pushing aside the still unopened requests for money, I turned on the television set, avoiding the commercial stations which are always swarming with people who want money, and tuned to the noncommercial calm of Channel 13 for education and uplift, only to discover that—you guessed it—Channel 13 wanted money. Channel 13 threatened to keep interrupting the education and uplift to tell me it wanted money until I gave it all the money it wanted.

It was tempting to cry out something shameful and unworthy—something like "I want money too!" I conquered the impulse, thanks to the wisdom of age, which has taught me it is undignified for a grown man to yell down a rain barrel.

Dugout Gasbag

"Hi, sports fans. This is Bill Bellclapper talking at you here today at the start of another baseball season. My guest on this edition of 'Dugout Gasbagger' is none other than W. J. Bryan 4th, the twenty-two-year-old sensation from Cal Tech who has been kicking this league in the shins ever since he signed in for a bonus said to be in excess of $375,000 a year. They call you one of the new breed, W.J. Would you be good enough to tell our audience what that means?"

"Man, how dense can you get! The new breed is a way of saying that we modern baseball players are altogether different from that bunch of boobs and hicks that you radio boobs have conned the kiddies of America into thinking of as great heroes in the past."

"Are you saying, W.J., that you yourself, for example, have little in common with someone like Babe Ruth?"

"In my book, he's Boob Ruth."

"Ha, ha! That's very funny, W.J. I suppose that as the new breed you have to be right up there on your toes all the time in the wit department."

"Of course. That's what I pay my ghostwriter for. He keeps me in witty lines—or at least in lines that pass for wit among the boobs who listen to broadcasters as dim as you."

"Ha, ha, ha! You're a laugh a second, W.J. How, in your estimation, has the game of baseball changed since the days of Ty Cobb, or, let's say, Mickey Mantle? I mean, has there been any—"

"Look, friend, I came on this show because my booking agent said I would have a chance to plug my new book. Now are we going to get to it so I can fatten up the royalty checks or are we going to waste the day talking about a lot of boob old-timers?"

"That's the way to talk, W.J.! And that, sports fans, is why they call him one of the new breed! Because he tells it as it is."

"*Like* it is, Bellcapper. I tell it *like* it is. It's easy to see that you never went to college; you can't even get your clichés straight. Now about the book, it's called 'Homeric Clout,' and it's all about me, and the girls I have to fight off when I'm not in the mood for love, and about how some of the older players wear dirty socks."

"That's a fantastic title, W.J. 'Homeric Clout.' That refers, I guess, to your fantastic ability to knock the old apple out of the ballpark."

"Man, you're not for real! 'Homeric Clout' is a reference to the way the club management helped me dodge the draft by getting me into the National Guard."

"Heh, heh, heh. You're really some kidder, W.J. The kids of America listening out there realize, of course, that you're just kidding about being a draft dodger. Actually, kids, W. J. Bryan 4th, like all the ballplayers on your favorite team, is a great American patriot, because you can't really ever make it to the big leagues if you're not patriotic and American, can you, W.J.? Now on another subject, when did you first realize that you were in love with baseball?"

"Actually, I don't like baseball very much, but I realized early in life that it was a good way to get into television. That's what I'd really like to do. If I can bat .350 the next few years I don't see how one of the networks can refuse to hire me. In the meantime, of course, baseball helps me sell a lot of books, so if broadcasting doesn't pan out I can always go into the publishing field."

"W.J., as one of the big bats expected to carry this club into the first division this season, would you tell the fans of America, and especially the kid fans, what goes through your mind when you hoist the old lumber and walk up there to bat against one of the really great ones like Tom Seaver or Denny McLain?"

"Well, naturally, I'm thinking mostly about my hair and whether it looks attractive hanging out from under the awful dead weight of that plastic batting helmet. I'd hate to be photographed hitting the game-winning home run with my hair hanging lank under my chin like a wet horse tail."

"Before we close, W.J., what reply do you have for these critics who say that $375,000 a year is too much to pay an arrogant youngster to train for a career in television or publishing?"

"Hey, Bellclapper, you can really cut a guy, can't you? Talking like that about me over the air is going to cost you, Dad. My lawyers will call you tomorrow. My booking agent will blacklist 'Dugout Gasbaggery' all over the league. What's more, you're getting a whole chapter in my next book—"

"And that, sports fans, is the voice of the new breed, and this is Bill Bellclapper talking at you and saying, 'If you want to be a champ, you've got to live like a champ.' Now here is some great news about soap—"

Postscript

Draft dodging was raised to high art among the privileged classes during the Vietnamese War. W. J. Bryan 4th seems to have benefited from the National Guard scam, which was used by many professional sports teams to keep their athletes out of harm's way.

Since it was unlikely that any National Guard unit would ever be called for combat duty, team managements regularly had fans among the National Guard brass enroll draft-vulnerable players in the hometown teams' local units. Thus Guard officers could show their loyalty to the team, and patriotic duty could be fulfilled without the home team losing a player. While being abused for taking refuge in the Guard instead of facing the draft, Vice-President Dan Quayle was gentleman enough not to point out that he was simply following the example of some of the most macho guys in the country.

In 1971 when this piece was written, Bryan's $375,000 salary seemed fantastic. By 1990, with many baseball players making more than $3 million a year, Bryan's $375,000 would place him near the bottom of baseball's salary scale.

Bitter Medicine

I went to the hospital. The cashier stopped me at the door. "You can't afford to come in here," she said. This was not news. Nobody can afford to go to a hospital anymore. The cost of medical care is so high that the average patient sent to surgery for a tonsillectomy is bankrupt before the doctor can get around to his second tonsil. This is why so many Americans nowadays have one tonsil out and one tonsil in.

I told the cashier I didn't want any medical care, but was just visiting. Visitor's admission was $20, which, as the ticket taker observed, was $5 cheaper than an orchestra seat for Liza Minelli's latest musical. The elevator ride was $7, so I used the stairs, which cost only $5.

At the top of the climb I was inhaling deeply. Technicians hurried me to an inhalation-testing room where a breath analyzer established that I was inhaling, in addition to air, the odors of floor wax, ether, iodine, toilet disinfectant, gift fruit baskets and adhesive tape.

Floor-wax odor cost me $10; ether, $50; iodine, $25; disinfectant, $20; gift fruit baskets, $15; and adhesive tape, $20. The air was free. There was a $100 charge for use of the inhalation-testing room, a $75 charge for use of the breath analyzer, and a $30 charge for the paper on which the bill was written. Naturally, I had to pay by check, having neglected to take out major hospital inhalation coverage.

Two guards restrained me in a corner of the corridor while a nurse phoned the bank to make sure I was not a bad-check artist. I was charged $40 for the guards, $25 for use of the corner, $10 for the telephone call, and $50 for the clean bill of financial health.

I went along the corridor toward the room occupied by my friend, a wealthy entrepreneur who had swallowed a fishbone during an expense-account lunch. For use of the corridor I was charged $50. Use of the overhead lights in the corridor cost me $20, and use of the heat from the radiators, $30. Since it would have cost $150 to enter my friend's room I stood outside and looked through the open door. Use of the open door for this purpose cost $15.

My friend was not there.

"Where is the man who swallowed the fishbone?" I asked a nurse. "The charge for information is $130," she said with an apologetic smile. The charge for the smile was $25 and the charge for its apologetic character was $40.

By this time, my bank balance was so low I was afraid I wouldn't be able to afford an exit. In fact, I would have made a run for the stairs and taken my chances against the accountant and treasurer if at that moment my wealthy friend had not appeared around a corner, fully dressed and sobbing.

His story, like the annals of the poor, was short and simple. He had been wiped out, possibly ruined. The fishbone had proved more elusive than the doctors had anticipated. They had been compelled to go into the esophagus, then into the stomach before they removed it.

By that time, however, his bank accounts had been consumed; his insurance exhausted; his airplane, yacht and cars sold at auction; and his estates in Maine, Delaware and Venezuela all lost. Though he had become penniless on the operating table, the hospital had refused to put him out until his incisions had been sewed and had even permitted him to keep the expensive clothes in which he had entered the place.

This, the hospital explained, was in line with medical ethics, for which the charge was $1,500. This friend has always been highly strung and it was not surprising that he broke down and wept in the administration office when told that, though a pauper, he had received the best medical care in the world.

The charge for use of the administration office was $100. The charge for weeping was $150. The administrator said he would waive the $300 charge for breaking down and send the rest of the bill to a collection agency. Escorting us to the door, he presented my friend with a gift from the hospital—a tin cup and a dozen pencils—and a piece of advice.

"Next time, get a divorce," he said, in a humorous vein. "It's cheaper than swallowing fishbones."

The charge for the tin cup was $50; for the pencils, $30; for the advice, $100, and for the humorous vein, which had been transplanted from a patient who had been hounded to death by a collection agency, $15,000.

Just Keep It to Yourself

He was wearing a $500 jacket and a cashmere sweater that would have had "Big Bucks" written all over it if it hadn't been too highbrow to carry on like a T-shirt.

He had just stepped out of a house that looked like about $3 million, though you couldn't tell from the front how big the swimming pool was or how many tennis courts it had.

With him came a dog that had been to one of the best dog finishing schools, as you could see from the blasé way it conducted itself in the company of a $500 jacket. You could tell that the man's first name was Edmond and that he liked to be called Ed, but hated being called Eddie.

He seemed to be taking the pooch for a walk, but I knew he was going to start talking before he got very far. Probably about dog biscuits, I figured, or tick removers. When you see a man walking vigorously during the television commercial pauses these days it's a lead-pipe cinch he is going to start chewing your ear.

This is the legacy of Lee Iacocca. Ever since Iacocca became famous as a vigorous talking walker on TV, television barkers have all walked while they talk.

Ed talked about his money. I am nervous with people who talk about their money. They intend either to make you feel guilty for not lending them $20, or to depress you by letting you know they've got enough to buy and sell you five times over.

Ed belonged to the latter school. Having glimpsed his house, jacket, sweater and dog, you didn't need to be told he was rolling in mighty sweet clover, but Ed was the kind of man who tells you anyhow.

The worst of it was, he didn't look a day older than twenty-

246

three, and since his civilized wardrobe made it clear that he was not in the rock-star profession, I assumed Ed must have inherited his millions.

Well I was wrong, because right away he looked me straight in the eye and announced that once he had been dumb and poor because he paid a lot of his money in taxes. Now he had got smart and rich.

It seems he had hired an outfit in the tax-dodging business, which had shown him how to keep his money for himself instead of contributing some of it to help defend the country, make life less miserable for the afflicted and provide police protection for the luxurious community he infested.

Then he said something like, "What matters is not how much you make, you half-wit. It's how much you keep."

With that he strolled away and dropped an envelope in the mailbox. It was his tax return. Ed hadn't come out to walk his dog and talk tick remover. He had come out to mail his tax return and boast that he was home tax free.

I was stunned by this squalid spectacle of a deadbeat so shameless that he was willing to boast about being a rotten citizen, so stunned that I missed the name of the company that had helped him achieve such disgrace.

A few nights later, though, Ed and his uptown dog appeared again looking like several million dollars. Again Ed headed for the mailbox with the tax return that would break the President's poor heart. Again he leered at me.

"So, you poor sap, still boobing it up by the tube instead of huddling with experts who can show you how to evade your obligations to the country without breaking a single law, eh?"

"But Ed," I cried, "don't you feel like a rotten human being when you realize you haven't even contributed to the cost of stopping the elm blight in these incredibly beautiful trees gracing this fantastically lovely street you live on?"

"Wise up, creep," he said. "It's not how much you make. It's how much you keep, and I keep it all."

Again he was gone before I caught the name of the expert tax finaglers who had furnished him in cashmere and canine elegance.

Nights passed. No Ed. Perhaps he had learned shame. Maybe he had remembered something his poor dead mother told him years ago, I said to myself one night by the TV set, when, lo, who popped out of a $3 million house wearing a $500 jacket accompanied by a finishing school dog. . . ?

"Sure I remember what the old lady told me," he said. "'Sonny boy,' she said, 'don't ever let the bleeding hearts tell you there's anything wrong with beating the tax leeches out of every cent you can, as long as you keep it legal.'"

Yes, yes, I realized too late that those were the words any truly loving American mother would have whispered to her son with her final breath.

Next time Ed showed up I apologized for having thought of him as a cheap deadbeat. I had been a fool not to lay in plenty of depreciation and untaxable income, I confessed, and so had missed the secret of happiness. Could he guide me back to the right path?

"It's not how much you make," said Ed. "It's how much you keep."

Killing Beethoven

One day a giant who lived in a castle in the sky dropped some magic seeds out the window. Upon waking next morning, he was astonished to see a huge beanstalk outside his window and, upon looking down, he saw that the beanstalk was rooted far below in the earth.

"What do you make of that beanstalk?" the giant asked his wife at breakfast.

"It's an open invitation for cat burglars to climb up here and steal the hen that lays golden eggs," she said.

"I'll fix that," said the giant, and took his pruning shears to the window.

Jack, having climbed heroically, had almost reached the window when he saw the giant lean out with the shears. "Hold on there, friend!" he shouted to the giant. "I have a free toaster for you."

The giant, who was a Reagan man, had already heard that there was no free lunch and believed it, and from that philosophical premise he had gone on to the conclusion that there were no free toasters either. Startled by seeing his philosophy confounded, he let Jack in the window and they fell into long conversation. Jack was working his pocket calculator when the giant's wife interrupted.

"Why aren't you at the piano working on your new symphony?" she asked the giant.

"There's more to life than writing symphonies," said the giant. "Do you realize we could be getting more than twelve percent interest, tax free up to $2,000, simply by letting a bank hold the hen's golden eggs for one year?"

"Plus this marvelous toaster absolutely free," said Jack.

The giant's wife glared in disapproval. "Interest is for loan sharks, bankers and the Swiss," she told him. "Giants can't beat the gnomes of Zurich at their own game."

To please his wife, the giant sent Jack back down the beanstalk and sat at the piano to wrestle with the theme for his largo movement, but he was unable to concentrate on the music. Each half note he struck reminded him that half the profits of a successful symphony could be taxed away unless he sheltered his income.

That night while his wife slept the giant slipped down the beanstalk with his hen and phoned Jack, who put him in touch with a tax lawyer named Ben.

Next morning his wife discovered the hen was missing when she went for two eggs to boil for breakfast. "Calm down," the giant said. "Jack has the whole week's supply of eggs in an All Savers account and Ben is putting the hen in a tax shelter."

His wife asked what they were going to eat.

"High off the hog from now on," the giant replied. "No more of those golden eggs sunny side up, golden eggs poached, golden eggs over easy and scrambled. From now on, baby, it's caviar off the foldout table in the Mercedes. Our nest hen is sheltered. With Ben's know-how I can make a million off the new symphony and Uncle Sam will still owe me money."

The giant felt so good about high tax-free interest and tax

dodges that he didn't work on his symphony all day, or the next day, or the next week. His wife was berating him for giving up his work when Ben dropped in via the beanstalk.

"Giving up the piano is the smartest thing you've done all week, big fellow," Ben said. "In symphonies you gain from nothing with the new tax code. You need a new line of work."

"My husband is an artist," said the wife.

"The Medicis are dead, madam," Ben explained. "Art is no longer a government-supported activity. If Michelangelo were living today he wouldn't be chipping marble. He'd be depreciating the quarry."

On Ben's advice the giant gave up symphony writing and undertook a career at depreciating his hen. It was such lucrative work that he was able to afford six telephones and sat around the castle all day telephoning New York, Europe and Asia about the price of golden-egg layers and minute fluctuations in the interest rate.

One day between calls he wandered over to the piano and tried to play "Chopsticks," but discovered he had forgotten the fingering. On a whim he decided to go down the beanstalk and take a few piano lessons. After descending, however, he found that all the piano teachers were tied up watching their money funds, and he started up the beanstalk, planning to purchase Vladimir Horowitz with his tax-free interest savings.

Months of sedentary telephone labor had left the giant so weakened that he faltered half a mile up the beanstalk and crashed fatally to earth. He has depreciated nicely ever since.

Those Killer Bills

Speaking of money, friend, when is the last time you paid your own hotel bill? With your own money, I mean. If, like me, you haven't done so for years, you are in for a shock when you go down to the cashier, say, "My bill, please," and receive a document stating that you owe $128.58. And not for an entire week's stay either.

Yes, it is now possible to owe $128.58 for spending a single night in a hotel. I am not making this up. For one night, $128.58! I did it recently: $128.58. In my first full-time job I had to work four weeks to earn $128.58.

Sure, I realize money has decayed since then. The dollar is no longer a dollar; we must think of it as a trifle, like the Yugoslavian dinar, the Polish zloty. Usually it is easy to do so, because the dollars we toss around like play money are not our very own dollars.

Consider the typical medical bill. Persons with very little money are regularly presented with medical bills so stupendous that they ought to fall prostrate and expire in front of hospital cash registers, yet they do not. Why? Because medical bills usually don't have to be paid with one's very own money. Insurance companies pay them, or possibly the Government. Most people probably don't even look very closely at these killer bills.

Same with hotel bills. Nowadays, hotels work on the theory that every guest in the house is on an expense account, and that anyone who isn't is either filthy rich or insane. It is the expense-account guest who establishes the market, though. If it's not the guest's money that's being spent, why should the guest care how heavily you soak whoever is paying his way?

Many hotels and restaurants, in fact, raise their prices to outrageous levels to satisfy their customers since expense-account people find that the more contemptuously they treat other people's money, the more the world admires them.

I have always been too small-time for the lavish life. This is why the hotel bill recently paid with my very own money was only for $128.58, for in New York, where I paid this breathtaking bill, hotels for truly gracious expense-account living may charge $128.58 for a haircut, and another $50 if you want a singe.

This hotel, though, is modest by Manhattan standards. I'd stayed there before, but always on expenses, so was unprepared for the pain when the cashier presented the bill to be paid with my very own money.

"$128.58? This can't be my bill."

He insisted it was. I studied it. The room price was $110. Amazingly, there was an added charge of $9.08 listed as "State Sales Tax."

"This sales tax, it's wrong," I said. "I didn't buy anything in the hotel."

"The State of New York considers you purchased the use of a room for one night and, therefore, became liable for sales tax on a $110 purchase," said the cashier.

"So what's this extra $5.50 you added for 'Occupancy Tax'?"

"That," said the cashier, "is New York City's recently imposed five percent occupancy tax. It is levied on all hotel rooms."

Did he mean to say that the State of New York, after taxing me $9.08 for purchasing the use of the room, had then authorized New York City to tax me $5.50 for occupying it? Did the State of New York expect me to purchase the use of a room and not occupy it?

Did the State of New York think people traveled to Manhattan and rented a hotel room so they could stand out on the sidewalk all night pointing to the hotel and telling passers-by, "I've purchased the use of a room in that hotel but have no intention of occupying it"?

The cashier said there was no point in becoming hysterical.

"Do you mean if I hadn't occupied the room they'd have charged me a nonoccupancy tax, and then there would have been some point in getting hysterical?" No reply.

And what was this $4 added to the $9.08 state sales and the city's recently imposed $5.50 occupancy tax, bringing the total tax to $18.58 or about 17 percent on the room?

"That," said the cashier, "is New York City's old occupancy tax."

I said committing occupancy must be considered a terrible, addictive vice in New York since they seemed to tax it as heavily as liquor and cigarettes.

"There is no need to be bitter, sir," said the cashier. "Your expense-account auditor will understand and forgive our local tax gouges."

"But I'm not on expenses," I sobbed.

He gasped, went white, recoiled. "Paying your very own money? Surely . . . surely you joke! It's not done. Just isn't . . . ever . . . done. . . ." He swayed alarmingly, and collapsed prostrate before the cash register. I didn't stay to see if he expired. If he did I imagine he paid a stiff expiration tax.

Backward Reels the Mind

So many things work in reverse nowadays. "Saturday Night Fever" is an example. It took fire as a record and turned into a movie. Movies used to turn into records, then into posters, then into T-shirts, then into bubble gum.

Richard Nixon's memoirs, a $2 million publishing enterprise, began as a Presidency. Presidencies used to begin as books and still do—Jimmy Carter's "Why Not the Best?" for example—but nowadays the book that turns into a Presidency seems to be merely a small part of the grander plan to turn the Presidency into a multimillion-dollar book bonanza.

Although Mr. Nixon is being abused for this, he is not the first to do the trick. Lyndon Johnson took an agreeable sum from C.B.S. for a book-and-television contract. Gerald Ford and Henry Kissinger turned public eminence into dandy financial incomes from N.B.C. television. So many of the Watergate gang have converted crime into hard covers that it sometimes seems the whole Watergate business was a publishing scheme to turn Government workers into big-selling authors. Even Calvin Coolidge published an autobiography. It was slender.

More surprising, perhaps, was Julius Caesar's innocence about the financial possibilities of public office at the time he wrote his history of the conquest of Gaul. This may have been because Caesar had an out-of-date agent at the time he went to Gaul, an old-timer known as Marcellus of Naples.

Being of restless temperament, Caesar had decided to conquer Gaul for the exercise. "Why Gaul?" asked Marcellus. "Because it's there," Caesar said. Marcellus advised him to keep some notes for a possible book. These were the basis of his great work which he summarized in the words "I came, I saw, I conquered," thereby establishing a level of immodesty from which he never lapsed.

The book was a small *succès d'estime* and attracted the attention of Flavius of Syracuse, the hottest agent in the Republic. "With your ego and that clipped prose style," Flavius wrote him, "you are ready for the big bucks, Caesar." (I translate freely from the Latin here; Flavius's precise words were "ready for the big *denariuses,*" the *denarius* being the coin in which royalties were paid.)

Caesar, meanwhile, had become restless again and was planning to conquer Dacia or Cappadocia as soon as he found out which had the more agreeable climate. Flavius made a personal call.

"Julius," he said, "the book on Gaul bombed because the Roman reader is bored with places like Gaul. Say 'Gaul' to the average Roman, he thinks you're talking about his bladder. Dacia and Cappadocia—worse. They sound like somebody sneezing."

"My business is conquering places, not selling books," Caesar replied.

"Then conquer something interesting," Flavius proposed. "Something that will give you a book so big you can retire afterward and spend the rest of your life rolling in *denariuses.*"

Caesar asked what. Flavius said Rome. "Move into Rome, toss out the Senate and make yourself Emperor."

Caesar pointed out that this would change the course of history. "History, schmistory!" scoffed Flavius. "The purpose of history is best-sellers. Anyhow, after you've got material for the book you can retire to Capri and turn it all back over to the Senate."

The idea tempted Caesar. History, after all, would take care of itself, but who would take care of Caesar in his old age when the *denariuses* stopped coming in from the public payroll? What's more, the climate in Rome was more congenial than Dacia's or Cappadocia's, and the headwaiters at the best restaurants all knew him.

He told his friends Brutus and Cassius and urged them to get in touch with Flavius who could steer them into the kind of public activities that paid off in royalties. They misunderstood. Unaware that Caesar intended to overthrow the Republic only long enough to get material for his big book, they assassinated him while he was in the midst of telling them what his contract provided.

He was speaking of the five research assistants, ten scribes, free parchment and gorgeous office space provided by his publisher, but he had saved the best for last. "Et tu, Brutus," he grinned, referring to the two-million-*denarius* advance. The knives fell, but a great tradition had been born.

It was Shakespeare who finally cashed in on Caesar's big book. Shakespeare could have made ten times as much if he had overthrown Queen Elizabeth instead of fooling around with the theater, but he was afraid his writing style would ruin him in politics. He used subordinate clauses.

Penury Gets You Nowhere

We drove all day to New England. Desperate for rest, we came in the gray New England night to Hyannis, a vast conurbation of motels occupying what once was Cape Cod.

These were not motels where you backed the station wagon up to a door, shoveled children, turtles, cats, luggage and Grandmother into the room and were checked in by an owner who forecast fog with the help of his corns and offered a pull at his private bourbon bottle by way of welcome.

They don't make motels like that anymore, so we pulled into one that looked slightly smaller than Kennedy Airport. My first impressions were of glass, glitz and grandeur.

A survey of the parking spaces suggested there might be a vacant room or two, and possibly as many as 1,500. This promised big bargains. Not for nothing do my children refer to me, when they think I'm out of earshot, as "Old El Cheapo."

On this journey I had left the children behind after explaining that people in their thirties couldn't go everyplace Mommy and Daddy went. Thus I had only my wife to exult at after seeing those acres of empty parking space. This was not entirely satisfactory since my wife was not reared on the wisdom of Benjamin Franklin. Her motto is "A penny saved is worthless, but a credit card is a swell day in town."

So when I said the motel would be so glad to see us that we might get a room for $15, she said, "New England in October is colder than the shores of the Baltic."

"Meaning?" I said.

"Get a room, not a pup tent by the swimming pool," she said.

I pulled up behind a gigantic German car suitable for delivering Conrad Veidt and Erich von Stroheim to depraved parties in Berlin. I estimated the car's value at $82,000 new, which it was.

Through the lobby's glass doors I could see the car's occupants checking in. They were dressed in the sinister leathery-tweedy style. This, combined with their vast Teutonic automobile, betrayed them as a team of television technicians, doubtless sent into the New England gray to shoot a TV commercial for pneumonia.

Such people tend to run up prices, since they are making free with other people's money, but I was cheered, upon entering the lobby, to hear the room clerk say, "Yes, the discount will be given to all three of you."

Men after my own heart, I thought, taking their place at the desk. A room for the night? Yes, luckily for me, there did happen to be a room for the night. The price was $125.

"But that's without the discount," the clerk said.

"And how much discount are you offering?"

"What discounts are you entitled to?" she replied.

"I'm entitled to the same discounts everybody else is entitled to," I said, probably too belligerently.

"Of course, sir." She was putting on the voice she used for soothing maniacs until the police arrived. "I mean, do you claim the senior citizen's discount, a corporate discount or a regular-customer discount?"

"I'll take them all," I said.

"May I see your discount cards, please?"

I don't have any discount cards. I am not a senior citizen and refuse to become one. "I am a citizen," I said. "Neither junior, senior nor emeritus, but a citizen nevertheless. I will take the simple citizen's discount."

"There is no citizen's discount," she said. "Only a senior citizen's discount."

Astounding! "How do you expect me to afford to pay the Social Security taxes that support senior citizens if I cannot even get a citizen's discount?"

"Perhaps you are entitled to one of our big corporate discounts."

"Though owned by a corporation, I am myself not corporate, but merely human."

"I'm sorry," she said, "but there is no discount for human. Unless of course you carry the Attila the Hun International Motel Discount Card."

"Look," I said. "I'm cheap, my career is on the downhill slope, gin does nothing for me anymore, and I wish I'd headed south where it's warm instead of New England where it's gray. Isn't there something there that qualifies me for a discount?"

The police were entering now. My wife was right behind. "How much?" she asked.

The clerk said $125. "Sold," said my wife, handing over a credit card and making my banker's day by adding another 18 percent to the cost of living on the wrong side of the discount gap.

The Whats Ride Up Front

People who regularly sit back in steerage when they make an airplane voyage often ask what goes on among us elegant folk up in first class after the curtains are drawn. Baccarat at $16,000 a hand, the laying of lascivious hands on the stewardess, exchanges of inside stock-exchange information worth a king's ransom—such are the impressions of our activities likely to be drawn by second-class passengers when they see the curtain being dropped to shield us from second-class prying.

Romantic as these illusions may seem, they are not half so interesting as what we are really up to.

The first thing we all do, as soon as the cabin is sealed and the second-class passengers are curtained off behind us, is laugh. Sitting there with our seat belts fastened, observing the no smoking sign, we have a good laugh.

What we are laughing at is the dumbness of the passengers in second class. They are so dumb that they think we are stupid enough to pay higher fares than they pay just to ride in first class, when actually, we are not paying anything at all.

Except for Rothschilds and madmen, all first-class passengers travel on expense accounts. Our companies pay for our tickets and take a tax deduction for a business expense. Result: Due to our flying first class, Uncle Sam's income declines; to make it up, he raises the tax rate on the kind of people who fly second class.

So, we are riding in the best seats in the machine, free. Thanks to the crowd in second class who are paying the bill. And they do not even have enough capacity for outrage to ask why they have to pay extra for their drinks while ours come free.

258

Who would not laugh?

After the good laugh, we all get acquainted, and the process sounds like this:

"I'm in insurance."

"Well, I'm in automobiles."

"Automobiles, eh? I'm a brilliant young scientist myself."

And we all tell each other what institutions own us.

"I'm with Ford."

"Oh, yeah, well I'm with Bank of America, see!"

"Who cares? I happen to be a brilliant hard-nosed young White House insider with rave notices in Newsweek magazine."

We in first class have corporate identity by the yard. If you, incidentally, happen to lack strong corporate identity, you may not be altogether happy in first class.

A few years ago on a flight between Seattle ("I'm in airplanes") and Dallas ("I'm with Consolidated Tax Shelters"), there was a man with such a weak corporate identity that when the passenger beside him asked who he was, he told him who he was.

Occasionally, you see, the stranger beside you says "Who are you?" instead of "Who are you with?" or "What are you in?" or "What do you do?" This does not mean that he wants to know who you are. It is simply his way of asking you to define your position in corporate America, to give an indication of your relative corporate importance and, in general, to let everyone know whether you have a vital position in one of the more revered American bureaucracies and, therefore, deserve attention, or whether you can be ignored for lack of corporate status.

Well, the passenger turned to the man and asked, "Who are you?"

And the fellow replied, "Being incurably romantic, I like to fancy myself a frustrated poet, but the fact, I am afraid, is that I am merely a failed idealist, made unduly melancholy by the passage of too many fruitless years, though not so melancholy that I no longer love women nor hate what old men do to the young, nor . . ."

"There is a passenger with us who will not say what organization he is with," cried the man beside him.

The stewardess urged us not to be alarmed, but other passengers were crowding into the aisle. Angry cries rang through the compartment.

"If he's got nothing to be ashamed of, why doesn't he identify his bureaucracy?"

"What are you anyhow, mister," asked an assistant to the executive secretary of a large chain of private police shops.

"I'm not a what," the offender explained. "A what is a thing, or a part of a thing. A who is a person. I am a who."

Here was a pariah without shame, and we let him know how we felt. We explained that everybody had to be a part of a thing to qualify for first class. And that if anyone chose to ignore his whatness out of false pride in a dubious whoness, we would rather not talk to him. It left all of us depressed all the way to Dallas ("I'm in oil depletion").

A Taxpayer's Prayer

Prayer to a baleful god:

O mighty Internal Revenue, who turneth the labor of man to ashes, we thank thee for the multitude of thy forms which thou hast set before us and for the infinite confusion of thy commandments which multiplieth the fortunes of lawyer and accountant alike.

For thy mercy in granting us exemptions for our beloved kin, we thank thee. Blessed be thy computer. Praised be thy everlasting mercy which taketh not all, but leaveth a sweet residue wherewith to render thanks to state and city.

Grant that this sacrifice not be found insufficient unto thy auditor. Let our arithmetic be correct, that thy computer not rise up in fury to smite us with thy dreadful penalty and interest payments.

O thou, who springeth from the tender loins of the Senate

Finance Committee and the ever-powerful House Ways and Means Committee, thou who setteth a full Pentagon before us, strike us not if we have failed to sign our returns on the proper line.

Bless and keep our Social Security numbers that we may never forget them, lest we lose the power to communicate with thee.

Though thy mercy be exceedingly finite, extend it, we pray thee, to our deductions, so that we may continue to walk in the dark shadow of the landlord and fear no eviction.

Grant that the sums we have spent upon lawyers to interpret thy word be not misspent, and that the sums we have made over to mathematicians to do thy calculus be not misplaced. Yea, though we falter in meeting thy wishes, it is not by wanton intent to deceive but by our poor want of appreciation of thy marvelous law, which surpasseth all understanding.

Lay thy blessing upon our file cabinets and upon the receipts therein. Look upon our records and find them faithfully kept and lovingly stored against the time of the audit.

Have pity upon us for the illnesses that failed to generate sufficient medical expenses to qualify us for medical deductions.

All this we ask in full humility, O Internal Revenue, for we know the awful scourge thy power can lay upon the arrogant and the deceitful. Grateful are we for the toil thou grantest us to perform untaxed, for thus we are enabled to continue enjoying coffee and pants with which to shelter the leg against the winter's blast.

Of every five days' labor, two are performed for thy sake, and for the sake of Governor and of Mayor, but of all these, thy share is the greatest.

Let Monday and Tuesday of every week satisfy thee, O great taxer. Grant that we not be asked to give thee Wednesday, too. Look upon our oil bills and take not our Wednesdays, we pray thee.

If we offend thee, stay thy fury. Send not thy dread agents with their powerful liens to seize our cars and our places of abode and our pants.

Let not thy prosecutors bind us in chains, but content thyself with lashing us with penalties and interest payments, and leaving us our cars and our pants, wherewith we may travel from bank to bank in decent mode to beg the sustenance you require.

Look upon us, O Internal Revenue, and see our terror, and know that thou art mighty while we are mere impecunious clay on a dark passage from earned income to Social Security with no tax shelter to protect us along the way.

Grant us indulgence, if not deduction, for our depreciation, which proceeds faster with the passing years.

Touch us with the blessing of the advantageous rate on capital-gains income. Give us the joy of tax-free municipal bonds.

Let us be a gigantic corporation so that we may plow all our income back into developing ourselves and owe only $18.63 in tax.

Amen.

The Easiest Money

Ronald Reagan came out of the White House rested up and raring to go. During his first week out in the world of free enterprise he signed up to write a memoir, compile a book of his speeches and go on the lecture circuit.

Ron, old buddy, believe me on this one because I know what I am talking about. You were entitled to pay me no mind when I told you how to run the country, and I didn't resent it, because as my relatives all asked at one time or another, "How many countries have you run, big shot?"

What you are getting into now, though, I do know about. I have done the lecture circuit. I have written memoirs. I have compiled collections of past utterances.

Any one of these things can be done without killing yourself. A man with incredible stamina could even do two of them without breaking down. But nobody, Ron, nobody can do all three, including fellows who can't get through a cabinet meeting without nodding off.

First, I'd forget the lecturing. The papers say you can get maybe $50,000 per lecture. Wow, they say: That's good pay for thirty minutes of idle chatter. But is it?

Before you even see the $50,000, a lecture agent takes 30 percent. Leaves you $35,000. Half of the $35,000 then goes to various governments in taxes, plus interest, penalties and psychic costs of being menaced and browbeaten by auditors of aforesaid governments. Leaves you $17,500.

If Bush really leaves the tax rate on big incomes at 28 percent (unlikely), you could net even more than $17,500. Provided, of course, your home state, city and county don't boost their own rates to compensate for what Washington no longer sends them.

All right, even $17,500 isn't bad for thirty minutes' work. Except you can't do it in just thirty minutes, because getting to the job site almost certainly means flying.

Ron, baby, have you used any of the commercial airlines since the deregulating experts got through with them? It can take all day to get to a $17,500 job, and all day can be forever when you spend it wondering if one of the engines might drop off en route. Then, after you do the job you've got to fly all over again to get home.

To make things worse, everybody will think you're getting away with the whole $50,000 mentioned in the papers. They don't know about the agent's $15,000. Don't know about the President's, the Governor's, the mayor's and the County Commissioners' $17,500.

"He is disgustingly overpaid," they will say, never realizing that you are not disgustingly overpaid, just outrageously overpaid. Sad to say, Ron, but a lot of misinformed, envious people are going to start disliking you.

Who needs lecturing at $17,500 a time when you can stay home—no dreary airports, no antique engines, no missed connections at O'Hare Airport—and work on the memoir for $5 million.

That's only the papers' guess about what you're getting for

the memoir, but let's say it's merely $3 million for the memoir while the other $2 million is for the collection of old speeches.

Even the mere $3 million for the memoir makes it senseless to use up your time, energy and luck lecturing at $17,500. Here's why: Unlike the lecture agent who takes 30 percent, a literary agent takes only 10 percent. Leaves you $2.7 million. Set aside half for taxes. Leaves you $1.35 million.

To make that much money on the lecture circuit, you'd have to deliver seventy-seven lectures. That means at least 154 airplane trips, but probably lots more than that, with hundreds of hours of additional plane-change agony at O'Hare, Atlanta, etc.

Obviously, smart ex-Presidents will stay home and do the memoir. Except that writing a memoir is no fun because first you have to learn to work a word processor. Then you have to sit alone in a room with the shades drawn, not talking to anybody, just studying the inside of your skull, going through old papers, thinking about the past.

Thinking about the past, reading old documents, never able to talk to anybody while you work—this is the road to deep depression, to Outer Melancholia. Who needs $1.35 million that bad, right, Ron?

Especially when the collection of old speeches will earn you $2 million. Subtract agent's 10 percent, leaves $1.8 million. Subtract half for taxes, leaves $900,000.

The beauty part? You don't even have to write the speeches. You never had to write the speeches. Somebody else wrote them for you, remember? All you have to do is paste them together and mail them to the printer, then nod off until the check comes in. It's your kind of work, baby.

PLACES I'VE BEEN

In 1963 and 1964 I spent a lot of time traveling around the country. The column was still an infant, and I was trying different things, searching for congenial material.

At that time the hippies were still around and criss-crossing the continent for the pure joy of getting away from wherever it was they came from. They were the vanguard of something new that was shaking Americans out of their staid 1950ish contentment. It was all right to say you were going in search of America, not pompous as it would sound nowadays.

My travels lacked the romance of the hippies' adventures with jalopy and motorcycle. I was thirty-seven, thirty-eight years old, married, and had three children and a mortgage. Most of the traveling was done by car, often with wife, children and heavy luggage. The car was usually a big Buick sedan. Sometimes I took the trains from the East Coast to Denver or Albuquerque and rented cars to go on to Oregon or California.

I took the children on a couple of cross-country train trips, too. It seemed important that they see the country at ground level so they wouldn't grow up thinking it was as small and boring as a six-hour airplane snooze through cloudland. I wanted them to realize what a tremendous journey it had been for people to cross a continent with horse-drawn wagons. I was in love with the grandeur and variety of America and wanted the children to be touched by it too.

The goal of these travels was to find material for newspaper columns of the "Whither America?" type. I soon discovered it was useless for column purposes to wander casually around chatting with people casually met. This produced the sort of material

267

provided by a farmer in Ohio who, asked what he thought were the great problems facing America, talked for twenty minutes about a boom in the crow population. Stopping for lunch in southern Indiana, I discovered a region where they served your hamburger slathered in mayonnaise unless you told the waitress to hold the mayo. I gave up the hunt for revelation and wrote low-pressure reports on the places I was passing through.

Reading these pieces twenty-five years later, I was struck by a sense of calm that seemed to suffuse them. As it turned out, this was the ominous calm before the storm, for the great disasters of the 1960's and 1970's were already in the air.

The earliest of these columns were written a few months before the assassination of President Kennedy. Even then, we were already in the Vietnam War, though oblivious to what that could mean. In California Richard Nixon, having just lost his bid for the governorship, had held his "last press conference" and told the reporters "you won't have Nixon to kick around anymore" because he was through with politics. Scattered around the country were faint hints that conservatism was being reborn, very faint hints. In Florida the Federal treasury was pouring billions into the project for landing men on the moon, and nobody was saying we couldn't afford it.

The possibility that conservatives would actually run the Government someday, that Nixon would ever return from the dead, that Vietnam would tear the country as nothing had torn it since the Civil War, that we would not only land men on the moon but do it so often that Americans would complain about having their soap operas interrupted for live TV from the moon—all this was inconceivable when I was thirty-eight, thirty-nine years old and listening to talk of crows and showing my children America from the dome car of the California Zephyr.

For this reason, these pieces felt to me like the news from America at the final moment of its age of glory. So I was startled when a friend said the impression with which they left him was of a time of almost unremitting bleakness.

"Instead of feeling like 'the news from America at the final moment of its age of glory,'" he wrote, "they seem to me like a frightening depiction of the barrenness and sterility that, quite apart from the Vietnam War, made some sort of revolution or violent protest inevitable within the decade."

So I read them again and thought maybe he had a point. Maybe that talk about an "age of glory" was just sentimental malarkey produced by discovering these reports from the time of my youth. It is terribly easy to confuse one's youth with the nation's age of glory.

Reader, I leave it to you to judge.

Delaware Township, N.J.

The authentic American wilderness of the 1960's is not really in the primitive West any longer, but right here in Delaware Township. It is a wilderness of asphalt and exhaust gas, of neon monsters, roadside liquoramas and machines that do eerie things in the night.

This motel room, for example, has a slot machine beside the bed which, on receiving a quarter, activates machinery attached to the mattress. This is "The Famous Magic Fingers Massaging Assembly." Lie down, insert 25 cents and "it quickly carries you into the land of tingling relaxation and ease."

The children love it, as they love everything about this roadside world. Left to their own impulses, they would use up a month's allowance keeping the magic fingers massaging. Is there something unhealthy in letting children develop a taste for vibrating mattresses? In the old wilderness, they would have reveled in a bed of pine needles, but surely one must change with the times.

The new wilderness, of course, is not confined to Delaware Township. It flourishes all along the mid-Atlantic megalopolis in what used to be the rural or small-town areas separating the old cities of Washington, Baltimore, Philadelphia, New York and Boston.

Basically, it is Noplace-on-the-Highway. There are brand-new housing subdivisions along all the ridge lines and valleys, but the landscape is lonely and the atmosphere is heavy with the menace of savagery and violence. ("Criminal registration required," is the universal greeting sign in this section of Jersey.)

In all parts of the forest, the traveler is constantly harassed by the terrors of an unseen law. Signs warn of awful punishments for committing litter. Everywhere are stark warnings that speeders will lose their licenses. No one pays any attention, least of all the speeders.

Everybody cruises serenely at ten miles an hour over the posted limit, and the crank who doesn't becomes the object of intense motorist hostility. Out here in the dual-lane world, the man who stays on the speed limit is despised almost as deeply as the cad who wants to make a left turn or pull into traffic from a roadside frozen custard stand.

The driver who has not been on the road all winter quickly remembers the old lesson that, out here, you have to move with the pack or be hated. At twilight, when the nerves can stand it no longer, there is the welcoming motel sign.

The motel is never really any place at all, whether the stationery proclaims it Melbourne, Fla., or Ellsworth, Me. This one, for example, lies next to a filling station and a neon sign about forty feet high which says "Liquor."

A cellophane wrapper which says "This glass has been sanitized for your protection" also says that the location is Delaware Township. The landmarks confirm nothing. Down the road is the universal American roadside restaurant in the universal American glass-and-plastic architecture serving the universal American plastic roadside meal.

The motel, which the children find so exciting, is unpleasantly suggestive, despite all its comforts, of some science-fiction nightmare. The "sanitized" drinking glass, the "message light" on the phone that will start flashing red if there is a message. The barely audible breathing of invisible heat ducts.

And, outside the curtained glass wall, the distant cries of swimmers from the pool, which is domed in corrugated plastic and heated to permit year-round bathing.

And, worst of all, the children feeding quarters to the massaging mattress. It is probably unrealistic to expect them to prefer a bed of pine needles, but it would be comforting to see some of the values of the old wilderness preserved. The pursuit of happiness ought to end some place more ennobling than "the land of tingling relaxation and ease."

Cocoa Beach, Fla.

Life is strange here in the world of tomorrow, and the uninitiated visitor must expect to feel alien, lonely and baffled when he first arrives.

The men go barelegged and the women wear long pants. Everybody wears sunglasses, sleeps in a mechanically chilled air and talks in a new galactic slang.

Earnest bronzed men are forever saying things like "Gordo is in a very up condition" and announcing that they have just put a plastic liner in the sustainer turbo-pump. Weather forecasters sit around mumbling that they have three quarters of the earth "under surveillance."

Up the road at Cape Canaveral, the world of tomorrow becomes a futuristic landscape of radar dishes and gantry cranes busting out of a primitive waste of sand and palmetto where the armadillo and the rattlesnake still survive.

The billions that the Government is force feeding into the space program burst out of the Florida sand in gaunt extrusions of steel and concrete, and people are pouring into Brevard County to get at the moon payroll.

Approaching Canaveral by highway to the north, a motorist notices the changes in the tenor of the billboards just below Daytona Beach. Back there they are still absorbed in the America of the present—internal combustion engines at the race track, tourist homes, Whataburger stands.

But as the road heads, flat and fast, for Canaveral, signs testify to a border crossing. Edgewater, thirty-five miles north of

Cocoa, proclaims itself "Gateway to the Moon." Further on, Oak Hill, not to be outdone, introduces itself as "Gateway to the Universe."

At Cocoa there remain only vestigial traces of the tourist Florida, although on Cocoa Beach the motels are happy enough to entertain gawkers when there is no heavy rocket business afoot. Here, everything is earnest, urgent and ready for orbit.

This is a new Florida, and the big concentration of technicians may very possibly represent the truly new breed of American. (The New York Mets fan, surely, is an old-breed American.)

All this comes as a disappointment at first. The romance propagated about Cape Canaveral is misleading. The traveler comes as a pilgrim to see the poetry of man reaching for the stars; he finds instead a motel society built on cement blocks and nuts-and-bolts ideas.

Bureaucrat technicians, mimeograph machine specialists, public-relations men, motherly creatures in fishnet hose running the beer at the motel lounges, blond bombshells at dawn on the Cape's beaches—these are the people who impose personality on the world of tomorrow.

Very quickly, of course, the pilgrim becomes a vital realist. After his first twenty-four hours, he listens without outrage while a young engineer from Texas explains that "consumables" have been added to Cooper's capsule.

He knows it would be a serious mistake to ask what "consumables" are. It would produce a ten-minute lecture of staggering technicality. Helpful girls would appear with bales of old mimeographed press releases about "consumables."

He begins, at night, to look back upon his day as a time when he was "no go" on a morning shave, pecan pie at lunch and an afternoon swim, but "go" on beer with dinner and a trip to the motel gift shop.

By this time, he is no longer appalled when his beer is brought by the motherly creature in fishnet hose. He may even find himself striking up absurd conversations with engineers from Texas, to demonstrate a proper spirit.

"That electron flux measuring device in the capsule—does it have a pocket ion chamber?" Or, "In what orbit will the xenon light cease to be visible to the astronaut?"

They all reach this stage. When they do, they're solid citizens of the world of tomorrow.

Cocoa Beach, Fla.

Eventually the rockets will arrive and depart with timetable regularity.

A new generation of home owners will curse the noise and sue. Clocks will be set by the coming and going of the Mars Express. Small boys will be bored silly by old codgers rummaging through faded memories.

"You won't believe this, boy, but I can remember when the whole world used to come here and hold its breath, back when the first man went into space—"

Right now the rockets are risky vessels which run on uncertain schedules and produce strange emotions in the crowds that come to watch them. When there is a man aboard, as there was the other day when Gordon Cooper started his twenty-two orbits, the atmosphere is faintly suggestive of an Aztec sacrifice.

The eve is celebrated in revelry. Dawn finds the traffic bumper to bumper for miles leading into Cape Canaveral. By 7 A.M. the sun is a furious blast of white heat in an iron sky.

Inside, the Cape is planet by Disney. Miles of bone-white sand and scrub brush. Here and there, dish-eyed radar on windowless block houses peers accusingly into your soul. At the press site, an old American ritual is in progress; a movie is being shot.

"All right," an authoritative voice bawls, "everybody look over toward the launch site." The press site is an artificially created mound carpeted in beautiful golf-greens sod. The mound is enclosed by a circular gray fence. Bleachers to the rear.

It suggests a dog show enclosure. Amplifiers boom the countdown news. An electrified world map winks the route proposed for Cooper. TV sets stand in the sunlight, camera batteries, telephones.

"Now, everybody look toward the launch site again," the movie producer commands. He is producing a film for N.A.S.A. It will illustrate the splendor of the press facilities. Cooper's rocket is a delicate silver tower silhouetted two miles across the scrub.

Cooper lies strapped on his couch waiting. Everyone is aware of the sacrificial role he must play if things go badly, but the thought remains unspoken. The reporters kill the minutes in gossip, and admire the strange ladies who have turned up in the enclosure with press badges.

One affects the costume of early Hollywood, all crepe and elbow-length gloves. Another wears yellow toreador pants, gold Aladdin shoes, yellow sport shirt, yellow sports hair.

The air is full of small talk. Television voices keep saying "tension is mounting." The amplifier smothers the drama in trivia. "Tension is mounting," says a radio voice. "Essentially all the redundancy has been dropped," a man on television is explaining.

When the amplifier announces only five minutes until launch, conversations run down. People move quietly to the bleachers. The clock ticks through a great quiet, and for the first time you stare at the silver tower and give yourself up to thinking about the man on his couch, with all that fire and thunder about to explode beneath him.

The final seconds are counted away. The rocket erupts, rises trembling on a blinding pillar of fire. The Hollywood lady clutches a handkerchief to her mouth. Standing, her whole body shudders as the Atlas rises, gathering speed and power.

A shock of sound roars across the sand. It is the infuriated snarl of a thousand express trains coming at you with open throttles. Television has never captured it, nor the blinding intensity of the rocket fire.

In two minutes it is over and out of sight. The amplifier is droning out vital statistics and humdrum quickly returns. We are already becoming temperamentally prepared for the day when the rockets will arrive and depart with timetable regularity.

But for ten minutes or so, most of us can still feel the adventure of what is happening here, and when we become old codgers we will bore small boys silly recounting it.

New York City

It must be the eternal hick in all of us that makes us feel ill at ease and bullied in New York. We contemplate a visit here with all the misgivings of rustics about to match wits with the devils of Babylon.

Englishmen have the same provincial qualms about venturing into London. Outlanders of the Augustan empire probably felt the same fears about a visit to Rome, and the ancient Egyptians about a weekend in Thebes.

New Yorkers, naturally, cannot understand why anyone should be put off by their city. It is doubtful if many New Yorkers even realize that these strangers in their midst are seething with inner misery, dreading the arrogance of waiters and smarting under the imagined snubs of bellhops.

There is no rational explanation for this, but it is an incontestible fact of American life. Back home, we are all city people nowadays. Still, New York is so firmly embedded in the American memory as the big city that it has a mythical existence which makes the other towns seem commonplace by contrast.

Recently, a new defense has been evolved. You tell yourself that it is not your part of the country that is provincial, but New York. "Most provincial place in America," the going cliché has it. Variations on the theme have it that New York has "lost its charm," "sold its soul" and "let its old spirit die."

And then, "The theater's dying." "Third Avenue is ruined." "Times Square is a honky-tonk." "Central Park after dark is a no man's land." Washington, which has recently been betraying pretensions to urbanity, has begun to tell itself that the great center of American civilization has shifted from the Hudson to the Potomac.

And yet, if this is so, why do we still feel the emotional tug when the sweep of the turnpike suddenly reveals the first distant tracery of delicate gray towers rising through the mist? Why do we strain to find a conversational opening to tell the New Yorker that Washington's National Gallery is really quite a match for the Metropolitan, or that San Francisco is more charming by far, or that he doesn't know what traffic is until he has driven the Los Angeles freeways?

The galling thing is that these revelations rarely disturb the New Yorker at all. Very likely, he will be delighted to hear them, for he rarely envies other towns and is usually pleased to hear that they are doing well. He may even tell you that New York is going to the dogs and cunningly balm your provincial ego by announcing that you are fortunate to be able to live in Chicago or Phoenix or Hagerstown, Md.

The most irritating thing of all is that New Yorkers really don't care what you say about their city. Years of research in this field have turned up only one example of big-city chauvinism worth mentioning. That occurred years ago when a New Yorker, after listening to the conventional catalog of gripes, finally balked at being told that it was impossible to get a decent martini here. "Why," he exploded, "you can get the best martini in the whole damn world in New York City!"

The outburst was uncharacteristic of the breed. On balance, they are tolerant of the rustic's edgy criticism because they rarely harbor repressed desires to live in Chicago, Washington or Hagerstown and have none of the small-town pride that makes the Chicagoan, the Washingtonian or the Hagerstowner bridle if you suggest that his city is less than the most.

It is this imperturbable New Yorker's confidence in his own town's urbanity that shakes the confidence of the visitor and leaves him seething with small-town envy.

And so, when the bellhop snarls at the tip, as bellhops will everywhere, it is magnified into a symbol of New York ruthlessness. When the clip is applied in a joint, as clips are applied in joints around the world, the victim feels that the city has had him.

It is the hick in him, probably, the part of his soul that has hated cities from the time of Ur. You can't relieve it by telling him that "New York is a summer festival."

New York City

"Go to New York," said the voice of authority. "Look at it with a fresh pair of eyes."

Following instructions, proceeded to Manhattan by car, carrying usual luggage, two boys (ages eight and ten) and one fresh pair of eyes. Arrived at dinnertime in Yorkville. Everybody speaking German, buying German newspapers, German phonograph records, German plane and boat tickets. Streets very bumpy.

Dickered with a sinister headwaiter at German restaurant about cut-rate children's portions. Ate German dinner (wiener schnitzel) while German band played tangoes. Waxed enthusiastic for boys. "Isn't this New York great!" "I want to ride a subway," said eight-year-old. And so to bed.

Next day, headed downtown by car. Streets very bumpy everywhere. Car headed instinctively down the most boring street in the world. Park Avenue. Miles of glass walls on either side reflecting each other back and forth across street.

Arrived unutterably depressed at Greenwich Village. Everybody wearing picturesque old clothes. Tried to infuse boys with sense of intellectual excitement in the atmosphere. "Look at all these wonderful alienated artists!" "Square," said the ten-year-old.

Cruised through maze of evil alleys looking for Mafia members to impress children. No luck. Older boy advised younger: "Anyhow, all the tough gangsters hang out in Chicago." Arrived at Mott Street. Everybody speaking Chinese, dashing from

Chinese shop to Chinese shop. Old men standing around look-ing full of ancient wisdom.

"Think of all these Chinese living right here in New York!" "Cool!" "When can we ride a subway?"

Splendid view of harbor traffic and Statue of Liberty from Battery. Gave boys last dime to view statue through binoculars. Binoculars broken. Gobbled dime, then refused to operate. Felt swindled. Kicked binoculars. Mayor Wagner ought to get binoc-ulars fixed and smooth out the streets.

Bumped uptown to Empire State Building. Swarms of peo-ple in lobby asking attendant, "Is this the Empire State Build-ing?" Exhilarating view from eighty-sixth floor. Tourists all joking uneasily about building collapsing. Observatory windows at 102d floor filthy and scarred with initials.

Boys demanded souvenir. Bought brass replica of building for outrageous $3.50. Can buy far superior brass statuette of Abraham Lincoln for only $1 at New Salem, Ill. Outrageous. Slept for forty minutes at Hayden Planetarium. Dined well ($14.73 plus tip). And so to bed.

Next day, rode subways to and from Staten Island ferry. Boys ecstatic. Subway less bumpy than streets, but extremely difficult to use for everybody but natives. Idea of subway maps on station walls apparently hasn't crossed Atlantic from London and Paris. Why doesn't Mayor Wagner get subway maps up and have the Empire State Observatory windows cleaned?

Showed boys typical New York rush hour. Millions of glassy-eyed persons striding ruthlessly through subterranean steam. Very impressive. At sunset, proceeded to Times Square, an oversize street carnival. Stalls doing brisk business in wed-ding veils, hot dogs, zircons. Everybody selling steak dinners for $1.19.

Wondered where people get the faces they wear to Times Square. Thousands and thousands of faces in every model. Hun-gry, imbecilic, subversive faces. Cunning faces. Faces that leer. Sad faces. Ruined faces. Faces that would stop at nothing. Such faces would never be permitted to stay overnight in Washington, where a face has to submit to security screening.

Noted boys taking undue interest in prurient movie posters. Treated them to $1.19 steak dinner. Tried to communicate human drama of New York. "There are eight million stories of hope and heartbreak all around us here, boys!"

"Next summer you've got to take us to Disneyland."

Charleston, W. Va.

The road to West Virginia slopes up from the seaboard through the moneyed green pastures of the Virginia hunt country, through Middleburg where the rich Yankee émigrés ride to hounds, past Atoka where the billboards advertise "Polo Every Sunday."

This is the American landscape as it should be. We instinctively recognize it from our daydreams and a hundred back issues of Holiday magazine. Emerald meadows and white board fences.

The morning air is sweet with the wafting perfume of folding money. The telephone lines hum with the voices of squires talking to their brokers and of consequential men checking up on Washington.

And then, as the road climbs another mountain, something odd happens very abruptly. Virginia is suddenly gone. The road loops insanely toward a bottomless valley, and the melancholy of the Appalachians descends in layers.

Here the landscape is no longer curried and combed, but beautiful in a savage way, except where people have laid hands on it, and in these places it is scarred and sad. Jagged wounds disfigure it where miners have stripped the mountains' skin away to get at the coal, and gray wastes are piled by the creek beds.

The houses are no longer graceful, but merely serviceable. The people are no longer picturesque, but just rather poorly dressed. And out of the air, the radio picks the lugubrious chant of the rockabilly singer and the churchmen urging West Virginia to send money to relieve the poverty of Hong Kong.

West Virginians are tired of being told how poor they are. Ever since President Kennedy's 1960 campaign here jolted the American conscience, people have been traveling up from the fat rich seaboard to cluck over dying towns and undernourished children and defeated men, and West Virginians developed the sensitivity of a poor relation who has had too much Sunday-morning solicitude from rich cousins.

One response has been an impulse to put the artifacts of poverty out of sight and accentuate the positive. Here in Kanawha County, for example, a campaign is under way to tear down more than 500 abandoned shacks that mar the countryside.

Governor Barron is positively ebullient and can reel off figures to prove that 1962 was the best year economically in West Virginia history, that unemployment is down more than 50 percent under his administration and that new industry is finally arriving to free the mountains from the smothering embrace of coal.

The official message from the Governor's office here is that "the outlook for West Virginia has never been better than it is right now." Perhaps this is true. It is difficult to argue with statistics, but there are still 50,000 people out of work here, and most of them are useless to the present American economy.

Others are working for $6 a day in hazardous nonunion mining operations, digging coal from mines that have been abandoned because they couldn't be worked profitably at union wages.

But the most obvious testimony about West Virginia lies along the main roads between the Virginia hunt country and prospering Charleston. All the evidence of the great American boom is missing.

There are no new housing subdivisions in the towns, no new shopping centers or supermarkets, no new glass facades, no new schools, none of the monstrous new farming machines, no glittering glass motels.

At Charleston in the west, all this begins again, but Charleston is on the fringe. In the central counties, with the out-of-date buildings and the people wearing out-of-date clothes, it becomes apparent that the future has leapfrogged the Appalachians.

In places like Clarksburg and Grafton and Jane Lew, the American from megalopolis has the uneasy sensation of being displaced in time. They stir old memories of Depression towns in the 1930's.

It nags at the mind, and the mountain air is heavy with the sense of a fundamental American failure.

Gettysburg, Pa.

The chemistry of the American soil is sinister. Drench it in the blood of patriots and it brings forth a frozen custard stand.

Gettysburg is no exception. The battlefield nowadays is ringed in neon, wax museums, dioramas, cycloramas, the new instant motels, gimcrack dispensaries, two-bit battle flags, brass busts of Old Abe, tin bayonets and all the other paraphernalia of the Civil War tourist game.

The Wills House, where Lincoln touched up his speech for the cemetery dedication, has become a museum with two (not one, but two) life-size wax Lincolns. One grouping presents him with his wife and two of their children, none of whom appeared in Gettysburg. The other presents him alone in shirt sleeves in the bedroom, engrossed in the tragic blue funk commonly associated with the mythic Lincoln.

Poor Lincoln. The Civil War hagiographers deny him the right to humanity even in his bedroom. In the adjoining gift shop, one may buy a small plastic "camera" which, held to the eye and clicked, reveals Lincoln in portrait.

South of town, on Seminary Ridge, Robert E. Lee strides his metal charger (fine for climbing on the statue: up to $500) and gazes eternally toward the Bloody Angle at the Union center. In the mile of open ground between Lee and the Angle, the elite of Lee's army marched nobly to butchery and the Confederacy died and the Union was saved. In Lee's line of vision, beside Emmitsburg Road where Pickett's shattered line hurled itself up against the Federal cannon, the General now looks out on the inevitable custard stand.

All week long the tourist business has been brisk here, thanks to the concentration of politicians and pedagogues who have been praising and parsing the Gettysburg Address. Very little that is memorable seems to have been said.

The scholarly activity has centered on the quibbling over trivia that marks the true Civil War buff. How many speech drafts did Lincoln write? Which one did he deliver? How was the flag flown when he spoke? For the ceremonial reading Justice Michael Musmanno of the State Supreme Court, to whom the chore fell, surrendered to the electronic age by reading the speech to a tape recorder and having the canned version broadcast over the cemetery's public-address system.

The troubling question of Gettysburg, however, is whether the order that was imposed here in blood was moral or political, and few of the celebrants—except perhaps Secretary Dean Rusk—seemed as certain of the answer as Lincoln had been a century ago.

The battlefield itself answers no questions. At dusk in the plum sunsets of these raw November evenings it is studded with grotesque marble monuments and metal silhouettes of old generals. The field where Pickett's line came is terrifying . . . a mile of open ground ideal for butchery. What kept them coming? Surely not dedication to states' rights or slavery or hatred for the philosophic concept of union.

The only answers from the battlefield are those that explain every battle of every war: courage, discipline, foolhardiness, fear, resignation and conviction that somebody somewhere had a persuasive reason for requiring their deaths.

Lincoln did and managed to articulate it. The Confederacy was less fortunate in its leaders who could never agree on what the great cause really was. "It's all my fault," Lee said here when he saw his army shattered. But was it? And what had he lost?

The politicians still can't decide, and the Civil War centennial goes on feeding us on a thin gruel of romance and frozen custard.

Trinidad, Calif.

Near the Oregon state line a billboard exhorts the motorist to "be a super patriot—impeach Earl Warren."

The key word is "super." It discloses the mind of the West in its obsession with bigness. In places like Illinois and North Carolina believers in the devil theory of history content themselves with modest cries of "impeach Earl Warren." They assume that normal, regular-size patriots can do the job.

The concept of the super patriot doubtless leaves all but the most hyperthyroid Easterner uneasy, embodying as it does the suggestion that Paul Revere and Sam Adams (mere "patriots" in their own time) could not quite measure up to the conspiratorial challenge of 1964.

The Westerner, by contrast, comes naturally to the idea of the super Everything. His country is big and he is proud of it. Everything is super, from breakfast to conspiracy.

He is the antithesis of his cousin, the Southerner, who sees the traveler as an "outsider" and constantly falls into the defensive position of trying to justify the South. To the Westerner, a traveler may be a "stranger," but not for long, and if the stranger comes from some small-scale world like the East or Dixie, the Westerner feels pity for him as someone who has never lived in grandeur.

"How do you like it out here in God's country?" he will ask you with earnest heartiness. Or, in the mountain meadows of Colorado, he will inhale huge lungfuls of the sharp thin air and sigh like a man who has found Paradise. "The big country makes you feel like a man!"

Bigness is the order of things. Trout, steak and pork chops are standard breakfast offerings from the Rockies to the Cascades, with huge mounds of greasy fried potatoes as inedible as grits in Alabama.

The Salt Lake is the greatest. "Hell, we are on the shores of the Pacific," Jim Bridger said when he discovered it in 1824. The ocean is the greatest on earth and the streams that flow down from the mountains are alive with super fish.

The trees are not only the biggest but the oldest. Some stood here when Egypt was ruled by Pharaoh. Without leaving the roadside, a traveler can embrace a tree fifty feet in circumference.

Super trucks haul them to sawmills down super Alpine roads beaming with gigantic flowers. Roses as big as cabbages.

In California the West now has the nation's super state. It has the biggest car population in the world. Naturally it celebrated the Fourth of July by scoring the biggest traffic death toll in the country.

In the super country it seems only natural that men are engaged by nothing less than super conspiracy calling for super patriots to fight super villains. And so it is.

The car radio picks a staccato of anxious voices out of the air. From Utah west the air crackles with warnings of impending socialism and worse. There is Billy James Hargis, "speaking for Jesus Christ and against socialism," with a guest speaker to warn the West to beware of the Supreme Court.

Dr. Carl McIntyre's broadcasts alert southern Idaho. "Anti-Communists are worse than Communists as far as the State Department is concerned," he declares, asking why it grants visas to "Russian spies" but not to Madame Nhu.

From southern Utah comes the voice of "Know Your Enemy," suggesting why General Eisenhower was reluctant to support Governor Scranton. Eisenhower, the voice explained, may have feared that certain commentators would document his activities in behalf of Communism over the past thirty years if he resisted Senator Goldwater.

It is very hard to avoid the super perspective out in God's country.

Aboard Goldwater
Campaign Train

This is the strangest way to make a President. What they did, you see, was to put 200 people on this curious train and haul the thing over the Appalachians and then drag it slowly through hundreds and hundreds of miles of cornfields.

Well, in any case, it is the strangest thing. The train rolls through the cornfields while the politicians sit inside drinking coffee and listening to "The Stars and Stripes Forever" on squawk boxes. Every hour or so, the thing stops and all the coffee-soaked politicians are put off and another shift is put aboard.

Everybody else jumps off the train and runs to the rear. The man who wants to be President comes out the back door, and everybody shouts, "We want Barry we want Barry we want Barry." "Well, you have him," says the man who wants to be President, and the crowd laughs. There is something very curious about this crowd. The faces never change. The train rolls through a hundred miles of cornfields and there, lo and behold, is the same crowd that wanted Barry at the last town. The woman carrying the sleeping baby, the old fellow with leathery ears, the jeering adolescent with L.B.J. placard.

All day long this crowd keeps reappearing at the back of the train and shouting, "We want Barry" and laughing when Barry says, "Well, you have him." Barry then warns about the "curious crew."

The "curious crew" is not the train crew. It is a group of people led by the other man who wants to be President. Sometimes Barry calls them by funny nicknames—Yo-yo McNamara,

285

the Secretary of Defense, and Orville Wrong, the Secretary of Agriculture, for example. This really makes the crowd howl.

"How do you think he's doing?" is a very popular question. People who don't want Barry say he is doing very badly, while people who do want him say the crowd has been great all day. It is impossible to ask Barry how he thinks he's doing for he never appears outside the car with the coffee-drinking politicians and maintains only the most formal relations with the rest of the train.

The other day—was it in Indiana or X?—he put on an engineer's hat and went forward to drive the train a while. He drives a train very smoothly. Should he fail to become President he would certainly make an adequate train driver.

It is odd. This sort of campaign gives a man an opportunity to demonstrate what kind of engineer he would be, but no chance to show how well he can run the country. As Barry might say, it is "curious."

Ah, the train is stopping again. This must be Mattoon, Ill., or perhaps Hammond, Ind. The last shift of local politicians is disembarking and the new one is getting on. Everyone is racing to the back. The crowd is at it again, shouting, "We want Barry." Barry is saying, "Well, you have him." The crowd is laughing. That eerie crowd. There is the woman carrying the sleeping baby. There is the old fellow with leathery ears. Could we be carrying this crowd in the baggage car?

Sometimes even Barry seems not quite real. In Indiana the other morning—or was it in Ohio last month?—he hailed the local Colgate toothpaste plant and declared that, if Government would stop harassing teen-agers and young married people, "there can be millions of these Colgates started across the country." A man afterward kept walking through the train asking where the country would get enough teeth to keep them all in business, but he was finally restrained and advised to go easy on the coffee.

It is curious here. Very curious. One has these fantasies, especially after nightfall. Perhaps it is the coffee and too much "Stars and Stripes Forever," but one has the gnawing suspicion that we are all doomed on this train.

Doomed to roll forever through the cornfields, listening to Barry say, "Well, you have him," seeing the old man with leathery ears day after day, week after week, year after year. And at night there are the dreams. Millions of toothpaste factories turning out billions of toothpaste tubes. It is a curious way to make a President.

Albuquerque, N.M.

It is hard to keep a clear head when you are caught inside a Presidential campaign.

From the outside, reading the headlines and watching television, it all seems so tidy. Barry says Lyndon believes in "daddyism." Lyndon says Barry is not fit to sit at the Washington end of the hot line. Neatly rounded-off crowds of thirty, fifty or a hundred thousand line routes, cheer, sulk, boo, clutch happily at candidatorial hands.

From a distance it looks crisp, exciting, cleanly dramatic. From inside it is something else. After twelve hours on the campaign plane, a simple recounting of what has happened sounds like a tale told by a madman. Well, to get to the point—

We left Washington at 3, were in Boston at 4 P.M. This, in itself, was ridiculous. It should take three hours at least to reach Boston and eight if you travel like a gentleman. This miracle of transportation is made possible by the jetliner, a kerosene-powered restaurant which feeds and oils 115 campaigners at altitudes above 30,000 feet while annihilating time.

At Logan Airport in Boston in an apricot sunlight politicians in black politicians' suits stroked cigars, shook hands and asked reporters to spell their names right while a band played "Mary Ann," a tune of the islands. The President's plane arrived. The President debarked to girlish squeals, was visible briefly in the bustle.

President, black-suited politicians and campaigners crushed into limousines and buses, raced into Boston with brakes screeching, horns blowing, drivers cursing, and debouched among a herd of neighing police horses in Post Office Square. A crowd that may have been 50,000 or 350,000 as announced by the chief policeman murmured incoherently in the dark granite canyons.

The President began reading a prepared speech. The amplifiers failed, making it impossible to hear what he said. A woman screamed, fainted and had to be rescued by ambulance crews.

"You'd better get out of here before this crowd breaks through the police lines," advised a local policeman.

Everybody crushed into limousines and buses and raced to Logan Airport. The restaurant headed for Pittsburgh, food and oil flowing freely. Somewhere over Connecticut, or maybe New York, airborne policemen apprehended a man near the rear galley who announced that he was Chief Osceola of the Seminoles with a vital message for President Johnson.

Large crowds pressed to the rear galley to stare at the fellow. Stewardesses urged everyone to return to his seat to restore the restaurant's equilibrium. We all descended at Pittsburgh.

More politicians in black suits. More limousines and buses. More brake-screeching, horn-blowing, cursing. President lost to view. Crowds, if any, invisible in Pennsylvania night. Everybody filed into a huge dome where for one hour and four minutes the President spoke of absolutely everything while girls squealed and the mind reeled.

We all dashed back to our limousines and buses, raced to the airport. Brakes screeching, horns blowing, drivers cursing. The great restaurant soared through the vast moonless American night toward Evansville, Ind. Stewardesses of great loveliness served peanuts, olives and pickles. White House aides distributed mimeographed copies of speeches the President had made in Boston and Pittsburgh, speeches the President would make in Evansville, Albuquerque, Los Angeles.

The restaurant descended at Evansville in a shower of peanuts. The Evansville airport was dark and full of policemen looming out of the night with big gun holsters. Orion hung low on the horizon, snickering. From a great distance in a small harsh glare the President was visible. He said there were 30,000 people listening to him out in that darkness.

The restaurant swished up over the Ohio River and high out across the plains and desert for Albuquerque. It was 1 o'clock in the morning when it took off and the stewardesses were serving steak.

In the twelve hours since leaving Washington the President had campaigned effectively across the length of the continent, someone said. Without newspapers or television it is hard to say here precisely what, if anything, happened.

Washington, D.C.

Most of the commentary on the Smithsonian Institution's new Museum of History and Technology has emphasized the architectural failure of the building itself, but what should also be said is that the exhibits inside are an unqualified success.

The failure here has not been with Father and Grandfather and their forebears, whose worldly goods are on display, but with ourselves. Our own generation is unable to build a shelter worthy of housing what the old people have left us.

And the quality of what they have left is very high indeed. Item for item, they had us beat nine times out of ten when it came to taste and beauty. The 1918 Oldsmobile which is on display is a case in point. With its top raked at an angle just jaunty enough for a sporting man but not too immodest for a lady, it makes the 1964 cars look like overweight heifers.

Superiority is not confined to the automobiles. The gleaming green and silver steam locomotive, the Mack truck with its camel-nose hood and solid tires, the six-door electric trolleys and the lace delicacy of the Victorian San Francisco cable car— these came from a race of builders.

Even their gas pumps were beauties. The new museum has one. It is a tall and willowy red number with a breathtakingly tapered waist and, at head level, a clear glass cylinder where a man could watch his gasoline bubble about until it entered the hose.

What has become of this gracious and charming lady? Surely there is none of her soul left in that squat mercantile ogre mounted in cement at the gas station, with dollar signs for eye-balls and a squalid little tax computer where his heart should be.

Everybody will have more respect for his elders after seeing the new collection. The old European criticism that they were a crowd of drab materialists was partially wrong at least. Materialists they may have been, but as is made clear here, it was a materialism that produced much beauty and grace.

It was also materialism which aspired to endure, and this fact inevitably raises a troubling question about our own generation. What is our generation going to leave for the Smithsonian? What have we that will last long enough to interest our grandchildren?

Our goods fall apart after they are three years old; our houses after twenty. Our great buildings are done in glass and are designed to be torn down. We are leaving hardly even any personal written record of our passage here; letter writing is dying as our lives, instead, are talked out over the telephone. There is something sneaky about us. It is almost as if we were determined to come and go without leaving a footprint. It is fitting that this should be the generation for which total annihila-tion is at least feasible.

And yet there should be something we can leave so that our grandchildren and great-great-grandchildren can come back to us, in their maturity, and try to understand us properly, as we can now go to the Smithsonian and see our forebears with fresh perspective.

What artifacts will we be able to leave? A big jet, perhaps, which is beautiful as well as complex. An electronic computer, a complete unassembled stereo rig, an aerosol bomb, a tube of gentlemen's hair oil, a Princess telephone, an album of credit cards and, if nothing else at all, one beer can—empty.

To be properly exhibited, of course, in that remote day at the Smithsonian, the mid-twentieth-century collection should fall to pieces and need replacing after every three years. All, that is, except the beer can. This should lie forever, unrusting, on a beautiful green lawn.

THIS EERIE
NEWNESS

Nobody warned us about the New Age.

Nobody told us there would someday be yuppies.

Nobody warned us that lawyers were coming, thousands and thousands of lawyers, lawyers swarming thicker than plague locusts.

Nobody said we'd see a time when Americans could hardly speak American anymore, much less English.

Nobody said, "Take a good long last look at Main Street, everybody, because it's going to be moved out to the country, rebuilt with a roof over it and called a mall."

Nobody warned us there would be computers instead of arithmetic, CD players instead of Victrolas, electrically generated din instead of music, and cigarette terror instead of sexual inhibition.

Nobody told us there would be Japanese ingenuity instead of good old American know-how.

Nobody gave us any hint at all that the better world, the better life and the better future we were building were going to be weird, eerie and not at all what we had in mind.

Nobody warned us about the New Age.

For Want of an Amp

I was starved for music. I wanted to hear Bach toccatas and "Flat Foot Floogie with a Floy Floy." I wanted to hear Gilbert and Sullivan, a Haydn quartet and Jimmy Durante singing "Inka Dinka Doo."

The radio was useless. It offered only music to buy groceries by, music to blast your brains out by and the golden oldies of Sam the Sham and the Pharaohs. By filing my fingertips with sandpaper I could tune in highbrow radio stations, but that was no good either. When my soul craved Gregorian chants, these stations played Mahler symphonies; when my heart cried out for the songs of Ned Rorem, they mocked me with Handel's greatest hits.

The solution was clear: a phonograph. I owned the ruin of a phonograph, bought in 1949. It hadn't worked since the late 1960's when, maddened one night by the Rolling Stones, I threw an adolescent at it, struck Mick Jagger and shattered every spring in its body.

By the time the adolescents grew up and left home, replacing it had become a problem, for the phonograph had matured into an instrument only slightly less complex than the N.A.S.A. space shuttle, and I had always been backward in electrical engineering.

Hunger for music, though, impelled me to take the plunge. I went to a department store, pointed to the catalog picture of a machine and ordered it sent to my residence. It arrived last week. To be more precise, *they* arrived last week—four cardboard boxes whose contents bore suspicious resemblance to certain equipment Colin Clive once used to turn Boris Karloff into a guttural nincompoop with bolts in his skull.

294

I knew, of course, that phonographs were no longer called "phonographs." I even knew that the needle was no longer called a "needle." It was called a "stylus," which, if my seventh-grade Latin teacher was correct, meant "a writing tool." What's more, I knew that the whole mess boxed in cardboard was called a "sound system."

Though I had doubts about the philosophical underpinnings of an industry that would use a writing instrument and an entire system to tickle the ears with "Inka Dinka Doo," I didn't intend to be caught playing the old fogy by whining for the days when a simple hand crank and a Victrola could fill Grandmother's parlor with "Who Put the Overalls in Mrs. Murphy's Chowder?"

A man has to face progress like a man. Nowadays, so does a woman, unfortunately for her. I faced it by emptying the four boxes of sound system and studying the assembly directions.

These had apparently been translated literally from demotic Macedonian by a Serb who had flunked out of English and been placed in vocational school to study sound systemics. Not since my own college physics lab report on the torsion-pendulum experiment had I read such a masterpiece of transparent weaseling contrived to hide the author's utter ignorance of the subject at hand.

Hurling it aside, I applied pure reason to the assembly problem. There were two speakers, a cassette player, several miles of wire and two turntables. The two turntables unsettled me. I knew the delicious effect of stereo sound was obtained by placing two speakers apart from each other, but I hadn't realized that two records were needed to get results.

This was galling. I had only one record each of "Inka Dinka Doo" and "Flat Foot Floogie with a Floy Floy," and I didn't fancy the expense of buying two copies of every Gregorian chant, Haydn quartet and Bach toccata needed for my library.

There were astounding numbers of places to connect wires to the cassette player and the turntables, but only one connecting point on each speaker. Logic indicated the proper course. I connected one turntable to one speaker, the cassette player to the other speaker, and the second turntable to the cassette player.

This done, I plugged in the power cords from the cassette player and both turntables, placed "Inka Dinka Doo" on a turntable chosen at random and sat back to hear the immortal Durante. The ensuing silence was intense. It remained intense for several days in spite of rewiring labors that would have exhausted a Con Edison crew.

Awaking in the predawn one morning with a ravenous appetite for a salami sandwich, I descended to the refrigerator and found our neighborhood burglar gazing disgustedly at the sound system. "They swindled you, dad," he said. "They didn't send you an amp."

"An amp? I need an amp?"

"They messed up in the mailroom. Instead of sending you an amp, they sent a spare turntable."

I thanked him, apologized for not having a new TV set he could burgle, and asked if he intended to take the sound system. "Not without an amp," he said. "Better wake up, old-timer, or the world's going to cheat you blind."

An amp? An amp? Anybody have a Victrola for sale?

Lawyers for Cars

While Japan was producing automobiles the United States was producing lawyers. American lawyer production has more than doubled since 1960, with the result that there are now 612,000 on the market, or one lawyer for every 390 Americans.

On a per capita basis, this is twenty times the number of lawyers available in Japan. These figures are the basis of my "lawyer-for-cars" proposal for solving our trade problem with the Japanese.

As first proposed to the White House, my plan called for exporting one lawyer to Japan for every car Japan exports to the United States. The Japanese objected to this. They argued that we would need to keep at least 200,000 lawyers for ourselves, leaving only 412,000 for export.

On a one-for-one basis, they noted, Japan would be permitted to ship us only 412,000 cars, which is far below their present export level.

As I explained to the White House, the Japanese estimate was far off base. Since the United States could function very happily with no more than three dozen lawyers, we should be able to send Japan 611,964 lawyers by the end of the year.

Under State Department pressure, however, we sought to please the Japanese by changing the car-to-lawyer ratio to a three-for-one swap. We would ship 611,964 lawyers, they would ship 1,835,892 cars in the present year.

Moreover, we would change the ratio in future years, in view of the fact that after the initial shipment our exports would decline.

At present we produce only 35,000 new lawyers each year. We proposed annual shipments from these inventories of 34,998 new lawyers at an exchange rate of between 50 and 75 cars per lawyer.

At this stage the Japanese revealed that they had been toying with us. A letter from the Japanese Lawyer Import Commission said, "We are dismayed to find that the 611,964 lawyers you propose to ship us are almost totally ignorant of the engineering and production skills necessary for the making of superior automobiles and highly sophisticated electronic machinery."

If we would agree to put the lawyers through a ten-year retraining program, Japan would be prepared to consider a deal. "We do not believe this is an unreasonably long retraining period," they said, "since our studies show that to an American lawyer ten years is virtually no time at all."

Simultaneously, lawyers began to raise obstacles. I was swamped with legal paper. Writs, injunctions, orders to show cause, requests for postponement, suits for damages on grounds of invasion-of-lawyers.

Among the most annoying were the 376,000 writs of *habeas Japanus* ordering me to produce the Japanese Government for the taking of depositions in suits to be prosecuted against me for "slanderously and maliciously asserting" that a lawyer was worth no more than fifty to seventy-five cars.

Not surprisingly, all my other activities have been brought to a halt. Though I expect to prevail eventually when my cases are finally decided by the Supreme Court in the second quarter of the next century, this is no comfort to one whose only dream is to see the day when Japan will be as blessed with lawyers as the United States.

For this reason it pains me to be attacked as I was last week by the Japanese Minister of Motion. "There are certain Western schemers, envious of Japan's ability to keep moving ahead," he said.

"These schemers have plans for infesting our society with hundreds of thousands of men cunningly trained in the arts of stopping all constructive activity, of bringing entire societies to a dead standstill. Yes, I speak of lawyers.

"There are plans afoot for shipping us enough lawyers to stop all forward motion in Japan, as they have stopped it in a certain country I need not identify. They call this trading lawyers for cars. To understand its true nature, however, I suggest that you try to imagine what kind of car Japan might produce if beset by 611,964 lawyers."

Well, I've been trying to imagine it, and I don't think it would be that terrible. The tires might have each other tied up in court when you wanted to drive to the seashore; the engine might sue every time you forgot to change the oil on time, and the gear shift on the showroom model might charge you with discrimination if you tried to buy an automatic transmission, but at least it would be a car that knew its rights and was willing to pay for their defense.

This, and not the insensate march of economic success, is the essence of civilization. I hope Japan will try it. Maybe, to show our friendship, we could give them 100,000 lawyers outright, just to get them started.

Bye-bye, Silver Bullets

The Lone Ranger is through. Washed up. He stands in a Los Angeles law office. Oriental rugs underfoot. A Kandinsky on the wall. The desk rich and sleek, covered with writs, injunctions, habeas corpus, mandamus, certiorari, nolo contendere, duces tecum, bills of attainder.

The lawyer has handled people like the Lone Ranger before. The world is full of them if you are a lawyer. People who go around the country drawing down big jack by passing themselves off as the Lone Ranger, Popeye the Sailor Man, Boob McNutt, Secret Agent X-9, the Green Hornet.

"You're all washed up, Popeye," he tells them. Or, "O.K., Hornet, one more rendering of 'The Flight of the Bumble Bee,' and I'll slap you with so many injunctions you'll have to pawn your Orphan Annie decoder and Cocomalt shaker to pay your court costs."

The Lone Ranger is easier meat than most. He is getting old. He is sixty-four now. It shows. His mask is deeply wrinkled. Tonto urged him five years ago to see a plastic surgeon about having tucks taken in the eye slits, but the Lone Ranger refused. He is old-fashioned about too many things.

"I'll give it to you straight from the shoulder, Ranger," the lawyer says. "You're washed up. Over the hill."

The Lone Ranger's reflexes are slow. He would like to leap aboard his fiery horse with the speed of light and gallop away with a hearty "heigh-ho, Silver!" He cannot. The lawyer's receptionist made him leave Silver outside on account of the oriental rugs. The Lone Ranger can read the secrets of a cold campfire, but he is no match for the guile of receptionists.

299

The lawyer urges the Lone Ranger to look at himself. A wrinkled man in a world whose heart goes out only to smooth men.

"I don't smoke or drink," says the Ranger. "I work out every morning to keep my body trim."

The lawyer has heard it all before. These old crocks are all alike. "I still eats my spinach three times a day and avoids all heavy lifting to keep my upper arms skinnier than Slim Summerville," Popeye once told him.

"I'm not talking two-for-a-penny Mary Janes, Ranger," says the lawyer. "I'm talking big law. Now come across with that mask."

The Lone Ranger recoils. They always recoil at this stage of the interview. The lawyer remembers how the Phantom recoiled when ordered to come across with both his mask and his form-fitting rubber suit, remembers how ridiculous the Phantom looked when it had been peeled off him. His entire body wrinkled like hands left too long in hot dishwater.

The lawyer is not a cruel man. He remembers the years he sat by his television set, thumb in mouth, marveling at the Lone Ranger. Once, he wanted to grow up to be the Lone Ranger's sidekick and gallop behind him on a small gray stallion named Zirconium.

Life for the lawyer has been a series of disappointments, except for the oriental rugs and the Kandinsky and the cunning receptionist. In law school he had wanted to grow up to be Perry Mason and save the innocent from the noose and be admired afterward by Paul Drake and Della for refusing to take a fee.

Instead, here he was, pushing around heroes for getting long in the tooth. He hoped the Lone Ranger wouldn't cry. He couldn't stand it when they cried. He remembered the Katzenjammer Kids, doddering octogenarians, weeping like babies when he told them it was time for the nursing home.

"Ranger," he says, "promise me you won't cry and I'll try to explain."

"I feel like crying," the Lone Ranger says. "It's the worst I've ever felt in my life. But I won't cry. The Lone Ranger doesn't cry."

The lawyer explains that his client owns the rights to the

Lone Ranger and means to make a bundle from them. There was going to be a young, new Lone Ranger, a smooth man. Having a dilapidated old Lone Ranger galloping the plains is bad for the young, new, smooth-man Lone Ranger image necessary for the making of bundles.

"You're trying to tell me I'm not the Lone Ranger anymore?"

They always asked that. "You mean to tell me I'm not Flash Gordon anymore?" Flash had asked when ordered to hand over Emperor Ming and the Planet Mongo. And the lawyer had said, "That's right—you're just Buster Crabbe now."

It was the only legal answer. To the Ranger he says, "From now on, you're just Clayton Moore. Your revels now are ended. Turn in your mask and your silver bullets, your white hat and your faithful Tonto and your fiery steed with the speed of light."

"What will I do for a living from now on?" the ex-Lone Ranger asks. The lawyer explains that this is a question nobody has been able to answer satisfactorily to retirees. Many of them he says, find shuffleboard fulfilling.

When the Ranger leaves, the lawyer considers calling in his receptionist and Paul Drake and telling them he is refusing to take a fee for this case. Instead, he pushes the intercom button.

"You can send Buck Rogers in now," he says.

Power Lunch

Yes, I craved power. Had always craved power. Always wanted to exude power. Strong men and forceful women buckling to my iron will—that was my craving, and yet . . .

I shall be frank. Life had come to a dead end. Confronted with strong men, challenged by forceful women, I was the one who did the buckling. People who had power invited me to lunch for the pleasure of seeing me buckle.

The most sadistic was Buck Backbreaker, whose power was such a legend in the board rooms of eight continents that no one dared tell him there were only seven continents. Twice each month he commanded me to lunch for the sheer joy of seeing me buckle to his iron will.

I might be buckling still but for a book titled "Power Lunching," by E. Melvin Pinsel and Ligita Dienhart. It is subtitled "How You Can Profit from More Effective Business-Lunch Strategy." A more accurate subtitle would be "Everything You Always Needed to Know About Power but Machiavelli Wouldn't Tell You."

I had scarcely opened it when the explanation for my constant buckling to Buck Backbreaker's will leaped from the pages. I had been lunching on wimp food, whereas Backbreaker ate nothing but power food.

Of course! No wonder the waiters sneered as they took my lunch order for quiche, prune salad, cottage-cheese soufflé and date-nut bread. No wonder they trembled in awe as Buck ordered raw oysters, uncooked leeks and thirty-two-ounce sirloins.

Buck was ordering power foods; I was ordering wimp foods. The man who wants to have his way orders power food, and in big quantities. "The bigger the steak, the more *macho* it becomes"—that is the principle. Fortified with new knowledge, I was ready to spring a surprise on Mr. Backbreaker when next we lunched.

"I suppose you'll have the watercress salad and sautéed bean sprouts," he said, winking at the waiter, then adding, "By the way, while waiting for the food to come, take my shoes across the street to the cobbler like a good fellow and have them shined."

Ignoring the waiter's cackling, I said, "I'll have two pounds of chopped mutton, extremely rare, and an order of raw turnips on the side." Eating things raw is the very essence of power lunching, according to Pinsel and Dienhart. It is also "a very high power play to order the same thing as your guest in food and drink."

"Now if you'll give me your shoes," I said.

"Never mind my shoes," snarled Buck Backbreaker, suddenly aware that he was in for the power struggle of his life. "Let's talk merger."

"Order first," I suggested. What else could he do? Needing a very high power play, he could only order the same thing his guest had ordered. His complexion's shift from ruddy to gray betrayed a deep distaste for extremely rare chopped mutton, even in minute quantities, but it was not for nothing that he was called a legend in the board rooms of eight continents. He ordered the two-pound serving, complete with raw turnips.

"You mentioned merger," I said as he reached the half-pound point.

"Not right now," he gasped, dashing from the table. I mercifully ordered the waiters to remove his uneaten mutton during his absence and, when he returned, offered to take his necktie and vest across the street to the cleaner to have the stains removed.

His reply was the challenge of a wounded giant: "Lunch tomorrow at high noon. Be on time."

I arrived early to talk to the chef.

"I'll order first today," Buck announced. The entire corps of waiters surrounded us, aware that they were witnessing a battle of titans.

"I'll start with six raw abalones on the half shell, unpounded," Buck said. "Followed by rabbit tartare."

The waiter recoiled. "You mean rabbit meat raw and finely ground?"

"Not just rabbit meat. I want it made with jackrabbit meat."

Buck leered in triumph. Then the chef appeared. "I hope you won't think me unsporting for not emulating your order," I said to Buck, "but I was afraid you wouldn't feel like eating very powerfully today, so I had the chef do me something a little special."

"M'sieur," said the chef, lifting the lid from his concoction, "just as you ordered—a whole roasted alligator basted with a gallon of hog lard and garnished with cloves of raw garlic."

"Can I take your shoes out for a shine?" Buck asked. I had

brought a second pair of shoes, anticipating this gambit, and a wise move it was. He still hasn't returned.

Heaven in Asphalt

Mall:
Five hundred and fifty acres of asphalt-paved parking space easily accessed via off-on ramps connecting with three interstate highways and the historic and picturesque Old Ox Road, now broadened to handle six lanes of high-speed traffic for greater shopping convenience.

Four famous-name department stores, each featuring world-famous labels hand-sewn in such famous cities as Rome, Paris and London for the products of famous American manufacturers.

Six fast-food stand-up counters ready to serve the hamburger of your dreams.

A cutlery shop with dozens of varieties of everybody's favorite, the world-famous Swiss Army Cheese Slicer.

A branch of the internationally acclaimed Jeans R Pricey, whose boast is: "If you can't find yourself a pair of overpriced jeans in our boutique it's tough buns, sweetheart, because our hired help gets fired if they're caught waiting on customers."

Nine restaurants offering the gourmet delights of a dozen continents from state-of-the-art food-preparation centers where the latest in microwave-oven technology assures that your order will arrive at the table completely thawed.

A branch of the famed Octopus Book Chain, whose famous guarantee to you is: "Find a sales clerk in our shop who can identify Charles Dickens and we will give you a free copy of 'Little Dorrit' with every purchase of ten discounted best-sellers."

Philodendron galore.

Earmuffs for jogging.

A Kitchen Madness store stocked with thousands of irresistibly chic kitchen items so unnecessary and so expensive that they are rarely found outside the kitchens of Westchester County's richest inside-trading gourmandisers. (How about a set of artichoke-initializing molds that enable you to serve each of your dinner guests a personalized artichoke bearing his own monogram?)

Feet killing you? Absolutely exhausted? No wonder after you've walked our 217 miles of stone corridors breathing our electronically recirculated antique air. Relax and feel your shopping zest revive while enjoying some of the movies playing in our amazing twenty-four-theater cinema complex (all screens large enough for comfortable viewing without binoculars).

No, our electronically recirculated antique air is not sold on the premises but comes from an exclusive dealer in Camden, N.J., who guarantees it was found in barrels sealed tight before air pollution was invented. He sells "only to the trade," which means decorators. You are cautioned not to pack our air into plastic bags or jars and try leaving the premises with them, as we are prepared to prosecute airlifters mercilessly.

$60-per-pound chocolates.

Puree of Jerome Kern and Richard Rodgers oozing from concealed amplifiers.

The famous country-fabric boutique.

The famous Milady's Slipper footwear boutique.

Forty-three famous boutiques staffed by sales clerks employed only after passing the most rigorous tests of their ability to fly into a rage when customers interrupt their private telephone conversations.

Three jewelers.

A "family dentistry" office.

An eyeglasses emporium.

Your fourteen-year-old daughter's dream of Paradise? Or your own vision of Hell? Neither: It is another great branch of the internationally famous Tower of Babel ("We Go Straight for the Cochlea") Record and Earbuster chain, without which no mall is complete. To enjoy soul-stirring screams of laughter, ask one of the children in charge to help you find a record of John McCormack singing "Silver Threads Among the Gold," "When You and I Were Young, Maggie" and "Under the Bamboo Tree."

Three branches of nationally famous banks, all of which offer the famous "Hello Sucker Credit Card" emblazoned with that magic respect-getter of a slogan, "Get those hands up and come across with 18 percent interest."

Two greeting-card stores.

While-U-Shop Autocare with complete change of tires, batteries, floor mats, oil filter, exhaust pipes, fake foxtails for radio aerial, plastic religious icons for dashboard mounting, plus you-name-it, plus everything for motorcycles.

Fifty thousand candles.

A miasma of perfume.

Booties for cats.

Ice cream and doughnuts.

Fantastic appliance bargains in brand names sounding suspiciously un-Japanese.

Losing the Hair Game

I am not kidding when I tell you that before World War II millions of Americans washed their hair with any soap that came to hand. It is in the history books. You can look it up. They used the same soap for hair that they used for face, hands and everything else.

Sure there was shampoo. But that was for the few. Poor people who had to wash their hair with bath soap made fun of rich people who used shampoo. When they saw one of the rich few lathering up from a shampoo jar, they yelled, "Shampew is for the few, but shampoo is for the foo."

As you can see, it was a silly time. Shampoo researchers had to put up with ridicule and abuse. Many couldn't take it and abandoned the shampoo research laboratories to work in labs where America was trying to beat the Nazis to the secret of producing a deodorizing foot powder. America won that race, thank heaven. Unfortunately, the men who did the job went back to shampoo after the war and ended forever that carefree era when an American's hair could find happiness alone in a shower with nothing but a cake of Lifebuoy.

We entered the age of dull, lifeless film. Dull, lifeless film was what the shampoo trust said would blight your hair if you washed it with soap.

Shampoo had arrived. How disagreeable it made life. Early shampoos required the customer to make decisions he was utterly unqualified to make. The typical shampoo came in three varieties: "For Oily Hair," "For Dry Hair," "For Regular Hair."

I have never known whether my hair was oily, dry or regular. From the first, I hated the idea that it might be oily. The thought of those millions of hairs up there on the scalp, each one secreting disgusting little globules of oil, could make me squirm with embarrassment.

Even if you did have oily hair, how could anybody bear to let the drugstore clerk know? I dreaded the smirk with which he would respond "Give me the shampoo for oily hair, please." Even having dry hair would be better than that, though dry hair sounded suspiciously arid, as though it went with harsh, austere people who didn't have any juice in them.

Well, naturally I took the shampoo "For Regular Hair." After all, my hair seemed to be as regular as most hair. Though I stayed with the regular, I always had an uneasy feeling that I was not getting full value because I really needed "oily" or "dry."

Nowadays washing your hair has become so complicated that I never do it without the advice of a lawyer. The complexity began to get out of hand when the shampoo labs discovered the "hair conditioner."

This is a liquid of dense viscosity that is sometimes put on the hair after the shampoo has been rinsed out, although some shampoos have the stuff built right in. In this case you get the scrubbing action of the shampoo and conditioning action of the dense viscous liquid all at the same time.

One question, of course, is how can you tell whether your hair needs the simultaneous shampoo-conditioning or the serial treatment with the conditioner not being applied until the shampoo is rinsed out. And that is only one question. Another is: What is a conditioner anyhow?

I have tried sundry conditioners with queer results. Some leave my hair feeling as if it had been larded with bear grease. Others make my hair yearn to be washed again with bath soap an hour or two after a shampoo and conditioner treatment.

Did I mention that with a conditioner you are giving yourself a "treatment"?

Here is how terrible this situation can become:

I have here three plastic containers picked at random off a shelf. The first says "Conditioning Shampoo For Dry Hair And Scalp." The second says "Shampoo Frequent-Use." Is the first batch unsuitable for frequent use? Will the second cause catastrophe on a dry scalp? Why do you need a degree in scalp soap from M.I.T. to wash your hair?

The third container is marked simply "Limp Hair." It contains not limp hair but a pink liquid described as a "quinine conditioner for dry, lifeless hair." This container is clearly trying to insult me. It is "Made in France," I see. Probably by some eminently sensible Frenchman who washes his hair in the bathwater.

A Smoke-free Diet

Since using this space recently to describe the miseries afflicting me since I stopped smoking 361 days ago, I have been inundated with expert opinion. Almost all the experts agree that the constant strangling sensation I suffer in neck and waist is not the result of a mysterious shrinkage of clothing, as I suppose, but is caused by food-fueled expansion of the fatty tissues.

This strikes me as bunk. Is it sensible to suppose that a stomach might crave more food intake simply because a set of lungs with which it happened to be associated suddenly had its smoke cut off?

It's my guess that the average stomach doesn't care one way or the other about the lungs' smoke supply, but even if it did, would it go on a food binge because the smoke stopped?

Stomach and lungs, after all, are close neighbors; living next door to lungs that are constantly full of smoke must affect a stomach the way living across the street from a burning dump would affect you and me. I mean, we might be pleased when the city stopped the burning, but we wouldn't start eating Thanksgiving dinner three times daily for a whole year, would we?

Enough of physiological philosophy. Back to the experts. Though thousands have submitted diagnoses of "overeating," "gluttony" and "obesity," only one has mentioned the baffling perpetual cold that set in when the cigarettes stopped.

He does not blame the cold on overeating, but his report is not cheering: My only hope for relief lies in years of rinsing the sinus passages daily with a salt-water solution. The process, he says, is difficult and uncomfortable. Not a physician, he declines to elaborate, but suggests I seek medical advice.

I think not, since he says the procedure may have to be repeated daily for years to eliminate a really well-entrenched cold like mine. Most people can get used to a constantly running nose, but having salt water pumped through your sinus tubes day after day for years seems a dispiriting way to spend a lifetime.

I am not stubbornly resisting all advice to diet. Though I believe it is nonsense, I am not too intolerant to experiment. I should note that I have always been a modest eater and remained so after giving up cigarettes.

To be sure, after conquering the habit, I increased food consumption slightly for health reasons: Having been unnaturally thin all my life, I was afraid of suffering a dangerous weight loss once I stopped taking in the four or five pounds of smoke that I had been carrying around for years.

To guard against this, I added a bowl of oatmeal topped with sliced banana to my normal breakfast, began eating dessert at lunch (usually a not terribly big slice of mince pie), and, just before bedtime, consuming a bowl of ice cream and, once in a while, a toasted muffin with butter and blackberry jam, followed on very rare occasions by a couple of pieces of cold fried chicken.

One morning after having to call my two grown sons to help me get my belt buckled, I acceded to their argument that the diet experts might know what they were talking about and decided to test them. After all the other miseries that had resulted from giving up smoking, surely I could put up with dieting.

Frankly, I did not undertake this popular American discipline in good spirit, but with feelings of profound malice toward all those antismoking health zealots who had assured me that giving up the butts would make me feel like a million dollars.

They hadn't told me about the perpetual cold that would ensue, had they? So it wasn't surprising that they hadn't bothered to say, "And by the way, you're going to suffer terrible distress around the waist and neck due to acute fabric shrinkage."

Why should I have expected them to say, "And while we're at it, maybe we'd better mention that you're never going to be able to eat a decent meal again, or even enjoy a bowl of ice cream followed by a nice jam-covered muffin and a few pieces of fried chicken just before bedtime"?

For the last two days, I have been living exclusively on grapefruit, lettuce, tunafish, skim milk, unsweetened tea and a sustaining sense of superiority over the man four offices down who still smokes.

I'd love to catch him lighting a cigarette in a restaurant so I could make a scene demanding my right to dine in smoke-free air. There has to be some reward for all the misery caused by giving up cigarettes, doesn't there?

No? Ah well, at least I've lost all craving for tobacco and shall probably never smoke again, and isn't it great? Lettuce, tunafish, pain in the waist, running nose . . .

Great, just great.

Where Have All the Ulcers Gone?

The papers say the American stomach ulcer is becoming an endangered species. The incidence of ulcers, both peptic and duodenal, has declined so notably in recent years that doctors can no longer assemble enough patients to obtain significant data about causes and treatment.

As one who grew up in the age when stomach ulcer was the badge of success, I lament this news as another symptom of a world changing for the worse, in a category with the death of John Wayne, incessant baseball strikes and the passing of the Democratic party.

In my boyhood, which was not that long ago, the stomach ulcer was so widely viewed as evidence of success that people who didn't have one often faked it. President Truman once destroyed a critic with the sneer that he held only a three-ulcer job. Everybody understood that twist of the knife. Important men had jobs that gave them ten or twelve ulcers. Only pipsqueaks could be fulfilled in three-ulcer jobs.

The assumption was that ulcers were caused by tension and heavy bouts of dynamic decision making. The more ulcerated your gastrointestinal organs, the more respect you deserved. Among the male elders in my family, there was lively competition to see who could validly claim the worst ulcers, and despite the otherwise excessively good table manners which were enforced in our household, thunderous and indecorous belching was justified on grounds that it indicated an honorably parlous state of stomach ulceration.

311

In recent years, heart attack has replaced the stomach ulcer as the medical badge of the overworked male. Except that it eliminates belching as a form of social boasting, this strikes me as a definite step backward.

The stomach ulcer is not the only medical problem in decline. Acute appendicitis, once almost as common as athlete's foot, appears to have become a rare affliction. Thirty years ago, every other boy in the locker room flaunted an appendectomy scar on his abdomen, and every adolescent bellyache posed the terrifying possibility of surgery.

I recall the family doctor, after two or three visits to treat me for the green-apple agonies, announcing, "If this happens again, we'll take him in and have that appendix out." After that, I kept mum about stomach cramps and avoided the knife.

For older women, the great ailment was "gall bladder." Someone was always headed for the operating table for "gall bladder." I took it for granted that one of the miseries to which middle age doomed the female sex was gall-bladder surgery. In the past fifteen or twenty years, however, I can't recall meeting or hearing of a single woman who was having her gall bladder excised.

Could this be because surgeons have become so fascinated with their marvelous new operations that they have no interest in such sophomoric stuff as appendix and gall-bladder removal except in the most critical cases? That would surely be too cynical a supposition about a noble and dedicated profession. Still, I now know a lot more people who have recently had open-heart surgery than have recently had a gall bladder or appendix removed.

Another medical problem that seems to be on the wane is broken arm. In my boyhood, it was hard to assemble nine boys for baseball without having at least one with an arm in a cast supported by an over-the-shoulder sling. When was the last time you saw a boy with his arm in a sling? I have to think back to the Eisenhower Administration.

Part of the explanation may be that new bone-setting techniques have eliminated the cast and sling, but part also, I suspect, is that boys no longer climb things like trees, cliffs and buildings for amusement. In my observation, based on long residence in New York, gunshot wound is a far more common ailment of modern boyhood than broken arm.

This may also help explain the almost total disappearance of black eye. At one time, a boy who reached the age of courtship without ever having had a black eye would have been ruled off the course of romance on grounds that he had not yet undergone the rites of manhood. Nowadays, you can travel among hordes for months without ever seeing a young man sporting a shiner.

I assume this does not indicate a decline in the nation's virility level, but only a change in the ways in which youth expresses its exuberance. Very likely, I suspect, the reason the boy on the subway doesn't have a black eye is that he has a handsomely patched stab wound concealed by his shirt.

But let us not think on in this unhappy vein. It was bad enough in the old days when such thoughts could give you an ulcer. Now they could lead to a heart attack. Such is medical progress.

Fear of Interfacing

Just like you, I too was once afraid of computers. What a silly fear it was. With a few hours of study, I have grasped the essential simplicity underlying the operation of these delightful machines and look forward to spending many happy years with my home computer as soon as I can afford one. To help others enjoy this pleasure, let me show how easily the computer can be mastered.

First, you have the hardware. This is pretty much like the brain housed in your skull—an ingenious mechanism capable of great activity, but so complicated that only a handful of specialists have the slightest idea how it works.

Do you know how your brain works? What the cerebellum does when the memory is activated? How many times per second the membrane pulsates during lobotomy? Of course not. And it doesn't bother you, does it? So why go all to pieces because the computer is so complicated only a Ph.D. from M.I.T. can understand it?

Relax, just the way you relax about your brain, and say, "Sure it's complicated, but it works, doesn't it?"

Now you are ready to move on to the software. As you noted during infancy, the brain isn't worth ten cents if you don't put something into it. Sure, after you've jumped out of the crib a few times and cracked your head, it's going to let you know that jumping out of cribs is misguided activity. But if you want it to do something interesting such as weaseling money out of a guilt-ridden rich relative you have to put some complicated information into it.

This is called "software." Software comes on floppy disks. You put the floppy disk into the brain and instantly the infant stops jumping out of the crib and starts carrying on like a college graduate.

Let's say you want to know the cube root of 7. All you do is put in the floppy disk marked "Cube Root," fiddle around with a sort of typewriter keyboard and, presto, you get the answer on a little television screen. Sometimes, of course, it doesn't give you the answer, but snaps back with some insolent remark like "You're not making any sense, dummy." Remember, once the floppy disk goes in, you are dealing with a college graduate, so don't expect to get away with anything.

What it's telling you is that you haven't worked the keyboard accurately. Do it right next time and the machine will print the cube root of 7 on its television screen. It could be wrong, of course, but since you probably haven't the faintest notion how to find the cube root of 7 on your own, you'll have to take the machine's word for it.

But how in the world could it give a wrong answer? you will ask. The answer is "Garbage in, garbage out." If the floppy disk has been instructed as poorly in finding cube roots as you were in high-school math class, its answer is going to be just as wrong as the one you get while licking your pencil over a yellow pad.

This brings us to one of the first warnings about using your home computer: Don't put in garbage if you want it to be more reliable than the typical human product of a standard American education.

All very well, someone will say, but what about ROM's? The answer is: Make sure your computer has plenty of ROM's if you intend to do the big jobs. The same goes for RAM's, although it depends, of course, on just how big a job you have in mind.

If you want to handle something like a N.A.S.A. space probe, which is unlikely if you're working with a home computer, I'd recommend all the ROM's you can get and tell them not to spare the RAM's either. I'd make sure they gave me plenty of K's, too. A computer without any K's, as they say in Silicon Valley, is like a 1947 Chevy without a foxtail on the aerial.

The number of K's you'll want for your particular job will depend on the quality of your interface. Interface quality may seem confusing at first, as indeed it is, though actually we're not talking about anything much more elaborate than the face that goes with the brain.

In human terms, someone like Paul Newman has a very high-quality face and a brain to match. Thus, we might say that Paul Newman has high interface quality, though it is very difficult, unfortunately, to conclude whether this means he can find the cube root of 7.

The question, of course, is why he would want to find the cube root of 7. If he did he'd probably be swamped with female mathematicians willing to find it for him in a flash in exchange for an ice-cream soda at the corner drugstore.

But this has taken us far afield from interface, which is not a bad place to be, since I particularly want to move ahead to the kludge. Why do people have so much trouble understanding the kludge? What is a kludge, after all, but not enough K's, not enough ROM's, not enough RAM's, poor-quality interface and too few bytes to go around? Have I explained yet about the bytes?

Without bytes—well, what good would the floppy disks be without bytes? They're these things located right here under the—hey, what's this? Don't seem to be any bytes down here.

Let's start from the top. With the hardware and the software . . .

Naked Ignorance

It was supposed to be healthy or honest, possibly both, when nudity went public and actors started standing around on stage and screen without a stitch on. Nobody was sufficiently far-sighted to warn that it would also make us dumber, but that seems to be what happened.

How else explain the horror stories emanating from the American campus about college students who can't tell you where the Pacific Ocean is, much less Japan? When public undress was taboo in the United States the dumbest kid in fifth grade could not only locate the Pacific Ocean, he could also pinpoint the location of several islands in it whose residents wore practically nothing at all.

This he knew from studying the National Geographic, a magazine considered such hot stuff by the corduroy-knickers set that it was studied with the same intensity a later generation was to lavish on Playboy and R-rated movies.

If you were curious about how people looked undressed— and who wasn't?—the National Geographic was the basic source of information. In the course of the research, a good deal of other information rubbed off the page onto the student.

By seventh or eighth grade, and certainly long before college, American youth had extensive knowledge of geography. When they grew up and had to fight World War II and somebody told them to go attack Japan, they did it very effectively because they knew where Japan was.

By contrast, half the California college students examined in a recent study did not know where Japan was. Forty-five per-

cent of Maryland high-school seniors who were asked recently to
pencil the United States in on a world map couldn't do it. The
whereabouts of their own country was a mystery to them.

Presumably if World War II broke out tomorrow, the Marines might invade Long Island, the Army Air Corps bomb Kansas City and the Navy shell San Francisco.

The issue is about trade-offs. Grant for argument's sake
that shedding the taboo against commonplace nudity made for a
healthier, more honest society. By eliminating the incentive for
young people to learn geography, however, it also made for a
dumber society.

Which is better: healthier, more honest, but dumb? Or sex-
ually inhibited, hypocritical about the human body, but able to
distinguish Kansas City from Japan when on bombing assign-
ments?

Hard choices like this are always involved when progress is
at stake. The problem is that we can rarely foresee the trade-off
until the progress has afflicted us irreversibly. Who could have
foreseen that the wonderful new honesty and health we gained
by making nudity commonplace would stop American youth
from studying the National Geographic, thereby producing an
alarming increase in national dumbness?

There was no real opposition to the National Geographic's
fondness for pictures of people undressed. Nothing to compare
with campaigns waged by social and moral uplifters nowadays.
No pornography commissions appointed by the Attorney General to hustle the church vote by denouncing magazines that
publish pictures of undressed people.

Far from being harassed by uplifters, the National Geographic was recommended by schoolteachers and pious uncles.
It was one of those things like milk, eggs, butter and sunshine
that were then foolishly said to be good for you.

The grown-ups knew about the pictures of undressed humans, but were never heard to disapprove of the Geographic
because of them. That was probably because adults of that be-
nighted, inhibited, repressed age, the age before Playboy, were
more sophisticated than today's adults.

The undressed people in the Geographic always looked
pretty much like the undressed people I saw later in life: not

special. I think adults who recommended the National Geographic remembered what fifth-graders were curious about and thought the wise policy was to calm them down by letting them see the real thing: nothing special.

More than that, though, the adults probably thought a little prurience could be useful if it lured the children into contact with the Geographic's heavy educational content. Let the kids peek, but only where there's a chance they can learn about something besides the unspecial quality of the human shape.

Nowadays you cruise through acres of entertainment nudity and come back so dumb you don't even know where your own country is, much less Japan.

The Heart of Superman

Some Hollywood hype artists came around not long ago. Slick fellows in purple sunglasses and $20 after-shave. Seems they're making this movie about Superman and as part of the hype they want to write me up, all about the fellow who hired Superman onto The Daily Planet, whether Superman could type with all ten fingers or was just a hunt-and-peck man—that sort of thing.

I put the dogs on them. Not because I've got anything against old Superman. Just that, as an old city editor, I know you can't trust a man in purple sunglasses to get the facts straight. He's too busy enjoying being stared at to keep his mind on business.

The first thing they asked me was why I hired Superman. That's when I turned the dogs loose. I knew they wouldn't like the answer. The fact is I hired him because he was willing to work for $20 a week, which was $2.50 less than the going rate for reporters.

You've got to remember, this was back in the Depression.

That's what people forget about Superman. He was strictly a Depression figure. That's why I can't understand why they're making a movie about him nowadays. You take a bunch of people who expect to earn $300 a week just for graduating from college, a bunch of people whose idea of a hero is their cocaine salesman, and how do you expect them to lay out ticket money on an old-fashioned square like Superman?

Anyhow, this well-put-up kid with blue hair and fusspot eyeglasses comes in and says he wants to go to work and will take $20 a week. Pretty soon I can see he's not even worth $10 a week. We have a dame on the staff named Lois who cannot find her way to the morgue without a street map, and even she is scooping the kid.

The managing editor says why don't I fire the big lummox and get a real reporter. And I say to him, "Ed, relax. This is only police news. It's not like we're asking him to cover Hitler or Chamberlain or the Depression or something that matters."

But the truth is, I am soft on the big oaf. The fact is, he is a gentleman. He wears a necktie and says "Please," and "Thank you." This is another reason I think it's nuts to make a movie about him for modern audiences. The only time anybody has seen a gentleman in the last thirty years is on "The Late Show" when William Powell is playing the butler in "My Man Godfrey."

What I like about the kid best of all is his innocence. His second or third day on the job, one of the copyboys comes to me and says, "You know that new guy with the blue hair? He's wearing bright blue long johns and a red cape under his blue serge suit."

Well, I figure maybe he is—you know—a little this way, if you get my meaning, so I have one of the old-timers check him out. After all, though The Planet is a newspaper, we are not totally dumb and blind.

A few days later this old-timer comes back and says, "Nothing to worry about. He's from Krypton. They dress that way on Krypton."

"Any odd habits?" I ask. "If you get my meaning."

"Aside from flying under his own power after stripping

down to his blue long johns in a telephone booth, he's perfectly normal."

So I say, "Flying, huh? What's that all about?" And, of course, he tells me the big ox has superhuman strength and likes to fly around intervening in the police news. He is obviously an overgrown Boy Scout, of which your average newspaper staff even in those days had very few, believe me.

I figure it is no worse having him flying around town doing good deeds than it is having a halfway decent reporter zonked out on boilermakers at the Calvert Bar, especially since he never asks for a raise. What's more, I like his modesty. He is as modest as Joe Palooka and Joe Louis rolled into one. That's another reason I can't figure making a modern movie about the big lug. I haven't seen a hero without a big mouth since Tom Mix and the Old Wrangler were canceled on radio.

Well, I told the staff they'd better humor him and pretend not to notice that he was really flying around town in a blue union suit being modest, civilized, gentlemanly and too timid with the girls to show them his etchings. It was softness on my part, but I couldn't help it. I figured he was a credit to his race.

Then the war came along and everybody got interested in the real news and, afterward, he began to date badly as gentlemen went out of style. I finally had to put him out on early retirement to make room for a reporter who understood economics. Never figured he'd make a comeback in this day and age. Not an old Depression antique like Superman.

Keeping out of Touch

I used to keep up with things. Keeping up with things seemed important. Vital. American. People who did it were on the ball, with it, on their toes, wide awake. No moss grew on them. They had moxie. They were in touch, *au courant,* plugged in. They knew the score.

I wanted to be praiseworthy like that, so I kept up with things. I could name all of Artie Shaw's wives, tell you how many weeks "Elmer's Tune" had been on the Hit Parade and explain how to tell a Buick's age by counting the holes on the side of its hood.

I knew the Yankees should have brought Charlie Keller up from the Newark Bears before the Yankees knew it, knew the Japanese were behaving badly in Manchuria before the makers of War Cards Bubble Gum knew it, knew that Ann ("The Oomph Girl") Sheridan was said to be a descendant of the Civil War hero General Philip Sheridan before other kids on the block knew what the Civil War was.

I am reminded of this because I just had to ask somebody, "Who or what is Cyndi Lauper?"

A disk jockey on radio had been talking as though Cyndi Lauper must be as well known as the Washington Monument. That was annoying. Nine chances out of ten he hadn't the slightest notion who Charlie Keller was, yet here he was, raving as though all humanity would naturally know of Cyndi Lauper.

Anyhow, I asked around and learned who Cyndi Lauper was (wears funny hair and sings) and how to spell it. I do that once in a while when smitten by the old urge to keep up with things. A year ago I found out who Michael Jackson was after a woman I know said her five-year-old daughter, a real charmer, was in love with him.

A man who could win that girl's heart must be worth keeping up with, I thought. The first person I asked wanted me to be ashamed of myself for not knowing who Michael Jackson was. Didn't I know anything? Didn't I know that Michael Jackson had just raked in $1 million or $5 million—I forget which—for making a TV commercial for a big cola company?

Apparently, Jackson was the biggest heist artist since Jesse James. Fortunately, the person who straightened me out was my son. No need to take abuse from him, so when he tried telling me I'd better start keeping up with things or I would soon be as outmoded as Lawrence Welk, I said, "O.K., sonny boy, name all of Artie Shaw's wives," just to teach him humility.

What's wrong with being as outmoded as Lawrence Welk? Admittedly, Welkian music is not the Budapest String Quartet's music, but at least it is music you can whistle, which cannot be said of either the Budapest String Quartet's or Cyndi Lauper's music.

Sneers at Lawrence Welk usually come from people who keep up with things. I no longer see the point of keeping up with most things. I first experienced doubts when Eddie Fisher and Debbie Reynolds were getting divorced so Eddie could marry Elizabeth Taylor.

Eddie looked to me like a potential multimarrier. That bothered me. Artie Shaw was quieting down matrimonially at that time, and I was grateful to him for making it easier to keep up with things. Now suddenly here was Eddie looking as if he might pick up where Artie was leaving off.

For the first time, it occurred to me there might be a lot of things that were not worth keeping up with. This was a moment of liberation.

To this day I do not know how many times Eddie has married. I do know, however, that Eddie Fisher gave me my first glimpse of what freedom could be, and that has made him one of my heroes. Soon thereafter, I was not keeping up with so many things that I had time to read Henry James. What's the use of knowing who Cyndi Lauper is if you've never heard of Daisy Miller?

How, you may ask, can I propound such deep questions after a life wasted learning about the wives of Artie Shaw, Buick holes, "Elmer's Tune" and the genealogy of "The Oomph Girl"? The answer is that age has brought me wisdom, just as the old folks used to say it would.

Age demonstrated that people who can't stop keeping up with things are doomed to become tedious old bores. If you doubt it, come to my house some evening and hear me recite the wives of Artie Shaw, recount Charlie Keller's statistics with the Newark Bears, reminisce about "The Oomph Girl" and whistle "Elmer's Tune," along with several hundred other songs from the Hit Parade.

I predict you will beg for mercy before I get around to telling you about Cyndi Lauper (wears funny hair and sings) and Michael Jackson (also sings but has lost a glove).

THERE'S A
COUNTRY IN MY
CELLAR

In the summer of 1954 I had been in England for a year and a half, so was naturally eager to see old friends the instant I got back to Baltimore. I was dying to tell them about the Tower of London, describe my weekends with belted earls and in a hundred other ways turn them green with envy.

The boat had scarcely docked before I was on the telephone explaining my intentions.

Yes, said a dear friend, I must come to his house and do that the very next night. He would assemble a few people, and we would have a dandy reunion.

I arrived primed to show them how cosmopolitan a man could become once he escaped Baltimore, but before we were done with handshaking and cheery hellos I detected an impatience among them. They were happy to see me, all right, but their minds were elsewhere.

That elsewhere was a huge television set which dominated the room. It had been on when I came in, showing the sort of vaudeville that used to accompany movies in the flossier film houses before Hollywood went bust. This seemed odd. In my experience, serious people never watched television except when sitting at a bar contemplating a glass of beer with their brains turned off. Something strange had happened while I was in England.

Television was not new to me. It had been a common piece of American saloon furniture before I'd left for London, and low-income people were then already buying sets on the installment plan so they could watch professional wrestling at home and keep children sedated. A group of convivial friends sitting

325

in the parlor staring silently at television, however, was unheard of in those days. Yet now, eighteen months later, this was obviously what my friends had been up to. What's more, having properly welcomed me home, they wanted to resume.

They had been watching the most wonderful show: Sid Caesar. It was on every Saturday night. Absolutely wonderful. Hadn't I heard of it? No? Then I must sit down and watch. I would be amazed at how wonderful television had become.

We all sat down, and for the next forty minutes or so looked at the set, just as people used to sit and look at the radio when Franklin Roosevelt delivered a "fireside chat." Conversation ceased among us; the box did all the talking. I date the start of the television age from that Saturday night when I first realized that Americans would now rather commune with furniture than with each other.

Since then it has become clear that television was the most revolutionary event of the century. Its importance was in a class with the discovery of gunpowder and the invention of the printing press, which had changed the human condition for centuries afterward. So too with television. After television the world could never again be as it was before I came back from London.

Humanity would no longer sit on the front steps and chat, or rock on the front porch and ponder silently, or gather in the parlor to see if human friction might brighten the evening. From now on, humanity would hunker down in dim rooms, sitting alone or in silent groups, which is the same thing, watching pictures flicker on electronic furniture.

Being a reactionary, I did the laughable thing and tried resisting the irresistible force of the revolution. It seemed monstrous that this thing, this insolent boxed tube, should be permitted to yammer incessantly night and day in my house. It was like having your house occupied by a mad, hyperthyroid salesman forever dipping into a bottomless satchel to pull out his wares: headache pills, deodorants, soap, beer, lipstick, foot powder, hair oil, auto batteries, razor blades, toilet paper, tire chains, canned soup, cockroach poisons, the whole sad produce of a continent ravaged for profit.

My strategy for fighting the beast grew more and more frantic. I banned the television set from the dining room, then banned viewing anywhere in the house during mealtimes. I put limits on the household's viewing time. I forbade people to look at the most mindless situation comedies, which at this time were usually about a sappy old dad who issued foolish orders that everyone ignored because he was a jerk, but they loved him anyhow.

It was futile, all futile. It was like forbidding people to breathe the air. Television was the environment we lived in. For instance:

It was a late Sunday-morning breakfast with the children. One of them, defying the rule against television during meal hours, had sneaked to the far side of the house. I heard the characteristic piercing cry of the thing, rose from the table to go turn it off and met my son rushing toward the dining room shouting, "They just shot Oswald on television!"

The whole family rushed to the set. Who cares about the silly edicts of reactionary, out-of-date old Dad when the whole family can stand around the set watching Oswald get shot again and again? Not old Dad.

America was happening on television, and if you weren't watching it you were missing America.

I finally accepted the truth in 1972 at Miami Beach where I'd gone to write about the Republican convention nominating Richard Nixon for his second term. I gave it up and went home after the second day. There was no point in being at Miami Beach. The convention had been written in advance as a television script with every event timed to the minute for maximum television effect.

Here was a revelation: The convention wasn't happening at the convention site. It was happening back home on millions of television screens. If I wanted to see the real thing I would have to go home, sprawl out on the couch and turn on the TV. I flew out of Miami next day and was at home that night in time to witness the superb television moment when Sammy Davis Jr. dashed down a ramp and clamped Nixon in a bear hug.

It was a moment that existed only for television, which needs a constant supply of moments as desperately as Count Dracula needs blood. It was the kind of moment—ten seconds that shake the world—that would come to be known under the masterful Reagan as a "sound bite."

"See there," it told televiewers who might have been uneasy about the Nixon people's flirtation with Southern segregationists—"See how famous blacks like Sammy Davis Jr. love and trust Dick Nixon."

Politics in America had turned into television. Elections were designed very much like television advertising campaigns aimed at selling an appealing image to the home viewer. The sensible way to cover them was by watching television.

At this time I was living in Washington in a house with a cellar. When television started threatening to take over our lives I had ordered the set moved down there. The cellar was just remote enough and just inhospitable enough, I thought, to make people ask, "Is this show really worth descending into the pit for?"

When politics was afoot in America I spent a lot of time in that cellar, usually alone since the rest of my family is no more interested in politics than you are. I never felt lonely down there, though. It was where America was happening.

Bad News from the Cellar

The campaign existed only on television. I could go to the cellar and light the box and, lo, the campaign would be right there. "Look," I would say to the cat, who always goes to the cellar with me when I descend for a stiff bout of television, "look, there is a man with immensely telegenic teeth in a northern snowstorm, and I'll bet he is running for President on our very own television box."

He was, of course. The cat knew it, and it bored her. All television politics bores her. She lives only for football, as the campaign lives only for television. Speaking confidentially, I do not like this about the campaign. It makes me suspicious. It is perfectly natural for Kojak to live only for television, but I become uneasy when I see a campaign acting as if it has Kojak envy.

This is why, back in January, I began keeping an eye on the campaign. Ah, those primaries! Night after night, down there in the cellar, and all those hundreds and hundreds of telegenic teeth getting on and off airplanes. But only on television! These embarking and disembarking teeth were as much a fixture of our cellar box as armistices in Lebanon and instant relief from acid indigestion.

When I pushed the button, they ceased to exist, those teeth. I would ascend to the upper world, race outside. The real world! Life! Life! I would be in contact with life out there. Real people with real dogs committing insouciant nuisances on real sidewalks. But not a single emplaning or deplaning jaw of telegenic teeth anywhere in sight.

Carter, Reagan, Ford, Udall, Bayh. Had I uttered any of those great teethogenic names in the real world, I should probably have been placed under observation for possible television fatigue, for everyone knew they had no more reality than the family hour, and considerably less than Johnny Carson.

As the year wore on—wore on? rotted away is more like it—I began sneaky reconnaissance sorties out of the cellar. By that time, both conventions had been held on television, and both parties had nominated the teeth of their choice. Surely, I thought, now the thing will have to make the leap from television to reality.

But no! When I closed the switch on Cronkite, Chancellor and Reasoner, the campaign vanished as rapidly as acid indigestion in the grip of the latest stomach-acid neutralizer. In the real world, not a single billboard, not a bumper sticker, not a campaign button, not even a chintzy window poster proclaiming the excellence of these teeth as opposed to those teeth.

Nothing! Absolutely nothing!

One day I saw a lot of policemen on the street. They said they thought the President was planning to drive by. I wondered if he would be a little ten-inch President slightly out of focus with a chameleon complexion capable of unnerving changes from green to orange around the cheekbones. I waited and waited, and after a while, noting that nobody else except the cops was waiting, I hurried back to the cellar where, in no time at all, I was able to see the President driving down the street. He was only ten inches tall and was completely green.

The cat was disgusted with the increasing amounts of television time being consumed by the campaign. She did not share my alarm about the gravity of this development but simply showed her disdain by going to sleep at once whenever any of the campaigning teeth came on to discourse upon their owner's excellence.

Good citizenship—not to mention reasonable paranoia—seemed to me to demand more aggressive measures. And so, after a long futile search for the campaign out in the real world, I tried to telephone it.

"Campaign headquarters," said the voice at the end of the line.

"I want to speak to the campaign," I said.

"The campaign's out," said the voice.

This was reassuring. "Out where?" I asked, thinking I might rush out in time to catch it and have a word with it.

"It's not exactly 'out,'" said the voice, "so much as it's 'on.' It's out being on television, if you get the nuance."

That was when Ford, Carter, Mondale, Dole and those League of Women Voters people all began lurking right inside the tube, just daring you to turn the thing on so they could go on and on for hours inside the box. It made you want to break down and cry. In fact, the cat did cry one night. I knew what she was thinking. These teeth are going to replace football on television, she was thinking, which will be like never having anything on the tube any more but important messages about acid indigestion.

I turned off the campaign and went up to the real world, leaving the cat in tears. It was very dead out there. End-of-the-world silence. And all up the block, blue lights glowing inside windowed cells, everybody was locked in, watching the campaign. Little ten-inch men doing tiny little media things inside little boxes. Inside little boxes! Little boxes! Boxes!

The Forked-Tongue Phrase Book

How to translate our campaigning politicians:

"My fellow Americans."—"Anybody who switches to the channel showing the movie is unpatriotic."

"It's wonderful to be back in the American heartland"—"What's the name of this dump?"

"Let's look at the record."—"Let's not."

"Peace with honor."—"War."

"Never has democratic government been more gravely endangered."—"My polls show I am likely to get beaten."

"These zealots of the radical left."—"Put me down as a champion of motherhood."

"Without regard to race, creed or color."—"Ho hum."

"Many people have asked me to spell out my position on American policy toward subsidies for the rectified juice industry."—"My ghostwriter thinks there's some political mileage in this, so I agreed to try it."

"Let us remember that these young people are the citizens of tomorrow."—"At present, however, they are still just kids."

"On the way over here a little girl came up to me and said . . ."—"This isn't really true, of course, but my television adviser says it is good for my image to tell anecdotes like this."

"I will never stoop to smear and innuendo."—"The polls show I have it won if I play it cool."

"Let us not judge a man by the way he cuts his hair."—"I

331

trust everyone has noticed that my opponent has not cut his for more than a year."

"My opponent's religion should not be an issue in this campaign, and I will never heed the advice of those who urge me to make it an issue."—"In case it has not been generally observed here, I would like to point out that he adheres to a minority sect with extremely odd views on transubstantiation."

"And standing there in that kibbutz, I said . . ."—"No Arab, I."

"My opponent has sought to sell himself as though he were a powder for the relief of acid indigestion, through use of the most expensive campaign of television huckstering in the history of American government. This crass commercial cheapening of public office is a vice in which I shall never indulge."—"I am in desperate need of funds to purchase television time."

"As Walter Bagehot once said of politics . . ."—"Will any intellectuals in the audience please note that I have a ghostwriter who knows who Walter Bagehot is and will tell me if I want to know."

"The disgruntled young must learn to work effectively within the system for the reforms they so ardently desire."—"Do as I say and in time you may be elected to public office to do as I do."

". . . and I pledge myself to the defense of the Constitution of the United States."—"Upon being elected, I shall immediately offer six amendments to the Constitution to do away with certain unconstitutional provisions now embedded in that document, and to make constitutional certain practices which it now, unfortunately, forbids."

"How wonderful it is to get away from Washington and be back here with the people!"—"At least it gives my liver that rest the doctor ordered."

"Now, I'm going to be perfectly honest about this."—"Oh no I'm not."

At Last, a Candordate

My fellow Americans:

Painful as it is for me to speak to you on television, because of my distaste for talking to machinery, I have chosen this way to announce to you today that I shall be a candidate for President of the United States.

My reason for using television is not flattering to you. To be honest about it, I have been advised that a great many of you whose votes I shall need rarely read anything more adult than the television schedules, and that it would be impossible to communicate with you except through this piece of furniture you are now watching. I believe this to be true.

I tell you this, though some of you will doubtless be offended by it, because I believe it is time to re-establish trust between the American people and their Government. This can only be done if the man at the very apex of Government, the President, will follow a policy of pure candor in dealing with you, the people.

In line with this policy, I must tell you that I am wearing a heavy application of cosmetics around my eyes and mouth, and on my cheeks. The purpose of this makeup is to deceive you with the impression that I am younger, less worn and less fatigued than, in fact, I am.

The gray spots in my hair have been dyed for the same reason. My hair style, this suit I am wearing, this shirt and this necktie were all selected by a committee of men and women who are professional experts in manipulating public opinion and enticing you to buy things you don't need.

I was strongly advised by these professionals not to appear

333

on television at all, but to hire a performer who looked more like a potentially great leader than I do, and to have him appear pretending to be me.

I rejected this proposal because I deplore the recent trend which has turned so many of our great actors into performers for television commercials, and it would break my heart to see members of this great profession reduced to playing politicians in political campaigns.

I must also inform you that I am not now sitting in a studio speaking to you. My advisers told me that to make this announcement "live" would be dangerous. I might make some natural gesture, such as rubbing my nose or scratching my chin, which would betray my natural nervousness under stress.

For this reason, this speech was recorded two weeks ago. Seventeen versions were taped. Snippets of nine of them were spliced together to create this announcement of my Presidential candidacy, which you are now hearing. I do not know where I am at this moment, but if it is being shown in prime evening time, as I hope, the chances are excellent that I am sitting at home with a large snifter of brandy, thoroughly enjoying myself on television.

I tell you this because I think it important for you to know that I am just as vain as the next man. I do most certainly enjoy seeing myself on television, even when I do not look much like me, as in this particular appearance.

I also enjoy seeing my picture in newspapers and magazines, and I am certain that I would enjoy the sensation of knowing that my words and acts were being discussed around the earth every day. I like the idea of everybody having to stand up when I walk into the room.

Frankly, ladies and gentlemen, I like to feel important, and one of the reasons I want to be President is to satisfy my vanity. It will almost certainly be an important factor in my decision—if I am elected—to run for a second term.

In my effort to be entirely honest with you, I am not going to overemphasize my interest in the vacation possibilities of the Presidency. Frankly, the knowledge that, as President, I would have my own jetliner and helicopters, chauffeured limousines and yacht, as well as sundry vacation White Houses in climates of my choosing—all these make the Presidency far more attractive to me than it would be if it required one to ride to work on the bus and offered only a two-week vacation in the family station wagon.

I would never, however, accept any job simply because the fringe benefits were excellent. For me, a job must also be absorbing, interesting and rich in ego gratification and pay a good salary.

The Presidency appeals to me on all these grounds. It would be immensely absorbing to me to fly to all the vacation spas for conferences with Prime Ministers, other Presidents, Chancellors and the more debonair dictators.

It would be both interesting and gratifying to see the most brilliant minds of the Ivy League sparkle and glisten at my command. The salary is excellent. Even if I served only one term, it would solve the serious financial problem of my children's educations. The expense account, needless to say, is superb, and free housing will be a godsend, since mortgage payments, utilities and upkeep on my present house are now so high that I have not been able to afford a suit in the past three years.

In all honesty, I have no program as yet. Any program I may announce before the election will almost surely be abandoned if I am elected. All I promise is complete honesty and absolute refusal to try to deceive you. My advisers tell me that not one in twenty among you will vote for such a candidate, and, in all honesty, I must tell you that I believe them.

No Curiosity Filled the Cats

Down to the cellar we went and lit up the horror box. The President was playing the piano again. This time at the Grand Ole Opry. "God Bless America." He plays badly, perhaps by design, for he is a man of design, fearful of the natural gesture, careful to contrive cocoons of image protecting the private man from public grasp.

If he could play like Paderewski, who was also a President, he would not dare it in public. Wrong image. Long hair, Beethoven's "Appassionata," highbrow music, tender sensibility—it would never play in Peoria, as they used to say around the White House in the glory autumn of 1972. In any case, he did not play the piano well at the Grand Ole Opry. It is O.K. to like Presidents who play the piano if they do not do it well.

What are we doing down in this cellar with the box lit? A continuing experiment. Can cats be made to look at television? And if not, why? Do cats have some higher critical faculty? They are intensely interested in everything else that occurs in this house, but so far they have absolutely refused to look at television.

The cats are not the least interested in observing the President of the United States at the keyboard in Nashville. Just the other day we had the President on this same box playing the piano at the White House in accompaniment to Pearl Bailey, and the cats gave it not a single glance. It is probably because they have no sense of history, no taste for irony, no ugly obsession with the intricate processes by which men are destroyed in the public arena.

With any sense of history at all, they might have paused to reflect that this outburst of public piano was pointedly reminiscent of Harry Truman, who also did turns at the keyboard. In his agony President Nixon was working to spin yet another image for the public's distraction: embattled, feisty Harry, who walked with kings but had the common touch.

Richard Nixon's admiration for Truman extends back twenty years when he used to quote Truman's homily about getting out of the kitchen if you can't stand the heat. Even now with Nixon's polls on the bottom, Nixon loyalists cleave to Truman, whose polls were just as bad. And here we are, lighting the box to find him doing a Truman.

Well, Truman was a natural man and Nixon is an image spinner. Twenty-six months ago, on top of the world, he was Big

Brother. The American people were like children, he told an interviewer. Discipline was what they needed. Had to learn that instant gratification of every wish was not the route to a healthy polity. Now, on the ropes, here he is in the cellar. Harry Truman, free spirit and battler against heavy odds, piano-pounder to an amused populace.

Who is Nixon really? The cats are blind to the mystery. With irony they might see at least that this piano playing is, well, *interesting* because done by a man who in his Disraeli manifestation dreamed of the generation of peace. The nobility of the dream and the clownishness of this public straining to play the nice guy do not play in the cellar, although this particular cellar is admittedly not Peoria.

The images are out of joint. If the cats had the slightest sensitivity, they would surely see, wouldn't they? that something terrible is happening on this very box which they refuse to consider. A man is being destroyed. Or is it only a cocoon of images that is being torn to pieces? And if so, will we find that there is nobody inside the cocoon? That the cocoon has absorbed the man and left nothing but images—all illusions without juice? Disraeli, Truman, Big Brother, A. Mitchell Palmer, Babbitt, Lincoln, King Charles I, Scipio Africanus standing between Western civilization and Asiatic Hannibal.

It is dreadful to see this happening in the cellar. He was there the other night for what is called a news conference, although no one confers and no news occurs. The cats would not watch. One tried to hold them, to make them confront the screen, but the grip failed as the mind became absorbed in the appalling nature of the spectacle, and soon the cats had fled to the laundry tubs to torment the crickets.

Next day the papers said the President had not done badly. Well . . . perhaps so, if one considered the thing as yet another exercise in image projection. There were moments of dynamism at which image critics might have said yes, he is projecting Presidentialism very well, very Theodore Rooseveltish.

Looking for the man, however, one saw a sad, groggy figure who had taken a brutal pummeling and was going on grit alone. If the Watergate thing were a prizefight, it would have been stopped long ago. There in the cellar it seemed that he had already taken such punishment that the damage would surely be permanent. It is truly a horror box we have down there.

Afterward, much later, patience brought us Morris—or is it Maurice?—television's feline cat-food salesman. The cats were rushed to the screen, eyes front. Surely they would show a flicker of interest in one of their own.

They did not. Cats, it seems, have no stomach for witnessing the debasement of their species. Strange creatures.

Postscript

Careful readers may be puzzled about a difference between the cats in the cellar while Mr. Nixon played the piano and the cat in the cellar a few pages back who wept because she feared television might replace football with politicians. The cats who watched Nixon had no interest in watching anything at all on television, including football.

In these years our house supported a variety of cats with a variety of tastes. Different cats joined me in the cellar at different times. A few pages up ahead I will be found watching politicians with a mouse. "What a brave mouse," you may say, "to hang around the TV set with so many cats in residence."

The truth is duller. By the time of the mouse, all cats had been carried away by our daughter. My wife and I had also been carried away, by moving van, to New York, where practically nobody can afford a cellar. The room I watched in there was a combination kitchen, dining room, parlor, foyer, coat closet, and mud room. This was a very typical New York sort of room, except that ours had a mouse. Most have cockroaches.

And All of Us So Cool

The candidates were so cool, so detached. We were soon reassured that this night they would make no mess in Philadelphia, take no risks, rouse no passions. One was reminded of those "surgical air strikes" that used to be performed on Hanoi. Objectives attained without bloodshed, courtesy of American technical proficiency. Everything neat, controlled. A surgical strike on the American electorate to drop ten-ton images into the national brain.

The sense of detachment from the event deepened as the first half-hour eroded into the second half hour. We hunkered down against a sleet storm of bewildering statistical data. Budget deficits, tax-revenue projections for 1981, the comparative veto rates of Roosevelt, Nixon, Ford. Yes, yes, these men walked easily among decimal points. They were cool in the presence of statistics of astounding arguability. It had to be admired, even though the statistics engorged the nonpresidential brain with puzzlement and the urge to doze.

Surely many of these splendidly precise statistics were being invented on the spur of the moment. No matter. In televisionland we are all sophisticated enough now to realize that every statistic has an equal and opposite statistic somewhere in the universe. It is not a candidate's favorite statistic per se that engages us, but the assurance with which he can use it.

We are testing the candidates for self-confidence, for "Presidentiality" in statistical bombardment. It doesn't really matter if their statistics be homemade. What settles the business is the cool with which they are dropped.

And so, as the second half hour treads the decimaled path

toward the third half hour, we become aware of being locked into a tacit conspiracy with the candidates. We know their statistics go to nothing of importance, and they know we know, and we know they know we know.

There is total but unspoken agreement that the "debate," the arguments which are being mustered here, are of only the slightest importance.

As in some primitive ritual, we all agree—candidates and onlookers—to pretend we are involved in a debate, although the real exercise is a test of style and manners. Which of the competitors can better execute the intricate maneuvers prescribed by a largely irrelevant ritual?

This accounts for the curious lack of passion in both performers. Even when Ford accuses Carter of inconsistency, it is done in a flat, emotionless, game-playing style. The delivery has the tuneless ring of an old press release from the Republican National Committee. Just so, when Carter has an opportunity to set pulses pounding by denouncing the Nixon pardon, he dances delicately around the invitation like a maiden skirting a bog.

We judge that both men judge us to be drained of desire for passion in public life, to be looking for Presidents who are cool and noninflammable. They present themselves as passionless technocrats using an English singularly devoid of poetry, metaphor and even coherent forthright declaration.

Caught up in the conspiracy, we watch their coolness with fine technical understanding and, in the final half hour, begin asking each other for technical judgments. How well is Carter exploiting the event to improve our image of him? Is Ford's television manner sufficiently self-confident to make us sense him as "Presidential"?

It is quite extraordinary. Here we are, fully aware that we are being manipulated by image projectionists, yet happily asking ourselves how obligingly we are submitting to the manipulation. It is as though a rat running a maze were more interested in the psychologist's charts on his behavior than in getting the cheese at the goal line.

This night, however, there is a reassuring human event. The television sound breaks down. So much technical splendor on the platform, and such a comic display of technology's whimsical imperfections in the sound box. We are abruptly thrust back into the imperfect human world, and the bogus quality of the event overtakes us.

We, after all, inhabit a world where things are always breaking down at crucial instants. We are suddenly reminded that neither of these cool political technicians has made much allusion all night to this world.

Neither has given any sign that we live in a country with race problems. Not a word about the anguish of cities which house 70 percent of the population. Nothing about the fade-out of the school system, the intolerable costs of college education, the breakdown of public transportation.

At some point in the long interruption, a television voice struggling to fill time, talks of the heavy makeup on Ford and Carter. It is so heavy, he notes, that "they don't look like themselves." It takes me back to a time of open-coffin funerals when the critics would pass judgment at the bier. "He looks just like himself," was the line of praise. He had to look very bad indeed to earn the line, "He doesn't look like himself."

I went to a mirror during the interlude, but couldn't decide whether I looked like myself or not.

No Business Like *What* Business?

About midnight a man appeared on the television screen in the cellar of our house to tell about a killing he had committed. Everybody else in the house had gone to bed. I mention this because the odd aspect of this whole business, looking back on it, was one watcher's personal reaction to this midnight of television and, in order to convey any sense at all of the peculiarity of the thing, I have to give you a glimpse of my personal situation.

Everybody else, then, was in bed. What is curious is that it never occurred to me to race upstairs and rouse anyone. Here was a man going on in great detail right there in our cellar about this killing he had performed, yet it seemed no more worth disturbing the house for than if it had been another Phyllis Diller appearance.

It was the Dick Cavett show and it had begun, as usual, with Dick's monologue, and a promise of pleasant anesthesia as Dick read off the cast of show-biz people on hand to plug their various enterprises.

Brian Bedford came first. He is in a play in New York and seemed agreeable. Agreeability is a virtue at midnight in the cellar, at least in our house, and since there is too little of it, Brian was a welcome guest.

He and Dick kept smiling, even through one rocky passage about a suicide. One felt headache and reality slinking off in defeat; one sensed the settling of the facial muscles into a fixed, fatigued smile. That smile, the cat could have told you, was a smile seen only on the best midnights down in that cellar, a smile that said, "All is, for this brief moment, right with the world."

Brian and Dick paused while several brief films were run. Most of them argued that this or that spot on the body gave off unpleasant odors and showed expensive aerosol sprays which would make the offending flesh smell like a chemistry lab. It was ridiculous stuff but amusing in a dumb way.

Then Dick was back with his next guest. He introduced Captain Bob Marasco. The audience applauded. Down in our cellar, the pleased smile may have shown a trace of frown. Captain Marasco? The name was vaguely familiar. Was it somebody who had just made a new Andy Warhol movie?

It was not. Dick said that Captain Marasco, who lived in Bloomfield, N.J., was a former Green Beret officer who had been charged by the Army some time ago with murdering a Vietnamese man and then discharged from the service after the murder charge had been dropped.

A few days before his guest appearance with Dick, Bob had told The New York Times that he had, in fact, killed the Vietnamese in question, who he said was a triple espionage agent. Dick quickly filled in his audience on this background, and Bob, who had a lot of poise on camera, began to tell about the killing.

In the opening phase, I did not listen so much as I looked. That is the norm when you get a new personality on the talk shows. Bob appeared to be a tall, broad-shouldered, athletic young man. His clothing style was mod without being odd. "Carefully groomed" would be the cliché. A careful man, a methodical man. Perhaps even a finicky, fastidious man when it came to details. Very neat in his habits one would guess. A good worker.

Bob's account of the killing seemed to bear this out. He answered Dick's questions with details that a less fastidious man might have glossed over in his recitation. Yes, Bob said, Dick was right: two shots in the fellow's head. Of course, he had been pumped full of morphine before the shooting, which made it as humanitarian as you could possibly make something as awkward as killing a man, Bob volunteered.

Dick looked slightly aghast and held up a shampoo. Brief films were shown to sell consumer goods. This was not too dull, this talk with Bob. Would Dick cut it short to bring on Patsy Kelly, who was playing in "No, No, Nanette"?

Gosh, all the talk shows had somebody from "No, No, Nanette," but how many nights did anybody come up with a guest like Bob?

The show was back. Good! Dick was going to keep Bob talking. What do you do now for a living? he asked Bob. Bob smiled slightly, knowing he was going to get a laugh, already indicating he would rather not. He said he sold life insurance. The audience laughed. Brian, who was still there, looked white and wilted, although this may just have been a faulty video tube.

Dick asked about putting the body in a mail sack and weighting it with tire irons and dumping it from a rowboat into several hundred feet of water in the China Sea, and he asked why Bob thought the body had not been found. Bob smiled the smile of a man who knew something unpleasant and said the waters were "shark-infested."

Brian asked how Bob could possibly have done it. Bob said he had what amounted to an official execution order from the C.I.A. An order to "eliminate with extreme prejudice." Everybody who worked with the C.I.A. knew what that meant, Bob said. He had done it to serve his country, to serve us in the audience, to serve me down there in my cellar. He was not telling it now for profit, was not making any money, in fact, from his story. He just wanted us to know what duty we were all exacting from our Army.

There was a station break. A brief film showed a liquid that did a terrific job of cleaning a toilet. By 1 A.M. Bob had begun to pall and when Dick went off I dialed with a yawn in search of an old movie. Later, going up to bed, there was a moment on the steps when the numbness lifted momentarily, and I marveled, for just an instant, that the TV set never turned into a cobra and bit us.

Pair of Country Slickers

It is late at night, but maybe not as late as it seems. Maybe it seems later than it is because Walter Mondale is bowling. The spectacle of a man running for President by bowling can leave you disoriented.

But then, maybe it really is late, for the mouse is out. I don't know how long the mouse has been staring at me, because I have been too busy staring at Walter Mondale bowling. I think he is bowling in Queens.

"He wouldn't bowl in Manhattan, would he?"

This is addressed to the mouse, and if I am talking to the mouse it must be very late at night.

"I mean, if a man's running for President, he would bowl in Queens, visit a synagogue in Brooklyn and drink a Perrier with lime in Manhattan."

The mouse has grown comfortable with me, but he never converses. He likes my companionship, and I like his. I used to have a cat who sat with me and watched men run for President, and she never talked either, but she died shortly after the 1980 campaign, died happily too, for she was enchanted by Ronald Reagan.

I didn't know how I'd get through the 1984 campaign until the mouse came along, but now, with companionship again to see me through, I believe we're going to make it. The mouse sneers as Walter Mondale's bowling ball rumbles down the alley, knocks down seven pins and leaves three standing.

I have to explain politics to the mouse:

"What he's doing, you see, is, he's showing the voters of Queens he can't bowl any better than most of them can, so they won't have to worry about having a President who'll invite them to the White House bowling alley and humiliate them by rolling a perfect 300."

Walter Mondale is replaced by a man with a ruined auto transmission, which is repaired perfectly in thirty seconds. He is replaced by a young man who is grinning smugly at the prospect of dying because he has so much more life insurance than I have.

"Neither of those men will ever be President," I tell the mouse. "Too many voters feel inferior to people who can get their cars repaired without six trips back to the shop, and nobody likes a guy who's just itching to die."

Senator Gary Hart replaces a third loser, some bird whose car is so sexy that women can't keep their hands off him. Senator Hart is saying he will move the American Embassy in Israel from Tel Aviv to Jerusalem.

The mouse gives me a puzzled look, which I interpret to mean, "Is Hart making a play for the moving men's vote?" A shrewd question, too, for moving men are a big part of the New York population. I can imagine Freddie Feddeck who moves me and my twenty tons of books every other month leaping on the Hart band van, thinking, "First he'll move the Tel Aviv Embassy to Jerusalem, then the London Embassy to Manchester, then the Rome Embassy to Naples, then . . ."

Yes, Hart's hint of eternal full employment for moving men cannot be taken lightly, but the mouse is missing the main point. He is a very young mouse. He does not remember Estes Kefauver.

"Hart's promise to move that embassy reminds me of Estes Kefauver," I say. "Running for President, Estes drifted into a northern Minnesota town, dead tired in the dead of night—this was back in '56—and was led into a packed hall, and his advance man said, 'This crowd is full of Indians,' and Estes said, 'What's their problem?' and the advance man looked at him the way you'd look at a half-wit and said, 'Damn it, Estes, they're Indians!'"

The mouse didn't get it.

"Look," I tell him, "you've got this Colorado, cowboy-boots Hart, groggy with fatigue, and they haul him into New York and tell him there's a big Jewish vote here, and he says, 'What's their problem?' so somebody tells him, 'They're miserable because our embassy is located in Tel Aviv instead of Jerusalem.' He's treating them like Estes going after the Indian vote."

Time passes. Hours. Possibly days. You lose track of everything when men are running for President in the parlor. When, for example, did the mouse get up on the kitchen counter and put his nose right up to the action like that? He has spotted a huge cheese while all I have noticed is Walter Mondale.

Yes, Walter Mondale is running for President in a West Side delicatessen. From the ceiling hang dozens of salamis. Corned beef, salami, lox surround him. The mouse is trying to get at the cheese, but Walter Mondale is in the way.

Gary Hart is in an Irish bar. "What's their problem?" he must have asked, for he is telling the customers how he will unite Northern Ireland to the Republic. Uninterested in beer, the mouse has dozed off.

Prescript

President Reagan brought us to the ultimate: America As Total Television. During his governance the printed word simply ceased to matter. White House dynamos had once telephoned newspapers to complain about unfair reporting. Not anymore. Now they telephoned television network bosses. Even then it wasn't poor reporting they complained about, but poor pictures.

A network reporter who thought her report on shortcomings in Reaganland would anger the President's cadres was amazed when the man in charge of propaganda thanked her for doing them a good turn. But, she said, that was a tough piece of reporting.

Oh, the words may have been, said the gentleman, but on television words didn't matter. What mattered were pictures. And the pictures had been wonderful.

At this stage the sales techniques had become so subtle that you didn't know you were being sold anything. Fortunately, cable television produced shopping channels at this very moment. Watching one before switching to the news sharpened the wits so you could understand what the government was really peddling.

"Star Wars" Mania

Now at last "Star Wars" can be yours.

You have read about "Star Wars" in the newspapers.

You have heard about "Star Wars" on television.

You have seen famous men rave about what "Star Wars" has meant to them.

Here is a typical letter from Mr. C.K., president of a large munitions plant in one of the most famous states of the Union:

"After I was indicted on charges of being a cheap chiseler just because a few bookkeeping errors resulted in a $35-million overcharge to the Pentagon," he writes, "it looked like I would have to go to the end of the line for the big military contracts. Then I saw President Reagan selling 'Star Wars' on TV, and today I have a new lease on life."

Yes, friends, Mr. C.K. not only has a new lease on life, he also has his claws into one sweet and juicy deal that calls for bouncing a laser beam off an earth-orbiting target of Army surplus uniforms.

Does that sound like fun? You bet it does. But Mr. C.K.

didn't go into "Star Wars" just for fun alone. No, ma'am. He also gets a Federal guarantee that no matter how much money "Star Wars" pays him, he will not be required to pay any tax whatever on that money until "Star Wars" is absolutely and entirely completed.

And when do you think that will be, Mother?

If you said "never," you have a naughty mind in addition to a natural instinct for knowing which Federal trough to get your snout into to avoid those unpleasant tax payments every April.

All right, I know what you're hearing, Mother. Right there in your parlor at this very moment, Dad is raising a lot of questions, isn't he?

Dad is saying, "I don't see why I have to put out a lot of dough for 'Star Wars' when we still haven't used up that whole case of Peruna that door-to-door salesman talked me into back in 1947."

That's all right, Dad. Dads are supposed to raise questions like that. That's why the good Lord made dads. But have you ever asked yourself this question? Isn't President Reagan a dad?

Isn't Secretary of Defense Weinberger a dad?

And what about those generals and colonels and public-relations officers in the Pentagon? Aren't most of them dads, just like most of those far-seeing, fun-loving Congressmen who have already O.K.'d hundreds of millions to buy "Star Wars"?

Are you going to say all those dads are wrong? Do you want to be the only dad who says we don't need "Star Wars" as long as the Peruna holds out?

Of course you don't. Listen to what Mr. M.J., a former doubting dad of Moline, Ill., writes to the makers of "Star Wars":

"I was formerly a doubting dad and then I saw a little girl with a crayon on TV illustrate what fun it would be to have 'Star Wars.' Next day I called the 'Star Wars' salesman and told him I'd been a fool because I wanted to keep my money to send my daughter to college, but now I wanted them to take it for 'Star Wars.'"

Yes, folks, Mr. M.J., former doubting dad, got his priorities straight at last. That's why the money for his daughter's college education has already been delivered to the crack scientific laboratories of a famous munitions plant in California where cheap chiselers will soon be providing hilariously amusing alibis for spending it on Caribbean vacations. And that, Dad, is just a small sample of the fun available through "Star Wars."

Now I hear a skeptic out there saying, "Sure, we all want to provide cheap chiselers with Caribbean vacations, but just exactly what is this 'Star Wars' that's going to make their chiseling so fruitful?"

Well, Mr. Skeptic, I suppose you've heard of the H-bomb and the kind of people who've got their hands on it and what they'd like to do if they could get away with it.

That's right, Mother, you tell Mr. Skeptic. They'd like to bounce those bombs right off America's noodle. Thank heaven for "Star Wars." Do you know what you get with "Star Wars," Mr. Skeptic? A big umbrella all over America.

When those people, and I mention no names, aim their bombs at our noodle, "Star Wars" catches them between the umbrella ribs and bounces them right back where they came from. Does that sound like fun? If you laughed last time you saw a hog try to walk on ice, wait until you see "Star Wars" bounce those bombs back to the workers' paradise.

So for thousands of laughs phone the White House, Pentagon or Congress right away and tell them you want "Star Wars," or send a certified check or money order immediately to the cheap chiseler of your choice.

Remember, for a daringly different way to put life into that tired old military industrial complex—"Star Wars"!

WE'RE LOSING CONTACT, CAPTAIN

Here are some fussy pieces about the low state of the mother tongue. I can't help the fussiness. It's the nature of writers to be fussy on this subject. They tend to love words too much, so become testy when words are abused, as they almost always are wherever English is spoken, which is practically everywhere nowadays.

Most English speakers do not have the writer's short fuse about seeing or hearing their language brutalized. This is the main reason, I suspect, that English is becoming the world's universal tongue: English-speaking natives don't care how badly others speak English as long as they speak it. French, once considered likely to become the world's lingua franca, has lost popularity because those who are born speaking it reject this liberal attitude and become depressed, insulted or insufferable when their language is ill used.

In defense of fussiness, I merely point out that the present age's simple-minded love affair with communications may soon make it impossible for anybody to tell what is on anybody else's mind. That's because what we call communications nowadays is mostly just racket and commotion. Telephones ring, fax machines quiver, bullhorns vibrate, computers beep, radios blare, television sets shout. . . .

Most ideas are too fragile to survive this uproar long enough to make the journey from one person to another. Words become a minor part of the racket and are not to be taken too seriously. President Reagan, hailed as "The Great Communicator," was usually incoherent when talking Presidential business without a speech-writer's text. What he communicated was

353

a sense of this or that—a sense of confidence, of well-being, of being a nice fellow, of being trustworthy, of being . . . well, a helluva fellow, that's all. Which is not an idea, but only an impression.

Since most of us are illiterate in mathematics, words remain the best tools available for letting each other know what we have in mind. With its intimidating mixture of noise and gesture aimed at creating impressions, feelings, senses and images, the communications gargantua debases the currency of the word and endangers our ability to . . . well, to communicate with each other if we come across something the world ought to know about in no uncertain terms.

Going in for Jefferson

It is the 26th of June. Thomas Jefferson has only eight more days to get the Declaration of Independence written for the Fourth of July, and so far he has written only one sentence. It is seventy-one words long. The boos of the spectators in Philadelphia cascade down from the grandstands as he struggles to move his quill into the second sentence.

The fans are throwing grog bottles onto his desk and chanting, "Bye-bye, Tom!" It is clear they want a ghostwriter to go in for Jefferson. Let's try to move our microphone through the debris and get a word with this courageous but embattled young Virginian. Tom! Tom! Here he is, ladies and gentlemen: the fellow from Monticello!

"Not right now, please. It's very hard to write with so much commotion going on."

And you proved it, Tom Jefferson, with that opening sentence. Seventy-one words long! Are you going to be able to shorten the sentences from here on in, Tom, and get more punch into your attack?

"I have a beautiful sentence blocked out as a follow-up, and it will run only thirty-five words. Maybe thirty-six if you count 'self-evident' as two words."

Could you tell the patriots of America right now what that sentence is, Tom Jefferson?

"We hold these truths to be self-evident—"

Hold it right there, Tom.

"You don't like the opening?"

It doesn't sound official, Tom. This is a serious official document you're working on. You can't just tell people you hold truths to be self-evident. You've got to make it sound like you've had all the resources of the country overwhelming you with data. Give me that quill and I'll show you what I mean.

There. Now read that, Tom Jefferson.

"'Public opinion polls and highly classified scientific research strongly indicate that a substantial majority supports the contention that there can be little or no credible opposition to the following philosophical assertions—'"

Listen to those fans roar, Tom! At last we're moving the ball for independence!

"But this sentence, aside from its appearing to have been translated directly from Urdu, is already thirty-one words long, and we haven't yet stated which philosophical assertions enjoy indications of the substantial majority support specified in our contention of negligible credible opposition."

Tell us what they are, Tom, and we'll add them on.

"That all men are created equal, that they are endowed by their Creator with certain unalienable rights, that among these are Life, Liberty and the pursuit of Happiness."

O.K., I'll put it in the mother tongue for you. There— Read that.

"Are you an agent of King George?"

Read it, Tom, and listen to that crowd roar.

"'That the totality of persons of both sexes—'"

You can't say "all men," Tom. That's sexist. And you don't want to say "all." It doesn't sound as official as "the totality of." Read on.

"'That the totality of persons of both sexes partake of equality at parturition—'"

Now that makes it sound like we've been to college, Tom.

"'—that they possess a quantum of rights, accruing through the circumstance of birth, which, in the absence of a final determination as to the existence of a divine Creator with the aforesaid rights-endowment capability, it would be counterproductive to ascribe to said putative Creator in view of the fact that such pursuit of questions of origin could only open Pandora's box, revealing a basket of snakes which would leave us with a mare's nest in which we might throw out the baby with the bath water.'"

The crowd loves it, Tom. Listen to those grandstands go wild.

"But it's not English."

Of course not, Tom. That's why they love it. It's American.

"Never!"

You have seen the future, Tom, and it writes American.

"Then why did they boo my opening sentence because of a mere seventy-one words?"

Because they could understand it, Tom. When you go to seventy-one words you've got to be incomprehensible to be respected. If you're going to make sense in American, you've got to do it in short bursts.

"Fabulous!"

Terrific, Tom! You've got it! The perfect first sentence for the declaration.

"Wow! I mean. Really. You know?"

Ladies and gentlemen, the greatest! Tom Jefferson!

New Age Babble

The company providing our cable-television service has just accessed me with a print communication, or, as the old-timers used to say, "sent me a letter."

It says the price of the cable service has been "adjusted." It doesn't say who adjusted it. Could the watchman have fallen asleep, permitting some rascal to sneak in and adjust the price?

Hah! I know what "the price has been adjusted" means in New Age Babble. It means "price is going up." I don't whine about prices going up. That's what prices do. What I object to is being told the price has been "adjusted."

What's wrong with companies that can't come right out and say, "Folks, the price is going up again"? They can't believe we're so dumb we don't know that "price adjustment" is New Age Babble meaning "price rise."

My theory is that companies are run nowadays by people who enjoy talking New Age Babble. Maybe they now have to talk that way to get to the top, the way you had to talk weird in advertising agencies in the old, old days to show you were on the ball.

Yes, there really was a time when adult human beings could be taken seriously after saying, "Let's run it up the flag-pole and see if anybody salutes."

My theory is that people who talk New Age Babble nowadays are forced to use it to get ahead and, after talking it among themselves long enough, forget that they are talking silly.

Fellow Americans, do we really want to be accessed by communications? Send me a letter or call me on the telephone, but access me not by communication devices: This is my plea, and I might as well be talking to the west wall.

Or, as a New Age Babbler might put it, "might as well try to impact the west wall." The New Age is the age of impacting.

Systems are constantly not only impacting, but also being impacted. Processes also get a lot of action, impact-wise. For instance, not long ago I was startled to hear a man on "The MacNeil/Lehrer NewsHour" call a cigarette a "nicotine-delivery system."

In New Age Babble, however, I was not startled; something far more ponderous had happened. My impression-input system had been impacted by the man's long-winded synonym for "cigarette."

There's hardly anything that a New Age Babbler can't convert into a dreary, dull, mind-numbing, excruciatingly boring system. Take the automobile. In New Age Babble it is not a car; it's an individually operable, quadri-wheeled, internal-combustion, surface transportation system.

This curiosity constantly experiences processes. If it sits at the curb, it is because it has undergone the parking process. If it balks and refuses to work, into the garage it goes for the repair process. The repair process ends with the owner's bank account being impacted by a bill.

The New Age Babbler spends much of his life in situations. If the mechanic's bill bankrupts him, he enters a bankruptcy situation. If he resorts to embezzlement to save himself, he is involved in an embezzlement situation.

If he escapes with millions to South America, he settles into a South American situation. There he probably enters the language-study process so he can figure out how big a price adjustment will follow the latest print communication to impact his mail slot.

There is another theory, incidentally about why people speak New Age Babble. This is, that its speakers really do think we're too dumb to know what they're saying.

The evidence always adduced for this theory is the Reagan Administration's invention of the term "revenue enhancement." I always assumed this was a joke produced by some wise guy at the Treasury who had to talk about getting more tax money in an era when the President had said he wouldn't let taxes rise.

Joke or not, every American smart enough to cope with Form 1040 instantly knew that "revenue enhancement" was just a flannel-mouth synonym for "tax boosts."

Speaking of taxes, "Read my lips" is not New Age Babble but something quite different, though perhaps equally annoying—especially to President Bush, who must now live with it. It is the kind of talk that seems vital and dynamic during campaign excitements, but is seen as merely tiresome or embarrassing when political fever subsides.

Another example: "The (insert letter of alphabet) Word." Before the 1988 Presidential campaign, it was "the C word," referring to cancer; in the campaign, "the L word." Recently I've seen "the M word" (referring to "Minimalist") and "the R word" ("Recession"). It's become "the E. A. phrase" ("Enough already!").

The Risings Tide

There was a heavy onset of Daylight Savings Time over the weekend. On Saturday anchorfolks on Channels 2 and 4 both warned New York that Daylight Savings Time was imminent.

Ignoring them, I started searching the radio dial for Jerry Lee Lewis or the Big Bopper, only to come up with a doctor who was saying something medical and uninteresting about Daylight Savings Time.

"The world isn't really coming unhinged," I said at bedtime. "It's just normal Saturday breakdown."

Sunday morning. Finally got to front page of Saturday's Washington Post: "Daylight Savings Time," it said, would start soon.

So it hadn't been just normal Saturday breakdown after all. No. It was continuing. In fact, the thing seemed to be infecting me because I heard myself saying out loud, "It's continuings."

"Whose continuings are you talking about?" asked my wife, who had started the morning with The New York Times. "And if you're talking again about the continuings of Marcel Proust's 'Remembrance of Things Past,' kindly talk to yourself while I finish this article about a crisis in a young women's finishing school."

"A young women's finishings school," I blurted.

She gave me one of those are-you-all-right looks and said, very firmly, "Young women's finishing school."

When corrected I don't normally carry on the way many husbands do, which probably explains why the police so rarely visit us in their official capacity. This time, though, I was in the power of something bigger than either of us. It was called English Usage.

"If anchorpeople, doctors and The Washington Post can shamelessly say 'Daylight Savings Time,'" I explained, "I have a perfect right to say 'young women's finishings school.'"

She resumed reading. "Do you realize," I asked, "that just yesterday, all over this part of America we had Eastern Standards Time?"

"Eastern Standard Time, not Eastern Standards Time," she said through gritted voice.

"And then at two o'clock this morning," I went on, "Eastern Standards Time slipped away and was replaced by Daylight Savings Time."

Astonishingly, she seemed uninterested in the eerie condition that engulfed us. "Am I right in believing you have to save at least two daylights before you can have daylight savings?" I asked.

She ignored me now, as she had always done when I used to cross-examine radio commercials in which hysterical people talk about making "a savings" by buying something. For many years I had been puzzled by the mathematical question implicit in these commercials: To wit, how could money be saved by spending it?

Eventually I realized I'd been misled by a faulty understanding of the advertising tongue. "A savings," which I had presumed to be an illiterate's way of saying "a saving," obviously had nothing whatever to do with saving. It was a term, probably from Old Norse by the look of it, which meant "monetary expenditure."

Until I grasped this, however, I always cried out when one of these radio spendthrifts started raving about "a savings" made by blowing the bank account. And what I always cried out was, "How can you save money by spending it?"

In those days at first she used to say, "It does no good to talk to the radio, you know." Of course it didn't. I knew that. Still it made me feel better. The radio seemed to be talking to me on the assumption that I was an imbecile. It felt good snarling back at it, telling it where to get off.

I wanted to hear my wife shout out in support, but she was afraid the neighbors would think her peculiar, I suppose, for very soon she began ignoring it when I talked back to the radio. Just as she was ignoring me now.

"Attention must be paid," I said. "Unless somebody notices when anchorpeople, doctors and The Washington Post start talking about Daylight Savings Time, we may all end up talking about young women's finishings schools, worrying whether the U.S. Army is an effective fightings machine and singing about how wonderful we will all feel on that great gettings-up morning."

"Listen," she said. "If you're trying to say the world must be getting really dumb when smart people like anchorfolks, doctors and The Washington Post go around uttering illiteracies like 'Daylight Savings Time,' go ahead and say it so we can have a little quiet while I read this piece about the development of these new miracle fertilizing agents."

"Miracle fertilizings agents," I said.

Don't Tell Old Pharaoh

Isn't there anybody left in the United States who feels himself the victim of injustice?

The question comes to mind because of the heavy volume of complaint lately in which spokesmen for the American discontented, speaking for large ill-defined constituencies, talk about their oppression. No group with an ax to grind is socially aggrieved these days, or politically abused, or economically cheated. They are invariably oppressed.

What they really are, of course, is afflicted; they are suffering from the fearful late twentieth-century epidemic of verbal bloat. The victim of verbal bloat is incapable of saying that the economic short-changing the country has given him is "injustice"; he must call it "oppression."

Verbal bloat is often justified by its sufferers on ground that the only way to draw attention to a grievance these days is to scream, pound the table and blow up the chicken house. In short, by abandoning reason. The people who argue this line are usually the same people who complain that the world is becoming an insane asylum.

There are practical reasons for rejecting their defense. The overstated argument distracts attention from the merits of the case and focuses it, instead, on the absurdity of the overstatement. Man's first landing on the moon, for example, was a splendid event, but when President Nixon, in a seizure of verbal excess, called it the greatest happening since Creation, silliness threatened to break out all over.

There are differences between Creation and mankind's splendid moments, one of them being a certain weight within the word "Creation" which leaves us feeling that it was an event beyond man's capacity to duplicate.

In the same way, there are differences between injustice and oppression. Oppression is another word of great weight, but here the sense of weight is cold, cruel, stony, the weight of pyramids bearing down on a humanity without hope of mercy or justice.

Is it this hopelessness that we are supposed to feel when women liberationists speak of the "oppression" of women in the United States? Surely not. A sensible case exists that women as a group are subject to certain unjust exploitations. Fine. Let's do something about it.

One good way to distract attention from the justice of doing something about it, however, is to bring up the subject of "oppression." Here is a typical example of how verbal bloat works to damage the cause it professes to serve.

First, the disinterested mind, which might have been hospitable to correcting injustice, is sidetracked into pondering the vast stony weight of the word "oppression."

"Oppression," it muses. "Slaves toiling hopelessly for Pharaoh with no hope this side of death. Surely the women I encounter are in no such predicament. Neither, surely, can be these women who are writing books, telling the television audience and complaining to newspapers that they are oppressed. Oppressed people are not permitted to write books and have no access to either television or press."

Somebody, this methodical mind may conclude, is doing an

outrageous overselling job in the manner of TV salespitchery, which minds everywhere have learned to discount at huge rates for nonsense. Is it fair, then, to slander those who conclude, "Women's liberation? Oppression? Baloney!"

Another unhappy result, of course, is to leave American men with a sense of discontent. If they are to think of American women as "oppressed," they must inevitably inquire, "Who is the oppressor?" The answer they are likely to supply for themselves is: "American men; to wit, me!"

Now it is very hard for the average American man to take very seriously the idea of himself as oppressor.

His knowledge of oppressors has been formed by Cecil B. DeMille. An oppressor is an overweight fellow, usually wearing sheets or metal, who lies around on cushions drinking wine and being fed grapes by beautiful slave girls. Periodically, he snaps his fingers and has Victor Mature tortured.

Nobody at this stage of television criticism needs to be reminded how much at variance this is with the true role of the American man. Oppressor? He might love to be. But what is he, in fact? With excessive self-pity but some justification, he tells himself, "Bill-payer! Woman-server! Child-supporter! House-lackey!" And so on. Of course it's foolish, but that's not the point.

The aim was to stir him to fight injustice. The result has been to make him yearn for the oppressor's stone.

Dry as Dust

A thirty-two-year-old man polled at random reports he has never said, "Before you could say Jack Robinson" and doubts that he ever will. Here are some other lively phrases he has never used:

"Spent money like a drunken sailor";
"Slower than molasses in January";
"Hotter than the hinges of hell."

The poll was conducted to confirm my observation that Americans don't talk as colorfully as they used to. I have a couple of theories why this is so.

One is that since the social ban on dirty talk was dropped in the 1960's, the subsequent generation has been too busy talking dirty to cultivate the art of talking colorfully. Another is that the collapse of education aimed at civilizing people has created a population as ignorant of poetry as it is of history and geography.

Traditional colorful speech was built on an instinct for and a pleasure in two poetic devices, simile and metaphor. If you have a tin ear when it comes to poetry, you're not likely to say a runner is "faster than greased lightning" or to describe a miser as "tighter than a Pullman window."

That about the difficulty of opening a Pullman window illustrates the point here. True, most people under age forty nowadays can't be expected to go around saying "tighter than a Pullman window." They are airplane people, not railroad people, but airplane travel, for all its horrors, has spawned few if any cliché metaphors and similes.

Ever hear anybody say "sore as a stewardess's feet," "phonier than an airline schedule," "madder than a bumped passenger on the Fourth of July weekend"?

Since the airplane generation doesn't convert experience into poetry, those with a taste for talk slightly better than humdrum are left with the old standbys for soreness, fraudulence and high dudgeon: "sore as a boil," "phonier than a three-dollar bill," "mad as a wet hen."

Another point: "sore as a stewardess's feet" won't do. It's sexist. The sexism police would pounce on anybody who said it. Those toilers in the sky aren't "stewardesses" anymore. They are "flight attendants," and many are now male, and what do you mean saying "stewardess's feet" as though only female feet got sore pounding those aisles in the sky?

All this is death to poetic impulse. You become so worried about committing a sociological faux pas that you haven't the wit left to discuss soreness entertainingly, unless you think "sore as flight attendants' feet, whatever their sex" is a clever bit of self-expression. And of course you don't.

Someone will surely object that "sore as a boil," "phonier than a three-dollar bill" and "mad as a wet hen" are clichés. This is not an argument against them. Admittedly, their staleness does little to freshen up talk about subjects (soreness, fraudulence, high dudgeon) that have—let's face it—been talked to death.

In uttering them, however, the talker is at least making the effort to get out of the old soreness, fraudulence and high-dudgeon ruts. In making a virtue of economy and understatement in writing, the great Ernest Hemingway unfortunately infected the spoken language with a weakness for drabness of expression.

One result has been the decline of the cliché simile and metaphor in conversation. It is rare nowadays to hear of anyone who is free as a bird, pretty as a picture, stubborn as a mule, strong as a horse, dumb as an ox, dull as dishwater, quiet as a mouse, poor as a church mouse, straight as an arrow, smart as a whip, sharp as a tack, sick as a dog, brave as a lion, bright as a button, dead as a doornail, crooked as a snake's back, pale as a ghost, white as a sheet, red as a beet, green as grass, sly as a fox, crazy as a bedbug, mad as a hatter, nutty as a fruitcake or as honest as the day is long.

No longer do people persist until hell freezes over. Nothing anymore is plain as the nose on your face, nothing simple as pie. Nothing is a piece of cake. No one anymore has a memory like an elephant, or goes all around Robin Hood's barn, or comes out of it smelling like roses.

No longer is there a man you can go to the well with. No longer does anyone throw a punch quick as a flash at somebody bold as brass, felling him like a ton of bricks and leaving him out like a light.

Does anyone still work like a dog? Is anyone still treated like a dog? Does it still rain cats and dogs? Not since Hector was a pup. That's why there is no one left who is too dumb to come in out of the rain.

I trust this makes everything far from clear as crystal.

So Long, American Pie

Browsing in The New Yorker, I find two distinguished citizens expressing faith in the singular American character of apple pie.

They are:

William Buckley, author, publisher, columnist and once candidate for Mayor of New York ("Municipal graft is as American as apple pie"), and

Benjamin Ward, New York City Police Commissioner ("Racism is as American as apple pie").

The weakness of both statements consists in their assumption that apple pie has a unique Americanitude, or Americanness, or Americanhood. This is no longer true, though it once was.

The very essence of apple pie nowadays is its frozenness. Modern apple pie is manufactured and frozen in pie factories and shipped by refrigerator transports to grocery freezers. Buyers keep it in a home freezer until it's thawed for eating.

Instead of saying "as American as apple pie," it would obviously be more accurate to say "as cold as apple pie."

This could be a blessing, incidentally, for tough-detective fiction, which needs some fresh clichés. For instance: "Somebody's roscoe had put three slugs through his ticker. He was as cold as apple pie."

"As American as apple pie" becomes distinctly unflattering once we recognize apple pie for what it is today. Who wants our national warmth, charm and lovability likened to frigid pastry?

The glorious Americanhood of apple pie derived from the long-gone time when it was baked at home by Mom. This apple pie was usually called, especially in movies, "Mom's apple pie."

The America of that time could produce "Mom's apple

pie" because it was economically better off than today's America. In that America a single breadwinner could earn enough to pay the rent and support three children and a car, luxuries barely affordable nowadays even to two-income households.

That meant Mom didn't have to go out to work, but could stay home mastering the art of baking "Mom's apple pie." And a good thing, too, as survivors of the World War II era know.

The precious things that American men went off to fight for in that war included not only the Brooklyn Dodgers and the two-pants suit, but also "Mom's apple pie," symbolizing home, hearth and mother, even though the pie wasn't always so great.

Would they have fought so resolutely, one wonders, if the Dodgers had already been shipped west for big profiteering bucks, if the two-pants suit had gone the way of high-button shoes, if "Mom's apple pie" had been a frozen-food division of a leveraged Wall Street buyout?

It is not just the frozenness of today's product that makes it archaic to say "as American as apple pie." It is also the hygienic disrepute which humiliates all pastry nowadays, at least among the under-forty population worrying zealously about its weight, blood pressure, cholesterol level, lung capacity, liver function, eyeball clarity, muscle tone, hormonal harmony, joint elasticity, perspiration rate, kidney tension, bile-duct flexibility and plenty more.

Apple pie is one of the things that the new American is supposed to abhor and avoid, like glazed doughnuts, coconut cake, chocolate mousse, Sacher torte, banana cream pie and stacks of hot pancakes floating in swamps of melted butter and maple syrup.

"As lethal as apple pie" is more appropriate to the modern age than "as American as apple pie."

(Another boon to detective prose here. Example: "'Kiss me,' she panted. 'Kiss me.' I knew what she wanted, all right. 'You want me to kill your husband for you, don't you?' I said, crushing her lips against mine. Her kiss was as lethal as apple pie.")

Why then do men as civilized as Mr. Buckley and Commissioner Ward persist in pronouncing things like municipal graft and racism "as American as apple pie"?

Because there is nothing harder to part with than a dead cliché. What we need is a new cliché. It must be built around some object so quintessentially and indisputably unique to America that we immediately recognize its rightness.

Dashiell Hammett got off a fine one back in the gangster age when he wrote "as American as a sawed-off shotgun." Note how much better Hammett's line makes Buckley and Ward sound on graft and racism: "as American as a sawed-off shotgun."

True, sawed-off shotguns are almost as outmoded as apple pie now that children tote Uzi machine pistols and Kalashnikov assault weapons. We need a new, absolutely up-to-date cliché appropriate to a gentler, kinder, heavier-armed age.

A frozen apple pie to the person submitting the best new cliché.

Postscript

The country turned out to be swarming with people who wanted a free frozen apple pie, but none of the entries was worth even a frostbitten toe. I wrote a column announcing that since my own entry was the best of the lot I had awarded the pie to myself. I declined to disclose what my entry was, explaining that doing so would only provoke a great deal of ill-tempered mail from sore losers. No new entries, please. The pie has been eaten.

Overworked Anatomy

"The seminar in anatomical clichés in American literature is now in session, gentlemen. I am available for questions. Smith?"

"What colors distinguish the human body in American writing, professor?"

"The human body is most commonly red as a beet, white as a sheet, purple with rage and green with envy. It is frequently immersed in a blue funk, unless its eyes are shielded by rose-colored glasses.

Who knows what colors the body assumes when it enters politics? Smith?"

"In politics, sir, the human anatomy comes in four colors: black, lily white, red and pink."

"Not pink, Smith. The body may be pinko or parlor pink, but pink has been out of style for twenty years. Where is the heart worn, Jenkins?"

"On the sleeve, sir."

"Excellent. Name the places where the finger, the foot, the nose and the ear are most commonly found."

"The finger, sir, is usually found in the pie or in the dike. The foot is almost invariably located in the door or in the mouth. The nose is stuck into another person's business or kept to the grindstone, while the ear is kept to the ground."

"Very good. Now, can anyone tell me why the heart, though it is worn on the sleeve, is so often hard to find in its customary place? O'Hara?"

"The heart goes out a great deal, sir."

"Exactly. What is the climactic state of this vital literary organ when it refuses to go out, O'Hara?"

"Cold-hearted, sir."

"Of course. But suppose it goes out constantly?"

"In that case, sir, it is a heart as big as all outdoors."

"Who can identify the metallic parts of the body? Epstein?"

"The tin ear and the steel-trap mind, sir."

"What about the brassy cheek, the iron fist, the leaden eyes, the bronze back, the silver tongue, the golden voice and the cast-iron stomach, Epstein? Perhaps a student of your kidney feels more at home with the internal organs. What is the invariable literary condition of the gall?"

"Unmitigated, sir."

"And what must a writer always do with the spleen?"

"The spleen is always vented."

"What parlous state of the internal organs accounts for cowardice in the sufferer?"

"He is lily-livered. He lacks the stomach. He has no guts and is faint-hearted. His heart, in fact, may be in his mouth. Internal body malfunction leaves him with cold feet."

"Very good. What, by contrast, do the veins of the brave man contain?"

"He has ice water in his veins, sir."

"Which makes him—?"

"A cool customer."

"Now, Howard, what remarkable appurtenance does a clever man wear on his shoulders?"

"He has a head on his shoulders, sir."

"And what is the shape of his head?"

"He is level-headed."

"When wasn't he born, and what condition behind his ears does this account for?"

"He wasn't born yesterday, sir. He is not still wet behind the ears."

"On what anatomical part will persons who trifle with him be thrown out?"

"They will be thrown out on their ear."

"With the consequence that—?"

"They will soon be out at the elbow, down at the heel and up to the knees in hot water."

"Not bad, Howard. Now, to close for today, will you quickly recite twelve of the anatomical parts most vital to American literature, McDonald?"

"Yes, sir. The keen eye, the sharp nose, the dead hand, the bleeding heart, the high liver, the accusing finger, the razor tongue, the cold voice, the hot head, the weak knee, the goose-flesh, and the mailed fist."

"Thank you, McDonald. In our next seminar, you will come prepared to discuss the out-of-joint nose, putting the foot down, the streak of decency, swallowed pride and the cold shoulder. Until tomorrow."

Postscript

I hope there are still a few people alive who spot the anatomy quiz above as a theft from the idea bank of Frank Sullivan, one of the superior humorists of not all that long ago. Sullivan created Doctor Arbuthnot, the cliché expert, and interviewed him frequently for The New Yorker in the dialogue form used above. Many other writers have stolen Sullivan's technique to prove they couldn't do it half as well, so I thought, "Who am I not to plagiarize as shamefully as my fellow artists, especially since it can only make Sullivan look good in the comparison?"

A Farewell to Loins

Out of the attic where she had been rummaging among my secret treasures came a dear, sweet child with a novel published thirty years ago and tucked away almost ever since for clandestine reading on a dim night in February.

"What are loins?" she asked.

"Give me that book," I said.

She didn't. "Somebody has underlined this sentence," she said, reading: "'In her loins she felt the ancient hunger stirring.'"

The innocent curiosity on her face left no doubt that the

sentence meant absolutely nothing to her; that she, in fact, had not an inkling of what loins were. Oh, she was old enough, all right, to know that a loin was something we might have in the deep freeze, but why a heroine should sense ancient hunger stirring in her grocery cache was beyond her comprehension.

This child, though beneficiary of progressive sex education in the public-school system and voracious consumer of modern anatomical potboilers and R-rated films, was utterly ignorant of loins.

Well, I am nothing if not enlightened in my willingness to tell children all. I laughed a very superior laugh. "Never heard of loins, eh?" (Very superior laughter.) "What do they teach you at the movies these days, anyhow?"

I savored this rare opportunity to have the drop on the Pepsi generation, then relented and said, "Loins are—"

At that instant I became aware that I didn't know what loins are, that I had never known what loins were. Loins were— well, *loins*!

It was like trying to tell somebody what ham hocks are. People who know what ham hocks are have a hard time telling people who don't. They take ham hocks for granted, have never tried to explain ham hocks. If somebody asks, "What are ham hocks?" they can only answer, "Ham hocks? Well—they're ham hocks, for God's sake!"

Loins, let me quickly add for the benefit of youngsters in the audience, have nothing to do with ham hocks. Nowadays, I gather, loins don't even exist anymore, but at one time they were absolutely indispensable anatomy to all authors of books intended to steam the eyeglasses, as well as books dealing with men of heroic iron.

The latter were forever girding their loins. In fact, that was all they did to their loins so far as I could determine. What was the first thing they thought of when confronted with the necessity to whomp the tar out of some offending rascal? Their loins. And what did they do to their loins? They girded them.

I was never able to envision a girding. I assumed it involved wrapping something tightly, as in a girdle, but I rejected the image of Achilles and Hector lacing girdles around their loins, not only because it seemed effeminate but also because I couldn't imagine precisely where their loins were located.

That was a nice quality about loins. You never knew exactly what they were. The literary evidence suggested they were located somewhere in the middle third of the torso, but whether they were interior or exterior and precisely what they looked like were mysteries.

The mystery was deepened by their obvious versatility. On one hand, loins could be girded; on the other, they were also subject to curious internal sensations. This was particularly so in the case of women whose loins were capable of feeling ancient hunger stirring, irresistible yearning and similar appetites of a distinctly lubricious character.

Modern writers seem to have abandoned loins. I am now on page 223 of a fairly typical novel of the sort that sells 750,000 copies in hard cover alone and have yet to encounter loins anywhere.

Every chapter canvasses both male and female carcasses with a thoroughness that would awe a surgeon, but in all that endless description of the human parts there is not a single mention of the loins. Nor do I encounter loins in any of the dozens of similar concoctions, which I read strictly to stay abreast of trends in modern literature, you understand.

I take this to reflect a slavish obedience to modern literature's dictum that novelists always call a liver a liver, a kidney a kidney, a pancreas a pancreas, and so on. I also assume that these writers, with their staggering knowledge of the human corpus, would call loins loins if there were any loins to be described. That they never do so persuades me that loins no longer exist.

Very well. I do not resist the march of knowledge. I concede that the heroine about whom the child asked me felt ancient hunger stirring in her ileum, her esophagus, her capillaries perhaps, though it makes her less interesting, since I am not her physician. But what can strong men gird if not their loins? Their hips, I suppose. "Fierce Achilles girded his hips." Forget it, Homer.

THE OLD
CUISINE

I was utterly unprepared for the gourmet revolution that started in the 1960's. My idea of good eating at that time was a thick piece of cold fried country ham embedded between two pieces of heavily buttered white bread. To cut the salt, big glasses of tap water provided the ideal libation. If you were a drinking man, as I then was, a gin martini straight up with an olive might be sipped between gulps of tap water.

Had you come upon me enjoying this meal, you would not have made spoilsport remarks about the evils of cholesterol, salt, bleached flour and gin. Since the gourmet revolution had not begun, people were not yet rude enough for such behavior.

Nor would you have asked what I thought of the meal. The theory that meals exist chiefly to be criticized by refined palates was not propounded until the onset of the gourmet revolution.

That I would one day eat something called radicchio and be expected to gush ecstatically about goat cheese would have seemed as unlikely as a shortstop making $3 million a year.

Being finicky about food was lower-class before the gourmet revolution. It was the very best people, after all, who were responsible for the terrible food served in country clubs, yacht clubs and exclusive town clubs operated by the uptown swells. The only people who ate well were stockyard workers, seafood merchants, farmers and families of recent immigrants who remembered how to prepare the food of their ancestors.

The gourmet revolution produced striking curiosities. For

377

instance, at the same time Americans were discovering that food could be more than fodder, they were also switching from the good old home-cooked fodder like Mother used to make to the new thawed fodder trucked by eighteen-wheelers to fast-food restaurants.

I would be hurt if anyone thought I was just a fodder eater before the revolution. A sandwich of cold fried country ham on white may not qualify as elegant eating in the Périgord, but it is so clearly superior to goat cheese that I refuse to waste time arguing the point. Yet, for two or three years in the 1980's you didn't dare accept a dinner invitation from New York's flossiest hostesses unless you were willing to face down a piece of vile goat cheese between the veal obbligato and the Belgian endive.

Shortly before this there had been the Era of the Practically Uncooked Vegetables. This had something to do with *nouvelle cuisine,* which had something to do with cooking everything so that it had no taste. These miserable, tasteless, practically un-cooked vegetables were the gourmet revolution at its worst. Yet I was sneered at—yes, *sneered at!*—for pointing out that for splendid vegetable eating nothing could beat a mess of new po-tatoes, green beans and fresh corn, all boiled, then simmered and marinated for two days in a pot full of ham bones.

No, I am not completely down on the gourmet revolution. As the pieces here should prove, I am much concerned with food and hold strong opinions about it. I would much rather write about the glory of raspberry preserves and the deficiency of cauliflower than the brilliance of the chairman of the Republi-can National Committee and the defects of our foreign-trade policy.

As explained a few pages farther on, I am the product of a kitchen culture. Even today, sitting in the kitchen of an evening eating Stilton cheese and crackers and envying my wife's mas-tery of the Cuisinart, I often find myself wondering, What would life be without eating and drinking? Almost as bad as life with-out television, I'll bet.

Slice of Life

How to carve a turkey:

Assemble the following tools—carving knife, stone for sharpening carving knife, hot water, soap, wash cloth, two bath towels, barbells, meat cleaver.

If the house lacks a meat cleaver, an ax may be substituted. If it is, add bandages, sutures and iodine to above list.

Begin by moving the turkey from roasting pan to a suitable carving area. This is done by inserting the carving knife into the posterior stuffed area of the turkey and the knife-sharpening stone into the stuffed area under the neck.

Thus skewered, the turkey may be lifted out of the hot grease with relative safety. Should the turkey drop to the floor, however, remove the knife and stone, roll the turkey gingerly into the two bath towels, wrap them several times around it and lift the encased fowl to the carving place.

You are now ready to begin carving. Sharpen the knife on the stone and insert it where the thigh joins the torso. If you do this correctly, which is improbable, the knife will almost immediately encounter a barrier of bone and gristle.

This may very well be the joint. It could, however, be your thumb. If not, execute a vigorous sawing motion until satisfied that the knife has been defeated.

Withdraw the knife and ask someone nearby, in as testy a manner as possible, why the knives at your house are not kept in better carving condition.

Exercise the biceps and forearms by lifting barbells until they are strong enough for you to tackle the leg joint with bare hands.

379

Wrapping one hand firmly around the thigh, seize the turkey's torso in the other and scream. Run cold water over hands to relieve pain of burns.

Now, take a bath towel in each hand and repeat the above maneuver. The entire leg should snap away from the chassis with a distinct crack, and the rest of the turkey, obedient to Newton's law about equal and opposite reactions, should roll in the opposite direction, which means that if you are carving at the table the turkey will probably come to rest in someone's lap.

Get the turkey out of the lap with as little fuss as possible, and concentrate on the leg. Use the meat cleaver to sever the sinewy leather which binds the thigh to the drumstick.

If using the alternate, ax method, this operation should be performed on a cement walk outside the house in order to preserve the table.

Repeat the above operation on the turkey's uncarved side. You now have two thighs and two drumsticks. Using the wash cloth, soap and hot water, bathe thoroughly and, if possible, go to a movie.

Otherwise, look each person in the eye and say, "I don't suppose anyone wants white meat."

If compelled to carve the breast anyhow, sharpen the knife on the stone again with sufficient awkwardness to tip over the gravy bowl on the person who started the stampede for white meat.

While everyone is rushing about to mop the gravy off her slacks, hack at the turkey breast until it starts crumbling off the carcass in ugly chunks.

The alternative method for carving white meat is to visit around the neighborhood until you find someone who has a good carving knife and borrow it, if you find one, which is unlikely.

This method enables you to watch the football game on neighbors' television sets and also creates the possibility that somebody back at your table will grow tired of waiting and do the carving herself.

In this case, upon returning home, cast a pained stare upon the mound of chopped white meat that has been hacked out by the family carving knife and refuse to do any more carving that day. No one who cares about the artistry of carving can be expected to work upon the mutilations of amateurs, and it would be a betrayal of the carver's art to do so.

Prescript

In 1975 a public-television station running one of those inescapable fund-raisers was auctioning fancy goods to the highest bidder. Among them was a dinner for two at the restaurant of the buyer's choice. The winning bidder was Craig Claiborne. He chose to dine in Paris and afterward wrote a famous account for The New York Times of eating a meal that cost $4,000.

After I read this description of eating at its ultimate, the inevitable column was obvious. It was the easiest I've ever written, rattling out of the typewriter in forty-five minutes, though I needed more time to ponder the dessert course. Later that day I put my problem to a friend's young daughter. What was the most appalling dessert she could think of? Without hesitation she specified the delicacy described in the next-to-last paragraph.

When the column was written in 1975, references to washing down the food with a 1975 Diet Pepsi and a 1975 Gilbey's Gin did not sound so elegant as they do in 1990. Let me, therefore, make it clear that I do not have a cellar stocked with vintage gin and Pepsi-Cola.

This was not only the easiest piece I've ever written, but also the most popular. People still write requesting copies.

Francs and Beans

As chance would have it, the very evening Craig Claiborne ate his historic $4,000 dinner for two with thirty-one dishes and nine wines in Paris, a Lucullan repast for one was prepared and consumed in New York by this correspondent, no slouch himself when it comes to titillating the palate.

Mr. Claiborne won his meal in a television fund-raising auction and had it professionally prepared. Mine was created from spur-of-the-moment inspiration, necessitated when I discovered a note on the stove saying, "Am eating out with Dora and Imogene—make dinner for yourself." It was from the person who regularly does the cooking at my house and, though disconcerted at first, I quickly rose to the challenge.

The meal opened with a 1975 Diet Pepsi served in a disposable bottle. Although its bouquet was negligible, its distinct metallic aftertaste evoked memories of tin cans one had licked experimentally in the first flush of childhood's curiosity.

To create the balance of tastes so cherished by the epicurean palate, I followed with a *pâté de fruites de nuts of Georgia,* prepared according to my own recipe. A half-inch layer of creamy-style peanut butter is troweled onto a graham cracker, then half a banana is crudely diced and pressed firmly into the peanut butter and cemented in place as it were by a second graham cracker.

The accompanying drink was cold milk served in a wide-brimmed jelly glass. This is essential to proper consumption of the pâté, since the entire confection must be dipped into the milk to soften it for eating. In making the presentation to the mouth, one must beware lest the milk-soaked portion of the sandwich fall onto the necktie. Thus, seasoned gourmandisers follow the old maxim of the Breton chefs and "bring the mouth to the jelly glass."

At this point in the meal, the stomach was ready for serious eating, and I prepared beans with bacon grease, a dish I perfected in 1937 while developing my *cuisine du dépression.*

The dish is started by placing a pan over a very high flame until it becomes dangerously hot. A can of Heinz's pork and beans is then emptied into the pan and allowed to char until it reaches the consistency of hardening concrete. Three strips of bacon are fried to crisps, and when the beans have formed huge dense clots firmly welded to the pan, the bacon grease is poured in and stirred vigorously with a large screwdriver.

This not only adds flavor but also loosens some of the beans from the side of the pan. Leaving the flame high, I stirred in a three-day-old spaghetti sauce found in the refrigerator, added a sprinkle of chili powder, a large dollop of Major Grey's chutney and a tablespoon of bicarbonate of soda to make the whole dish rise.

Beans with bacon grease is always eaten from the pan with a tablespoon while standing over the kitchen sink. The pan must be thrown away immediately. The correct drink with this dish is a straight shot of room-temperature gin. I had a Gilbey's, 1975, which was superb.

For the meat course, I had fried bologna *à la Nutley, Nouveau Jersey.* Six slices of A&P bologna were placed in an ungreased frying pan over maximum heat and held down by a long fork until the entire house filled with smoke. The bologna was turned, fried the same length of time on the other side, then served on air-filled white bread with thick lashings of mayonnaise.

The correct drink for fried bologna *à la Nutley, Nouveau Jersey,* is a 1927 Nehi Cola, but since my cellar, alas, had none, I had to make do with a second shot of Gilbey's 1975.

The cheese course was deliciously simple—a single slice of Kraft's individually wrapped yellow sandwich cheese, which was flavored by vigorous rubbing over the bottom of the frying pan to soak up the rich bologna juices. Wine being absolutely *de rigueur* with cheese, I chose a 1974 Muscatel, flavored with a maraschino cherry, and afterward cleared my palate with three pickled martini onions.

It was time for the fruit. I chose a Del Monte tinned pear, which, regrettably, slipped from the spoon and fell on the floor, necessitating its being blotted with a paper towel to remove cat hairs. To compensate for the resulting loss of pear syrup, I dipped it lightly in hot-dog relish, which created a unique flavor.

With the pear I drank two shots of Gilbey's 1975 and one shot of Wolfschmidt vodka (non-vintage), the Gilbey's having been exhausted.

At last it was time for the dish the entire meal had been building toward—dessert. With a paring knife, I ripped into a fresh package of Oreos, produced a bowl of My-T-Fine chocolate pudding which had been coagulating in the refrigerator for days and, using a potato masher, crushed a dozen Oreos into the pudding. It was immense.

Between mouthfuls, I sipped a tall, bubbling tumbler of cool Bromo-Seltzer, and finished with six ounces of Maalox. It couldn't have been better.

The Gallic Gang

Many persons have been surprised to learn that the French are deeply involved in the international heroin traffic. Those who keep an eye on criminal circles, however, have been aware for some time that the dreaded French underworld organization known as the "Ma Fia" has been tightening its dirty grasp on the vice of five continents.

Little is known about the Ma Fia, because of the code of silence ("Ze Code de la Taciturnité") which all new members are required to sign in menu ink on the day they are initiated. Punishment for violating the code is swift and harsh. When, for example, Armand ("Greasy Jake") Vieux-Hochfort told Toulon police where they could recover a hijacked shipment of Dijon mustard, Ma Fia hoodlums poured all his mineral water into the Seine and secretly refilled the bottles with tap water.

In the United States the Ma Fia is organized in twelve tightly knit groups in which personal relationships are remarkably like those in a big, highly disciplined family. These groups are called "Plumes."

The biggest and richest, covering Brooklyn and New Jersey, is the famous Plume de Ma Tante, headed by Pierre Bouboulet. It has been warring recently with the Plume de Mon Oncle, which governs the Hoboken and Manhattan territories.

Just three weeks ago, three members of Bouboulet's Plume were trapped in an East Side restaurant and served garlic sauce on their mousses. New York police say the job bore all the earmarks of a Jean-Pierre ("The Chef") Flaubert operation.

"The Chef," who earned his nickname years ago by inviting seventeen members of the Chicago Plume to dinner in a garage and serving them poisoned mushrooms, has been arrested many times but never convicted.

The F.B.I. proved that he was the man who invented the handwriting on French menus and even showed how he did it—with chicken feet dipped in watered blueberry juice—but the evidence was thrown out when the defense showed that the F.B.I. had obtained it by bugging "The Chef's" apron.

Life in the Ma Fia can be extremely dangerous, since there are seventeen specific offenses for which Plume captains may order executions.

When a member commits one of the capital offenses the Plume captain goes to the cash register and asks his wife for fifty cents in dimes. She says, "I just gave you fifty cents last week. How do you expect me to make ends meet in this business if all you do while I sit here keeping the help from robbing us blind is loaf around at the bar drinking up the best wine and taking fifty cents to call up those bums you run around with?"

He explains that he has got to telephone the top five lieutenants of the Plume and tell them to come to a judgment. His wife tells him to get his hand out of the cash register or she will give him a judgment on the back of his hand.

If the Plume captain can get to the cash register when his wife is reprimanding the bartender, the judgment is made and the violator is invited to dinner. After a magnificent hot hors d'oeuvre and a soup that is superb beyond description, the entree is brought in. It is a plate of hot dogs and beans. The judged man customarily blanches and mumbles "Sacre bleu!" because he knows that when the Plume captain serves hot dogs and beans it means that the guest has been doomed.

René de Gabardine, whose tips helped police capture a ring of Bronx perfume bootleggers last year, was later tried by his Plume and ordered to take his wife to Paris and buy her a new wardrobe. De Gabardine, confronted with this sentence, broke. He took his own life next day by opening his wrists in a tub of American champagne.

Pre-Gourmet Adventures in Eating

How many people out there are old enough to remember the fried seafood platter? You don't see the fried seafood platter in restaurants very often anymore, do you? And when you go to somebody's house for dinner, that somebody doesn't surprise and delight you these days with the fried seafood platter, right?

That's because restaurants and home-cooking specialists have all gone "gourmet," whatever that means, and it must mean something because there are a lot of mouth-watering dishes that these "gourmet" cooking authorities refuse to cook. Turnips and carrots mashed with butter, for example.

You simply cannot get turnips and carrots mashed with butter anymore, unless you dismantle some "gourmet" cook's New England boiled dinner, scrape away the cabbage and mash the turnips and carrots right there on your plate with a huge dollop of butter, adding plenty of salt and pepper.

It is still possible, if you have good sources of information and a full tank of gasoline, to find a fried seafood platter. In fact, a few days ago, the craving came on me so strongly that I motored 250 miles to a place in Massachusetts known only to me and a few dozen other persons of rarefied taste, which serves a genuine early American fried seafood platter unmutilated by truffles, garlic, hollandaise sauce or freshly ground green peppercorns.

Why is it so hard for modern cooks to prepare this dish? Its basic element is batter. You add a couple of oysters, a shrimp or two and several large fragments of fish. It doesn't matter what variety of fish, since you can't taste the fish anyhow once it has been agglutinated in the batter.

The point is: You are not supposed to taste the fish. The whole trick is the batter. And the trick there is: You are not supposed to taste the batter either.

In the kitchen of my Massachusetts hideaway they understand all this perfectly. Like the great fried seafood platter cooks of yore, they keep a vat of boiling grease at the ready. The waiter enters the kitchen: "Guy wants the seafood platter," he says. The cook wraps the treasures of the sea in about six yards of batter, drops the whole business into the grease, lets the vat sizzle and roar and walks away to read a magazine.

You know what he's waiting for? He's waiting for all that grease to soak into the batter and marinate it with the great smells of all the other foods that have been cooked in it for the past week. When it turns golden brown, he shovels it onto a plate, shouts, "One fried seafood platter ready for the long-distance traveler!" and the waiter rushes it to the table.

Now, the best part: the smelling of the hot grease sizzling in the batter. After that brings the taste buds to life, sink a fork into a morsel of the viscous mass and embark on the highway to heartburn.

An oddity of the fried seafood platter is that appetite begins to flag after the third or fourth mouthful. This is because the heat oozes out of the batter very rapidly. Once the cooling process begins, you start to taste the food, and after that boredom is never long in arriving.

The secret of enjoying a fried seafood platter is to smell it and bolt as much of it as possible before taste sets in. After that it is not much to chew about.

However—and this is a bonus—you can spend a lot of time trying to locate the oysters inside the batter. This is no task for beginners. The oysters, rarely larger than a quarter, are commonly buried in a chunk of batter no smaller than Muhammad Ali's fist. If the batter is sufficiently glutinous, it takes a veteran fried-seafood-platter eater to tell whether the object finally uncovered by open-batter surgery is an oyster or merely a fragment of boiled apron added by the chef to excite the restaurant critics.

Critics of the fried seafood platter always complain that it is all aroma and heat. I say this is only half the story. The aroma and heat are worth the price of a trip to Massachusetts during those first few moments, but there is more than aroma and heat. There is grease. There is the quest for the oyster. There is the pleasure, after the batter has cooled and the tastelessness of the seafood has been exposed, of offering to trade your dining companion a forkful of batter-coated mystery for one of his lobster claws.

And finally, at 3 A.M., there are those pains in the chest and the sweet comfort of realizing that they do not signal the coronary attack promised you by the hostess who watched you mash butter into turnips and carrots, but only dear old fried-seafood-platter indigestion.

Kitchen People

I'm a kitchen person. When invited to somebody's house, I get uneasy at being ushered into the parlor and urged to sit down. There's something about a parlor that makes me gloomy. In the world I come from, the parlor was the room where the dead were laid out for burial. No amount of cheese dip on crackers can overpower the distinct odor of tuberoses that parlors stir from my brain.

Usually, of course, the people who invite you want only to show off the parlor. It has just been redecorated, or there's a new rug they're proud of. Maybe an expensive lamp designed by an artist in Milan. After passing the appropriate compliments, it may be all right to get up and move around.

If so, I rise quickly and roam toward the kitchen. Not without worrying that I've messed up the parlor, though. I know I've dented the couch cushions by sitting on them. I hope my trousers haven't left any dust on the upholstery. In the world I come from, people who dented the parlor couch cushions and left dusty imprints on the furniture were almost as odious as people who rested the backs of their heads on the chair fabric and left hair-oil stains.

It is only in the kitchen that I can feel at home. It ought to be a kitchen big enough to hold a table so you can play pinochle or do the crossword puzzle while the cooking is going on. It ought to have a radio that can pick up a baseball game, a bowl full of cake icing convenient for finger dipping and a stock of fresh celery and rat cheese within easy reach of the pinochle game.

For perfection I would add (1) a squalling child or two who can be told to shut up or be banished to the parlor, (2) a telephone that rings off and on with pleas from relatives hoping to cadge money and (3) a cook snarling that the table isn't going to be fit to eat on if the cardplayers don't stop spilling beer.

Yes, this kitchen should be eaten in, for it is the house's social center, and never mind that it may have a dining room. The only time I can eat in a dining room without feeling miserable is at 3 P.M. on a Sunday afternoon, and, even then, only if that meal is called "Sunday dinner" and consists of fried chicken.

As a kitchen person, I may be thought hard to please, at least by dining-room people. Dining-room people ascribe great importance to heavy silver, heavy linen and heavy crystal. Evenings at their houses are exercises in weight lifting.

What's worse, they live in constant fear: fear that bandits

will burst in and steal the silver at gunpoint, fear that a guest
will shatter a valuable glass and stain the priceless linen. I don't
blame them.

Being tight with a dollar myself, I was never tempted to
become a dining-room person. It has cost me dearly. Once when
I was young, poor and without prospects of success, a friend
who knew how to get ahead brought a rich contractor to my
place, thinking this plutocrat might take to my charms and offer
me a profitable job.

Later I learned he had such a job to offer; he needed a man
of the world to bribe members of the legislature. I showed my
imposing guest to the kitchen, sat him down conveniently close
to the celery and rat cheese and served him a bourbon and ginger ale in a jelly glass.

"You don't serve drinks in a jelly glass," my friend groaned
afterward, but I'm not sure this was why the job wasn't offered.
I think it was because of the silverware I set before him, a fork
filched from a Greyhound Terminal lunchroom and a tin spoon
bent out of shape by the baby.

Parlor people, I know, have passed the word that I am simply "unpresentable." I believe this verdict was first circulated by
Walter Lippmann, a man of immense charm and cultivation,
who invited me for dinner when I was still ambitious to scale the
social heights of Washington.

Though Lippmann was gracious, we both recognized immediately that rooms divided us. Lippmann, with his customary
brilliance, instantly saw that I was a kitchen person; and I—
sadly, because I worshipped Lippmann—knew at once that he
was a parlor person.

A polished host, Lippmann offered to show his house almost as soon as I entered and, after looking into his library, I
said, "Where's the kitchen?"

That noble face did not flicker, but I could tell instantly
that Lippmann was astounded and puzzled. It took me a second
or two more to realize that Lippmann had only the vaguest notion of where his kitchen was located. He did find it after a
search, though, and we stepped through the door. The people
working there stared in amazement, occasioned, I suppose, by
the shock of seeing two strange men wandering in their domain.

Obviously, Walter Lippmann lived and died in a world where no undertaker had ever ruled the parlor, where it was perfectly all right to dent the couch cushions, to lounge around in dusty trousers and even to lean an oil-soaked scalp against the back of the wing chair.

He was a splendid man, but he was a parlor man, and I was a kitchen man and, being a wise man, he did not invite me again. For that, I liked him even more.

The Magical Root Beer

When I was a child we always had homemade root beer at Christmas. Making it required yeast, a lot of sugar, quantities of water and a bottle of root-beer extract, which was then easy to find in the neighborhood grocery.

My mother stirred everything together in a big dishpan and, I suppose, put it on the stove to encourage all the ingredients to cleave together, though I cannot remember this for certain. It just seems the brew would have to cook a bit, wouldn't it?

In any case, she eventually poured it into Mason jars and capped them, but not tightly. If the caps were on too tight, the gas created by the yeast turned the jar into a modest explosive device.

An exploding root-beer jar didn't yield serious megatonnage, but it left a lot of broken glass in a puddle of root beer on the floor. This was not just a nuisance, but also a small tragedy, for the finished root beer was glorious stuff to drink and losing any of the limited supply dampened the spirit with sadness.

The trick was to get the caps on the jars just so. If too tight, the jars exploded with a thud. Too loose, and all the gas would leak out, so there would be none of the delightful bubbles that gave the drink its spirited bite.

Twisting them to the ideal position must have required fingertip sensitivity fit for a safecracker, and my mother had it, for she rarely had more than one or two explosions per season.

After the root beer survived what she called the "settling down" phase, the caps were screwed down tight, and the product went into the icebox. Chilled, it was a fit libation to a holiday that, for me, was entirely about magical wonders, despite exhortations from my mother and various Sunday-school teachers to "remember whose birthday we're celebrating."

I was immune to all efforts to awe me about the religious aspect of Christmas. That was for Easter. Christmas was a time for enjoying rituals of happiness, like the making of the root beer, and worrying about the explosions, and looking forward to tasting it.

After growing up, I heard it said that Christmas exploited children's greed, but that is surely wrong. A child's delight at this gaudy time in the dark pit of the year arises from a sense that something wonderful is about to happen. Santa Claus is not just another salesman; he is a philosopher teaching children that dwelling on life's possibilities can do more to improve the spirit than dwelling on life's inevitabilities can.

For me the root beer was as essential to a proper Christmas as pine trees, the jingle of Salvation Army bells and the human crush in the ten-cent store. It was part of the commotion that seemed to promise rapture just around the corner.

The season produced a lovely surge of good humor, maybe even optimism, in my mother, my uncles and aunts, and in most of the grown-ups I encountered. Along my magazine route, customers who were cool, surly or forbidding the rest of the year were suddenly in such good moods that they might give me an extra nickel when paying for their Saturday Evening Posts.

The homemade root beer was involved with all this wonder, and stayed involved long after I had wised up about that corrupt old Santa Claus and learned that life's inevitabilities are so absolutely inevitable that they leave little room for possibilities.

Still, a closet optimist perhaps, I had got married. We then had children. One December day I heard myself asking my wife, "What is Christmas without homemade root beer?"

Root beer made no magic for her, but she understood the question. In childhood she had passed dim Christmases yearning for a happening so wonderful that it could never happen to anyone. How nice it must have been for her to find someone whose yearning could be fulfilled with root beer.

She found the extract, which was no longer easy to find, and followed directions in the box, even taking pains about tightening the caps on the Mason jars. Unluckily, her fingertips were not made for cracking safes.

A night or two after the marvelous-to-be root beer was put in the cellar for the "settling down," we were seated in the parlor when we heard the first dull thud below. Not all of the others exploded that night. By loosening the caps, we saved two or three, but they were flat as tap water, and the children cried for factory-bottled ginger ale.

We didn't try again, but yielded instead to one of life's smaller inevitabilities: Remembered happiness can never be recovered, even at Christmas.

Postscript

The root-beer ritual obviously had something to do with a wish to restore my soul to the innocence it enjoyed in childhood. Drinks are often involved with such religious impulses arising on festival occasions, but the drink is likely to be wine or whiskey rather than root beer.

The drink that obviously satisfies the nation's spiritual needs as fully as a drink can, is neither wine, whiskey nor root beer. It is beer. I dislike beer. I can afford to because I'm allergic to something in it. At a typical beer-drinking ritual, say a profes-

sional football or baseball game, I am aware that a vast beer culture exists in America and that I am an outsider to it, an alien in a nation of beer guzzlers.

The public actions of people in the grip of beer astonish and worry me. In stadiums they assault visiting ballplayers. Driving about the countryside they hurl cans at people and landscapes. In railroad waiting rooms they do not finish drinking their beer but leave puddles of it here and there. Whether this is some instinctual reflex like the cat's habit of spraying to mark his territory, whether it is part of some beerish pagan ritual, or whether it is a malicious deed aimed at punishing the aliens among them, I cannot say.

A Muddle in a Puddle

At Penn Station in New York I sat in a puddle of beer.

I had not intended to sit in a puddle of beer. My family will swear to that. I can imagine any of them in the witness chair:

"Puddle of beer? Nyah, the old man didn't say nothing about going to Penn Station to sit in a puddle of beer. He said he was just going there to catch the train to Washington."

Furthermore, I do not like to sit in puddles of beer and had never done so before, since I had always suspected that sitting in a puddle of beer would make the seat of my best slacks give off an odor that would attract bar rags.

Imagine my amazement then to discover myself in the Penn Station waiting room sitting in a puddle of beer. This particular puddle of beer had been poured into the contour depression of a waiting-room chair seat, by whom or why I could only guess. Nor did I think of guessing at first.

My first thoughts came in the following sequence:

1—I am sitting in a puddle of liquid.

2—This being New York, the nature of the liquid puddle now penetrating my best slacks and soaking my underwear could be truly unspeakable.

3—Now I understand why, though every other seat around me is occupied, and hundreds of other people are standing around me desperate with fatigue, this seat alone was not taken until I sat down.

4—The fumes rising around me are very similar to fumes that used to fill the barracks early on Sunday mornings in 1943, which means that the puddle I'm sitting in is almost certainly a puddle of beer.

5—This being New York, and this being the Penn Station waiting room, I ought to be thankful that the puddle is merely a puddle of beer.

All these thoughts were thought in a fraction of an instant, but as my brain cooled I dealt swiftly and calmly with the main policy problem confronting a man who has just sat in a puddle of beer in the presence of a large audience.

Problem: Should that man leap up screaming curses?

Of course not. The hundreds of people pointedly not looking at me had doubtless watched intently (without looking) while I sat in the puddle of beer. Obviously, every one of them knew the puddle of beer was there, and any one could have spoken out as one human might speak to another.

"Wouldn't sit there if I was you, mister, 'cause there's a puddle of beer there, y'see."

Not one had said that, yet surely, even in New York, not all could be poor dumb wordless beasts utterly indifferent to a fellow traveler wearing his best slacks. Only two possibilities could explain their apparent brutality:

One, the person who had poured the puddle of beer was heavily armed and had announced that anyone who tried to prevent me from sitting in it would be instantly rubbed out.

Two, the puddle-of-beer pourer was an entertainer hired by the railroad to amuse passengers waiting for trains that were far behind schedule. This clown, after pouring the puddle of beer, had promised everybody a big laugh when, discovering that my best slacks had been ruined, I leaped up screaming curses.

Contingency One meant there was an armed maniacal

beer-puddle pourer, possibly with his finger on the trigger. Any abrupt movement, such as leaping, might be fatal.

Contingency Two, though less dangerous, meant that hundreds of waiting passengers were now waiting not for their trains, but for me to leap up cursing, so they could collapse in laughter.

It is a terrible confession to make, but I hated my fellow passengers then, loathed them for their eagerness to laugh at my ruined pants, detested them for despicable sheep who hadn't enough character even to warn a good, decent, kind man against sitting in a puddle of beer. I would never, never satisfy their craving for a good laugh.

And so I sat there, as though I sat in puddles of beer three times every day and all night long while watching television.

The expression on my face, I hope, said, "Ah, how nice to find a good comfy puddle of beer in the depot waiting room."

When osmosis had lifted the puddle of beer through my nether garments and up into the woof and warp of my best jacket, I rose with the calmly dripping dignity befitting a traveler to Washington. And when I arrived there the cab driver said, "Ah, you're from New York, I smell."

SPEAKING
PERSONALLY

Finally, here are some pieces in which I was giving away a little more of myself than a newspaper reader needs from a columnist. A columnist should not do this, but sometimes you cannot help it.

I think of a car dealer who ran for the Senate out West thirty years ago. Since he was low on mental wattage, the party geniuses in Washington placed him in the custody of technicians who engineered his every move and wrote every word of his speeches. One day near the end of the campaign, he was carried away by an enthusiastic audience. Finishing the heavy labor of reading his ghostwritten speech, he laid it aside, smiled out at the throng and said, "Now I'd like to say a few words of my own." He lost the election.

If you write a column like mine, the urge to say a few words of your own now and then can be just as fatal, yet it is irresistible. In my case this is because I am constantly putting on false faces, adopting personalities that fit the type of person who, in my judgment, can most effectively speak a particular column. Today's column may best be told by an imbecile, tomorrow's by foxy grandpa, the next one by a foolish know-it-all, the next by a hopeless mossback, the next by the greatest essayist since Montaigne, and so on through the full human catastrophe.

I'm trying to create a sense of a particular and maybe peculiar human being who is at grips with whatever narrow part of the world we are talking about that day. The reader should be amused by this personality, or contemptuous of it, or superior to it, or outraged by it, or fond of it, or respectful, or sick and tired of it, or any of the hundreds of other responses one person has to another. The important thing is that the reader respond. The reader with no response becomes a non-reader.

In creating these varied personalities, these voices that talk the columns, I don't try to go beyond cartoon and caricature. Working in an 800-word space, subtlety is out of the question. You can't perform a ballet in a telephone booth. Still, now and then a man becomes impatient when the public sees him only as a caricature. He feels an overwhelming compulsion to say a few words of his own. So we get these pieces that follow.

None is so intimate that it might better have been confined to the confessional. By the standards of movie-actor memoirs these are milksop stuff. The urge to let it all hang out has nothing to do with the urge to say a few words of your own. Letting it all hang out is nothing but exhibitionism, which distracts the reader from understanding anything interesting about the exhibitor. "The women a man sleeps with," as H. L. Mencken observed, "make charming episodes in his life, but it is seldom they influence the main course of it."

What the following pieces reveal is a somewhat staid, conservative fellow gone a bit long in the tooth and, therefore, starting to believe that it was a better world when he was a youth. Who doesn't?

He has discovered that practically everything we are taught when we are young will turn out to be wrong by the time we become old. Doesn't everybody discover this if he lives long enough? Nothing astonishing there.

Melancholy has eaten into our subject's marrow. I like that. A touch of melancholy is becoming in a man once he is old enough to recoil from a New Year's Eve celebration, as the author of "Gone with the Philco" recoils despite the prospect of a chance to kiss his tormentor's wife. A person with no melancholy is a person who loves life too little to be saddened when he learns it cannot go on forever.

Too much melancholy, on the other hand, is as insufferable as unrelieved gaiety. I am pleased to notice that it gives way to curmudgeonly fury under the lashing of one disagreeable letter too many from Churlish Reader—Samantha, in this case.

Notice, though, that even when cutting loose he cannot entirely abandon his habit of hiding in a self-caricature. Who is supposed to be telling the story in that column about the summer of 1939, a sad memory of a blissless childhood? Is it just another bad Hemingway parodist talking? Or is the columnist trying to parody his own all too comparable style? If so, why does he apply a humor device to such a sober memory of childhood?

Could it be that he was completely out of control while writing it because the clock read five minutes to deadline and he was working under the influence of desperation?

The Summer of '39

That summer we played step ball until dark and ate fried fish for supper and, afterward, hung out at Sommers's confectionary store. Schmidt, whose old man had money, bought himself a milkshake two or three times a week to put on weight for football, and we would go inside and watch him drink it and listen to Frank Sinatra on the juke box and argue about Hitler.

Afterward a gang would wander up out of the park and beat us up. Sometimes, if a girl came by, Wimpy would pick me up by the heels and hold me upside down to show her how strong he was. Then I would go home and kill some cockroaches because it was too hot to sleep.

Everybody killed cockroaches late into the night that summer. Schmidt said it was a good way to sharpen the reflexes for football, but it was also something to pass the time in the terrible heat. At 2 o'clock in the morning, front steps along the street were filled with people breathing heavily from the heat and from their labors against the cockroaches.

Opened windows and doors everywhere intensified the sense of early morning community. You could hear the man who

lived in the back alley beating his wife and the woman who lived
next door beating her son for shoplifting. He had served time in
the reformatory and carried a switchblade and was taken away
in a police wagon one night during a wake.

The wake was being held in the downstairs apartment of
our house where the tenants took in funerals whenever an em-
balmer, to whom they were distantly related, had an overflow in
his regular establishment. People came from blocks around to
eat boiled shrimp, drink whiskey and admire his work. Schmidt
used to sneak in long after midnight because he said the spectacle of death heightened his determination to live every moment
to the hilt, which was essential to success in football.

Afterward, Wimpy would come by and we would go upstairs and kill a few cockroaches or listen to the man in the alley
beating his wife.

One night after eating the fried fish for supper, several of
us decided to go down to Jockubaitis's Drug Store near the park
and beat up some other kids, but there was nobody there but a
beautiful girl, and Wimpy picked me up by the heels and held
me upside down to show her how strong he was, and I found a
nickel on the sidewalk.

Wendell, who was always breaking everybody up with his
wit, said I was now rich enough to weigh myself three times and
buy a Hearst newspaper, and we went back to Sommers's confectionary store, and pretty soon a dozen guys from Jockubaitis's Drug Store came by and beat us up.

The beautiful girl came with them and said I was the one
who had taken her nickel, and they held me upside down by the
heels to show me how strong they were. Schmidt got away unscarred and credited his escape to his fast football legs.

After that, the summer got hotter. People were so drained
by the heat they lacked the strength to go on killing the cockroaches. The asphalt streets began to melt, and the neighborhood tree, which was in the next block, turned brown and
died. Mr. Arcati, who lived upstairs and wanted to be a policeman, fired his revolver out the window one night and got an
eviction notice. He said he had only been shooting at cockroaches and demanded to know why the authorities didn't crack
down on the first-floor tenants for holding funerals without a
license.

In this awful heat, the beautiful girl from Jockubaitis's Drug Store appeared one night at the hall on the corner where bingo games were held nightly, and I dug out my Saturday movie money and went inside and won two cans of vegetable shortening, and handed them to her. She was damp with perspiration and deeply touched.

Later on the sidewalk, she confessed she had never been to a wake, and after midnight, when boiled shrimp and whiskey had loosened the mournful discipline of the bereaved, we sneaked in and stood on the fringe of the festivities. Walking home in the rich, damp moonlight, she said it seemed funny seeing me right end up.

I told her she looked funny, too, and our hands touched, and when her father greeted us at her door demanding to know what she was doing coming home at that hour of the night with stolen vegetable shortening, she said it was all my fault, and he held me upside down by the heels until her big brother came and beat me up.

It cooled in September, and the war began in Europe. Later Wimpy joined the Marines and was killed. He was a strong guy, too. Schmidt got his weight up to 147 pounds and made the third string. Wendell got appendicitis but recovered. I still see things upside down a good bit of the time.

On the Death of a Hard Master

None of the obituaries on the death of The Saturday Evening Post saw fit to salute those of us who began our careers in its service. In those days, which must have been, oh, about 1935, Tuesday morning invariably began with a depressing bundle of Saturday Evening Posts, neatly bound in brown paper and smelling of fresh ink, lying on the front steps, a deadweight on a soul that yearned to soar.

That depressing bundle represented duty, hideous, distasteful and loathsome to the nine-year-old who would have to sell its contents, would have to find thirty-five or forty unbelievably beneficent adults willing each to part with the sum of five cents before there could be any stickball playing or snowball fighting or ring-a-levio after school that week.

Older heads assured us that the sacrifice of freedom was well made in that cause of learning about work—this was the Depression—but as we sat in school Tuesdays, dreading the 3:15 bell that would propel us into capitalistic activity, we cultivated a distaste for work that has stayed with us the rest of our lives and a distaste for The Saturday Evening Post that lingered into middle age.

The Post was not a hot seller, at least in the type of community where nine-year-olds were expected to help earn their keep. True Story was what the ladies of the community wanted; its spurious confessions about rendezvous in rumble seats that came to no good—invariably illustrated with posed photographs revealing a flash of garter—must have spoken of a remote romantic world to women sitting under unshaded light bulbs in kitchens of landlord green.

In any case, The Post, with its Norman Rockwell vision of sweet, greening America and Iowa Republicanism, was hard selling. The men preferred Liberty (reading time for this story: three minutes, seventeen seconds), now defunct these many years.

This sociological wisdom was embedded in the mind as you put on roller skates on Tuesday afternoon, slung the canvas bag of Posts over the shoulder and set off to ring doorbells. "Want to buy a Saturday Evening Post?" (The sales pitch was distinctively soft, when not downright defeated.) "Haven't you got True Story?" "The Post, never read it. Why don't you sell Liberty?"

In a town of 30,000 persons, 35 door-to-door sales was a good week. It usually took four or five days to sell the whole bundle, and the net profit was twenty-five cents. (Not bad in the economy of the 1930's; you could buy three apples for a nickel.)

The Post outlived a great many things that we associate with it in remembering the ordeal of having to sell it. Things like Liberty magazine and three apples for a nickel and roller skates. (Why don't children roller-skate anymore?)

It also outlived landlord green, the unshaded light bulb, the rumble seat and the boy peddler. Recalling that time, those of us who endured it will probably remember that it was supposed that unpleasant work, like selling The Saturday Evening Post in a society hungering for True Story, would ultimately prove beneficial to us.

We were misled. There were undoubtedly a few benefits. We learned early that poor people living in ugliness and despair prefer romantic escapism to hard-headed Republican virtues, and we learned that work is not all it's cracked up to be when it is imposed on you, like a sentence, by the economy.

Yet many persons, who endured it during the Depression, will protest, and do so regularly to their children, that young people today would be a superior lot if they had had some practical experience of hardship. This is the traditional boast of the parent, heard down through the generations, that he is a better fellow than his offspring because things were harder when he was a child.

It is not to be taken seriously, yet it has become such a commonplace among parents who spent their childhood in the Depression that many of their children have developed a sentimental longing for the Depression.

You used to see them all over the country trying to re-create the Depression through simulated poverty, as though suspicious that the accident of birth in good times had deprived them of an edifying experience.

The Depression was expensive by then. Ragged old imitation furs from the 1930's retailed in the flossier boutiques at twice their original cost. Rental prices for imitation slum housing around campuses were three and four times a laborer's salary in 1935. And what did the seekers have for their money? A plastic Depression, its phoniness betrayed by their own preference for Ramparts over True Story.

The Depression was not everybody having a ball and being picturesque. It was not being able to play ring-a-levio until you sold thirty-five copies of The Saturday Evening Post. It was a dead weight on souls that yearned to soar.

Youthful Ambitions

Once upon a time, or in 1942 if you prefer, high schools graduated their sweaty produce in June. Now the car-crash roundups in the press suggest they favor May, and why not? It's a whole new world out there at Hudson High and oodles more fun, I gather, than it was when Jack Armstrong and I were reading Ovid when the Latin teacher was looking and Spicy Detective when he wasn't.

Mention vice and we would have thought of the senior prom. Had we been asked to stand before all America on the Donahue show and discuss teen-age pregnancy, both Jack and I would have died of incredulity, embarrassment or stage fright.

The senior prom was awful enough. For one thing, I couldn't dance. I had intended all year to learn to dance so I could revel at the senior prom, but had been too busy to get around to it.

This meant I would have to find a girl who didn't mind dancing with a person who couldn't dance. No easy task, especially since I found it painfully difficult to speak to any female except my mother, aunts and sisters.

Another difficulty: I had no car. Since the California way of life had not yet been invented, the high-school student's natural right to ride to school in his own car did not exist. The number of car owners in the average high school was slightly smaller than the number of students under indictment for armed robbery.

Many students, though, could cadge a loan of the parents' car for glorious occasions. Here again I was at a disadvantage, since my mother had no car. There was a kind uncle who might lend me his car if I could drive, which I couldn't.

I had intended to learn to drive so I could try to borrow his car for the senior prom, but had been too busy to get around to it. This meant I would have to find a girl willing not only to go to the dance with a nondancer, but also to go on the trolley car.

Believe it or not, I agonized over this situation for months of fretful nights before good sense came to the rescue and I said, "To heck with the senior prom."

At that time heck was still good enough for high-school boys, though we were capable of stronger talk when showing off. Very soon most of us would learn to speak almost as gaudily as today's junior-high kids.

For the commencement I rented a band-leader tuxedo (white jacket), sat in a steamy auditorium with several hundred other wilting youths and sweated buckets while the Mayor of Baltimore talked incomprehensibly for hours.

It was a segregated world we inhabited. My high school was for white males only. The yearbook editors insisted that everybody have an "ambition," and almost all 542 graduates they photographed confessed without jokey self-consciousness that they did indeed have "ambitions."

"To study medicine" and "to study law" were popular. So was "to be an accountant." Alvin Udoff wanted "to be an actor," Bud Crawford, "to study radio," and Jake Abramowitz, "to be an announcer."

Reading these confessions of boyhood dreams is a bit jolting forty-five years later, for it suggests a powerful determination to make a serious run at life in a way that has become fashionable to mock in young people today.

"To enter business"—dozens of them say that. Others are more idiosyncratic. "To be a commercial pilot." "To play pro baseball." "To be a machinist." Paul Shapiro wanted "to be an author." Earl Morey wanted "to study theology."

"To enter the diplomatic corps," said Charles Sussman. "To be an orchestra drummer," said Murray Heine. "A violinist," said Julius Scheir. "To be a rabbi," said Eugene Rosenberg. "A teacher," said Charles McIntyre. "An aviator," said Gordon Ward.

"Aeronautics," "stenography," "physics," "surgery," "bacteriology," "an entomologist," "a printer," "a toolmaker."

These kids were not fooling around. Here's Rowan LeCompte: ambitious to become "a designer of stained glass." His stained-glass windows today are part of the glory of the National Cathedral in Washington. These kids were determined on success while they were still kids and not ashamed to say so. A hundred listed as their "ambition" simply "to be a success."

A great many went to the war in the next year or two and lost the power to say heck with pleasing boyish innocence. Many doubtless became successes and learned in the 1960's to tolerate and even love children who told them success was a shabby and contemptible goal.

I was above such squalor. True, for "ambition" I put down "to be a newspaper columnist," but as usual I was just fooling around.

Reeking of Savoir-faire

The observance of the one hundredth anniversary of the tuxedo evoked painful memories for me of a long ago when I yearned to pass for a man of the world. My dream then was to be suave and sophisticated and to reek of savoir-faire.

I would never have spoken such words except in mocking tones, but silently I acknowledged that "suave," "sophisticated" and "savoir-faire" were precisely what I longed to be. There is a fine antique English expression for this condition: I wanted to "rise above my station."

This was tedious work. Many barriers had to be overcome, including the formidable tuxedo barrier.

In my branch of society, nobody ever "dressed for dinner" in the sense that movie characters "dressed for dinner"; that is, men in tuxedos and women tinkling in diamonds. In my social sector, a man was "dressed for dinner" if he yielded to his wife's pleas to stop coming to supper in his undershirt on steamy summer evenings and agreed to slip into his work shirt before sitting down.

Herb Gardner has correctly noted that the generation born between the wars "went to the movies to learn how to live our lives." As a small Jujube chewer, I had watched men like Lyle Talbot, Paul Muni, George Brent and even Wallace Beery wear the tuxedo as coolly as I wore a sweatshirt.

Clearly the tuxedo was the ultimate male garment. Wearing it with poise marked even the ostensibly rough-hewn (Wallace Beery) as a man of suavity, sophistication and savoir-faire. The movies were explicit. Those who did not master the tuxedo would never shine at the Astor.

But where did you practice? There was high-school commencement, of course. High-school boys always graduated in rental tuxedos with clip-on bow ties and white jackets, which made the experience seem doubly fake, because in movies white tuxedo jackets were worn only by band musicians and characters in Somerset Maugham movies about toffs in the monsoon belt.

Late in the college years, when the social-climbing madness was intense, I accepted an invitation to join a fraternity. Such is the folly in which a man may wallow when he seeks to rise above his station. The foolishness of the initiation ritual to which I willingly submitted now seems too embarrassing to describe beyond saying that it required a tuxedo.

The rental shop provided everything it took to create suavity, sophistication and savoir-faire. Everything but the shoes.

Unless you're a seasoned tuxedo wearer, you don't think about tuxedo shoes until it's too late. Consequently, I had to wear the only black shoes I possessed: wing tips with a lot of those fake holes all over the toes and sides. Because I hadn't yet grasped the importance of shoe upkeep to social schemers, the holes in the soles of these shoes were not fake.

Upon reporting for the ritual, I immediately realized that I was the only member of this fraternity who had not been fitted for his first tuxedo the day he entered nursery school.

It was the first time I had ever seen grown men wearing patent leather shoes. In my world, a man wearing patent leather shoes would have seemed only slightly less peculiar than a man wearing a tutu to the bingo game at Lithuanian Hall.

Complete humiliation ensued when we initiates were commanded to kneel before the sacred something-or-other, for kneeling meant exposing to the initiators' view the holes in my shoes.

Several years passed before I mustered courage to face the tuxedo problem again. I was to go to a job in London. The pay was low but the expense-account generous. I could travel first class by ocean liner. This meant "dressing for dinner" in the first-class dining room.

At last I bought a tuxedo, with everything. Including tuxedo shoes. Leaving the haberdashery, I ran into a suave, sophisticated acquaintance. "I've just bought my first tuxedo," I said.

"Never call it a 'tuxedo,'" he said. "The word betrays you as a vulgar bourgeois social climber. The proper terms are 'dinner jacket' and/or 'black tie.'"

I have always been grateful for insults when they were for my own good, so for years thereafter I recoiled whenever I heard some vulgar bourgeois speak of his "tuxedo" and prided myself upon the civilized delicacy with which I invariably said, "Is it black tie?" instead of, "Should I wear a tux?"

Man's social foolishness changes with time. Now I boast that my dinner jacket is an off-the-rack model from a no-prestige haberdashery in North Jersey. This announces that I am too full of savoir-faire to bother having my tailor run up a silk dinner jacket.

Sophisticated men go with the social flow. I, for example, am now shopping for patent leather shoes. If you see me at a bingo parlor wearing a tutu, be good enough to tap me on the shoulder, remind me where I come from and send me on home.

Tired of That Old You?

Here is a letter from a woman who raises a difficult question: "Dear Sir,

"Somewhat late in life—in the nick of time, as Noel Coward wrote of Mrs. Wentworth-Brewster's discovery that 'life was for living'—I have discovered that I am a conservative, and I wonder if there is any political organization which is on my side.

"I am not talking about what the newspapers nowadays call 'conservatism,' a doctrine whose followers, so far as I can make out, like war, despise the poor and want power concentrated firmly in one man (the President), while making it easier for his constabulary to put me in jail. Perhaps I can make myself clearer if I tell you how I discovered my own conservatism.

"The instrument, as it is so often the instrument that changes our lives, was the television set. The Presidential campaign had just been interrupted for an important message from its sponsor, and this, of course, turned out to be several important messages, as it always does. One of the several was a commercial aimed at stimulating milk sales. It promised that there would be 'a new you coming' if I would only drink a glass of milk.

"I use the word 'promised' because the man who had written the commercial clearly assumed that everyone who would watch it disliked himself so thoroughly that the prospect of 'a new you' arriving after milk ingestion would be pleasurable to contemplate.

"Frankly, I was far more disposed to regard his message as a warning. I am not a bit persuaded that a new me would be any improvement on the present me. The present me is not, I concede, a construction in human felicity. There are many faults. I am prolix in letters, to cite an obvious one. I am a shade smug. I don't like people very much, and so forth. I could go on, but never mind.

"My point is that, flawed though the present me may be, my experience of that inescapable American marketing phenomenon, newness, compels me to believe that the new me would almost certainly break down easier, wear out faster, emit even worse pollution and contain more plastic than the present me.

"In short, it suddenly occurred to me that I like me pretty much the way I am. As the Presidential campaign returned following the messages, my mind was too absorbed with this fresh discovery about myself to follow the political folderol.

"I was a person who distrusted newness. This certainly put

me out of the American mainstream, for almost everything advertised on television was praised for its newness, and I disliked or distrusted almost all of it, from the new frozen chicken croquettes to the new instant coffee miracle.

"These claims for newness, it seemed to me, were a smokescreen for unpleasant facts; to wit, that you can hardly get a decent piece of fresh farm-raised chicken which tastes like chicken anymore, and that a decent cup of coffee made in a percolator will probably be equally hard to find before much longer.

"It was not just the middlebrow television audience that was in thrall to depressing, misleading newness, I perceived. The intellectuals were forever talking about the new this and the new that, on the unquestioned assumption that what was new must naturally be splendid.

"I tested my responses to a number of the things that are being urged upon me nowadays on grounds that their newness makes them better than they might otherwise be. There was the New Politics. I didn't like it, because it looked to me exactly like the Old Politics, which I heartily disliked.

"I didn't think much of the New Journalism either. When I buy a paper I want to get yesterday's scores, not the scorekeeper's attempts to improve on Dostoevsky.

"The New Left, aside from being terribly dressed, struck me as decidedly inferior to the present left, or the Old Left, or whatever it is to be called, because it had no system of thought to inform its activities and, so, had neither program nor intellectual creed for its opponents to oppose.

"Am I making myself at all clear? I like leftists who can be argued with and newspapers that tell me what happened yesterday. I like politics that I can heartily dislike at first blush without having to dispose of a lot of nonsense about, ah, these being different, better, more marvelous politics, because they are new.

"I like chicken that tastes like chicken. I like coffee that tastes like coffee. I can live fairly well with the present me, and do not want a new one. In short, I rather like the world the way it is, although certain changes are, of course, essential. Is it possible for me to find others like me willing to form—I shudder at the word—a movement?

"Sincerely,"

Back to the Dump

When I was a boy everybody urged me to get plenty of sunshine, so I got plenty of sunshine for a long time. One day while I was absorbing July sun as fast as I could, a doctor asked what I thought I was doing.

"Getting plenty of sunshine," I said.

"Are you mad?" he replied.

No, I was not mad, just slow to catch up with life's revisions. Getting plenty of sunshine had been declared dangerous while I was out to lunch. I revised my store of knowledge. Now I get only small droppers of sunshine extracted from the half hour just before sunset.

When I was old enough to notice that girls were pleasantly different from boys, my mother told me the facts of life. "You must always treat a woman like a lady," she said. So for a long time I went through life treating women like ladies.

One day while I was helping a woman into her coat, another woman asked me what I thought I was doing.

"Treating a woman like a lady," I said.

"Are you mad?" she replied.

No, I was not mad, but my interrogator was furious. I had been out to lunch during one of life's revisions and missed the announcement that it was swinish to treat a woman like a lady. I discarded another piece of my childhood education. Now I treat women like ticking bombs.

When I was seventeen and for many years afterward, I admired Franklin and Eleanor Roosevelt as the ideal couple. One evening I had an encounter with a ticking bomb, and contemplated behaving like a fool, but rejected the impulse because we weren't married.

"What do you think you're doing?" she asked as I fled. I told her that someday I wanted to be half of a couple as ideal as Franklin and Eleanor Roosevelt.

"Are you mad?" she replied.

No, not mad. I had been out to lunch during another of life's revisions and, so, had missed the disclosure that Eleanor didn't get along well with Franklin and that Franklin fooled around when she was out of town. Another part of my youthful education went to the dump, but too late. By then, age had brought its inevitable energy crisis and I had begun to prefer napping to behaving like a fool.

Perhaps it was not age that defeated me, though. Maybe it was fatigue caused by the constant trips to the dump to discard everything I'd learned in the first half of my life. Life seemed to be an educator's practical joke in which you spent the first half learning and the second half learning that everything you learned in the first half was wrong.

The trips to the dump became more and more frequent. There I lugged the old precept that a hearty breakfast of bacon and eggs was good for me.

I also hauled away the old lesson that it was racist to refer to people of African ancestry as "black." One windy night, I hoisted up the cherished teaching that every American had a duty to drive a two-ton, eight-cylinder automobile with room enough inside for a steamer trunk and the whole darn family, and staggered off to the dump. That was a heavy night's work and left me bent in spine and spirit.

At about this time, movie actors began running for President, astronauts began flying around the planet to get from one desert to another and people began renting one-bedroom apartments for $2,000 a month. Out to the dump went important fragments of my education which had made me believe that movie actors existed to be browbeaten by Congressional investigators, that if you've seen one cactus you've seen them all, and that $2,000 a month ought to buy you a controlling interest in the Gritti Palace Hotel.

No wonder I was tired. And then, a terrible fear seized me. If everything I'd learned in life's first half had to go to the dump, wasn't it inevitable that everything I was learning in the second half would also have to go?

A crushing thought. I'm not getting any younger. I've had the stamina so far to heave out everything I learned in youth, but if everything I've learned since has to go in the next twenty-five years I'll be too feeble for the job.

I'm sitting here right now wondering what present certainties might have to be junked before the century is out. My conviction that President Reagan is a nice guy, for instance. Will some whippersnapper someday say, "If you hadn't been out to lunch again, old-timer, you'd have read the recent book reporting that Reagan had to be dosed on jolly pills to control his passion for kicking orphans"?

And there's my present fear that the nuclear weapons race could kill us all. Some people already say I wouldn't have that fear if the Russians hadn't manipulated my brain. I think that's silly right now. Considering all the other people I know are manipulating my brain, I don't see how the Russians could get a crack at it. But you never know. Someday I might have to learn that I wasn't really afraid of nuclear war at all, but only under the sway of Moscow Svengalis.

It wouldn't surprise me. Live long enough and you'll eventually be wrong about everything.

No More Orange Motorcycles

One of the first things I ever got for Christmas was an iron motorcycle with a sidecar and an iron policeman mounted on the saddle. Motorcycle, sidecar and policeman were all orange. The policeman could be removed from the motorcycle seat, but he was frozen perpetually in the seated position—arms spread to grasp the handlebars—and looked silly almost everyplace else except on the edge of a pie pan.

Next, I got an ocean liner which looked more or less like the Titanic and sank just as inexorably on every voyage across the bathtub. Time passed, and I got Big Little Books and Oz books, which I enjoyed because teachers said they would rot my mind.

One year, I discovered the pleasure of standing on Wilsengoff's grocery-store corner and watching girls go by without letting them notice I was watching. For Christmas that year, I got a used bicycle with balloon tires.

Time kept passing, and I got a board game called "Bulls and Bears." You sold short, cornered vanadium and made a killing in utilities. At that time, I still got English walnuts and tangerines for Christmas, too, so that year wasn't a total loss. Still, you could tell something vital was running out.

Christmas marched on. I got two neckties, an Arrow shirt, a large bottle of Vaseline hair tonic and a recording of Ravel's "Boléro," conducted by André Kostelanetz.

I became sour and disagreeable as Christmases persisted in recurring every 365 days—except in leap years, when they arrived a day later. This did not stop the getting. I got socks, I got subscriptions to the National Geographic, Collier's and The New Republic, and I got gloves.

Then I got after-shave lotion and a shoeshine kit.

One Christmas, I got a scarf, six undershirts, a styptic pencil and a leatherbound book for recording telephone numbers and addresses.

The country began to boom and so did Christmas. In a quick flurry of Christmases, I got a radio, a hi-fi set, the nine symphonies of Beethoven conducted by Leonard Bernstein, a case of beer and a compass to attach to the car's windshield so I could tell what direction I was driving.

The direction was always the same: directly toward another Christmas.

I got a dispatch case, an unabridged dictionary, a camel's hair coat, a Swiss watch, English shoes, an assortment of German sausages, an Italian cookbook and a Japanese cassette player and recorder.

The following Christmas, there was an odd pause. You could sense people thinking, could feel imaginations failing. I got a deerstalker cap.

The next Christmas was even less memorable. I got an assortment of Swiss cheeses, gift wrapped.

Several Christmases passed before I noticed that something was different. I first remarked this the Christmas I got a rocking chair and a packet of marvelously treated paper for cleaning bifocals.

Next Christmas, I got a large, handsome jar of hair pomade guaranteed to conceal the gray in less than three weeks.

Then I got an electronic gadget for changing the television station without getting out of the rocking chair, as well as a case of Geritol and a pair of tickets to the taping of "The Lawrence Welk Show."

Christmas after that was puzzling at first. Bounding out of bed to dash downstairs to see what Santa had brought, I was stopped by one of the children—a huge brute with the odor of Christmas Eve's bibulations still clinging to his beard. "You don't have to use the stairs anymore, Dad," he said. "Look what Santa Claus brought you." It was one of those stair-rail elevators where you sit down, push a button and get a free ride.

I sat down and took the ride. Sitting there in slow descent, I was reminded of a Christmas long ago when I got an iron motorcycle with an iron policeman mounted in its saddle. I did not straighten up at ride's end, but preserving my seated posture, I moved toward the Christmas tree for the annual surprises.

The lad seemed troubled by this strange posture. "Gosh, Dad," he said, "we went to a lot of trouble to get you an autographed copy of 'How to Avoid Probate' this Christmas, but it's not too late to find a wheelchair down at the hospital."

"That won't be necessary," I said. "The edge of a pie pan will do just fine." And I took the gift crate of vitamin pills with a smile, because I was remembering about the Titanic.

Because It's Here

Dear Samantha:

I've been in a quandary, and if you think there's nothing duller than six months on Easter Island, wait until you spend three days in a quandary. But golly, woman (does anybody but me still say "golly"?), what's a man to do when a girl (person?) like you writes words like: "Please spare the public your usual dim-witted New Year's Day column"?

Frankly, Samantha, I think your criticism is unfair. Several people to whom I mentioned it all agree that my usual New Year's Day column is no more dim-witted than anybody else's. Even you have to admit that my 1923 New Year's Day column— The Hilarious Mock Almanac—is still a classic. Some of its best lines—"If silence is golden, how come cats aren't rich?" and "A bird in the bush is better than two on your head"—were reprinted in the Mock Almanac Anthology of 1949.

I don't mean to sound defensive. Listen, Samantha, I don't like having to write the annual New Year's Day column any more than you like reading it. All I want to know is why women nowadays have names like Samantha. This is no criticism of you. You can't help it if you have to go through life signing poison-pen letters with "Samantha." But be honest with yourself now: Don't you think the world has gone steadily downhill ever since parents stopped naming their children Lucy and Dorothy and started naming them Samantha?

It's ideas like that—exciting, original ideas—which you probably have in mind when complaining about "the twaddle content" of my usual New Year's Day column. Here you betray a sad incomprehension of New Year's Day, for New Year's Day,

Samantha, is twaddle, just as surely as Al Pacino is "Bobby Deerfield," Marlon Brando is "The Godfather" and desire is the name of the game.

The game whose name is desire, in case you don't know, happens to be football. And what is New Year's Day? Football. Three long weeks of football. And what is football? I will tell you, Samantha, what football is: Football is twaddle.

If this sounds disjointed, forgive me. It would sound jointed if I hadn't interrupted myself seven times already to bang my head against the wall in an effort to produce a New Year's Day column that might meet your standards.

But then, your standards probably don't want to be met. They probably want to be called for at the house or the apartment or wherever they live. I've known women like that. "Meet me at the corner of Fifth and Elm, and we'll catch a movie and then have some shepherd's pie," you say to them.

"I don't meet men on street corners," they say. "You can call for me at my house." That means you have to be introduced to their parents. "Pleased to meet you, Father Oliver . . . a genuine pleasure, Mother Oliver, ma'am. . . . Honorable? Of course my intentions are honorable."

Is that what your standards propose to put my New Year's Day column through if it tries to meet them? From the snooty tone of your letter, I suspect your standards are pretty la-di-da, which probably means their parents are even more so. Why should my New Year's Day column have to be subjected to that?

I can hear them now. "But my dear, this column has much too high a twaddle content to be entrusted with our precious standards."

I hope all this doesn't strike you as ill-tempered, Samantha, because I am not ill-tempered. I am well-tempered, as well-tempered as Wanda Landowska's clavichord. I do not write churlish letters to wretched hacks caviling at them because it is their ponderous duty to compose the usual New Year's Day column. And why not? Because I am well-tempered, thanks to expert tempering twice weekly by an osteopath on the Upper West Side.

This gentleman, incidentally, admires my usual New Year's Day column. Since nobody feels like reading a newspaper on New Year's Day, he says, the ideal paper should contain plenty of material that can be skipped without loss to mind or spirit, which characteristic, he assures me, has always distinguished my perennial January 1 effusion.

I conclude, however, that this is not good enough for you, my dear woman of the tart pen. You want wisdom, profundity, weight, heavy breathing about the state of the cosmos, and you are willing to raise lumps on my skull to obtain it.

No, I am not angry. Not cross with you. All I have to say is, Why should I wear out my brain just to gratify a few soreheads like you who are too highbrow for the honest twaddle that satisfies their fellow citizens on this unutterable day?

Sincerely yours,

Gone with the Philco

It's New Year's Eve, and he wakes up feeling blue. He's seen too many New Year's Eves now and he's jaded with them and he hates that—being jaded, I mean. He hates people saying he's "jaded" with this and that, has hated it ever since he told Ben Cooper he never wanted to see another "I Love Lucy" as long as he lived, and Ben said, "You've become jaded."

He'd heard a lot about being jaded since then. Just last week when he told his wife he didn't care to walk out on the Seattle-Denver football game for a ride in the new Mercedes Ben Cooper gave himself for Christmas, his wife had said he was jaded.

People made it sound shameful to be jaded, but what was so terrible about being uninterested in things you enjoyed when you were a kid? He'd probably enjoyed playing with tin cans when he was a baby. He couldn't remember for sure, but he probably had. A year or so ago he tried to put the needle into Ben Cooper by saying, "Ben, I wouldn't walk into the next room right now for the chance to play with tin cans—you think I'm jaded?"

Ben had looked at him the way people look at you when they start to wonder if you're drifting out of the mainstream of America. Ben's look was that look that says to itself, "The old fellow's starting to do more thinking than is good for him; we'd better try to get him looking at more television."

But now it's New Year's Eve, and it's going to be New Year's Eve all day, and he thinks, "Maybe I really am jaded." It's hard to argue with that blue feeling. The magic is gone, he thinks, and wishes he hadn't thought it, because he's tired of characters in bad plays, bad movies and bad novels talking about "the magic," saying, "the magic is starting," and "the magic is gone."

But there was magic once on New Year's Eve. It came out of the radio. New Year's Eve was the night his mother let him sit up as late as he wanted, listening to the radio until 1, 2, 3 o'clock in the morning. Lying there in the parlor with the Christmas tree still lit, he listened to the arrival of the New Year in New York, then an hour later in Chicago, and thought of it moving across the continent like a great mass of brand new time, until it finally reached California.

There was something magical and marvelous about this huge block of newness moving relentlessly around the planet until the whole earth was wrapped in a brand new suit of time. And when he finally went to bed he felt that when he woke up, the world would be new and fresh and filled with opportunity to start all over and get things right. Maybe he could even raise his arithmetic grade to a B; maybe develop his biceps with York barbells so he wouldn't have to be pushed around anymore by Sleepin' Moses, the neighborhood bully.

Yes, that was magic all right. But now it's been a long time gone. Gone with Guy Lombardo and the Royal Canadians, whose "Auld Lang Syne" broadcast from the ballroom of New York's Roosevelt Hotel had always signaled the arrival of new opportunity in the eastern time zone.

Now on the morning of this latest New Year's Eve, he thinks of Guy Lombardo and remembers laughing when somebody said, after Lombardo's death, "Guy Lombardo has gone and taken New Year's Eve with him."

Why had he laughed? Maybe because it was so true. Yet Guy was still escorting New Year's onto the East Coast long after the magic had vanished. Guy was playing that New Year's Eve when, to avoid the ritual midnight kissing at a big party, he had fled to a quiet room and listened to a friend confess that his life had become empty and purposeless. Later the friend divorced and left his family.

Too many New Year's Eve parties lately had been like that, with friends straining for gaiety to mask their knowledge that the world was not going to be new and fresh in the morning and filled with opportunity to start over and get things right this time.

Now, on this latest New Year's Eve, coming down to breakfast, that's what he dreads—tonight's party with old friends. He'll have to enjoy it, whether it's enjoyable or not. And maybe he will. But he can't be sure, because he knows his friends, people like Ben Cooper, will be watching him to see how jaded he's become.

He's feeling like a man facing a terrible test. Can he maintain an impressive level of gaiety past midnight, despite what he knows: that Guy Lombardo took the magic with him and that tomorrow morning he's going to be just as dumb at arithmetic as he is today?

Breakfast coffee brightens his outlook; a good breakfast dispels a lot of the jade from his mind. "Yes, yes," he thinks, "I will have to fake the gaiety, all right, but that needn't be all bad." Pretending to be giddy with joy at midnight, he can probably get away with that warm kiss he has lately wanted to give Ben Cooper's wife, Myrna. That might disclose a new opportunity for both of them in the New Year.

He knows it won't, of course, and is grateful it won't. He's jaded, you see—the lucky devil.

At Rope's End

People are more fed up than usual. I noticed it at Sunday dinner with the family. The whole family was all fed up. They were fed up with the Iran-contra hearings, which had just ended, and fed

up with Congress for not letting the President do what he
wanted to do.

My family is solidly Reagan Republican in politics, but they
were fed up with the President's stories about the Iran-contra
business. Except for me, they all thought these stories were lies
and were fed up with a great President like Reagan being reduced to telling them.

I started to tell them why I thought the President was not
lying, but quit upon noticing that everybody was scowling silently over the crab cakes and ham. From lifelong association
with my family, I knew what that scowl meant. It meant they
were fed up.

Fed up with having the crab cakes and ham ruined by the
Old Political Wiseguy who was always telling the rest of the family they didn't know what they were talking about because they
lived in Baltimore whereas he had once lived in Washington.

They were fed up with Washington. They were fed up with
know-it-alls trying to tell them it was a mistake to be fed up
because the situation wasn't as bad as it looked.

They knew how bad the situation was. They lived in it
every day, and they were fed up with it.

They were fed up with me always knifing good President
Reagan with sly little thrusts. It was bad enough that they had to
admit the President was lying. Having to put up with the Old
Political Wiseguy saying the President didn't have to lie because
nobody thought it worthwhile telling him what was going on—
they were fed up with that stuff.

I stayed too late enjoying the satiation and got caught in
Sunday-night homecoming traffic on Helldriver's Boulevard,
also known as the Washington Beltway. The cars were steaming
with fed-up drivers and fed-up passengers.

They were racing bumper-to-bumper at seventy miles per
hour because they were fed up with the highway, fed up with the
weekend, fed up with their cars, fed up with the people inside
their cars, and fed up with the cars all around them for going
only seventy miles an hour and not getting out of the way so
they could get home.

The passenger in my car said she was fed up with me taking
her on Helldriver's Boulevard because she was fed up with feel-

ing that she was going to die every time she had Sunday dinner with my family.

I was pretty fed up myself with that kind of talk. In going to the family dinner, hadn't I driven her through the nightmare of exurban Maryland and Virginia with their slowpoke roads and hideous housing tracts? I had done that in spite of being fed up with those ugly miles and miles of cornfield condominiums.

At home it was not too late to catch yet another rerun of "Upstairs, Downstairs" on television. In the old days when we watched the reruns it was nice because they reminded us of our childhoods, when we had seen "Upstairs, Downstairs" before it became a rerun. Now, though, we were both fed up with it.

Anyhow, it was on public television, and you could never tell about public television. It might be waging one of its periodic attempts to crush the human spirit by holding a fund-raising marathon. We were fed up with fund-raising marathons. It was television's equivalent of junk mail.

Is there anybody who isn't fed up with junk mail? If Californians were as fed up with junk mail as I am, instead of shooting each other from moving automobiles they would all be in the backyard shooting their junk mail.

As a political junkie, I cannot sleep without a fix, so I turned on the tape of something the VCR recorded the night before. It was one of those shout-and-pout panel shows in which famous newspaper types compete for most-fed-up honors.

One famous journalist was fed up with the President, another fed up with Western Europe, and a third so fed up with the Ayatollah that he thought everybody should let Iran know we're sick and tired and aren't going to take it anymore, and get in our cars and shoot the old man if he puts one more mine into the Persian Gulf before the Pentagon remembers to build some minesweepers.

Or something in that vein. My mind always wanders when they get sick and tired like that and aren't going to take it anymore. This usually means my mind is fed up and wants to be turned off, so I always go to bed, even though I'm fed up with sleeping.

WORDS TO LIVE BY

Now Hear This

Have a nice day.
No left turn.
Buy some right away.
Yield.
Take inches off your waistline.
Keep off the grass.
Think.
Don't leave home without them.
Read up to 2,500 words a minute in just six weeks.
Curb your dog.
Conserve energy.
Vote.
No smoking.
Fasten seat belts.
Save the dolphins.
Save the bay.
Walk.
Wait.
Have exact change ready.
Get clothes twice as white.
Stop.
Fight pollution.
Love it or leave it.
Try some today.
Quiet.
Smile.
Take two aspirins.
Brush after every meal.
Keep right.
Fight cancer.
Fight heart disease.
Fight multiple sclerosis.
Fight diabetes.
Fight high blood pressure.
Fight lung disease.
Fight birth defects.
Get two cents off.
Fight unsightly tummy bulge.
Boycott the whale killers.
Save.

Fly now, pay later.
Don't miss it.
Spay your cat.
Stand back.
Keep moving.
Slow.
Maintain speed.
Wait for dial tone.
Ring bell.
Watch out for deer.
See your dealer.
Beware of dog.
Do it today.
Support your police department.
Give the United Way.
Mail early.
Keep off median strip.
Be a Big Brother.
Enter.
Exit.
Keep out.
Sign all forms in quadruplicate.
Remember the Maine.
Remember Pearl Harbor.
Enclose stub with check.
Do not send cash in mail.
Pay cash here.
Subscribe today.
Grasp handrail.
Flush.
No tipping.
Think bluefish.
Think catfish.
Think tennis.
No loitering.
Step down.
No littering or spitting.
Say good-by to razor nicks.
Look years younger.
Give.
Move up.
Move to the rear.
Avoid last minute rush.
Do not touch.

"The Becoming Looseness of Doom" is adapted from a commencement speech delivered at Hamilton College in the spring of 1969. "The Excellence of Welby Stitch Jr." appeared in the March 21, 1969, issue of Life magazine. The columns and news stories included here appeared in The New York Times of the following dates:

A Sadness of Team and Pants (12/26/87)
Badlands (5/9/76)

ROOTS
Summer Beyond Wish (7/4/78)
The Incredible Shrinking Life (12/15/79)
Alert on Dangerous Turf (4/18/84)
Moseying Around (9/20/81)
Making It (6/26/83)
Who Wouldn't Love New York? (4/8/78)
Dangerous to the Last Drop (12/13/87)
Justice in the Grass (5/26/87)
Burgville Marches On (8/23/87)

SERIOUS NONSENSE
Stranger Than Orwell (9/1/79)
The Case of Vinous Inflation (4/21/73)
So You're Thinking of Cloning (3/11/78)
Looking Up Trouble (8/11/85)
Count Your Miseries (8/27/83)
Boneless Sunday (2/3/74)
Bearing a Burden (8/10/86)
Little Red Riding Hood Revisited (1/13/80)
Lawn Treason (4/28/70)
Crashing Into Crosswordland (1/19/75)
Fanchismo (12/5/71)
Murder Most Foul (12/9/79)
How Shall I Dear Thee? (4/15/81)
The Great Whale's Mistake (6/23/74)

1968
Let's Keep This Show off the Road (3/14/68)
Nightmare out of the Attic (6/6/68)
Mourners (6/8/68)
They Line the Tracks to Say Good-by (6/9/68)
On the Southbound Train (6/11/68)
That Time When Minutes Last Hours (8/8/68)
Beleaguered in the Mainstream (8/27/68)
A Macabre Atmosphere Pervades the Convention (8/28/68)
The City That Fascinated Itself (9/1/68)
Just the Varnished Truth, Please (9/29/68)

AGE OF GOLD

The Golden Spouse	(10/2/79)
Ermine, Skin and Bones	(1/31/81)
The Common Touch	(12/10/80)
Dugout Gasbag	(4/6/71)
Bitter Medicine	(1/15/78)
Just Keep It to Yourself	(4/13/86)
Killing Beethoven	(10/10/81)
Those Killer Bills	(10/12/86)
Backward Reels the Mind	(5/6/78)
Penury Gets You Nowhere	(11/1/86)
The Whats Ride Up Front	(10/1/70)
A Taxpayer's Prayer	(4/10/77)
The Easiest Money	(2/1/89)

PLACES I'VE BEEN

Delaware Township, N.J.	(4/13/63)
Cocoa Beach, Fla.	(5/16/63)
Cocoa Beach, Fla.	(5/18/63)
New York City	(8/8/63)
New York City	(8/10/63)
Charleston, W.Va.	(8/22/63)
Gettysburg, Pa.	(11/21/63)
Trinidad, Calif.	(7/9/64)
Aboard Goldwater Campaign Train	(10/4/64)
Albuquerque, N.M.	(10/29/64)
Washington, D.C.	(1/28/64)

THIS EERIE NEWNESS

For Want of an Amp	(1/15/84)
Lawyers for Cars	(6/8/83)
Bye-Bye, Silver Bullets	(9/4/79)
Power Lunch	(6/3/84)
Heaven in Asphalt	(3/17/87)
Losing the Hair Game	(8/8/84)
A Smoke-Free Diet	(5/26/85)
Where Have All the Ulcers Gone	(8/16/81)
Fear of Interfacing	(1/23/83)
Naked Ignorance	(1/16/88)
The Heart of Superman	(12/17/78)
Keeping Out of Touch	(11/9/86)

THERE'S A COUNTRY IN MY CELLAR

WE'RE LOSING CONTACT, CAPTAIN

THE OLD CUISINE

SPEAKING PERSONALLY

WORDS TO LIVE BY